The Tories and the People
1880–1935

For Fran and Hannah

The Tories and the People
1880–1935

MARTIN PUGH

Basil Blackwell

© Martin Pugh 1985

First published 1985

Basil Blackwell Ltd
108 Cowley Road, Oxford OX4 1JF, UK

Basil Blackwell Inc.
432 Park Avenue South, Suite 1505,
New York, NY 10016, USA

British Library Cataloguing in Publication Data

Pugh, Martin
    The Tories and the people 1880–1935.
    1. Conservative Party—History
    I. Title
    324.24104'09   JN1129.C72
    ISBN 0–631–13806–4

Library of Congress Cataloging in Publication Data

Pugh, Martin.
    The Tories and the people, 1880–1935

    Bibliography: p.
    Includes index.
    1. Tories, English—History. 2. Conservative Party
(Great Britain)—History. I. Title.
JN1129.T7P8 1985   324.24104'09   85–9065
ISBN 0–631–13806–4

Typeset by System 4 Associates, Gerrards Cross, Bucks
Printed in Great Britain by The Bath Press Ltd, Bath

Contents

Contents

Tables, Maps and Plates

PLATES

Acknowledgements

I am particularly grateful to Norman McCord and Brian Harrison for their critical comments on various chapters of this book, and to David Cannadine, Roy Foster, Patrick Joyce, Simon Lloyd, Roland Quinault, John Ramsden, Elizabeth Redgate and Mike Winstanley for advice on points of detail. I have benefited greatly by reading the theses and dissertations written by Dennis Dean, S. A. Hogg, Sandra Holton, Patrick Joyce, Leon Kitchen, Helen Mathers, Dilwyn Porter, Roland Quinault, John Ramsden, Duncan Ross and David Gray Smith. Members of Historical Association branches in northern England and of university history groups at Newcastle, Edinburgh, Cambridge, Oxford, Leeds, Durham and the Open University heard papers on aspects of the work and contributed valuable questions and comments on it.

The assistance of Pat Murrell and Richard Wellings in gathering some of the material for the book was much appreciated. Tracking down source material on the Primrose League has been a major operation and I am glad to record my thanks to the following people who helped in finding it and making it available: His Grace the Duke of Beaufort, Mrs Anne Bennett, Dr Tony Donajgrodozki, George Lane Fox, The Rt. Hon. Lord Harris, Mrs E. M. Hawley, Miss Ann Hay, Mrs Josie M. Hutchinson, The Rt. Hon. Lord Home of the Hirsel, The Rt. Hon. the Earl of Lonsdale, His Grace the Duke of Norfolk, Lady Violet Powell, Stephen Stacey, The Hon. G. R. Strutt and Mr R. H. Harcourt Williams. I am particularly grateful for permission to reproduce material in the possession of Miss Elsie Pedley of Grinton (plate 6), the Trustees of the Lonsdale Estate Trust (plates 2 and 3), Gloucestershire CRO (plate 4) and Suffolk CRO (plate 1). I gladly acknowledge the assistance rendered by the staff of Birmingham Public Library, the Bodleian Library, Blenheim Palace Estates Office, Churchill College Cambridge, Labour Party Archives, the Mitchell Library, the NRA (Scotland), the National Library of Scotland, Nottingham University Library, the Northumberland Estate Office, Reading University Library, and the county record offices for Buckinghamshire, Cardiganshire, Cleveland, Cumbria, Dorset, Gloucestershire,

Durham, Essex, Hertfordshire, Lancashire, Northamptonshire, Northumberland, Oxfordshire, Shropshire, Suffolk and Yorkshire.

It is a matter of serious regret that I have been denied access to the papers of the 27th Earl of Crawford and Balcarres at the John Rylands Library, Manchester.

Finally, but not least, I am grateful for the financial assistance received from the British Academy's Small Grants Research Fund and Newcastle University Staff Travel Fund.

Introduction

Like the poor, the Conservatives are always with us. While their opponents divide and coalesce, expand and contract in provoking and exciting ways, they appear to remain the constant element in the British political system. Perhaps this explains why academics have largely failed to devote to Conservatism the attention which its record of success might be expected to merit. Yet there is nothing inevitable in the evolution of the Conservative versus Liberal pattern of Victorian politics into the Conservative versus Labour pattern which characterized the mid-twentieth century. Britain did not develop a system dominated by a Social Democratic majority in which the Conservatives were reduced to a mere rump, nor one in which Liberal and Labour forces contended for power; but one sees no *fundamental* obstacle to the emergence of such patterns. Conservatives survived by conscious adaptation as well as through luck, but the process of change on the right has characteristically been obscured under a blanket of traditionalism. Hence one of the themes of the present volume is the peculiar mixture of innovation and antiquarianism entailed in the politics of the Primrose League, which provided Conservatives with a reassuring and an efficacious means of transition from the narrow world of parliamentary politics and tight local elites to twentieth-century conditions.

However, it has long been assumed by students of politics that the emergence of mass political parties, integral to the society which supports them, is inherently bound up with left-wing movements, while right-wing politics remains a matter of parliamentary elites whose contact with their supporters resembles their visits to the dentist − occasional and painful, if ultimately necessary.[1] Empirically such distinctions make little sense, at least in the British context. The late Victorians fully appreciated that Conservatism derived much of its strength from its ramifications throughout British society. 'Politics, after all, has a social basis,' as one correspondent of the *Primrose League Gazette* summed it up.[2] In a backhanded compliment, the *Manchester Guardian* pointed to the 'subtle work of demoralization' perpetrated by the Primrose League: 'It is really the first systematic attempt on a great scale to render the exercise of a democratic franchise a matter not of conviction but of fashion.'[3] Ostrogorski paid slightly cynical tribute to the league for surpassing the Conservative Party organization in numbers and in fighting strength. But apart from Janet Robb's 1942 study there has been no examination of the league during the twentieth century. Professor Hanham perceived its significance in his fine study of the political system, but his own work covered a slightly earlier period. Since then we have had few, but excellent, attempts to extend our picture of the popular basis of Conservatism, notably Professor Cornford's discussion of social class and the constituencies, the work of John Garrard and Patrick Joyce, who have pointed to the capacity for social integration in Victorian Conservatism, and the contributors to Longman's *History of the Conservative Party* series, Robert Stewart and John Ramsden.[4]

Yet popular Conservatism remains a somewhat elusive and under-studied phenomenon, perhaps partly because Conservative historians have, on the whole, been interested in high politics, and uncomfortable about the grassroots manifestations of Conservatism. In the centenary year of the Primrose League, Professor Gash fenced uneasily with the suggestion that under its aegis artisans and duchesses met one another regularly: 'How often these exotic encounters took place is not known', he observed, moving rapidly on to other matters.[5] On the other hand those who are interested in popular movements have concentrated on the strengths and weaknesses of the Labour and Liberal forces, and the result has been a somewhat unbalanced impression of historical development. Historians of socialism, often suspicious of political leadership, tend to exaggerate the significance of the rank and file. Consequently a tiny organization such as the ILP has attracted a disproportionate share of the attention of researchers. It is a sobering thought that the total paid membership of the ILP in 1900 has been put at 6,000, a figure equivalent to the paid membership of the Primrose League in Bolton at that time![6] The detailed evidence of local Primrose League habitations throughout England, Wales and Scotland presented in chapter 5 and the appendices of this book, though incomplete, should encourage students to attempt to correct the imbalance. The Conservative half of society is still largely awaiting its historians.

In its hey-day — the 1880s and 1890s — when it was the largest political organization in Britain, the Primrose League capitalized on Conservatism as much as a social force in British society as a strictly political one. Reaching well beyond the confines of traditional political organizations, it recruited non-voters as well as voters, the apathetic as well as the political, women as well as men, children as well as adults, and the working class as well as the middle class. Both the size of its female support and the role played by women as leaders and activists in the League rather than simply as passive followers, surely calls for some modification of our perspective on women in modern British history. Inevitably the explosion of work on women's studies in recent years has concentrated attention upon articulate radical minorities, so that, as with labour history, we are in some danger of missing the big battalions. If one is looking for feminists one will not find many among the ranks of the Primrose League; but one will find the more typical woman in all classes who was not entirely content with her allotted role, yet unwilling to repudiate it. If we can understand such women we may understand both the timing and the limited nature of the emancipation which their sex has experienced in modern Britain. Moreover, the study of women's history, however necessary as a first step, must not become an esoteric interest practised only by the initiated. If it does nothing else, a study of the league reminds us that women have long been in the mainstream of political life notwithstanding their formal exclusion from voting.

Ultimately, Conservatism has proved comparatively elusive because, as Dr Harrison has pointed out, its real strength often lies in silence.[7] The historian is therefore less likely to be able to depict Conservatism satisfactorily either as doctrine or as party programme, but is obliged to look into the informal, underlying conservatism which reveals itself in ill-defined but widespread phenomena like patriotism, monarchism and imperialism. Recently we have been sharply reminded of the continuity between our own age and the Victorian era in terms of such popular sentiments. During the last fifteen years a series of major royal occasions including the investiture of the Prince of Wales, the Queen's Silver Jubilee, and the marriage of the Prince of Wales to Lady Diana Spencer, has evoked a wave of deep emotion for which it is hard to find a parallel. Similarly, anyone who thought that nationalism had withered in the post-war world will have been thoroughly disillusioned by the experience of the Falklands War, which underlined how easily patriotism can be appropriated by governments, and how effectively external conflicts can distract attention from social and economic discontent. Even if nationalism or monarchism were to be dismissed as mere contrivances of the mass media, which would be very unwise, their survival would still suggest that the popular sentiments characteristic of the era of Lord Salisbury remain only just beneath the surface of British society.

1

The Conservative Dilemma

The nineteenth century was not a comfortable time for British Conservatives. Except for a few fleeting years in the 1840s, they never appeared to be swimming with the tide of human affairs; instead, they fought a protracted rearguard action, often with skill and stubbornness but sometimes with resignation bordering on fatalism. Rarely did Conservative politics exhibit the optimism which Whigs, Radicals and Socialists commonly displayed. Even the triumphs of Disraeli and the comfortable victories of Salisbury were diminished by a pervasive apprehension, almost a fear, about the future. Up to a point this mood was an asset, in that it enabled Conservatives to speak to similar opinion in the country, and it is probably no accident that the three phases in which Conservatives enjoyed secure office followed upon or co-incided with widespread alarm among the solid citizens who comprised much of the electorate. The Liverpool-Wellington era was a sharp reaction to external and internal upheavals unleashed by the revolution on the continent; Peel's reign from 1841 to 1846 reflected a desire to limit the consequences of 1832 and a fear of Chartist agitations; and the Disraeli-Salisbury era after 1874 represented the coalescence of middle-class property with aristocratic interests at a time of growing democracy and alarming military weakness.

Throughout the century the status quo seemed to be threatened by four kinds of pressure: the inexorable spread of industrialization which raised up a wealthy middle class susceptible to alliance with the lower orders against the traditional rulers; a burgeoning of religious dissent which promised to overtake the established Church numerically and disputed its status; a marked, if sporadic, advance towards one man, one vote; and the emergence in Ireland of an organized nationalism which carried the seeds of imperial disintegration. In the face of these challenges Conservatives instinctively sought to organize their defence around the monarchy, the House of Lords and landed interests, the Church, the Empire and the Union. The question was how. The approach of the so-called 'ultras' involved resisting each reform to the end and trying to reverse it subsequently. Though in their youth men like Salisbury flirted with reaction, it was not seriously pursued; few, for example, really wanted to restore the Corn Laws. At the opposite extreme were those who accepted change as inevitable and wished to manoeuvre to obtain the most beneficial type of reform, which sometimes meant risking a Conservative initiative in order to forestall a damaging radical one. For them timing was of the essence, for only when change seemed inevitable would Conservative supporters themselves acquiesce; moreover, a premature measure would only trigger off further tinkering instead of imposing a final solution; in this sense the 1867 reform act failed. Contrary to impressions, Salisbury became quite adept at this technique, as shown by his judicious innovations over the redistribution of seats in 1884–5 and over County Councils in 1888–9. Conversely, the women's suffrage issue, which tempted some Conservatives to a pre-emptive strike, was judged unripe and too divisive. The intermediate, and more typical strategy simply involved obstructing reform for as long as possible, then accepting defeat and quitting the last ditch expeditiously so as to fight effectively under the new rules. Thus, after the demoralizing experience of 1830–2 the Party rallied and climbed back to office after three general elections within a decade.

Such strategies involved two distinct but closely related issues: the substance of Conservative policy and the means best suited to promote it. Obviously, Conservative objectives could not indefinitely be secured without winning elections; but, as the rules governing electoral conflict changed, support had to be won from larger and different social groups. Would the have-nots vote for a party concerned to defend the haves? And if they did, would not their support in itself require some modifications in the Party? Many Conservatives contemplated this with deep pessimism. For example, the backbenchers acquiesced in the franchise reform of 1867 largely because it left their own county electorate relatively unscathed; moreover, the consequence seemed to be to stimulate the radicalization of the Liberal Party's politics during 1868–74, which in turn drove more Palmerstonians towards the Conservatives. However, the ripples of 1867 kept spreading – the secret ballot, the 1883 Corrupt Practices Act and, most alarming of all, the extension of the household and lodger franchises to the counties in 1884. Many a Conservative squire panicked into thinking that the agricultural labourer was a natural radical with a history of rick-burning, Luddism, Chartism and dissent; in a competition for his vote Conservatives might be hopelessly outclassed.[1] In addition, many of the new county voters were in fact industrial workers like miners, whose enfranchisement had been delayed because they resided outside borough seats. 'My electorate is 11,500, over 7,000 new voters,' the young Curzon lamented of South Derbyshire. 'Of these between 4,000 and 5,000 are colliers and manufacturers and I haven't a chance with them. They won't even hear me...So certain am I to be beaten that I am planning a tour round the world.'[2] Curzon's pessimism proved justified, and along with dozens of other

Conservatives he was rejected by his county constituency in 1885. Indeed, Conservatives won only 119 out of the 377 county seats in that year; even among the 239 English county seats they carried only 105. Some seventy Conservative country gentlemen and sons of peers were defeated at this point and failed to return to the Commons.[3]

The ambitious chose to meet the dilemma by quitting rambling rural seats for compact urban and suburban constituencies (see chapter 6), for the latter were more likely to be equipped with a well-oiled machine and a local boss, made fewer demands upon the Member, were often more conveniently placed for London, and held a shrinking Liberal challenge. Other country gentlemen opted out of parliamentary politics and chose to pitch their energies into the struggle for the new County Councils, a sphere of government which had always been more congenial to them. But the most positive reaction arose from a perception that in order to win votes it was not always necessary to engage in a competition with the Radicals. Quite traditional Conservative causes could still triumph if handled boldly and not apologetically; nor did an effective machine have to be a carbon copy of the 'caucus'. These lessons were personified by Lord Randolph Churchill in the 1880s. Indeed, his significance for Conservatism has nothing to do with a *new* programme, but with pumping fresh life into traditional shibboleths, as Salisbury recognized.[4] In this sense the Primrose League was a true child of Churchill, and it proved well calculated to meet his party's need. For on matters of substance, unlike the National Union of Conservative Associations, the League never went beyond generalized beliefs about preserving the estates of the realm, the Church, the Monarchy and the Empire; and as an organization its deferential and hierarchical character could hardly have been more reassuring for men who had been dragged kicking and screaming into the nineteenth century, and contemplated the twentieth with apprehension.

TOWARDS AN ORGANIZATION

The traditional idea that modern organization descended upon the Conservative Party as a Disraelian inspiration around 1867–70 has been largely undermined by investigation of both earlier and later periods which suggest a far more gradual development. In fact, the problem lay not so much in an antipathy to organization as in a suspicion of central interference in constituency affairs. Country gentlemen felt only a loose attachment to party, while the party managers, such as they were, preferred to leave organization to ad hoc arrangements by key individuals for fear that a more formal, institutional structure might generate pressures or demands upon the parliamentary party. Basically the whole notion of converting voters to Conservatism was alien in the early and mid-nineteenth century; it seemed sufficient for a majority to be induced to vote for the right candidates by personal influence.

Under the stimulus of the First Reform Act several hundred constituency associations had sprung into life during the 1830s. These, however, were invariably mere extensions of aristocratic influence, with the result that as Conservative fortunes steadily improved up to 1841 the cost of maintaining the associations seemed to outweigh their usefulness, and many lapsed.[5] Francis Bonham, the party's first chief agent, encouraged the registration of supporters, produced candidates where required and sometimes assisted with expenses. However, the centre had very few resources, for benefactors largely preferred to contribute to a local interest. Moreover, Bonham's help was frequently not wanted. In two-member seats where one member was a Tory the London managers often attempted to get a second man alongside the first; as the minority party between 1846 and 1874 Conservatives were obliged to look for such opportunities. But the local constituency invariably adopted a quite different perspective. To introduce a second Conservative would force a contest where otherwise the sitting member might be returned unopposed; even the formation of a new party association could easily provoke local Liberals into counter-measures and a breaking of the unwritten truce over candidatures, which would cause great expense and might introduce 'politics' into community affairs.

On the other hand the campaigns of the Anti-Corn Law League undoubtedly stimulated the formation of county protection societies during the early 1840s, which led in turn to the revival of many of the defunct Conservative associations. They were to provide the basis of Conservative organization in the aftermath of the repeal in 1846, for most of the professional side of the machine, in the shape of party agents, had left along with the Peelites. Until the 1850s relatively little attempt was made to improve the system from London, partly from lack of funds but also from sheer lack of will; Derby in particular tended to accept the inevitability of a prolonged role in opposition as the Peelites merged with the Liberals. Yet despite such defeatism and the failure to win an election between 1841 and 1874, the protectionist Conservatives were soon within reasonable reach of power; indeed, by 1859 they were only about ten seats short of a majority. After 1853 things had begun to improve under Sir William Jolliffe, the Chief Whip, and Markham Spofforth as party agent. Like Bonham, they largely accepted the impossibility of managing county seats from London and sensibly concentrated their attention on boroughs where Conservatives were more likely to be cooperative and where gains might best be made.

In retrospect it seems clear that the towns provided the key to the modern revival of Conservatism, and, as with the Liberals, they pioneered more formal organizational methods. In 1863 the Earl of Shrewsbury founded a National Conservative Registration Association on his own initiative which gave way in 1866 to an official party version under Lord Nevill (later the Earl of

Abergavenny). This body, whose task was to maintain a registration agent in each county and a list of non-resident voters, represented the first of three branches of the modern party machine. The second was the National Union of Conservative and Constitutional Associations, launched in 1867, and the third the Conservative Central Office, set up in 1870.

Thus by the 1860s the question Conservative strategists were asking themselves was not whether to make changes, but how much innovation would suffice to transform a substantial minority force into a majority without detracting from the traditional character of the party. Although the 1867 franchise reform and the new National Union appear superficially to be bold attempts to outflank their opponents these were really of secondary importance. For Disraeli, the key requirement was a little judicious tinkering with the electoral system designed to make the existing Conservative vote count for more; prior to 1867 the counties, where the party's strength lay, sent only 162 MPs from a population of 11.5 million, while the boroughs with 8.5 million sent 334. Thus extra county representation, combined with a redrawing of boundaries so as to exclude urban elements from Tory county seats, was the essential objective – partly achieved by the Second Reform Act. Had the Conservatives been ready to take a gamble on their popular appeal they would have extended the new borough franchises to the counties in 1867; but instead it seemed safer to concentrate the changes in boroughs where they might discomfort the Liberal incumbents.

However, even before the Reform Act some Conservatives derived encouragement from their gains in industrial areas, especially Lancashire, in 1859 and 1865, and these gains were sustained in the 1868 election despite the Party's overall defeat. To both parties the new electors represented an unknown quantity which called for a constructive response. For Conservatives this took the form of workingmen's clubs and the National Union. Some of these clubs already enjoyed a long history, but the idea was to increase the number so that each ward of a town had its own modest premises within easy walking distance of the men's homes. A network of such clubs facilitated the task of agents in identifying Conservative voters, ensuring that they were registered and that they actually voted. To complement the social attractions of the clubs it became a common practice to establish Friendly or Benefit Societies, savings banks, and even building societies in association with them.[6] This had the advantage of attracting the politically uncommitted into the Conservative sphere and reinforcing purely political loyalty with certain material considerations.

Though an important asset, workingmen's clubs suffered similar drawbacks to the older associations in being conditional upon local initiatives and difficult to control from London. Hence the creation of the National Union under John Gorst in 1867 as a means of both co-ordinating and extending their role. However, the politicians were inclined to want to have things both ways: to enjoy the electoral advantages of the clubs but to deny them any real authority in the party through the National Union. Although the clubs themselves were not assertive, higher expectations were entertained among the constituency associations which the National Union actively promoted. By 1880 some 310 associations had affiliated − it was not yet compulsory to do so − as well as hundreds more clubs and registration societies. In this period the club and the association catered to different social classes. Even in Liverpool, where under Archibald Salvidge some 8,000 Conservative workingmen were enrolled, they remained quite separate from the party's ruling body, the Liverpool Constitutional Association.[7] Salvidge's skill and the exceptional strength of working-class Toryism in Liverpool gave them some influence over major matters like the selection of candidates, but this seems to have been untypical. By and large the party kept its rank and file supporters at arm's length by avoiding a low or even a uniform membership subscription. Consequently, where substantial membership figures were claimed they meant very little, because the 'members' had no obligation to pay to join, and therefore had no rights in the party. Participation most commonly took the form of subscribing to registration associations. Those who could afford it might pay to become a Vice-President and thus sit on the controlling bodies; in Keighley two guineas bought a seat on the General Committee,[8] while in West Derbyshire the Central Council cost give guineas.[9] Thus, although the ruling committees were often elected by the lower committees, ordinary Conservatives were unlikely to climb far up the ladder and control remained in the hands of small cliques. Not until the 1920s did the party move towards a formal system of membership and a low entrance fee, in sharp contrast to the Primrose League, which adopted this practice from the start.

Clearly the emergence of permanent local organizations presented several dilemmas for Conservatives. Was it right or even efficacious to segregate Conservative supporters along class lines? Disraeli himself was among those who considered it rather inconsistent with the best principles of the party. And how much independent authority should a body like the National Union command? The conventional parliamentary view held that the National Union should encourage and assist constituency activities, but had no rights of compulsion over local associations, nor any resources save those allocated by the party leaders. As a check on National Union ambitions, Disraeli created in 1870 an alternative focus of power in the Conservative Central Office, which disposed of the funds and nominated twelve members to the National Union's Council, but was itself appointed by the parliamentary leadership.

As a result of such restrictions the National Union has always enjoyed a reputation as the mere 'handmaiden' of the Conservative Party, burdened with duties but entrusted with little authority.[10] Yet for the late nineteenth century this is less than entirely accurate; during the 1880s and 1890s it proved a rather assertive handmaiden. From the start its function had been defined, even by Gorst, so as to exclude programmes and principles which were a matter of general agreement and therefore presumably not worth discussing, and to consist exclusively in devising the best methods for propagating Conservative objectives. However, in practice things were much less simple. The deferential workingmen who attended the early meetings soon gave way to a more bumptious and independent-minded type, as the annual conference minutes show. Even when addressing themselves to organizational matters delegates adopted a querulous and critical attitude towards the parliamentary leadership, which they blamed for giving insufficient attention, resources and rewards to the urban Conservatives they represented, and for failing to bring county Conservatism under the National Union's aegis. [11]

Nor was the National Union by any means silent on party policy. No doubt its conferences recycled the traditional platitudes and passed resolutions of confidence in the leader or government as a matter of course, but in this respect it was not significantly different from Liberal or, later, Labour practice; all three devoted much of their time to essentially ritual activity. Genuine policy debates on subjects inconvenient to the party leaders became quite common for the National Union during the 1880s and 1890s. For example, proposals for government assistance to workingmen who wished to buy their own homes met with considerable support; [12] this was precisely the kind of sectional pleading that the parliamentarians feared from such a body. Demands for restriction upon alien immigration, another working-class issue, won approval on seven occasions and eventually became the subject of legislation under Balfour in 1905. [13] Women's suffrage, which alarmed the leadership largely because it seemed so divisive, received Conference support on several occasions. [14] Perhaps most damaging of all in the end was the revival of protectionism, which began to surface in the 1880s in the form of 'fair trade' resolutions by Colonel Howard Vincent MP, and under the guise of 'Imperial Federation'; in 1886, for example, Curzon showed himself perfectly aware of the risks of using the National Union as a policy-making forum on such an issue: 'We meet here for discussion and not for dictation. This is a conference and not a caucus.' [15] As a result of its debates the National Union committed itself to a measure of tariff reform more than a decade before the parliamentary party shifted in that direction. Obviously the National Union in no sense made party policy; even the groundswell of protectionism required a lead from a major figure, and this did not come until Chamberlain's campaign in 1903. But the rapidity with which parliamentary Conservatism succumbed at that stage is a warning against depicting the party in the country as merely passive and deferential. While never the equal of the National Liberal Federation, the National Union differed only in degree. As its track record suggests, it had the potential to be very troublesome indeed. In this context the apprehension of Conservative leaders about such a supposedly anodyne organization was understandable, and their ready appreciation of an alternative mass organization of a different character − the Primrose League − becomes entirely intelligible.

THE NATIONAL UNION CONTROVERSY AND THE EMERGENCE OF THE LEAGUE 1883-4

In the aftermath of electoral defeat in 1880 the Conservatives entered a period of acute internal bickering and demoralization from which they did not fully emerge until the Home Rule crisis of 1886. With Disraeli's death in 1881 the party experienced an uncomfortable dual leadership of Sir Stafford Northcote in the Commons and Lord Salisbury in the Lords. In the early 1880s Northcote was widely considered the more likely permanent leader. Salisbury's record of resignation over the 1867 Reform Act still marked him as an extreme, inflexible and remote figure; the party had not yet discovered the attractions of an aloof aristocrat among a popular electorate. Meanwhile, inspiration flagged at the prospect of Northcote, still apparently deferential towards Gladstone, whose secretary he had once been. Far from recapturing the élan of Disraeli and his victory of 1874, the party seemed about to revert to the Derby era.

In these circumstances bolder spirits began to adopt their own initiatives. In the Commons, Lord Randolph Churchill, Sir Henry Drummond Wolff, John Gorst and A. J. Balfour formed what contemporaries dubbed the Fourth Party, which devoted itself to vitriolic and effective harassment of the Government, the underlying object being to embarrass their own front bench. Simultaneously, Conservatives in the National Union vented their irritation over the election defeat, which they ascribed to the unsympathetic response of the traditional leaders towards organization. Thus the natural target of criticism on both fronts was the hapless Northcote, and the cumulative effect of several years of controversy was to compound the impression that he could not cope with the stresses of leadership. That all this facilitated Salisbury's emergence as leader was almost certainly the intention of Churchill, if not of every member of the Fourth Party. Moreover, Salisbury himself signalled his appreciation by his early endorsement of their activities.[16] Churchill's preference for Salisbury is not surprising, despite the role he was playing. Both intended to preserve as much power as possible for the traditional aristocratic elite in the party. In so far as Lord Randolph had any definite and consistently held political opinions, which was not very far as his latest biographer has shown, they were very right wing even for a Conservative; the occasional 'Tory Democracy' speech was little more than a tactical manoeuvre.[17] Above all Lord Randolph was guided by self-interest. With a leader in the Lords there would be greater scope for rising figures like himself in the Commons; Salisbury's rather isolated position suggested that he would be easier to bargain with.

To co-ordinate the two strands of dissatisfaction in the country and in Parliament seemed a natural step. The link between the two was Gorst, who had been persuaded by W. H. Smith to attempt an overhaul of the party's electoral machinery once more, but had rapidly fallen foul of the local associations. The National Union was flattered when a man of Churchill's eminence adopted its cause, and by capitalizing on the Union's grievances he won another platform from which to bring his attack on Northcote to a climax. In 1883 Lord Randolph managed to win election to the Council of the National Union, albeit by a narrow margin, so that at the annual conference at Birmingham in October he was in a position to ventilate the Union's chief complaints: that it was denied control over finance, was inferior to the central council appointed by the party leaders, and was compelled to accept nominated members onto its own elected council. It was probably not clear even to Lord Randolph what he wanted to achieve by all this beyond personal advancement. As yet he was such a junior and inexperienced figure that he could not be confident that Salisbury would bother to reach a settlement with him, and in fact at this time he evidently discussed with family and friends the possibility of establishing a new party for the less hidebound Conservatives.[18] What emerged was the Primrose League − a party within a party. This initiative found Lord Randolph pulling three levers simultaneously during 1833–4 − Fourth Party, National Union and Primrose League − in the hope that one would make his political fortune before it was too late.

In April 1883 the occasion of the unveiling of a statue of Disraeli reminded the Fourth Party of an imperishable asset they might deploy in their current struggle. Both within the party and outside the memory of Disraeli seemed to evoke affection and respect. The original idea of harnessing such sentiment in some permanent institution is usually ascribed to Sir Henry Drummond Wolff,[19] but the initiatives leading to the wearing of primroses on 19th April arose from more obscure figures such as the India Office official Sir George Birdwood, who enlisted the support of some London clubs and newspaper editors.[20] During the summer and autumn, Wolff, Churchill and Gorst discussed the possibilities frequently at Lady Dorthy Nevill's luncheon parties;[21] they wisely involved Sir Algernon Borthwick who, as proprietor of the *Morning Post*, had already given the Fourth Party a good deal of editorial support and was to do the same for the Primrose League. Believing that his services to the Conservative cause had been insufficiently recognized by the leaders, Borthwick determined to attach himself to Churchill in the expectation of rising in his wake. The other pioneers of the league at this point were Sir William Hardman, Borthwick's editor; Sir Alfred Slade, a particularly sycophantic ally of Lord Randolph who also participated in the National Union struggle; Colonel Fred Burnaby, who contested Birmingham jointly with Churchill; F. Dixon Hartland MP, Sir Henry Hoare MP, Percy Mitford, Seager Hunt, and Churchill's brother-in-law Lord Wimborne. In short, the Primrose League at its inception represented yet another Fourth Party machination, based upon little but the clique of conspirators clustered around Churchill, hopeful of a share in his fortunes.

At a small meeting in the Carlton Club on 17 November 1883 the 'Primrose Tory League' was launched by Churchill, Gorst, Wolff and Slade, all now members of the National Union's Council, who constituted themselves the Grand Council of the new body. Their proclaimed object was to rectify 'the failure of Conservative and Constitutional Associations to suit the popular taste or to succeed in joining all classes together for political objects'. [22] Membership was declared open to all except atheists and enemies of the British Empire who would subscribe to the following:

> I declare, on my honour and faith, that I will devote my best ability to the maintenance of Religion, of the Estates of the Realm, and of the unity of the British Empire under our Sovereign...

Initially the four ringleaders tried to keep their names secret until more subscriptions had been raised, which only provoked irritation and amusement from their fellow politicians. In fact, the real character of the league took some time to evolve. When Gorst departed for India in November there went with him the possibility of creating a more effective version of the National Union, for the others had little real interest in such an organization. Undoubtedly Churchill's 1880 contest at Birmingham had underlined the inferiority of the Conservative electoral machine, while the appearance in 1883 of Gladstone's legislation against corrupt electoral practices made the mobilization of voluntary workers a matter of urgency. Such a need, the early leaguers believed, could simply not be met by the existing Conservative Associations which had 'degenerated to a mere congeries of cliques', as Claude Hay put it. [23] When, for example, Lady Hicks-Beach formed a habitation (local branch) in Gloucestershire, she explained that her intention was to ensure registration of voters and secure the loan of carriages at election times' [24] – thus clearly showing the pressure of the 1883 Act. Yet Lord Randolph, in so far as he had thought about it, envisaged the Primrose League as a semi-secret society of Conservative gentlemen of a younger, or at least livelier, disposition than the usual politicians – in short, an extra-parliamentary Fourth Party but not a mass organization. [25] Churchill, however, rapidly ceased to play a significant role. It was Wolff who stamped certain characteristic features on the new organization. Though he wanted a popular body, he looked for a different style to the imitation Liberalism of the National Union, and found it in some of the organizations already strongly supported in his Portsmouth constituency: Benefit Societies, the Orange Order and the Freemasons. [26] A hierarchical structure, underpinned by honours, badges and decorations, dressed up in quaint titles and dignified by ceremony and ritual, seemed to be part of the attraction of such bodies, which the League emulated with great

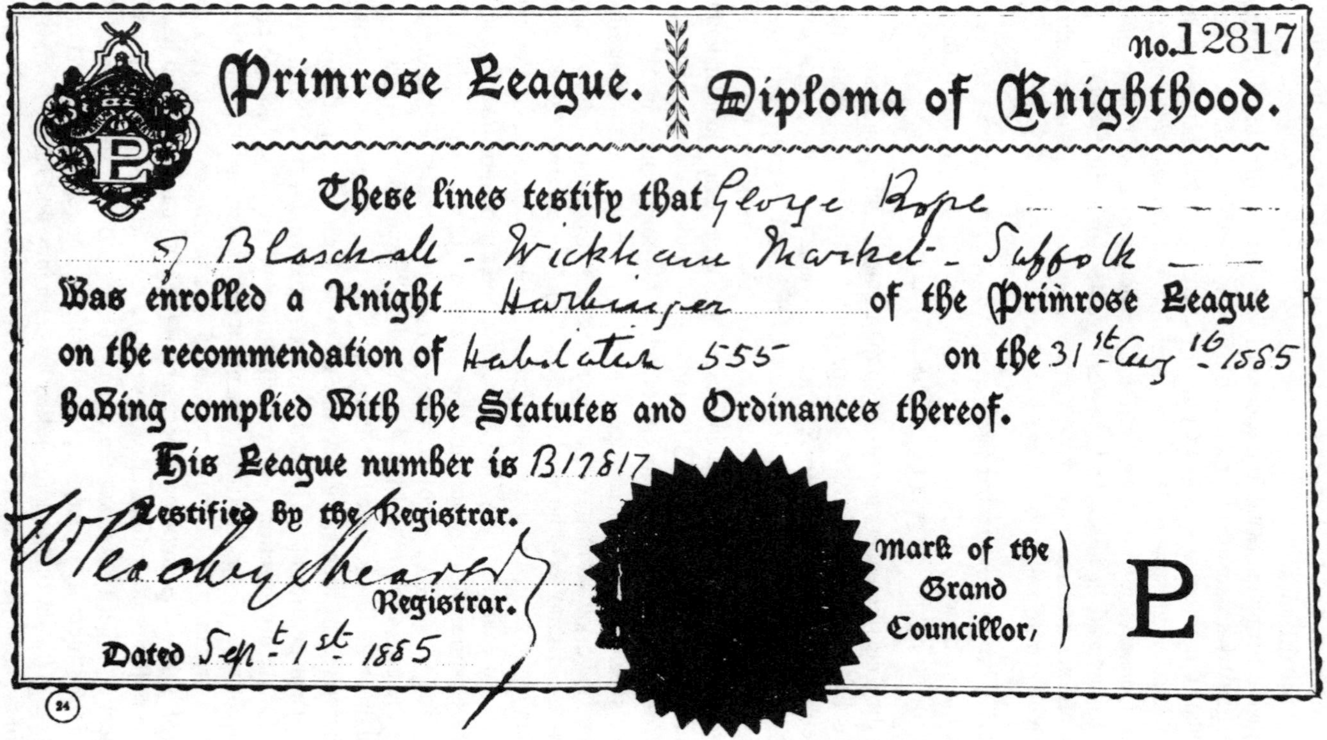
no. 12817

Primrose League. Diploma of Knighthood.

These lines testify that George Rope

of Blaxhall – Wickham Market – Suffolk

Was enrolled a Knight Harbinger of the Primrose League

on the recommendation of Habitation 555 on the 31st Aug 16 – 1885

having complied with the Statutes and Ordinances thereof.

His League number is B17817

Testified by the Registrar.

W Peakey Shearer

Registrar.

Dated Sept 1st 1885

Mark of the Grand Councillor, P L

Plate 1 The Primrose League: Diploma of Knighthood 1885

gusto. Wolff was also instrumental in opening the League to women and to Christians of all denominations including Catholics, groups that had hitherto not been much in evidence in the ranks of organized Conservatism.

However, the Primrose League remained cloaked in mystery over the winter and spring. Prominent dignitaries like the Duke of Portland were approached for donations and respectability, while both Salisbury and Northcote received invitations to become trustees. Northcote naturally suspected it as just another Churchill conspiracy, while Salisbury, who could afford to be generous, showed more warmth.[27] By 1884 there was a party interest at stake as well as a personal one. Negotiations between the Conservative and Liberal leaders over the franchise bill were leading towards an agreed, but drastic redistribution of the constituencies. In the fairly near future, therefore, a fresh election would be fought, in which the party would be grateful both for a popular organization and Lord Randolph's platform oratory. Thus for Salisbury, party and personal considerations required a settlement with Churchill over the tiresome National Union dispute, and they reached an accord in July 1884.

Apart from an agreement that all constituency associations must affiliate, there was little in this deal to please the National Union. Its powers were not changed, and Hicks-Beach took over from Earl Percy as Chairman. Perhaps the only significant point was the official recognition now given by the party leaders to the Primrose League. It may seem odd that a campaign which had ostensibly been waged to strengthen the National Union should have been concluded with the elevation of what appeared to be a rival, but it made good sense for both Salisbury and Churchill. The former had never had any intention of granting the National Union anything beyond its existing duties of disseminating propaganda and stimulating constituency organization.[28] That affiliation was now to be compulsory was itself a sign of his confidence that the Union would be more loyal than in the past. The basis for such confidence lay in Churchill's patent eagerness to accept a face-saving compromise which would allow him to abandon the National Union and take cabinet office in Salisbury's next administration. Both of these things he did. Those urban Conservatives who had been hoping for a real devolution of authority were disappointed; like Gorst and Northcote, they had been by-passed. To Salisbury accrued the credit for handling an intractable problem and turning a leading rebel into a loyal lieutenant. Moreover, in giving a boost to the Primrose League he was setting another rival against the National Union, and promoting a body which both ideologically and organizationally was far more congenial to him.

THE PRIMROSE LEAGUE AND THE PARTY

The dual system represented by the National Union and its constituency associations on one side, and the Primrose League and its habitations on the other, seems cumbersome and fragmented. In the local constituency a multiplicity of organizations might compete for support, including the Conservative Registration Association, Conservative Club, Conservative Workingmen's Club, Primrose League Habitation and Orange Lodge.[29] In practice, however, the dual structure suited the party's requirements rather well before 1914, with the league happily accepting the role of the 'preaching friars', in Salisbury's words, to the regular church of Conservatism; the two bodies complemented each other's efforts, and enjoyed a common personnel at the higher levels.

In the absence of official membership figures for the Conservative Party itself, one cannot be sure of the strength of the associations affiliated to the National Union, but few had a genuinely mass membership and many remained purely nominal; given the financial barriers and social exclusiveness of the official party it seems unlikely that numbers even approached those of the league. Both numerically and in terms of its social breadth the league comprised the popular wing of Conservatism. Contrary to first impressions, the league was not a purely rural phenomenon but enjoyed a very large membership in cities by the 1890s (see chapter 5). Unlike the party, it catered for women and, later, for children too; indeed, whole families sometimes joined up. Bridging the barriers of sex, age and class was always the proud boast of the league. To some extent its latent rivalry with the National Union was mitigated by a pretence on the part of the official body that the league was primarily a women's organization, a description which contained no more than an element of truth. Thus not until the Edwardian period were the two seen to be in direct competition for membership.

Another aspect which generated a little friction was the belief that the Primrose League diverted funds away from the party to mere social activities.[39] In fact the league's central organization functioned on a fairly modest income of around £7,000 in the the 1880s and 1890s; the bulk of the resources lay in the habitations. This of course reflected a traditional preference of Conservatives for patronizing local bodies; therefore it does not follow that in the absence of the league its resources would have found their way into national party coffers. In any case, during the 1890s the party was actually raising substantial though diminishing sums from Tory peers; any shortfall was more than compensated by the huge donations from businessmen. W. W. Astor's £20,500 in 1900 compares with £37,500 from all the peers in 1895, and £45,000 in 1892. Neither in late Victorian nor Edwardian times were the Conservatives nationally short of money.[31]

As far as policy was concerned the League developed no pretensions whatever. It was possible to submit resolutions for debate at Grand Habitation, but the discussions actually centred on the league's own operations and business. Meetings were crowned by an address from the Conservative leader, and motions of unbounded confidence in HM Government if Conservatives were in office. Political discussions clearly did take place at habitation level, but usually went no further. Detailed policies were simply regarded as out of bounds; instead, the league defined its political purpose in terms of the defence of a few general principles — Empire, Monarchy, Religion, the Estates of the Realm. Theoretically, much the same should have been true of the National Union, but as we have noted, its practice drifted towards that of the National Liberal Federation. In defining its position the league claimed no exclusive or inexorable relationship with the Conservative Party; whoever upheld the principles of the league might enjoy its support. This, of course, was a way of emphasizing their common ground with traditional Palmerstonian Liberals; a 'true' Liberal was therefore welcome to escape the radical panaceas gripping Gladstonian Liberalism. Conversely, the league maintained that it supported Conservatives only in so far as and for as long as they continued to uphold its principles. As critics pointed out, the league never actively worked for anyone who was not a Conservative, but until the twentieth century it firmly declined any binding commitment to the party as such. The corollary was that it enjoyed no formal representation on other Conservative institutions. Indeed, habitations which occasionally affiliated to the National Union were consistently instructed by Grand Council to desist.[32] This was not because they feared poaching but because of the need to recruit widely. After dropping the 'Tory' in its original title the league offered an ideal point of entry for groups and individuals gravitating towards Conservatism or becoming involved in politics for the first time.

This independence seemed awkward and unnecessary to some Conservatives, who would have preferred for the sake of simplicity and efficiency to bring the league under the auspices of the National Union.[33] However, before 1900 the politicians largely preferred the existing arrangements, for the league gave them the advantages of a mass organization without its drawbacks. It was self-financing. It showed little interest in propagating the details of Conservative legislative achievements or raising hopes of future programmes, as the National Union was prone to do. By confining itself to very traditional and generalized Conservative causes like the Empire it helped to channel the debate in the country into congenial courses; for if ever the parties engaged in a competition to offer the electors precise material benefits the Conservatives felt they would end up the losers. Moreover, because it refused any place in the structure of the party, the league never threatened to make demands upon the party. At elections it put its workers at the disposal of local Conservative agents to employ or not as they chose. It accepted the approved candidates on the basis of their presumed principles and, unlike the National Union, never raised embarrassing questions as to whether they ought to include more working-class men.

In the last resort the smooth running of the alliance depended simply on a considerable overlap of personnel between the two wings of Conservatism.

There were always some league members who regarded the party as too stuffy and exclusive, and some Conservatives who considered the league unduly frivolous or suspiciously feminist. But by and large co-operation flourished. At habitation level one finds 55 MPs acting as Ruling Councillors in 1900 and 32 peers as late as 1908.[34] At the top Northcote, Salisbury and in their turn Balfour, Curzon and Baldwin held the honorary title of Grand Master. The role of Chancellor was usually filled by a peer, a backbench MP or a junior minister (appendix I); while at the intermediate levels dozens of influential Conservatives played a role in the league as Ruling Councillor or Grand Councillor, and in the party as President or Chairman of the National Union (appendix II). A party whip from each house had joined Grand Council following official recognition in 1884 and by the 1890s fifteen to twenty MPs invariably accompanied them. Colonel Howard Vincent, H. C. Raikes, Ashmead Bartlett and Sir F. Dixon-Hartland were typical of MPs deeply involved in the Council of the National Union as well as the league. As a result the league, though a mass organization, manifested itself in reassuring and acceptable faces whose loyalty was not in doubt; indeed, the prevalence of peers suggested a reversion to the older pattern of local voluntarism loosely linked to Westminister − a felicitous illusion for those embarking on a transition to modern political practice.

2

The Politics of Social Integration

However impressive the support attracted by the Primrose League in its heyday, a suspicion lingers that it amounted to little more than a quaint curiosity, the last retreat of romantics, eccentrics and political lightweights. With its undisguised enthusiasm for social junketing, its defiantly archaic terminology, and the whimsicality of its very title, the league invited derision even from political allies. Nor are such impressions entirely erroneous. Its spirit and character were always that of a huge rearguard action; and ultimately, no doubt, its members so much enjoyed looking back and recapturing times long past that their grip on the present relaxed. Yet all this should not obscure the League's effective contribution to the *modernization* of right-wing politics in Britain. In the context of late Victorian Britain its antiquarianism was scarcely unusual, nor was this necessarily a defect for a Conservative movement at a time when the age of improvement was patently faltering. 'It is, in short, a return to ''Merrie England's'' traditions for the village folks. But mark! It is politics all the same.'[1]

In the 1880s, and for long afterwards, the 'Primrose' tag caused endless speculation, the significance of which may be quite briefly disposed of. Disraeli's love of primroses became widely known when, on his death in 1881, two wreaths composed of the flowers arrived from Queen Victoria bearing the words: 'His favourite flowers from Osborne, a tribute of affection from Queen Victoria.' As the first anniversary of his death approached, Sir George Birdwood, a civil servant at the India Office, suggested to the Secretary of St Stephen's Club that primroses be used as table decorations on 19th April. The club's committee turned down the idea, but other friends such as Lord Lytton wore them as 'Beaconsfield Buttonholes'. Birdwood wrote to several London newspapers on the subject and florists began to respond to the publicity by supplying more primroses. When the exercise was repeated in April 1883 an extensive sale was established.[2] For Disraeli's political heirs the fond link with the Crown represented a considerable political asset; yet while their opponents could not credibly question the signs of royal favour, they could disparage the connection by challenging the primrose itself. 'Tell me, Lady Dorothy,' Mr Gladstone pressed Lady Dorothy Nevill over dinner not long after Disraeli's death, 'upon your honour, have you ever heard Lord Beaconsfield express any particular fondness for the primrose?'[3] Despite having been a close friend and neighbour of the statesman for many years, she had to admit she had not. Though immensely satisfying to the Liberal leader this news did nothing to quell the belief in the connection between flower and politician. Those who picked meticulously through his novels for evidence found little more than a recommendation in *Lothair* that primroses made capital salads! However, the League periodically made it its business to unearth testimonies from Hughenden residents on the importance of these flowers.[4] The substance appears to be that the queen had sent Disraeli primroses and violets on more than one occasion during his lifetime, though she was not the first to do so.[5] Beyond that, one may surmise that he made known his fondness not for primroses as such, but for primroses that came from the queen.

THE RETURN TO CAMELOT

Any search for precise ideological connections between the league and the statesman is not particularly profitable. The point is that in 1883 Disraeli, now sanctified by death, served as a useful peg on which to hang a new Conservative organization. What the league obviously shared with him was sheer romanticism. At least something of the spirit of Young England clung to its early years, as indeed did one living link with the England of the 1840s, Lord John Manners, who was Seventh Duke of Rutland from 1888. Not surprisingly, aristocrats like Manners looked askance at the late Victorian Conservative Party. Protection was both dead and damned. Industralization continued to transform British society, while agriculture diminished and decayed. Even the Conservative ranks were being penetrated by latter-day Peelites – wealthy, urban and middle class. It was natural to look back with affection to a presumed era of stability based upon the relationship between a loyal people and the responsible English gentleman.

Thus at the outset the league chose to underline the importance it attached to the traditional gentleman by the terminology it adopted:

> This creation of a Tory democracy was raised from the spirit of emulation and honour of all classes of the genuine English volunteer type known to our forefathers as chivalry. Hence the Primrose League was formed on the basis of the old orders of knighthood.[6]

However, the league was far from unique in this respect. As one historian has reminded us, much of the Victorian and Edwardian era was characterized by a flourishing belief in codes of conduct appropriate to the English gentleman.[7] In its more colourful manifestations this mood took the form of revivals of medieval jousting tournaments, the first of which took place at Eglinton in 1837; another was held at Parham in Sussex in 1875, another planned at Taymouth in 1880, while in 1912 Earl's Court was the scene of a tournament organized by Lady Randolph Churchill. It was much the same spirit of romantic escapism that made so many Victorians relish the novels of Sir Walter Scott, idealize the clans and chiefs of the Scottish Highlands, and embellish their castles and homes in the Gothic style. Prince Albert himself sat for his portrait bedecked in armour, for however incongruous on such a staid bourgeois, this coincided with the queen's conception of her husband as a chivalrous knight.

What did this lost medieval world mean to Victorians as they glimpsed it through their pervading industrial smog? In the aftermath of the revolutionary and Napoleonic period it surely represented stability, a society firmly rooted in land ownership, the loyalty of the poor to the lords who defended them, the loyalty of the lords to their king, and a monarch supported by a powerful undivided church. Nor was this merely escapism: it underpinned a style of politics. In common with its rivals, Conservatism ransacked the past to serve the present. For Liberals the past served as a reminder of the virtues of Cromwellian England and the evils of absolute monarchy, still alive in Tsarist Russia, or of ancient barbarism, still flourishing among the Ottoman Turks. While socialists often shared these sentiments, some, like William Morris, found inspiration in the satisfying, skilled labour of smallscale pre-industrial society. The Conservative perspective on medievalism was different, but equally lively. At the Eglinton Tournament both the knights competing for honour and the spectators had been Tories.[8] Romantic manifestations of medievalism like castles and kings provided symbols of authority, particularly attractive to Conservatives in a century of perceived social change. Thus the emphasis which the league gave to the preservation of the estates of the realm, the central role of the monarch, the common interest of aristocrats and people, the lavish use of honours and titles, the rich visual appeal of its activities, and even its tolerant attitude towards the Catholic Church, reflected the various aspects of Victorian medievalism. In the context of the 1880s it never appeared quite as exotic as its critics liked to believe, but rather as a political expression of an established and familiar phenomenon.

The medieval spirit could most easily be recaptured by the archaic terminology adopted by the league's founders. There is at least circumstantial evidence for thinking that the league found its immediate source of stylistic apparatus in freemasonry, since key terms such as Grand Master, Warden and Chapter were common to both organizations. In fact, freemasonry itself owed much of its medievalism to the early connection with the Order of the Knights of St John, from whose own terminology the league seems to have borrowed freely — esquire, priory, serjeant-at-arms, and, most importantly, the idea of lay associates who might be male or female.[9] Membership of the league involved a pledge of loyalty, not quite comparable to masonic practice, but hardly usual for a political party at this time. In addition, during the first few months of its life, the league was shrouded in privacy and mystery as though its leaders were behaving in masonic fashion, though it never became a secret society as its opponents alleged. The two organizations also shared a common emphasis on fraternization between people of all classes, and a similar dedication to the establishment in general, and the royal family in particular. One also has a strong impression of a common membership between the league and freemasonry at the higher levels of society, in that men like Lord Henniker in Suffolk, Lord Addington in Buckinghamshire and Lord Ridley in Northumberland were prominent in both. In 1886 the Scottish Grand Council of the league agreed to hold its meetings on the same days as those of the Grand Lodge of Freemasonry for the convenience of its members.[10] All this should not be taken to imply any direct masonic inspiration behind the league. It is simply that during the twenty years prior to the league's creation, freemasonry had expanded very rapidly and, for reasons of social standing, many of those who were already masons found the league attractive. One study of politics in Sheffield has also suggested that Conservatives were more likely than Liberals to be attracted by the social side of freemasonry.[11]

All members of the Primrose League followed knightly example by taking a pledge to uphold and defend certain principles. During his first year a man was strictly a Knight Companion, then a Knight Harbinger, while ministers of religion were Knights Almoners. Dame, from madame, was said to be ancient designation for the wife of a baronet or knight, superseded by 'Lady' only during 'these later and more degenerate times'.[12] Initially the lower category of membership had been termed Esquire, and sometimes Companion, but these were dropped in 1885 in favour of Associate, probably because it was the only suitable word which would cover both sexes.[13] At the apex of the league's hierarchy stood the Grand Master, whose function was to preside over Grand Habitation once a year. Beneath him stood a chief executive figure, the Chancellor, supported by a salaried administrator, the Vice-Chancellor. Originally the founders contemplated calling the local branches 'lodges', but eventually rejected the idea on the grounds that the term's association with the Orange Order would alienate Catholics.[14] Instead they adopted the Middle English word Habitation. Led by a Ruling Councillor, the habitation relied heavily upon a large number of Wardens, each of whom regularly canvassed a small patch of its territory — a typical illustration of the league's capacity for obscuring the work of an efficient, modern political machine in archaic terminology. Habitations might be established only by the issue of a Warrant and a number by Grand Council, the ruling body of the league, whose formal

Habitation No. 1532

The Primrose League,

64, VICTORIA STREET, LONDON, S.W.

I, the undersigned, wish to join the _____ *Lowther* _____ HABITATION OF THE PRIMROSE LEAGUE, and I accordingly sign this Declaration and agree to pay such subscription per annum to the Habitation as is affixed to my name.

DECLARATION OF ASSOCIATE.

I declare on my honour and faith that I will devote my best ability to the maintenance of Religion, of the Estates of the Realm, and of the Imperial ascendency of the British Empire ; and that consistently with my allegiance to the Sovereign of these Realms, I will promote, with discretion and fidelity, the above objects, being those of The Primrose League.

Name in full _____ *Beatrice Todd* _____
(Mr., Mrs. or Miss).

Address _____ *(Miss)* _____

_____ *Mount Clifton Penrith* _____

Occupation _____

Date _____ *June 12ᵗʰ 1899* _____

Annual Subscription *3ᴰ*

(13)   Form to be filled up by Applicant.

Signature of Recruiting Member,

RSWoof

22-10-98.

Plate 2   *The Primrose League Declaration of Associate 1899*

instructions were Precepts, and to which the Knights and Dames paid annual Tribute. An additional payment of a guinea entitled a Dame to membership of the Grand Dames Council, soon retitled Ladies Grand Council, while for men the equivalent was to become a Knight Imperial in the Imperial Chapter under a Prior.

Imagination seems to have failed when the leaders considered the more utilitarian parts of the organization such as the salaried provincial secretaries who received the staid appelation District Agent, though the regions over which they presided recalled Anglo-Saxon England, perhaps slightly adjusted to suit the Victorian railway system:

North Northumbria:	Northumberland, Durham, North Yorkshire
South Northumbria:	East and West Ridings
Cumbria:	Cumberland, Westmorland, Lancashire
North Gwallia:	Flint, Cheshire, Anglesey, Denbigh, Caernarvon, Merioneth, Montgomery, Shropshire
West Gwallia:	Cardigan, Pembroke, Carmarthen, Radnor
East Gwallia:	Glamorgan, Brecon, Monmouth, Hereford
North Wessex:	Gloucester, Somerset
South Wessex:	Devon, Cornwall
Mercia:	Derby, Leicester, Nottingham, Lincoln, Rutland, Northampton, Stafford, Warwick, Worcester
East Anglia:	Norfolk, Suffolk, Cambridge, Huntingdon, parts of Essex
East Saxons:	Berkshire, Oxford, Buckingham, Bedford, Hertford, parts of Essex, Middlesex and Kent.
South Saxons:	Surrey, Sussex, Hampshire, Wiltshire, Dorset.

Many local habitations adopted historical figures as a way of fostering local pride and distinguishing an obscure locality; examples include 'King Arthur's Round Table' (Camelford), 'Hereward' (Littleport, Cambridgeshire), 'John o'Gaunt' (Hinckley and Thurnby, Leicestershire), 'Robin Hood' (Nottingham East and Eastwood, 'Robert the Bruce' (Lochmaben) and 'William Wallace' (Larbert). Alternatively the names of local houses and castles were adopted, such as 'Delapre' (Northampton), 'Kildrummy' (West Aberdeenshire), 'Powis' (Welshpool), 'Welbeck' (Nottinghamshire), and 'Ravensworth' (Gateshead).

Endlessly amusing as Primrose flummery was to its opponents, it nonetheless represented a significant element in the league's appeal; for the league's strength as a Conservative organization lay in its refusal to apologise for being traditional. Medieval symbolism may have distinguished the league from other political bodies, whose membership invariably remained modest if not exiguous, but this quality enabled it to speak to a wider constituency of romanticism and nostalgia than its more prosaic rivals. Conservative organizations like the National Union, which often seemed a pale imitation of the Radical caucus, were never likely to capitalize fully on this potential. Indeed, in so far as the real task for Conservatives lay in tapping the latent conservativism in the country, the Primrose League held the key: an appeal to the imagination.

THE GROWTH OF A MASS MEMBERSHIP

After its somewhat obscure inauguration in November 1883 the new organization faltered briefly. Not surprisingly, many potential members hesitated, for not only were the league's officers well below the first rank in Conservative circles, they also enjoyed a deserved reputation as mere cronies of Churchill. To join would therefore have been to exacerbate a schism in the party. By March 1884 only 46 habitations had been established, and the league urgently required a mark of approval from the party leadership. Meanwhile, Grand Council adopted a variety of stratagems designed to add lustre and momentum to the cause. The approach of spring prompted the secretary to negotiate with florists to supply plenty of primroses in time for the anniversary of Disraeli's death in April; those who cooperated gained the right to style themselves 'Florists to the League'.[15] In December 1883 they had shrewdly decided to permit women to join, as a result of which by May 1884 they were able to boast a number of titled ladies, apart from Churchill's wife and mother, among the members: the Duchess of Newcastle, the Marchioness of Waterford, the Countesses of Bective, Chesterfield, Desart, Jersey, Feversham, Lonsdale, Malmesbury and Shrewsbury, and Lady Gwendolen Cecil, Lady Campbell of Blythswood, Lady Henniker, Lady Rossmore and Lady Egremont. The League thus doubled its potential market at a stroke and began to tap the popular fascination for aristocracy.

Initially, the founders had clearly not envisaged a mass membership. However, signs of interest among the lower classes led to a reappraisal. The question was not tackled until March 1884, when Sir Alfred Slade reported that he had permitted 'on this occasion only, the admission of some working-men, by inadventure, without entrance fee'.[16] The decision to formalize this practice was, as Claude Hay later admitted, controversial, and drastically changed the nature of the enterprise.[17] By 1885 a dual system had been instituted whereby Knights and Dames paid 2/6 a year to Grand Council plus a subscription to their habitation, while Associates paid only a very small sum.[18]

Meanwhile, Grand Council continued to fish for big names. The Duchess of Sutherland complained to Sir Algernon Borthwick that her name was being used in connection with the league, 'the leaders of which are kept secret'.[19] Salisbury himself showed sympathy without commitment: 'Its objects are most excellent,' he commented on receiving a copy of the statutes 'I quite agree with you as to the supreme importance under present circumstances of volunteer effort at and between elections'.[20] Substantial sections of the peerage accepted membership, often without knowing quite what they were joining: the Duke of Portland, the Marquis of Abergavenny, the Earls of Hopetoun, Limerick, Orford and Kinnoull, Viscounts Curzon and Castlereagh, and Lord Wimborne. But the real turning-point came in July 1884 with the Churchill-Salisbury compromise which gave the green light to the orthodox partisans. At once a clutch of MPs entered the Grand Council, including Sir Michael Hicks Beach, G. Sclator Booth, Lord Elcho, Colonel Edmund King-Harman, W. T. Marriott, Lord Arthur Hill and Robert Bourke. At this point Grand Council took the goat by the horns by inviting Northcote as well as Salisbury to become patrons. Despite the former's suspicions, both agreed to be patrons. 'But I suppose we shall have no such commonplace name. What do you say to Vavasours?' asked Salisbury, evidently entering into the spirit of the enterprise. [21]

While the party leaders became Grand Masters, Churchill himself rapidly faded as an active participant. After August 1884 he rarely attended meetings, which is only partly explained by his absence in India during 1885. Though he remained a trustee of the league for the rest of his life he was thereafter seen only occasionally at major functions. Doubtless the league seemed scarcely more important to him than the National Union; once entrenched in cabinet he had little further use for either. But if Lord Randolph soon outgrew the league, the reverse was equally true. During 1885 its personnel increased so rapidly as to eclipse the original Fourth Party clique, though Borthwick, Hardman, Mitford and Dixon-Hartland continued to be prominently involved. Privately the league's leaders admitted to being 'very much shaken' by Churchill's abrupt resignation from the cabinet in 1886, but remained adamant that their principles would outlast the vicissitudes of any individual career. [22] Beyond welcoming his infrequent speeches as a sign of his return to the ranks, the league abstained from any temptation to offer him a platform from which to launch a fresh bid for power.

For the reasons already suggested, membership during the first six months barely reached one thousand; up to the spring of 1884 the league amounted to no more than Churchill's semi-secret society for Tory gentlemen, and only after the official establishment of Associate membership in April 1885 did a mass movement become possible; within seven months the Associates comprised two-thirds of total strength, and over 80 per cent within two years. Any explanation of the remarkable surge in membership during 1885–7 must not overlook the stimulus of two general elections. The first of these in November 1885 was most fortuitous from the league's point of view, for the excitement generated by the 'Unauthorized Programme' and the alleged threat to disestablish the Anglican Church could not have been better calculated to impress Conservatives with the relevance of its basic principles. Yet since the league was scarcely off the drawing-board it could not be blamed for the party's failure to perform better at the election; on the contrary, the defeats in the counties served to underline the need for a popular organization capable of mobilizing the Conservatives among the new electorate. While the prospect of disestablishment rapidly faded, an issue even better calculated to galvanize Conservatives emerged when Gladstone's son Herbert flew the famous Hawarden Kite in December, thereby making Irish Home Rule the dominating question of the day. This, and the second general election it brought in its wake, doubtless accounts for the extraordinarily, rapid expansion of the Primrose League during 1886, which brought half a million men and women on to its books by early 1887. Thereafter recruiting continued briskly, though in the early 1890s the pace slowed as Salisbury's government lost impetus.

Table 1   *The Primrose League: official enrolment figures 1884–1910*

	Knights	Dames	Associates	Habitations	Total
1884, 29 Mar.	747	153	57	46	957
1885, 31 Mar.	8,071	1,381	1,914	169	11,366
9 Sept.	13,122	4,471	8,610	–	26,203
28 Oct.	16,262	7,309	20,641	–	44,212
18 Nov.	18,583	9,913	34,567	–	63,062
16 Dec.	21,144	12,696	59,237	–	93,077
1886, 27 Jan.	23,891	15,245	84,775	–	123,911
24 Feb.	26,694	18,076	110,584	–	155,354
31 Mar.	30,206	21,365	149,266	1,200	200,837
1887, 31 Mar.	47,234	36,800	442,214	1,710	550,508
1888, 31 Mar.	54,580	42,791	575,235	1,877	672,616
1889, 31 Mar.	58,180	46,216	705,832	1,906	810,228
1890, 31 Mar.	60,795	48,796	801,261	2,081	910,852
1891, 31 Mar.	63,251	50,973	887,068	2,143	1,001,292
1901, 31 Mar.	75,260	64,906	1,416,473	2,392	1,556,639[a]
1910, 31 Mar.	87,235	80,038	1,885,746	2,645	2,053,019[a]

[a] For further evidence on the gap between enrolments and live membership at this time see chapter 7.

Like all political organizations the league tended to exaggerate its real membership. Inflation of the figures arose in broadly two ways. In the first place, as the Vice-Chancellor George Lane-Fox freely conceded, the totals published were, strictly speaking, figures for enrolments since the inception of the league rather than accurate figures of live membership each year.[23] Since habitations were not required to send a subscription for their Associates, who comprised nine-tenths of the total, there was no obvious incentive to weed out lapsed members. However, there existed a clear procedure for calculating actual current membership for which returns were to be made to headquarters every April – the end of the Primrose year. Local records show how the procedures were in fact followed. For example, Whitehaven's cumulative total of 1037 in April 1892 was reduced by 167 for those who had died or left the district, to 870 subscribing members. At Sowerby in 1888 the secretary recorded 591 from which were deducted 4 resignations, 6 deaths, 11 removals, 2 transfers to other habitations and 3 who could not be traced, which left a live list of 565.[24] One's impression is that this procedure was carried out more efficiently by large urban habitations than by lax rural ones, perhaps because a greater turnover of population made it more necessary. Certainly the habitations which competed for the annual awards of Champion Banners were obliged to demonstrate a meticulous record of membership movements, both losses and gains.

A greater source of exaggeration probably lay in the tendency to retain in the national totals the membership of habitations which had failed to make an annual return. Grand Council evidently preferred to leave inactive habitations on the books for several years before dropping them partly because it did not wish to offend and partly because the dormant ones frequently returned to life.[25] From 1892, when the novelty of the new organization had worn off, the authorities made it known that they were withdrawing warrants from defunct habitations, and this was carried out periodically with advice from provincial agents. Thus, despite an undeniable element of inflation, the figures brandished during the 1880s and 1890s are unlikely to have been grossly misleading; they paint a picture of the largest and most widely spread political organization of the time.

SOCIAL INTEGRATION

Why did the Primrose League manage to attain such a remarkable membership in its heyday? To a large extent because it offered politics in a far more enjoyable, intellectually undemanding form than its rivals within and outside Conservatism. This obvious characteristic should not be overlooked, for it helps to open up one aspect of political behaviour which has often remained closed to scholars. The late Victorians, being less blasé about a mass electorate than our own generation, were acutely aware of the non-political base upon which their whole political system rested. How many voters would give more than a moment's thought to the momentous issues put before them, or were equipped to make an informed judgement? Such doubts prompted copious attempts, especially after 1867, at building bridges between the remote world of Westminster and the workaday world inhabited by the electors and their families.[26] In essence, Primrose League habitations represented simply the most systematic expedient of this kind. Their success was conditional upon an acceptance that the politicians must meet the voters half way if they were to penetrate beyond the limited ranks of the party faithful; this meant adapting to and even integrating their activities with the ordinary social life of their supporters to some degree. Consequently habitations attempted to tread a careful path, aspiring to be political but not boring, educational but not 'improving', respectable but not censorious.

In pursuit of this objective, habitations cast their activity in the form of a rich array of social events and entertainments, both amateur and professional. Their meetings, in consequence, eventually acquired something of the combined character of a music hall, a harvest supper and a women's institute. For the Associate, membership of a habitation opened up a regular programme of events in each season of the year, in contrast to the sporadic, election-orientated activities of the party organizations. This programme invariably comprised four main elements: musical entertainments, dances, teas and summer fetes and excursions. Of these the first provided the staple event in the life of the habitation, especially during the autumn and winter months. Musical evenings and smoking concerts could be staged quite cheaply by using the talents of the best vocalists among the members, with a few piano solos, monologues, comic stories and animal imitations for variety; and a meeting of any kind was improved by contributions from anyone able to 'sing patriotic songs with good choruses so that the audience may join in'.[26] In time many habitations built up their own choirs, Christy minstrel troupes and brass bands. At a typical evening in January 1888 the 'Burnaby' Habitation in Walworth (London) reported:

> The proceedings opened with a piano forte solo ably rendered by Miss Daisy Pitt, followed by the 'Death of Nelson' in Mr Prince's best style, Mrs Schwetzuebel next giving 'The New Kingdom', succeeded by a recitation 'Rubinstein's Piano' vociferously encored, in response to which Mr Gill facetiously rendered the 'Roman Guide'. A new song 'A Mother's Love' (Wellsbourne) was then ably rendered by Mrs Marshall, Mr Court following with 'Dreaming', succeeded by Mr Arthur Bantick with 'Queen of the Earth' and Mrs Kessell 'My Little Sweetheart' (both encored), Miss Mitchell closing the first part with 'Daddy', capitally rendered. During the interval Mr Philip Johns (Chairman) addressed the audience on behalf of the habitation. . . . The second part of the programme was then proceeded with, Miss Daisy Pitt opening with a piano solo, 'Come Back to Erin', followed by Mr H. Prince with 'Once Again' (encored), Mrs Schwetzuebel, 'I Dreamed a Dream', Mrs S. Kessell, 'Come into the Garden Maud' (encored), Mr Marshall, 'A Winter's Story', Mr Arthur Bantick, 'Thy Sentinel Am I', all ably rendered, Miss Mitchell (a very promising little lady) concluding with 'I Shan't Go to School Any More' (encored).[28]

The success of this formula had much to do with the receptive social climate of the mid–1880s. For it was during the 1870s that the music hall had begun to occupy a central place in the cultural life of working and lower middle-class people in Britain.[29] By the time of the league's appearance music halls had largely shed their old reputation for vulgarity and obscenity, and instead provided entertainment of a kind considered suitable for women as well as men, yet which remained lively enough to be genuinely popular. This was precisely the character to which Primrose entertainments aspired. London, of course, was in the vanguard of this movement; but in the provinces, where the provision of music halls lagged behind, the league found itself ideally placed in the 1880s to capitalize upon a readymade interest.

Entertainments, whether held in the evenings or during the day, indoors or out, frequently included a lavish tea or picnic for the habitation's members. Sometimes such occasions degenerated into an undignified scrimmage for buns in the marquee at a garden party. But the typical arrangement was for some hundreds of people to sit down at separate tables each presided over by leading ladies who 'held trays' and preserved order and decorum; at a Halifax habitation in May 1890, for example, tea was served to 200 members under the aegis of eleven ladies – a fairly safe ratio. [30] The formula of tea at five or six, music from seven or eight, followed by a dance from ten until the early hours, proved an overwhelming attraction in both urban and rural areas; for few, whatever their politics, would relish being left out of such major events in the life of their immediate community.

Dancing proved to be a principal means of attracting younger members. A Grand Annual Ball at around 3/6 a ticket for gentlemen, (2/6 for ladies or 18/– for a family ticket) clearly catered to the better off. But at regular intervals throughout the year inexpensive dances took place to which members might be admitted free and non-members on payment of a few pence. In halls lavishly decorated with flowers, ferns, banners, flags and mottoes, dancing was invariably 'kept up with vigour' until two, three or four in the morning. Here again habitations managed to satisfy a keenly felt social need in the late nineteenth century. According to Charles Fenwick MP, the league was not only 'a tyrannical organization, a secret society', but also, 'a *matrimonial agency*' (my italics). [31] Though such jibes aroused predictable derision in Radical audiences they really underline the formidable attraction of the league at community level. For under its eminently respectable auspices both sexes might seize their opportunities for maximizing social intercourse.

A similar means of adapting to current tastes arose quite fortuitously during the 1890s in the shape of the 'safety bicycle', the manufacturers' answer to the need for a machine capable of carrying a woman in skirts with both propriety and safety. The ladies of the league, who were not on the whole among the 'New Women' of the decade, shunned the provocatively masculine forms of clothing advocated by the Rational Dress Society, but for them and many others the safety bicycle proved to be a great boon. Indeed by 1896, when annual British bicycle production rose to 750,000, a third of sales were for ladies' machines. [32] The underlying obstacle to a popular bicycle was social as much as technological: bikes were considered vulgar. However, their reputation seems to have been transformed by the discovery that fashionable Parisian society had adopted cycling as a pastime. [33] Thus the late Victorian cycling boom encompassed more than hardy Fabians and Clarion Cycling Clubs; family flocks of Cecils and Londonderrys also perambulated the countryside at this time.[34] And where the aristocracy led others might follow. 'Now that a better class of people are using the wheel,' pronounced the *Primrose League Gazette*, 'some good and practical work might be done in this way by wardens and others.'[35] For women in particular cycling represented an irresistible escape from the conventionally approved forms of exercise and recreation. Moreover, if undertaken *en masse* it ensured both immunity from the chaperone and safety from street urchins. Hence the popularity of cycling clubs. Characteristically, Grand Council responded by instituting a Primrose League Cycling Corps with its own rules and badges, under the Presidency of that distinguished freewheeler A. J. Balfour. Led by a Captain and a Lieutenant for every twenty members the local corps was open to any habitation member 'in possession of a bicycle'. As the mobile arm of its parent habitation, the cycling corps helped with tracing removals on the electoral register, contacting isolated voters and conveying messages between committee rooms.[36]

Summer brought the Primrose season to a spectacular climax in the shape of fetes and garden parties, often combined with mass excursions by specially chartered trains to the country seats of the aristocratic patrons of each habitation. Nominally light-hearted affairs, these occasions were in fact quite carefully conceived with political objectives in mind. Ruling Councillors believed that their role as political leaders of the community would gain strength if they were seen to be involved in the pleasures of the people as well as in their voting habits. One way of doing this lay in using their immense resources of land and houses to indulge popular curiosity about the lives of the rich and highborn. Until the latter part of Queen Victoria's reign it was comparatively rare for the private parks surrounding stately homes to be opened to the public, and the league was well placed to capture the novelty of a privileged visit.[37] The enjoyment of a memorable day spent in the grounds of a famous house in the presence of its gracious owner might help innoculate an increasingly urban population against the Radical characterization of the aristocracy as aloof, absentee and exploitative.

Furthermore, these summer activities were only one aspect of a wider effort at refining and domesticating popular leisure in Britain.[38] Without assuming that these efforts were wholly successful one must accept that the concatenation of a diverse railway system, additional leisure time and a growth of family spending power in this period greatly facilitated the strategy. For example, the tradition of the working-class seaside holiday began to be established in the late Victorian era, helped on by the introduction of the half-day Saturday in the 1870s, bank holidays in 1871, and one-week holidays in the 1890s, particularly in the cotton and engineering industries. From the employers' point of view these regular, family holidays and excursions appeared a desirable alternative to casual absenteeism and the older festivals and fairs, which attracted rowdiness and drunkenness. [39] A similar concern with respectable family leisure activities informed the League's summer strategy. Fetes, for example, should not 'contain the elements of vulgarity and noise, such as generally exist in swings, roundabouts, penny peep-shows etc., and yet. . . [they] should not be so distinctly elevating as to be pronounced dull'. [40] Approved alternatives included brass bands, punch-and-judy and the entertainments offered by professional magicians such as 'Professor Clarence' and others. In addition, there were horticultural and agricultural classes, the inevitable teas and dancing, and athletic competitions. Sports could even become the chief attraction. In July 1888 the Toxteth (Liverpool) habitation journeyed to Lymm in Cheshire for its Annual Pic-nic and a programme incorporating the following: flat races, egg-and-spoon races, three-legged race, throwing the cricket ball, potato race (ladies only), standing long jump, flat race for married ladies only, half mile walking race, 80 yards sack race, 100 yards flat race for ladies only, and a tug of war — 'married versus single, in which the gentlemen who were subject to home rule proved themselves more than a match for their single and less fortunate opponents'. [41] In this jocular but relentless emphasis on marriage and family one hears the authentic tones of a late Victorian institution. While the Toxteth sports and picnic was a modest affair for a single habitation, much more elaborate fetes, often combined with political rallies, were organized by groups of habitations. These would not have been feasible without the full development of branch line railways through most of the country by the late nineteenth century. For example, in the 1890s the Melbury Habitation in the depths of west Dorset drew attendances of 5,000 to the grounds of the Earl and Countess of Ilchester, largely by means of special trains which converged from Weymouth, Bridport, Yeovil and Abbotsbury; the organizers successfully demanded reduced fares from a reluctant railway company. [42] The prospect of a cheap excursion for families to whom railway travel was still a novelty rather than a habit helped to overcome any reservations they might have on political grounds.

The Primrose League's reputation for beer-and-skittles or, more accurately, tea-and-buns, should not be allowed to obscure its underlying political significance. The fundamental point is that the rhythm and pattern of the Primrose year sketched above was not primarily determined by the Westminster timetable, as was usually the case with political bodies, but reflected the seasonal life of its supporters. Inevitably some habitations, carried away by the exuberance of their social whirl, had to be reminded by Grand Council that entertainments were only a means not the object of the exercise. [43] For however trivial the functions might be, they were considered justified if they exposed large numbers of people to a political message, albeit briefly and superficially. Thus every concert, tea or garden party had to include its political speaker or lantern show. For one thing this element of instruction and propaganda provided a useful insurance against infringements of the law on corrupt electoral expenditure. Also, the league's founders were convinced that Conservatives had hitherto

☞ THE OFFICIALLY RECOGNIZED PRIMROSE LEAGUE ENTERTAINMENTS. ☜

If by my humble efforts, I succeed
To make the time pass pleasantly, and lighten care
With mirth, refinement and dexterity.
Then I've achieved the task I set myself. PROF. CLARENCE, K.P.L.

PROF. CLARENCE, K.P.L.

(THE ROYAL ILLUSIONIST, COURT PRESTIDIGITATEUR, HUMORIST, & CARICATURIST)

Has had the honour of giving his Entertainments before—

T.R.H.	The PRINCE and PRINCESS OF WALES (Three times)
T.R.H.	The DUKE and DUCHESS of EDINBURGH (Twice)
T.R.H.	The DUKE and DUCHESS of CONNAUGHT (Four times)
T.R.H.	The DUKE and DUCHESS of ALBANY (Once)
T.R.H.	The PRINCE and PRINCESS CHRISTIAN (Twice)
H.R.H.	The PRINCESS LOUISE (MARCHIONESS of LORNE) (Once)
H.R.H.	The PRINCESS FREDERICA of HANOVER (Twice)
H.R.H	The DUKE of CAMBRIDGE (Four times)

And was specially engaged by H.S.H. the Late KING OF PORTUGAL to visit Lisbon and give three performances at the Royal Palace in 1886 ; besides which Mr. Clarence has been favoured with hundreds of engagements by the Nobility, Clergy and Gentry, and has been annually engaged to perform at the Mansion House, London, by each succeeding Lord Mayor, since 1881 up to 1890,

And has perfectly successfully given 538 Primrose League Entertainments.

Testimonials.

The following was received from Mr. Deputy Arnold, who was entrusted by the Lord Mayor to arrange the Entertainments given at the Mansion House, London. E.C.:—

Mansion House, London. E.C., April 17th, 1890.

Prof. H. G. Clarence. Dear Sir. In again remitting cheque for the tenth time, I cannot refrain from once more expressing my unqualified gratification at the universal satisfaction and delight afforded to the juveniles and their adult friends with your remarkable Entertainment given at the Mansion House last evening. The Lord Mayor and the Lady Mayoress, and in fact everyone, enjoyed it, and Mrs. Clarence's charming addition to the usual repertoire— "The Doves at Home" was a brilliant success. Trusting that next year I may again welcome you upon a similar occasion, believe me to remain, yours truly, J. G. ARNOLD. (Tenth annual engagement).

Banbury Habitation, May 18, 1892.

Mr. H. G. Clarence. Dear Sir. The capital Entertainment given by Madame and yourself at our Primrose League Gathering gave entire satisfaction, not only to me but I can truly say to everyone present ; in fact many have since told me that they enjoyed it more than any we have had before, and a ruling Councillor of another Habitation who was present was so delighted with it, and asked for your address, deciding to engage you both forthwith. Sincerely hoping to have you down again, believe me, yours faithfully, J. S. FORTESCUE, Hon. Sec.

Trowbridge Habitation, May 5, 1892.

Prof. H. G. Clarence.—Dear Sir,- Your splendid Entertainment very largely contributed to make our Annual Primrose League gathering by far the most successful one we have ever had. Everybody was more than pleased. I enclose cheque, and thanking you myself for the performance, believe me, yours truly, T. HERBERT CLARK, Hon. Sec.

Brattleby, Habitation, May 23rd, 1892.

Professor H. G. Clarence gave one of his Entertainments under the auspices of the Local Habitation of the Primrose League. The performance was indeed excellent throughout and afforded unbounded amusement, interest, and delight to every member of the large audience present.—(Signed) J. H. WHITE, Rector of Brattleby, Lincoln.

Hundreds of Testimonials up to date, such as the above forwarded upon application to
PROF. CLARENCE, K.P.L., 6, JUNCTION ROAD, HOLLOWAY, LONDON, N.

*Plate 3a   Poster advertising officially recognized Primrose League
entertainments 1890*

PROGRAMME No. 4.

An Excellent. Enjoyable, and Clever Performance, forming a

POPULAR PRIMROSE ENTERTAINMENT

ENTITLED

MYSTERIA.

Part One.

Optical Illusions, Wonderful Conjuring,
Clever Sleight of Hand, and Capital Fun.

Exhibiting many Astonishing, Pleasing, and Mystifying Illusions and Experiments, presented in a way that never fails to please the old and young, the staid and jovial, alike.

Part Two.

Some Elegant Jugglery, Hindoo Marvels,
Chinese Mysteries, Japanese Wonders,
Egyptian Novelties, &c.

Fascinating, Enjoyable, and Refined, and Productive of a considerable amount of mirth and good humour.

WHEN SO DESIRED THIS ENTERTAINMENT CAN CONCLUDE WITH A FUNNY NEGRO PERFORMANCE.

TERMS—One Hour, £1 10s. One Hour and Half, £2. Two Hours, £2 10s. And travelling expenses for one person.

THE LONDON AND PROVINCIAL

ROYAL ENTERTAINMENT BUREAU,

ESTABLISHED 1868. (MANAGER, H. G. CLARENCE, K.P.L.,)

6, JUNCTION ROAD, HOLLOWAY, LONDON, N.

Provides the following at moderate inclusive terms for FETES, GALAS, &c., &c., &c.

ASSAULT-AT-ARMS and Athletic Sports

BALLOON Ascents and Parachutist's Drop from the Clouds.

CLOWN Cricketers, Conjurers and Characteristic Comic Singers.

DUETTISTS and Dancers, Lady Serios and Gentlemen Comics.

EQUILIBRISTS, Balancers, & Boneless Wonders.

FLYING Trapeze and Flying Ring Performers.

GYMNASTS, Acrobats, and Tumblers.

HORIZONTAL Bar Performers, and Vaulters.

INSTRUMENTALISTS, Hand Bell Ringers, and Vocalists.

JUGGLERS, Globe Walkers, and Stilt Dancers.

KNOCKABOUT Irish Comics, and Negro Artists.

LAUGHABLE Liliputians and Living Marionettes.

MUSICAL Grotesques, Clowns, and Mimics.

NONDESCRIPTS—A Very Novel Performance.

ORIENTAL Troupe of performing Arabs.

PUNCH & JUDY, Performing Dogs and Monkeys

QUICK Change and Protean Artistes.

ROPE Walkers and Dancers

SENSATIONAL Crack Shot Experts.

TRICK Bicycle Riders and Performers.

UNIQUE Performance with Bantam Fowls.

VENTRILOQUISTS and Farm-yard Imitators.

WIRE Walkers Dancers and Balancers.

XELLENT Artists in every other Branch of the Profession.

YIELDING Perfect Satisfaction in every respect

ZOUAVE Lightning Drill Artists, &c. &c. &c.

CHRISTY MINSTREL TROUPES of from Five to Twenty-five Artistes.
BRASS AND STRING BANDS, large or small, in or out of Uniform.
GRAND FIREWORK DISPLAYS, ILLUMINATIONS AND ORNAMENTATIONS, etc.

And every possible kind of attraction provided suitable for every occasion, either in or out of doors.

Kindly state the sum intended to be expended, when programmes and particulars appropriate to the requirments of the case will at once be forwarded. Permanent and only address, H. G. CLARENCE, K.P.L,
Junction Road, Holloway. London, N.

Plate 3b   Poster advertising officially recognized Primrose League
entertainments 1890

been singularly inept in tackling unsophisticated audiences on political subjects. With its ear to the ground the league often picked up the confusion and misapprehension of ordinary people; for example, to many people 'Home Rule' implied sending the Irish back home, while the Conservatives' 'National Union' suggested a trade union. Thus the Dames in particular took their educational role seriously, deploying simple and striking visual messages by means of lantern slides, limelight shows and *tableaux vivants*. But none of this could supplant the platform speech — provided it was of the right sort. It was often said, though not universally practised, that speakers 'must indeed be below the mean if they cannot say all they *need* say in from ten to fifteen minutes'. Consequently many an orator, sent down from London at some expense, found himself merely an item in the programme of a habitation's Entertainment, sandwiched ignominiously 'between a nigger song and a conjuror'![44] Undoubtedly many a Ruling Councillor indulged himself, or even herself, by inflicting lengthy orations upon their captive Associates, but the typical speech filled the function of an interval in the evening's proceedings, and was appreciated as such — provided it did not delay the next act.

The significance of the grassroots activities of the league must also be seen in the context of party political finance in the late nineteenth century. Part of the league's attraction for Conservative politicians lay in its capacity to finance itself. The league's modest central funds, drawn from the 2/6 paid by Knights and Dames and the guineas subscribed by members of Ladies Grand Council and the Knights Imperial, went on district agents' salaries, routine propaganda, and special items such as touring vans and new lantern shows. By and large, however, the financial resources were raised and spent locally. Yet the official income of habitations was limited to sums ranging from 1/- to 2/6 levied on Knights and Dames, plus the charges for Associates, who commonly paid 3d or 6d per annum, sometimes as much as 1/- or as little as 1d. At a time when a 'substantial meat tea' cost habitations around a shilling a head the Associate was clearly getting a bargain for his meagure subscription.

Habitation records for the 1880s and 1890s make it abundantly clear that events were frequently organized in expectation of a financial loss which could not be sustained by the habitation's funds. In these circumstances the officers simply sought donations as a matter of course.[45] In 1891 the St Albans constituency habitations spent £96 on a single political demonstration and promptly formed a list of subscribers to meet the bills.[46] This universal pattern varied regionally, in that areas with comparatively high family incomes, such as Lancashire, tended to charge Associates higher fees and made them pay a little for entertainments; many rural habitations, on the other hand, were virtually handing out charity. As early as 1886 the league in Croydon made the startling boast that it had 'taken the place of the Charity Organization Society' in its area.[47] Practice does seem to have changed over time. After the turn of the century, habitations that had offered teas, dances and fetes free to members for many years began to run up substantial deficits. They were pleasantly surprised to discover that the imposition of charges to members, and higher ones to non-members, far from deterring the crowds, generated profits.[48] In this way what had begun as a matter of lordly subsidy evolved into a tradition of fund-raising through social events that was carried over into the Conservative Associations by the Primrose Dames during the 1920s, to the lasting advantage of the party. It has been tentatively estimated that the typical Conservative constituency association spent some £350–400 per annum in the Edwardian period, of which over half was contributed by the MP or candidate.[49] The absence of accounts for more than a scattering of habitations out of the two and a half thousand makes generalization difficult for the Primrose League. In the 1890s the range of expenditure seems to have been from around £20 to £220 according to the size and spirit of the habitation. Of course many constituencies enjoyed half a dozen or more habitations, so that their total expenditure on the Conservative cause must often have equalled or exceeded that of the official party.

In this light one is entitled to be a little sceptical about the optimistic claims made for Gladstone's 1883 legislation against corrupt and illegal electoral practices. Essentially the act was designed to impose the responsibility for election expenditure upon a single agent, and to set strict limits on the nature and the extent of expenditure. It has been pronounced an 'unqualified success' in one recent study, which may be true in the sense that formal election expenditure dropped.[50] But it is further claimed that the real fall was greater than that indicated by declared expenses because of the reduced scope for *undeclared* expenditure. Contemporary Liberals had no such illusions and regularly accused the Primrose League of circumventing the 1883 Act. Where does the truth lie?

Clearly the league had been created with a view to generating the volunteer labour for which Conservatives had usually paid before 1883. In this sense its work was wholly in tune with the spirit of the legislation. However, the new situation was much more complicated. Initially, habitations had been advised to dissolve themselves for the period of an election campaign so as not to expose the Conservative agent to charges of excessive spending; but this was soon found to be unnecessary. Instead habitations simply suspended their meetings and advised members to place themselves at the disposal of the Conservative agent on an individual basis.[51] Dames in particular were counselled against making charitable visits to League members or canvassing streets for which they were District Visitors.[53] In practice the league seems to have been adept at devoting its resources, both financial and physical, to the Conservative cause without falling foul of the Act; this may be traced to three factors. In the first place, although the legislation limited expenditure on election campaigns, it failed to define precisely the point at which a campaign began. Certainly the occurrence of a vacancy or the issuing of a writ were taken to initiate the election; but the campaign was often held to have begun as soon as steps were taken to promote a particular candidate, which was sometimes several years before the election itself. [53] For the party organizations this could be very inhibiting. However, the person who eventually became the candidate might attend functions designed to promote his *party* as long as he had not formally been adopted by the association. The sharper the distinction between the individual and the cause the greater the safety. As Ruling Councillors, candidates could indulge freely in Primrose League gatherings which, under party auspices, could subsequently have been held to fall under election expenses.

Secondly, the law proscribed both bribery and *corrupt* treating; thus treating in the ordinary sense of providing food, drink or entertainment, was held to be *prima facie* innocent, and very strong evidence was required to obtain a conviction for such expenditure. Thirdly, and crucially for the league, meetings held under the auspices of a political organization or *bona fide* club for the purpose of propagating opinions and winning adherents might legitimately include refreshments even if supplied at below the cost price. Moreover, where such treating had become a customary element in a regular programme of functions held regardless of whether an election was in prospect or not, it proved virtually impossible to establish an *intention* to corruptly influence the recipients. [54]

Obviously habitations which could point to just such a regular annual pattern of events would escape the proscription on corrupt treating. Nonetheless they sailed very close to the wind. A good example of deliberate flouting of the spirit of the law is provided by the Melbury Habitation's summer fete in 1894. In his correspondence the habitation secretary made it abundantly clear that the fete served a party political purpose. [55] Previous fetes, he assured the new Conservative candidate for West Dorset, had been 'of immense value' to his predecessor, and 'I sincerely believe this (one) will be so to yours.' Thus he tried hard to obtain a front bench speaker on the grounds that the absence of a politician of this status had been the only weakness of earlier fetes. Yet such calculations had to be concealed when approaching the railway authorities for special trains and cheap fares for the occasion. When the company officials demurred about granting such concessions for a political function the secretary blandly contended that the fete was 'not necessarily of a political character' and kept quiet about the speakers he was arranging. Yet the only justification he could offer was that the function was open to supporters of both political parties. He proposed calling it a 'Unionist' rather than a 'Primrose' fete on the curious grounds that the former sounded less political, and concluded disingenuously: "in short, the Committee are anxious to make the day one of entire enjoyment and amusement, and to keep politics in the background.' In the event the Committee felt obliged to make concessions because they had printed posters advertising the cheap fares in anticipation of co-operation from the railway company, whose obstinacy threatened the whole enterprise. Moreover, the secretary appreciated the dangers of the law on corrupt treating. He admitted to the Conservative candidate that some might claim that the provision of free teas for hundreds of habitation members at the fete would invalidate his election. However, he swept the thought aside:

> Personally I don't believe it — for on two previous occasions a fete was given at Melbury to which the members were admitted free and were also given a rattling good tea by the Ilchesters. Farquharson — then candidate — was present on both occasions, and you will remember the Bridehead Habitation was brought over here free of cost.[56]

Such an example illustrates how the league could operate successfully on the fringes of the law because the *intention* to influence voters through treating, though present, was obscured. The election judges certainly considered expenditure of the kind undertaken at Melbury to be 'dubious' and even 'dangerous', but were reluctant to deem it corrupt treating; the spirit rather than the letter of the law was being infringed.[57] Where political parties indulged in similar practices they were more vulnerable because their intention seemed more obvious and blatant. Since the league remained constitutionally separate from the Conservative Party and could point to its habit of mixing social and political functions, it could risk lavish spending with impunity. As a result, despite Liberal fulminations, the league was infrequently brought into court and even then escaped where the parties were caught. This frustrating situation doubtless lay behind the eventual decision by the Liberals to create their own 'Liberal Social Council' as a vehicle for spending money on social events held under the aegis of such remaining Liberal peers as could be mustered — greatly to the amusement of the Primrose League.

Ultimately the significance of the Primrose League's brand of Conservatism lay in the extent to which it enabled Conservatives to escape from the narrow confines of the parliamentary milieu and sink roots in the lives of their supporters in the country. Already by 1880 several expedients had been adopted including workingmen's clubs, local Conservative friendly societies, and the practice among Conservative employers in some towns of using the factory or mill as a focus for political loyalty. In many ways the league was an attempt to extend and consolidate these initiatives. Habitations often used Conservative clubs for meetings and sometimes held joint events with their members. A Primrose League Benefit Society was established. Some urban habitations noticeably embodied the tradition of factory-based politics, such as the large Elswick Habitation in Newcastle-upon-Tyne which drew its members from the mechanics and engineers of Lord Armstrong's works. In contrast, the Conservative Associations themselves remained, with a few exceptions, essentially machines for registering the male, Conservative, parliamentary voters.

Although registration work and canvassing were frequently undertaken by the habitations, these functions represented only one aspect of their activities. Nor were they as exclusive, socially or politically, as the party organizations. Indeed, the habitations deliberately reached out to recruit from whole sections of society largely neglected by the party — non-Conservatives, women, non-voters and children.

Large as the league's membership was, the figures actually understate popular involvement in one sense, for habitations deliberately opened their doors to non-members, particularly in the 1880s when it seems to have been common for guests to accompany members to meetings. Non-members gladly availed themselves of the oppportunity to attend dances or join railway excursions to political rallies. For example, in 1897 the Lowther Habitation in Westmorland, though in decline by this time, took 133 members free to a Unionist rally at Levens Hall, while another 132 non-members paid 2/- each. [58] Obviously the ease of entry invited infiltration by political opponents happy to take advantage of the league's socializing. In the aftermath of elections habitations invariably reported that certain members had supported the Liberals. At Whitehaven fifteen individuals were identified in 1892, but only three of them turned out to be current members, and none of them voters. The council simply agreed to let the matter rest, 'Lady Lonsdale having expressed a wish to that effect.' [59] As late as 1910 habitations still sought advice from Grand Council as to what action *if any* should be taken in such cases [60] — a striking indication of an organization determined to avoid becoming an exclusive clique of party loyalists. The calculation was that ease of access would give the league an impressive size which, in itself, would tend to demoralize political opponents and would draw in the politically apathetic who simply feared being left out of local events. However, it is important to note that by 1910 Grand Council had begun to advise the expulsion of known opponents — a sign of the league's imminent absorption into the ranks of the regular army of Conservatism.

A second distinguishing characteristic, already noted, was the incorporation of women and men into the same organization at a time when it was normal either to ignore the former or at least to segregate them. Nearly half the total membership appears to have been female (see p. 49). Moreover, local registers paint a picture of membership as a *family* affair with husband and wife, unmarried siblings and children all enlisting. The roles of Ruling Councillor and Dame President were often filled by a husband and wife, brother and sister or father and daughter combination. More surprisingly, one finds a similar practice at a humbler level among the wardens. For example, there were four husband-and-wife teams among twenty-six wardens at Sowerby in 1887, five among thirty-one wardens at Elswick (Newcastle) in 1905, and seven among thirty at Jesmond (Newcastle) in 1906. [61]

A third feature concerns the electorate. Although the league devoted a good deal of time to identifying Conservative voters so that they might be registered, it was equally interested in educating the male non-voters in Conservative ideas. Unfortunately too little precise evidence survives to enable one to generalize about this element. Many membership registers included a separate column for recording those who were currently on the electoral roll. For the Garstang (Lancashire) Habitation, for example, some 284 male members were listed in the 1890s, but their electoral status was recorded in only 179 cases; of these 49 per cent were identified as non-voters. A more exhaustive record was maintained by the Primrose League Divisional Council in the St Albans constituency, which boasted 11 habitations in 1890–91. This shows 936 parliamentary voters among a total membership of 2,660 in ten of the habitations. However, since no separate return was made for the women in this total one can only estimate, from other habitations, that 49 per cent were female. This would mean a male membership of 1,357 among whom the non-voters would be 31 per cent.[62]

The fourth aspect is the way in which the league extended its range beyond the conventional age barrier to include children. The idea appears to have sprung up quite spontaneously during the early 1890s among some London habitations, notably in Hammersmith, Croydon and Dulwich, who simply decided to organize the sons and daughters of their members as 'Primrose Buds'.[63] No doubt this seemed a natural step for a generation which already devoted much energy to mobilizing and influencing the young through Sunday Schools and the more novel organizations such as the Boys' Brigade (1883) and the Church Lads' Brigade (1891),[64] both of which were spiritually compatible with the league. Eventually the 'Juvenile Branches' were incorporated into the league's formal structure; children of seven to sixteen years might join with their parents' consent, wore their own badge, and were supervised by a Dame who served as a Warden of the parent habitation.[65] Into a programme of outdoor sports, patriotic songs, first aid and 'hospital cooking' the Dames judiciously inserted instruction in the duties and privileges of citizenship and the principles of the Primrose League – in which the Buds were periodically examined (appendix III). Several urban habitations met an enthusiastic response, though whether from the children or their parents is difficult to tell; Croydon claimed 700 juveniles in 1900 and 950 by 1906, and Ecclesall (Sheffield) 650 in 1905, though for obvious reasons the annual turnover of membership was as high as 25 per cent.[66] What had begun as a minor element in the league received a considerable stimulus during the Edwardian period. As the league itself moved into decline it devoted increasing attention to youth work in order to counter what was seen as the growing influence of socialism in British society. In addition, the rapid expansion of the new Boy Scout Movement prompted moves for collaboration at branch level. The Bradford Juvenile Branch was the first to request permission to identify itself with the Scouts; and in 1909 the Boy Scout headquarters agreed to the establishment of troops based upon juvenile branches.[67] As a result the members of the Juvenile Branch of the 'Disraeli' (Bradford) Habitation styled themselves the First Primrose League Boy Scouts. This was a logical development. Founded in 1907, the Scouts had attained 100,000 members by 1910 and 150,000 by 1914, overtaking their older rivals in the process. Ideologically the two organizations shared a similar outlook. 'Remember, whether rich or poor, from castle or from slum, you are all Britons in the first place...You must sink your differences.' [68] Baden Powell's sentiments plainly echoed those of the league. Both, moreover, operated by harnessing a working and lower middle-class rank and file under the leadership of their social superiors. By 1913 the league reported some 259 Juvenile Branches with 65,000 members; there were 138,000 Boy Scouts (1912), 61,000 in the Boys Brigade (1912) and 36,000 in the Church Lads Brigade (1911). [69] Thus in the short term the league was, once again, capitalizing on a current fashion; in the longer term its Juveniles represent an important strand in the large youth organization of twentieth-century Conservatism.

These different dimensions to the Primrose League take us a long way from the merely quaint and romantic. Indeed, the evidence justifies some reconsideration of the conventional conception of British Conservatism as simply a narrowly based, traditional caucus party of parliamentary representation of the kind analysed by Maurice Duverger. [70] The form of Conservative organization considered here departs from the caucus type in a multitude of ways. First and fundamentally, it not only aimed to recruit membership very widely, but also succeeded to a large extent in crossing the boundaries of sex, class and age. Second, it incorporated non-electors. Third, its membership entailed formal enrolment with a signed pledge and a payment. Fourth, it adopted an educative and propagandist role. Fifth, its activities were continuous and regular, not determined by the pattern of parliamentary elections. Sixth, its meetings were gatherings of the rank and file members, not merely the ruling elite. And finally, it moved beyond the political sphere into the social life of its members.

Such characteristics have often been considered peculiar to parties of 'social integration' which are assumed to be necessarily *socialist* parties. [71] Whether any non-Conservative political movement closely approached this type is in fact arguable; all British parties fell seriously short in one way or another. In the case of Conservatism and the Primrose League the limitations are fairly clear. Sice the two were constitutionally separate, membership of the league was not to be equated with party membership; nor did the league enjoy any control over the decisions of the party, though many individuals exercised influence. Moreover, there must be some doubt as to how democratically the league functioned in view of the markedly deferential attitude shown towards leadership. However the habitation executive councils were the product of direct election by the members every April, and this was a functional, not a decorative, part of the structure. At the centre Grand Council was also elected, although it had a large co-opted element. The annual Grand Habitation meetings, at which the entire league was represented, occasionally generated critical debates on the functioning of the league, but hardly exercised any control over Grand Council. Like all party conferences they were largely ritual occasions for boosting morale and passing declarations of confidence in the leaders. Though these qualifications are not unimportant they do not seriously detract from the significance of the Primrose League as a systematic attempt to make political loyalty an integral part of the lives of a large number of people rather than the private language of an elite. That the party of the right should have accomplished this in Britain has not been sufficiently noticed by scholars. No other political party approached as closely to a party of social integration before 1900, and it must be doubtful whether any party came closer even after 1918.

3

Women and Conservative Politics

In March 1880 Constance Flower loyally attended her husband's adoption meeting as Liberal parliamentary candidate for the Brecon Boroughs. When it was discovered that no other lady was present she was obliged to conceal herself behind a screen: 'I could hear but was not visible.'[1] Her predicament is a reminder that the evolution of women's political role must be understood partly in terms of social class. For the conventions that so restricted Constance Flower were characteristically middle-class: in upper-class circles women had never been invisible nor distant from politics, which often permeated the daily lives of their households. Historical analysis of the women's movement in Britain has tended to focus on the initiatives of middle-class women in the mid-Victorian era, quite naturally in view of the dilemmas and prejudices such women encountered. Not until the Edwardian period has it been possible to draw working-class women into the explanation, and even then only to a minor extent. Thus duchesses continue to be at a discount in the historical marketplace. Yet in the Conservative half of British politics it was they who first breached the defences of male orthodoxy, thus paving the way for women with fewer social advantages. They have been neglected because they rarely presented a direct challenge — those who already had a foot in the citadel had less need to storm the barricades. To overlook them, however, is to forget the dependence of Victorian Conservatives upon women volunteers for parliamentary registration and electioneering, as well as the role of women as Conservative voters and local activists in the twentieth century. In this chapter we will consider the evolution of women from conventional hostesses to Primrose Dames, and their gradual effect in reconciling Conservatives to women in politics long before 1918.

THE VICTORIAN POLITICAL HOSTESS

In mid-Victorian England the natural role for a politically ambitious woman was that of political hostess. Success hinged upon possession of certain assets

— a wealthy husband, an imposing house near Westminster and a country seat — and upon certain attributes, notably beauty, charm and quick-wittedness. This last quality was perhaps the most important, for the hostess must engage her guests in serious discussion, not merely light-hearted banter, be ready to intervene to forestall a clash between rivals, and keep herself well informed about events as well as personalities. Even a routine day at Blenheim under the rule of Frances, Duchess of Marlborough, involved spending an hour or two studying the newspapers, otherwise a woman would fail to show 'an intelligent interest' in the protracted discussions in the evening.[2] Of course, politics was by no means compulsory in Society. Millicent, Dowager Duchess of Sutherland, pre-eminently a social hostess, threw grand Stafford House receptions often graced by a royal guest. Very few, among whom Theresa, Lady Londonderry stands out, operated as both social and political hostesses. During the second half of the century battle lines were drawn between a formidable phalanx of Conservative and Liberal Unionist ladies including the Marchionesses of Londonderry, Salisbury and Lansdowne, the Countess of Jersey, the Duchesses of Devonshire and Buccleuch, and Lady Dorothy Nevill, and on the Liberal side Lady Palmerston, the Countess of Waldegrave, Lady Spencer, Lady Tweedmouth, Lady Molesworth, Lady Cowper and Lady Beaumont.

Their social activities followed a regular annual pattern broadly determined by the parliamentary year, which commenced in February. However, February in London held little appeal, and much of Society kept away, like the queen herself, who clung to the seclusion of Windsor until Easter. Thus the London season in fact stretched from April to the end of July. These months saw huge receptions for several thousand guests packed into the febrile grandeur of Park Lane and Carlton Gardens where, amid the ceaseless political gossip, strategies formed and vanished with each turn of the kaleidoscope, and seedling reputations sprouted and withered from week to week. Early in August Parliament gratefully rose, so that those who had not already done so might escape to country houses and heather moors seeking relief from the oppressive treadmill of metropolitan gaiety. The guest with plenty of stamina might spend two or three weeks at each of a series of country-house parties, though towards the end of the century the innovation of the 'week-end' provided a less tedious alternative. By the 1890s many of the English upper classes were taking advantage of improved continental transport to spend part of the summer or autumn in Biarritz, on the Riviera, or at Carlsbad, Gastein, Marienbad or another of the spas of central Europe. Christmas and New Year would find them cosily immersed in the country, safely out of the London fog until spring, when a new political and social year summoned them back again.

Victorian hostesses naturally liked to believe that they wielded political influence, if only over individual reputations and advancements. An ambitious young MP might be flattered into loyalty, or suddenly dropped from the guest list for playing the rebel too often. Austen Chamberlain once claimed to be able to measure 'the state of his own political fortunes by the number of fingers, ranging from two to ten, which [Lady Londonderry] gave him when they met'.[3] Or the hostess might secure promotion for her husband or son by exercising her charms on the party leaders. For example, the sixth Marquis of Londonderry was widely considered to owe his elevation as Irish Viceroy in 1886 to his formidable wife rather than to his own slight talents, though his readiness to spend freely in Dublin was probably the decisive factor.[4] Even the seventh Marquis was said by the malicious F. E. Smith to be 'catering his way to the cabinet'. Inevitably such impressions are exaggerated by frustrated rivals. Francis, Lady Waldegrave, who was credited with great skill, failed for years to push her husband, Chichester Fortescue, beyond his undersecretaryship.

Undoubtedly Conservative leaders greatly valued the contribution of their hostesses to the party. Regular receptions for several hundred leading figures provided a substitute for the formal apparatus for communication which the party largely lacked; and at the very least the ladies consolidated the efforts of the whips in reconciling factions, deterring the disenchanted from rebellion and keeping the ambitious in hope.

However, during the 1880s the traditional role of the hostess began to diminish somewhat. Most Whigs gravitated towards the Conservatives, thereby endowing them with a huge preponderance of support in high society. In these circumstances the task of rallying the political elite required less effort; property coalesced instinctively. The challenge now lay in reconciling the traditional political world to pressures from below in the shape of a more comprehensive local and central organization. Not that the hostesses refused to accommodate themselves to change. It is estimated that whereas before the 1870s Society comprised a mere 500 families, by 1900 it included around 4,000 as the plutocrats gained entry.[5] The Irish Home Rule Members began their absorption into English life through Lady Waldegrave's hospitality; and the Conservative hostess Lady Dorothy Nevill had brought Joseph Chamberlain to her dinner table even before his debut at Chatsworth in 1886.[6] However, a Chamberlain might be absorbed without disturbing the life of Society, especially if he was keen to be; the caucus called for a different response.

In addition, the late nineteenth century witnessed a relaxation of the all-pervading masculinity of upper-class social life that was welcome to those women who had not succeeded as hostesses.[7] Many women had long found the riding and shooting at country house parties an interminable bore, and in order to provide company for them it became more usual to invite some non-shooting men. From this it was a logical step to include men of literary, artistic or scientific reputation, and some hostesses noticed that the men lingered less over their port before rejoining the ladies. Next, the game of bridge was adopted by both sexes as a means of filling the hours between afternoon tea and dressing for dinner. By the 1890s the guest could expect to be told to bring his bicycle as the fashion for cycling in mixed parties reached its height. All these practices are symptoms of the tendency towards a more balanced participation between the sexes in upper-class circles, a development which attained its most conspicuous form at gatherings of the 'Souls'.[8] Here the masculine virtues were at a discount, as men and women explored and exhibited their intellects and sensibilities on a comparatively equal footing. Not surprisingly one finds among the Souls a sprinkling of Primrose Leaguers — Willy and Ettie Grenfell (later Lord and Lady Desborough), the Earl and Countess of Pembroke, the Countess Brownlow, the Duke and Duchess of Rutland, the Marchioness of Plymouth, Lord and Lady Windsor, and the Duchess of Sutherland.

Such was the climate in which the leading ladies of the Primrose League came out. They were not moved by the kind of frustrations and restrictions suffered by middle-class women, rather by their own penchant for politics and an awareness of the potential for a wider public role which their socially advantaged position gave them. Yet any lady with a position to preserve naturally hesitated; she must find the right sort of public involvement. Charitable work offered vast scope, though it seemed slightly peripheral to the politically minded. A number of ladies, enthused by the fashionable notion of sallying forth to debarbarize the masses, found acceptable public outlets for their energies in organizations such as the Girls Friendly Society, founded in 1874.[9] Recruiting young females, the Girls Friendly Society sought to protect them from exploitation, encourage their training in domestic skills, and imbue them with religion, deference and loyalty to the queen, who was held up as a model of motherhood. In many ways the GFS is strongly reminiscent of the league. While it betrayed no trace of assertive feminism, its practical work for women and by women tended to foster the self-respect of their sex. Further, some of its leading figures, such as Lady Louisa Knightley, served their apprenticeship in the GFS in the 1870s before going on to the league in the 1880s. Innocuous as such involvement may seem to later generations of women, the experience loomed large at the time in the minds of *both* sexes: for Lady Knightley's husband originally forbade her to become GFS President. However, by 1884 she was addressing audiences of 5,000 girls: 'Dear me! I should have thought this such an event a few years ago. Now it comes quite in the day's work,' she wrote.[10]

For many upper-class women the Primrose League filled a huge gap in their lives, in that it combined the satisfaction of educational-philanthropic work, which was already available, with the challenge of electoral battles; moreover, they could indulge in league activity without losing caste or alienating themselves from male aristocratic society. This was possible largely because of their class and their orthodoxy. No one could mistake a Lady Jersey or a Lady Londonderry for one of the 'New Women' who so antagonized late Victorian males; on the contrary, they were lauded as successful women: that is, they were wives and mothers first and foremost. They could scarcely be represented as frustrated, failed women whose objectives would be subversive of the proper relations between the sexes. Although their public participation in political work was novel, it could be, and was, represented as essentially an extension of their existing role and as supportive of men's work. Since they also maintained their traditional function as hostesses these ladies preserved some sense of continuity, thereby mitigating any idea of a challenge to conventional notions about women's proper sphere in the minds of male politicians.

THE EMERGENCE OF THE DAMES

'It would seriously injure your influence if you were known to have influence,' Benjamin Jowett once told Florence Nightingale.[11] Perhaps in the same spirit many of the late Victorian female politicians conspired to preserve convention by filling their memoirs with accounts of charming, leisured lives filled by family, parties, gardening and the gentle arts; they sometimes omit entirely to mention the incessant round of public work which occupied much of their time.[12] The stereotyped view of men who go boldly out into the world and women who love to stay at home disintegrates upon close examination of several late Victorian marriages; four who were very active in the Primrose League illustrate a different relationship.

Frances, Duchess of Marlborough, was an intelligent, forceful woman, almost as prominent politically as her husband.[13] The Duke himself rose briefly to public attention when he became Viceroy in Ireland in 1876–80 so as to escape the social ostracism brought about by the Aylesford-Blandford scandal. During their Irish exile the Duchess took various initiatives designed to reconcile Catholics to the Union, and on being restored to Society she threw herself into electoral and league activity, while her husband sank back into obscurity. Even more formidable and politically motivated was Theresa, Lady Londonderry, whose husband was regarded as a nonentiy when sent to Dublin in 1886 at the age of thirty-four. During his period at the Board of Education she is supposed to have taken the chair at a departmental meeting despite his presence.[14] Tireless in both local and national politics as Conservative hostess and Primrose Dame, Lady Londonderry involved herself in most major issues before 1914 including Home Rule, tariff reform and the House of Lords. Margaret, Countess of Jersey, displayed a serious interest in current affairs from childhood; as a teenager she attended Commons debates on Gladstone's Irish Church Bill and filled pages of her journal with its provisions.[15] The seventh earl enjoyed minor roles as Lord-in-Waiting to the queen, spokesman on local government in the Lords, Postmaster General for one year, and finally as Governor of New South Wales. His wife, far more ambitious and persistent, could hardly get enough public work. Diligent at her school visiting and Mothers Unions, she also served as a Juvenile Court magistrate, was a staunch defender of free trade and a founder of the Victoria League and the Women's Anti-Suffrage League. Much praised as a public speaker, Lady Jersey, except when abroad, saw continuous activity in elections and the Primrose League up to the 1930s, when she was in her mid-eighties. Similarly Lady Knightley packed her life from youth to old age with public work including workhouse visiting, the county education committee, the Girls Friendly Society, the Primrose League, and the National Union of Women's Suffrage Societies. Sir Rainald Knightley, already an MP when they met, found himself debating Irish Church Disestablishment with her during their courtship. Forty years in parliament failed to give him the confidence and zest for electioneering which his wife brought to his flagging cause in the 1880s.[16]

Each of these husband and wife teams included a partner who tended to be home-loving, unambitious and easily exhausted by the stress of public work; in every case it was the male. The women, by contrast, comprise a phalanx of gracious but masterful, tough and persistent people who retained a lifelong fascination for politics both on the platform and in committee. Nonetheless one should not underestimate the magnitude of their initiative in the 1880s. At this time there existed no provision for a Conservative woman to join her party; nor did the party even recognize any women's organization until the Edwardian period. It had been no part of Lord Randolph Churchill's original conception that women should be involved in the Primrose League; the first advertisements invited 'gentlemen' to join. It is not entirely clear how Grand Council's decision to admit women arose. Lady Borthwick, the socially ambitous wife of Sir Algernon Borthwick, proprietor of the *Morning Post*, claimed to have been the first Dame properly enrolled. However, Lady Dorothy Nevill and her daughter Meresia may have been the first to be enrolled by Sir Henry Drummond Wolff as a result of dinner-table discussions at which the formation of the league had been plotted. Wolff, not Churchill, appeared at Blenheim to 'initiate' all the Churchill ladies, who according to Lady Randolph found the whole thing mildly amusing and looked askance at the 'Brummagem gaudy badges'.[17] When first approached the serious-minded Lady Knightley commented crisply: 'It all sounds rubbish, but the objects . . . are excellent. I can quite believe that the paraphernalia helps to keep Conservatives together − means, in short, an army of unpaid canvassers.'[18] Lord Salisbury's sentiments exactly.

Despite some initial scepticism titled ladies soon began to join in large numbers, as we have seen. However it would be wrong to assume a significant rank-and-file participation by women simply on the basis of a few prominent women at the top of the league. It is tempting to make such assumptions with, for example, the Independent Labour Party because of the presence of several well-known couples among the leadership – the Bruce Glasiers, Snowdens, MacDonalds and Pethick-Lawrences. Yet we appear to have no systematic evidence of female membership in the ILP branches few as they were; on the contrary the prejudice of male ILPers against women's involvement even in the Edwardian period is on record.[19]

In the case of the Primrose League, separate statistics for Knights and Dames (see p. 27) reveal the pattern for the higher class of membership; the ratio of Knights to Dames was three to one in September 1885, two to one by November 1885, three to two by January 1886 and five to four by March 1887. However, the vast majority of members were Associates, for whom no separate return by sex was made. Fortunately a number of the surviving habitation records include detailed membership registers which reveal the consistently high level of female involvement, and this is shown in table 2.

Table 2   Sex composition of habitation membership

Habitation	Male (%)	Female (%)	Sample	Years
'Mostyn', Llandudno	39.6	60.4	556	1888–91
Bishop's Castle				
(Shropshire)	46.5	53.5	155	1893–8
Sowerby (Yorkshire)	47.1	52.9	644	1888–9
Whitehaven	48.8	51.2	1,122	1889–97
Melbury (Dorset)	49.8	50.2	1,067	1886
'Scott' (Edinburgh)	50.0	50.0	388	1912
Nailsworth and Horsley				
(Gloucestershire)	53.5	46.5	159	1887
'Pennyman', Cleveland	54.9	45.1	1,050	1886–8
'Lowther' (Westmorland)	56.0	44.0	780	1886–9
Garstang (Lancashire)	57.5	42.5	494	1894–1909
Coln Valley				
(Gloucestershire)	74.2	25.8	182	1886–7
Total sample	51.3	48.7	6,597	

These findings are of considerable importance for social and political history. They obviously corroborate the impressionistic evidence of the Primrose League as an organization which catered to women; but what is more striking is that they show the league as a body which incorporated men and women rather than segregating them. Moreover, they suggest that the Primrose League – uniquely for a Victorian political institution – must have included hundreds of thousands of women in its ranks. Since no other political cause could rival this, their involvement surely throws some light on the political allegiance of women as voters in the twentieth century. And although these women should not be represented as part of a 'women's movement', to ignore them in the writing of women's history would be to adopt a wholly false perspective.

Numbers, however, are only part of the picture. The role played by women and their relationship with the male members is of equal importance. At local level some towns, for example Barnsley, Trowbridge, Brighton, Durham, Torquay and Wellington (Shropshire), had a 'Dames' habitation, that is, one run solely by Dames, along with a 'Knights' habitation. In addition there are a few examples of exclusively male habitations attached to clubs, for example the 'Abergavenny' (Constitutional Club in London), or to a university, such as the 'Iddesleigh' (Edinburgh University). This practice was, however, untypical, and was deprecated as inconsistent with the ideology of the league, which advocated the unity of divergent social groups through common activities and common interests. [20] After the first few years these separate habitations often amalgamated. Where they persisted the explanation may be that the local Conservative Association already had a large male membership and showed hostility to a competitor; even the highly successful 'Grantham Dames' Habitation in Croydon was single sex 'not entirely from choice'. [21]

In the typical mixed habitations the evidence shows that women were not merely passive footsoldiers marshalled under male leadership. Detailed information has been found for 1,274 habitations in England and Wales during 1887–9; in one in four of these the leading office of Ruling Councillor was occupied by a woman. In addition, it soon became the practice for those with a male Ruling Councillor to appoint a Dame President who was in effect his deputy and might run the organization while he became a figurehead. Other offices were even more likely to be held by women, particularly that of Hon. Secretary and Warden, perhaps because of the heavy demands they made on the holder's time. All the evidence tends to corroborate the impression of an organization in which women played an active, not merely a decorative or supportive, role. This stemmed naturally from the fact that the initiative for the establishment of habitations often originated with prominent ladies who felt little hesitation in enrolling men under their leadership. [22]

In its central organization the Primrose League was less obviously susceptible to female influence, for Grand Council remained in its original all-male condition until after the First World War, despite occasional suggestions that women should be represented. At an early stage the ladies decided that they could pursue their objectives quite satisfactorily by instituting their own Ladies Grand Council in March 1885. [23] Constitutionally the LGC was the creature of Grand Council and subordinate to it in all matters, though it enjoyed complete control over its own funds. [24] The ladies chose their own President and Vice-President and a fifteen-strong committee. The two bodies liaised through regular reports, and in deference to the ladies' interest in propaganda a Joint Literature

Table 3   Habitation officers

Habitation	Wardens			Executive Council		
	Men	Women	Year	Men	Women	Year
Sowerby (Yorkshire)	17	9	1887	7	4	1888
Whitehaven				6	4	1888
Elswick (Newcastle-upon-Tyne)	23	8	1905	16	8	1905
St Andrews (Newcastle-upon-Tyne)	12	6	1905	12	7	1905
Jesmond (Newcastle-upon-Tyne)	11	19	1906			
'Scott' (Edinburgh)				16	7	1898
Wokingham (Berkshire)	1	12	1887			
Garstang (Lancashire)	16	11	1897	13	3	1898
Melbury (Dorset)	8	12	1886			
Nailsworth and	4	6	1887	8	2	1887
Horsley (Gloucestershire)	6	7	1897	6	10	1899
Skipton (Yorkshire)	4	13	1890			

Committee was set up under Lady Jersey's chairmanship. Grand council seemed particularly sensitive about the LGC intervening between it and local habitations or individual members. This may reflect the fact that the ladies met more frequently and for a time effectively seized the initiative. Shrewdly making the most of their assets, the ladies organized drawing room functions for those who came up to London for the season each summer; fired with enthusiasm, their guests dispersed to their country residences to establish their own habitations in the autumn. In the early years, when habitations were still thin on the ground and the league lacked the resources to employ pro-fessional agents, this proved a useful way of speeding up recruitment. However, it doubtless gave the men a feeling of being by-passed.

On the other hand it was difficult to cavil at the successful expansion during 1885–7, and the LGC did in fact enjoy direct and regular communication with the habitations, as is abundantly clear from its minutes. As a result the LGC was often quick to identify areas and issues of political weakness, and served to some extent as a channel for criticisms and complaints to reach Grand Council.[25] It would therefore be a mistake to see the LGC merely as a gracious social gathering, though its members used such gatherings as weapons in the political battle they saw as their real function. As early as 1886 several of the men, perhaps reassured by the heavy defeat of the Gladstonians, wanted to minimize the political activities of the women and attempted to steer them in the direction of philanthropic work. But they refused to be fobbed off. The Duchess of Marlborough and Lady Randolph Churchill quickly announced that they declined to be confined to 'benevolent and philanthropic matters'.[26] The then Vice-Chancellor, Lord Harris, attempted to invoke the authority of Lord Randolph Churchill to bring his wife and mother to order, but apparently without success. Within a few years the league had nothing but praise for the women's political work. It would have been futile for Grand Council to risk antagonizing the powerhouse of the organization. Significantly, the LGC never had to go cap in hand to Grand Council, for ladies who joined it paid a guinea a year which was quite separate from tribute and habitation fees. As a result the LGC enjoyed an annual income of £1,400 or more by the 1890s, which, though not a large amount in itself, loomed large in the context of the league's central finances. Most of the money raised and spent through the league was subject to local control, so the central organization gratefully received an annual donation of around £800 from the LGC. With the rest of their money the ladies felt free to finance whatever new items of propaganda, such as lantern shows or touring vans, they thought necessary. Eventually the men copied the LGC by establishing a Knights Imperial, which Knights might join for a guinea a year. Never as successful as the LGC, perhaps because they were in more direct competiton with the Conservative Associations for subscribers, the Knights Imperial seem mainly to have entertained themselves at dinners.

THE PROPER SPHERE

It was one thing for ladies to occupy a leading role within the organization, quite another for them to fight the Conservative cause outside it. From the start the Dames intended something more than a private club for Conservative ladies − that, after all, was what was wrong with existing Conservative Associations; they wanted to face the public, which meant on the platform and on the doorstep. If anyone remembered in the 1880s the famous triumph of the duchesses who had kissed butchers in aid of Charles James Fox's election at Westminster in 1784, they would doubtless have considered it an eighteenth-century vulgarity mercifully extinct in the Victorian age. The Dames must act with complete propriety, if only to dispel the prevailing male belief that elections were such inherently rough and unsavoury affairs as to be incompatible with feminine participation. Although some ladies had taken part in their husbands' elections before the 1880s, the general election of 1885 stands out as the turning-point in this respect. The league in general, and the new LGC in particular, saw this as a fine opportunity to test themselves. Conservative candidates, faced with the menace of church disestablishment and the rest of Chamberlain's 'Unauthorized Programme', a new county electorate and drastically redrawn constituency boundries, needed all the assistance they could get. Lady Randolph Churchill's by-election campaign for her husband at Woodstock is well known, but a more significant sign was the Duchess of Marlborough's canvass in Birmingham at the general election, for it was an example set by a far more conventional and old-fashioned figure. Meanwhile Lady Knightley plunged into a five-month canvass of South Northamptonshire in a bid to save her husband's vulnerable seat.[27] Even in these circumstances, however, some Conservatives were so offended by such forwardness that the Chancellor of the league felt obliged to remind critics that Grand Council 'could not possibly prevent a lady canvassing for her husband.'[28] In short, if Sir Rainald Knightley could swallow his pride it was not for others to delimit the duties of husband and wife. Once the breach had been opened, middle-class women could follow with far less controversy than an independent initiative on their part would have caused. The pioneering image of the lady of the manor canvassing the tenants rapidly gave way to a much more modern pattern in which squads of thirty to fifty Dames systematically worked the streets of an urban or suburban constituency.

Both the increased electorate and the limitation on expenditure made this kind of volunteer canvass essential during and between campaigns. Significantly, it represented a natural extension of existing activities for many an upper-class lady. As Meresia Nevill, one of the earliest canvassers, put it: 'As a rule I consider women the best canvassers, in as much as they are used to district visiting. They have the habit of going among the poor, and speaking to (them) and hearing their wants.'[29] By comparison with a man, the lady canvasser stood a good chance of gaining entry to the voter's house and acquiring knowledge of his family's circumstances and interests; 'advice or opinion given concerning the social or parochial matters...often have a greater influence than political considerations in deciding votes.'[30] In the first instance the canvassers were often dealing with the non-voting wives but argued that 'the influence of the wives of the working men with their husbands is unbounded'.[31] Such a bold generalization must be treated sceptically, but the women-only canvass had its own value in that it was followed up with small-scale meetings often held in the women's homes at which Dames gained an appretriceship in public speaking. Also, in municipal elections where women comprised a significant element of the electorate, the Dames were sometimes made solely responsible for mobilizing them.[32] In the early years the women ratepayers often showed some reluctance to use their votes, but an approach from a lady who would offer to convey the hesitant to the poll in a private carriage during the day when polling was quiet, was well-calculated to succeed. In addition, the Dames' activities reflected a common Victorian interest in the possibilities of raising the condition of the urban population by exposing them to civilizing influences, a task for which educated ladies were thought to be especially suited. It mattered little from this point of view whether the

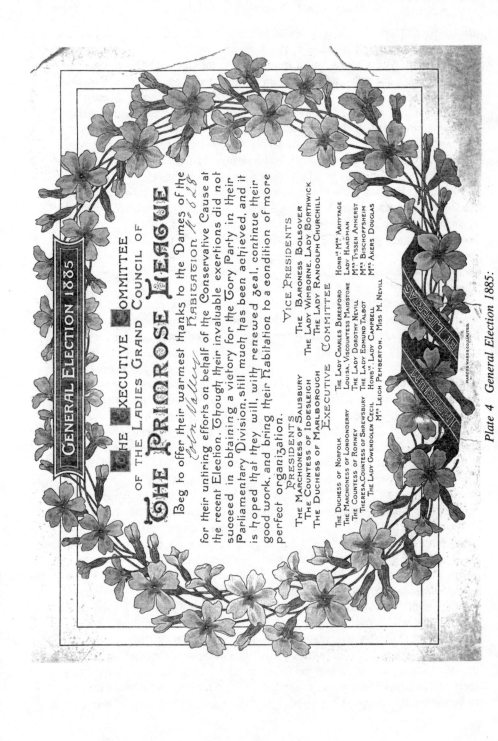

GENERAL ELECTION 1885

THE EXECUTIVE COMMITTEE
OF THE LADIES GRAND COUNCIL OF

THE PRIMROSE LEAGUE

Beg to offer their warmest thanks to the Dames of the
Colen Valley Habitation No 628
for their untiring efforts on behalf of the Conservative Cause at
the recent Election. Though their invaluable exertions did not
succeed in obtaining a victory for the Tory Party in their
Parliamentary Division, still much has been achieved, and it
is hoped that they will, with renewed zeal, continue their
good work, and bring their Habitation to a condition of more
perfect organization.

PRESIDENTS
THE MARCHIONESS OF SALISBURY
THE COUNTESS OF IDDESLEIGH
THE DUCHESS OF MARLBOROUGH

VICE PRESIDENTS
THE BARONESS BOLSOVER
THE LADY WIMBORNE. LADY BORTHWICK
THE LADY RANDOLPH CHURCHILL

EXECUTIVE COMMITTEE

THE DUCHESS OF NORFOLK
THE MARCHIONESS OF LONDONDERRY
THE COUNTESS OF ROMNEY
THERESA, COUNTESS OF SHREWSBURY
THE LADY GWENDOLEN CECIL

THE LADY CHARLES BERESFORD
LOUISA, VISCOUNTESS MAIDSTONE
THE LADY DOROTHY NEVILL
THE LADY EDMUND TALBOT
HONbLE LADY CAMPBELL
Mrs LEIGH PEMBERTON. MISS M. NEVILL

HONbLE Mrs ARMYTAGE
LADY HARDMAN
Mrs TYSSEN AMHERST
Mrs BISCHOFFSHEIM
Mrs AKERS DOUGLAS

IMPERIUM ET LIBERTAS

MARCUS WARD & CO LIMITED.

women were voters or not. When old-fashioned Tories grumbled about the league enrolling servant girls, the Dames invariably justified themselves on the grounds that the girls would learn loyalty, duty and self-respect and become better wives and mothers as a result; in the words of Baroness Henry de Worms (DP Toxteth Habitation):

> It is not an age when 'men must work and women must weep'. . . . Women need not neglect their homes because they share the aims and aspirations of their husbands or fathers or brothers . . . the more women interest themselves in subjects of universal importance, the happier their homes are likely to become. [33]

However, the Dames would not have been so formidable a weapon had they confined themselves to indirect influence through other women; they relished tackling the male electors too. As a woman of some social rank the Primrose Dame started with an advantage over the usual Conservative canvasser, who ran the danger of verbal abuse and even physical attack when venturing into working-class districts. She was much more likely to be treated with respect. When tackling the staunchest Radicals of Daventry Lady Knightley noted that she was always received 'with the same unvarying civility'. [34] Consequently when difficult or hostile territory had to be opened up to Conservatism, such as London's East End or the South Wales coalfields, the Dames were invariably employed as shock troops going in to establish bridgeheads for an official Conservative organization. Naturally the wise Dame avoided a patronizing or inquisitorial approach when tackling the male elector, especially in the more politically aware communities. Her advantage lay in the fact that her political visits carried no threat to his pride, for he enjoyed the superior status of parliamentary voter while the gracious lady appeared as the suppliant; if tactfully handled, this situation could only flatter him.

Thus an experienced team of Dames might relieve a Conservative agent of many of his burdens. With their plentiful leisure time they could devote the years between elections to building up an accurate picture of the party's reliable supporters by regular street canvasses; in some constituencies the wardens held the canvassing books and up-dated them every three months: 'a few men help occasionally, but it is found that lady visitors do more good.' [35] A laborious but vital task was to trace those voters who had moved house since the publication of the electoral register every January. When, for example, a by-election occurred in the marginal seat of Darlington in 1898, some eighty women of the local habitation worked the constituency, in which there were 720 removals in a total electorate of only 7,000; they traced all but thirty of them. [36] At general elections the Dames were also used particularly for rounding up the outvoters; indeed by the Edwardian period the LGC co-ordinated the outvoter campaign centrally on behalf of the Conservative Party with the enthusiastic approval of the party's chief agent. [37] Finally, the Dames were alive to some of the flaws in the system of registration which powerfully affected the performance of the parties. Only recently have historians begun to question the assumption that the disfranchised men, four out of every ten, were almost exclusively working class. [38] It has been shown that younger men, regardless of social class, encountered difficulty in being registered because of the lateness of marriage; they often either resided with their parents or took rooms, and consequently lacked any claim on the household qualification. However the alternative — the lodger franchise — proved an embarrassing option for respectable families in that it involved exposing the trivial details of one's personal life to examination in the Revision Courts. In the absence of some pressure to claim and sustain their qualification every year it was tempting to neglect electoral registration until marriage made it relatively easy. The Dames were certainly charged with trying to persuade the sons of middle-class families to make the effort much sooner. [39]

SUFFRAGE AND ANTI-SUFFRAGISM

No organization which incorporated so many women as the league could avoid making some contribution to the wider struggle over the political emancipation of women in Britain. But whether the contribution was a negative or a positive one is not immediately clear. For women the obstacle to enfranchisement was broadly twofold; they must persuade the men who enjoyed the power to bestow the vote, and they must demonstrate that the majority of women both deserved and wanted the vote. Most women, so the anti-suffragist argument ran, remained either apathetic about politics or unmoved by their unprivileged status; they simply left it to their husbands, fathers and brothers to vote in their place. Now the Primrose League undoubtedly tended to undermine sentiments of this kind, but not in a direct or deliberate way, for it was not corporately committed to women's suffrage. It challenged convention through its routine activities. Merely by seeking to inform women on political issues as though they were men, and by employing women in the role of instructors and leaders, it began to dissolve the whole notion of strictly separate spheres for the sexes, thirty years before the vote was won. In particular, the whole nature of the league's propaganda undermined a major pillar of anti-suffragism, namely the assumption that women, being dominated by personality and emotion, were incapable of comprehending the great questions of principle and issues of an abstract character. Twenty years of assiduous work by the Dames on behalf of causes regarded as fundamental to Conservatism — Empire, the Union with Ireland and the Anglican Establishment — rendered this rather absurd. More important, in co-operating loyally with the men they had made little attempt to force demands pertaining to women upon their colleagues; they had demonstrated that duties came before rights. This became the basis of the argument that women's suffrage, so far from being antipathetic to Conservatism, was a natural corollary to Conservatism.[40]

Naturally enough, many Dames believed that they played such an extensive informal role in politics that to deny them the formal right of voting was absurd. Activists such as Lady Knightley, Lady Borthwick, Lady Rayleigh and the Duchess of Sutherland took this view. Neither by instinct nor upbringing were they democrats; they had no quarrel with the prevailing Conservative view of the suffrage as a matter of personal fitness, not of individual rights; possession of property and payment of taxes remained valid criteria for electoral qualification, and plural voting a perfectly functional practice.[41] Lady Knightley, for example, shared her husband's opinion of Disraeli as an un-principled opportunist whose Reform Act had put 'all power into the hands of an uneducated mob!' Yet in the years between the second and third reform acts she learnt to come to terms with the situation. After a summer and autumn campaign throughout her husband's constituency in 1885 she finally accompanied him to the polling station; Sir Rainald went in to cast his vote for himself, and then: 'I felt − for the first time personally − the utter anomaly of my not having a vote.' By this time Sir Rainald, who had originally detested the idea of his wife appearing on a public platform of any kind, had to accept the general view in South Northamptonshire that his shaky seat had been saved by her efforts more than by his own popularity.[42] She went on to work for the National Union of Women's Suffrage Societies, while he closed his long parliamentary career in 1892 by voting for a women's suffrage bill.

However, Primrose League suffragists never tried to turn the organization into a wing of the suffrage movement, though many habitations, particularly in London, the north and Scotland, would probably have welcomed this.[43] Grand Council, faced with a potentially disruptive debate within its ranks, took refuge in the view that women's suffrage was no part of the objects of the league, a position it adopted on all divisive issues. The league as such therefore held no view, but individual members remained entirely free to take sides; nor would Grand Council intervene to stop habitations holding discussions on the question. As a result one finds some habitations being treated to anti-suffragist lectures by their ruling councillors, while others were entertaining speakers from the NUWSS and passing suffragist resolutions.[44]

Despite a groundswell of suffragism locally the league's first generation of leaders included some of the staunchest anti-suffragist women, notably Lady Jersey, Lady Londonderry, Lady Wimborne and the Duchess of Marlborough. To them the vote was indeed a mere formality which could scarcely add anything to the influence they claimed already; naturally many middle-class women did not see it this way and were prepared to condemn publicly those Dames who signed the anti-suffragist petition in 1889.[45] As time passed the position of the anti-suffragists undoubtedly grew anomalous. The Duchess of

Marlborough regularly inaugurated habitations with a declaration of her inability and reluctance to make the speech she was about to deliver; she disapproved, she said, of women participating in politics – except in exceptional circumstances such as the present time when the Church and religious education were under attack. [46] Exceptional and ephemeral circumstances somehow became usual, and soon the Duchess was heard to pronounce that while opposed to women's suffrage she advocated women's influence and 'hoped that the ladies present would exercise that influence upon everyone belonging to them in the shape of a man (Laughter)'. Other Dames tried to define precisely what was and was not a proper activity for a woman. For example, while condemning public speaking as vulgar and 'manifestly out of our province', they urged women to address 'small and homely gatherings'. [47] Of course such distinctions largely broke down. Homely gatherings of the league had a habit of turning into major functions. 'I hardly consider it a woman's place to address a large meeting such as this,' protested Lady Londonderry, not for the first or the last time; but she consoled herself, 'surely there is no nobler work for women than endeavouring to influence all those around to preserve the empire as our forefathers handed it down to us.' [48] In fact within a few years women speakers came to be taken for granted on Conservative platforms, and audiences often called for a speech from the candidate's wife. [49] Even Lady Jersey, who was good at it, defended the practice: 'Women whether they like it or not, are born members of the State...therefore it seems to us a matter of common sense that they should try and understand what is good for the State.' But, she added, 'We don't wish to govern the country...We want, so far as lies in our power, to assist in placing men in the Government who we think will lead our country in the paths of peace and prosperity.' [50]

Fine as this distinction between placing men in government and actually voting for them may be, Lady Jersey stuck to it for many years. In 1908 she took the lead in establishing the Women's National Anti-Suffrage League, a group which attracted similarly forceful and independent women such as Gertrude Bell the orientalist and traveller, and Mrs Humphry Ward the novelist, as well as other hostesses like Lady Glenconner, Lady Sheffield, Lady Ilchester and Lady Wantage. [51] Either because of their personal talents or because of their advantageous social status such ladies never felt the economic and political disabilities of many middle-class women. However, they enthusiastically supported women's role in local government both as electors and as councillors or guardians; again this distinction, which looked plausible to a generation brought up to equate social policy with local administration, steadily ceased to be realistic as traditional welfare functions became an integral part of central government. Moreover, when the women 'antis' amalgamated with the Men's Committee for Opposing Women's Suffrage in 1910 they were embarrassed by Curzon and Cromer's resolute hostility to women's municipal vote as merely the thin end of the wedge. Paradoxically the women antis were markedly superior to their male colleagues as propagandists and organizers, as Cromer himself admitted.[52] In 1908 they collected 337,000 signatures for an anti-suffragist petition and boasted 286 branches by 1914.[53] Meanwhile the men showed skill in raising money but never became much more than a clique of crusty old antis fuming away in their London clubs. It was all the more insulting for the women to discover that after the amalgamation of the two bodies the men insisted on retaining control.[54]

It has rightly been argued that the more the women antis allowed themselves to be provoked by Edwardian suffragette militancy into making their case publicly, the more they undermined it by advertising their undoubted political skills. Yet the Edwardian dilemma came simply as the climax of a long and futile attempt to reconcile their anti-suffragist principles with their practice both in the Primrose League and in municipal affairs. Their attitude seemed particularly anomalous in the light of changing views among Conservative men, who were by no means impervious to the significance of the Primrose Dames. By the late 1880s men were beginning to renounce their anti-suffragism on the grounds that the Dames had proved to their satisfaction that Conservative principles could be maintained by ladies 'without going out of their proper sphere'.[55] As one local newspaper commented editorially in 1887:

> The feeling that women have little to do with politics has been dispelled, for they show a desire and a right to have a voice and a vote in Imperial as well as municipal affairs, and it is to be hoped that the parliamentary franchise will not be witheld for any considerable time. Meanwhile, through the instrumentality of the Primrose League, they can continue to introduce the elements of brightness and gentleness and goodness into our political system, confident that the chivalrous and the gallant will be with them.[56]

Such evidence justifies some reconsideration of the traditional reputation of Conservatives for anti-suffragism; the hostility of the party activists and the MPs has been exaggerated, while conversely the sympathy of the party leaders has been overestimated. The National Union of Conservative Associations approved suffragist resolutions on seven occasions – 1887, 1889, 1891, 1894, 1907, 1908 and 1910 – as did the party in Scotland in 1887 and 1890. Obviously these conference decisions were not binding on the party, but they are a sign that the antis had begun to lose ground at an early stage. It is not difficult to see why the National Union should have been sympathetic. It tended to attract Conservatives who were keen on effective organization and winning elections; such people were in a good position to appreciate the contribution of Primrose Dames as workers and as potential voters. As a result, when the anti-suffragists eventually tried to mobilize their support in the Edwardian period they discovered that they were twenty years too late. By 1910 the National League for Opposing Women's Suffrage admitted to finding it all but impossible to obtain cooperation from Conservative agents in the constituencies.[57]

Nor were Conservative MPs quite so anti-suffragist as is often thought. In the absence of a party policy on the matter backbenchers felt at liberty to raise it in the Commons; indeed between 1884 and 1913 they were hardly less prominent in this respect than the Liberals. Conservative promoters of women's suffrage bills at this time included Sir Albert Rollit, F. Faithfull Begg, Sir Algernon Borthwick and Sir James Agg-Gardner, all of whom sat on the Grand Council of the league, in Borthwick's case as Chancellor. He did not hesitate to back up his bill with petitions from habitations despite the official neutrality of the league.[58] An analysis of the voting record of Conservative MPs between 1867 and 1913 undermines any simple generalization (see table 4). It suggests that the strength of anti-suffragism fluctuated between three distinct phases. From 1867 to 1883 Conservative suffragists were consistently outnumbered usually by three or four to one; this is the instinctive hostility of the old Conservatism. However, between 1884 and 1908 this pattern was emphatically reversed, in that suffragists formed a majority of those voting on every occasion but one. Naturally these bills were not expected to become law and it must have been tempting to record a token vote for the women; but the same is true for most of the earlier divisions too. No doubt many of the MPs who abstained were antis, but the fact that more antis abstained after 1884 than previously is not without significance. It suggests a party gradually and reluctantly coming to terms with the uncomfortable fact that it relied upon women's efforts to some degree for its success. The third period from 1909 is clearly more mixed. Matters were now complicated for two reasons. First, as the prospect of a women's franchise appeared imminent the question of party advantage became more acute; thus a number of the divisions were on bills from the radical side of the House which were much more democratic in scope than Conservatives would accept. Second, many MPs simply wanted to show by their votes that they could not be browbeaten by the suffragettes.

As evidence accumulated that Conservatives derived more benefit than their opponents from women's participation in politics, the balance of opinion inevitably moved slowly in favour of the suffragists. Was it entirely accidental that every Conservative leader from Disraeli onwards evinced public sympathy for women's enfranchisement? Though in a minority, Disraeli enjoyed support from Lord John Manners, Lord Sandon, Lord Caernarvon and Lord Randolph Churchill. His successors, Northcote and Salisbury, took the same line, as later did Balfour, Bonar Law and Baldwin.[59] 'I can conceive no argument by which (women) are excluded, 'Salisbury told a Primrose League audience in Edinburgh in 1888. 'It is obvious that they are abundantly as fit for it − by

Table 4 Conservative MPs in Commons divisions on Women's Suffrage Bills 1867–1913

Date	% For	% Against
20 May 1867	8.7	91.3
4 May 1870	43.1	56.9
12 May 1870	27.3	72.7
3 May 1871	33.1	66.9
1 May 1872	24.0	76.0
30 Apr 1873	31.0	69.0
8 Apr 1875	35.4	64.6
26 Apr 1876	28.5	71.5
19 June 1878	19.9	80.1
7 Mar 1879	15.6	84.5
6 July 1883	20.8	79.2
12 June 1884	77.2	22.8
25 Nov 1884	33.3	66.7
18 Feb 1886	62.4	37.6
27 Apr 1892	55.0	45.0
3 Feb 1897	57.3	42.7
16 Mar 1904	58.5	41.5
28 Feb 1908	51.8	48.2
19 Mar 1909	—	100.0
12 July 1910	43.0	57.0
5 May 1911	57.4	42.6
28 Mar 1912	35.8	64.2
12 July 1912	—	100.0
5 Nov 1912	55.5	44.5
6 May 1913	16.8	83.2

Percentages recalculated from Brian Harrison, *Separate Spheres*: *the Opposition to Women's Suffrage in Britain*, (1978), pp. 28–9, to exclude Liberal Unionists, who were more anti-suffragist than the Conservatives.

knowledge, by training, by character − as many who now possess the franchise, and their influence is likely to weigh. . .in the direction of morality and religion.'[60] Indeed the sympathy of some bishops and the formation of a Church League for Women's Suffrage ensured that suffragism would be central to Conservatism and not merely a fad. Significantly, although Salisbury's argument appears a typically Conservative one, it was by no means distinctively so at this time. Radical and Socialist suffragists had also begun to perceive men as the barbarous element in society and women as the civilizing force. Keir Hardie urged that the 'coming of the motherhood element into politics' would result in the state pursuing a compassionate, fraternal policy. [61] This reflected a certain shift of emphasis on the part of the constitutional suffragists towards the end of the century. Whereas in the 1860s women had argued on the basis of individual rights which must be common to both sexes, they now increasingly accepted the anti-feminist line that women did not possess entirely the same attributes as men. Woman was inevitably different by function and experience — essentially mother and housekeeper. However, this domesticity, so far from constituting a disqualification for politics, made women responsible and unselfish — more likely to be model citizens than men. In so far as women were absorbed by religion, morality, education, social welfare and temperance, so the extra dimension they could bring to politics must inevitably be of an improving, virtuous kind. In retrospect this conception of women's character is easy to belittle. But the point to remember here is that Conservative suffragism cannot be represented as an eccentric or reactionary view, for it appears to have reflected the general reorientation of suffragism at this time.

Naturally the value of the Conservative leaders' support was somewhat diminished by their reluctance to take up the question while actually in office with the sole exception of Stanley Baldwin in the 1920s. For this there is a twofold explanation. First, although they believed that propertied women were perfectly entitled to have a vote, they never regarded their exclusion as a gross abuse requiring urgent attention; it never seemed worth the controversy that legislation would surely provoke within the party. Thus they avoided any party policy on the subject, treating it as a matter for individual conscience. Secondly, the underlying difficulty lay in the fact that women's suffrage could not be considered in isolation from the rest of the parliamentary franchise. As a result of the reforms of 1867 and 1884, which had extended the householder and lodger franchises to boroughs and counties, approximately sixty per cent of adult men qualified. Married women might simply have been enfranchised as the wives of householders, and thus the road to adult suffrage would have been open. To Conservatives it seemed safe and proper to enfranchise women who possessed qualifications which would have entitled them to vote had they been men — 'equal suffrage' — which was also the position adopted by the women's societies. Thus Conservative backbench legislation usually envisaged enfranchising women who were inhabitant occupiers as owners or tenants of a dwelling house, tenement or building. This was the basis of the post-1869 local government franchise which applied only to single women until 1894, when married women were allowed to qualify in the same way though not in respect of the same property as their husbands. By 1892 some 503,000 women had gained a place on the municipal register in England, Wales and Scotland, which suggests that they would have comprised at least

10–15 per cent of the parliamentary electorate – more than enough to give a decisive advantage to one party.

But did the prospective gain justify the risks? According to Lady Salisbury a women's bill, however limited in scope, '*must* lead to manhood suffrage the moment the other side come in again. That is the worst of a Conservative majority passing Liberal measures.'[62] On the other hand, Lady Knightley insisted on the wisdom of enacting women's suffrage 'on a taxpaying basis before universal suffrage came into practical politics.'[63] She may well have been correct, in that if women had gained a modest foothold on the parliamentary franchise in the 1890s the issue would probably not have figured at all prominently in the Edwardian period. In the event, despite their fears in both 1867 and 1884, the Conservatives managed to survive and even flourish with the expanded electorate; the leaders therefore hesitated to interfere with the rules of a game they were winning. As a result they never faced acute pressure to legislate; and Salisbury could enjoy the luxury of flattering his lady activists by giving his support in principle, while placating the antis by doing nothing of substance.

After the turn of the century, however, what had been a relatively gentle debate turned into a fast-moving controversy in which the stakes were dangerously high. With the general collapse of Conservative popularity in the country during 1903–6 and the party's failure to recapture office in 1910, the old system lost much of its attraction. Now Conservatives gave serious consideration to all kinds of constitutional innovation, including the referendum and reform of the House of Lords. While the antis placed their confidence in Asquith's powers of obstruction to hold off the suffragist majority in his party and cabinet, many leading Conservatives inclined to a less risky and more positive approach. With the passage of the 1911 Parliament Act there was a real prospect of adult male suffrage and the abolition of plural voting; in this context the inclusion of propertied women on the register became an infinitely more serious prosposition than previously, for it was the one structural change likely to give Conservatives an electoral victory.

Since they were out of office from December 1905 the Conservatives did not have to bear the brunt of suffragette militancy; nonetheless, as awareness of women's role and aspirations was heightened under the impact of militancy so the party inevitably felt the disgruntlement of the women within its ranks. Lady Constance Lytton, a prominent suffragette who risked her life by fasting and enduring forcible feeding, was not the only Conservative lady to adopt militant methods. In 1907 Kensington Habitation had the temerity to call for an alliance with the WSPU, and in 1909 Streatham Habitation reported the arrest of two members for attempting to force an entrance to the House of Commons. When the 1910 general elections came, several habitations fell foul of Grand Council because of the reluctance of a number of Dames to work for anti-suffragist candidates.[64] Lady Betty Balfour, then Dame President of the Woking Habitation, went so far as to resign her office in protest against a speech by her MP, Donald MacMaster, in which he had declared the enfranchisement of women to be contrary to the interests of empire and constitution: 'To continue to work for a Member holding such views seems to me an absurdity', she wrote.[65] Female assertiveness also provoked some reaction from Conservative Associations who urged that men ought to withdraw from the Primrose League and ignore women members as being 'of no political use'.[66] Some male Associates probably did vote with their feet, at least by staying away from habitation meetings at this time, allegedly on the grounds that they felt unable to smoke or to dress comfortably in the presence of ladies.[67] Grand Council somewhat nervously encouraged habitations to respond by providing more separate gatherings for men at which they might smoke in peace, advice which undermined the whole basis of the league's work. In addition the fierce controversy over tariff reform in this period drew some women such as the free trader Lady Jersey into the limelight. A striking example of female political assertiveness was provided by the Countess of Ancaster, who publicly criticized the interference of the Tariff Reform League in areas where the Primrose League already operated, notwithstanding her husband's role in promoting tariff reform at this time.[68]

Clearly, then, neither the league nor the Conservative Party could expect to remain immune from the divisive argument over the role of women in politics; both militants and moderates naturally sought to bring pressure to bear on the leadership to settle the issue. But could Balfour be cajoled into a decisive stance? Christabel Pankhurst, who taxed him regularly on the subject, evidently hoped so. 'It is quite ludicrous,' he admitted, 'to attempt a distinction of ''principle'' between the adults of one sex and the adults of another.'[69] But while happy to discuss the matter on theoretical grounds he shrank from acting on his conclusions. Balfour hedged initially on the familiar grounds that most women were not yet keen to possess the vote; when women as a class felt conscious of their exclusion, government would cease to be government by consent, and only then would legislation become imperative. Further, Balfour hesitated to pronounce a policy on the suffrage for fear of imposing another division on a party already acutely divided over tariffs. To this Christabel briskly countered that divisions ceased once the leader spoke out! For once she may have been perceptive. For, as we have seen, there had been a long-term drift towards the suffrage within Conservatism, though this had little to do with Christabel's recent efforts; and during the war some of the supposedly staunch anti-suffragists were to surrender both in Lords and Commons, not because of a change of heart but because of the difficulty of opposing the official line.[70] A firm lead before 1914 would have rallied the suffragists throughout the party and would probably have cowed the already demoralized antis. But Balfour was not the man to do it; with his authority already undermined over tariff reform, and with three election defeats behind him he gave up the leadership in 1911.

Meanwhile, the constitutional suffragists held out an attractive strategy for winning the credit for enfranchising women and thus humiliating the Liberals. In 1907 Lord Lytton and Lord Robert Cecil joined the Men's League for Women's Suffrage and were prominent members of the parliamentary Conciliation Committee from 1910, as were a number of Primrose League MPs including Samuel Roberts, Claude Hay and Sir John Rolleston. The ladies, led by the Countess of Selborne and Lady Knightley, took a fresh initiative by establishing the Conservative and Unionist Women's Franchise Association in 1908; from the ranks of the Primrose League came Lady Betty Balfour, Lady Rayleigh, Lady Galloway, Lady Willoughby d'Eresby, the Duchess of Sutherland, Lady Hoare, Lady St Oswald, Lady Edward Spencer Churchill, Lady Mary Cooke, Lady Limerick and Lady Willoughby de Broke. They were the respectable face of Conservative Suffragism. Privately Lady Selborne, Lord Lytton and Lord Robert Cecil negotiated with Catherine Marshall of the NUWSS terms that might be acceptable to the Conservative Party, in particular a bill involving a referendum on women's suffrage, an idea which had already been adopted with respect to tariffs.[71] The real virtue of this for the NUWSS lay in its indirect effect on the Liberals, who by 1913 were in imminent danger of being outflanked by both their rivals. Continued silence by Conservatives on the issue, as Christabel Pankhurst pointed out, exacerbated the danger of the women's movement sliding towards Labour.[72] Up to a point her warnings were vindicated by the electoral pact between the NUWSS and the Labour Party in 1912 which in effect placed Conservative NUWSS members like Ladies Knightley, Selborne and Betty Balfour in the embarrassing position of aiding their party's enemies. Thus by 1913 the temptation to opt for a formal Conservative policy and outmanoeuvre the Liberals was quite strong; indeed the Conservative antis were so fearful of a commitment by the leaders that they contemplated forming a new pressure group specifically for Conservatives.[73] In 1914 the Party Chairman, Sir Arthur Steel-Maitland, showed a sudden interest in the details of the issue which further raised expectations.[74]

However, Bonar Law, despite his own careful support for the Conciliation Bill, hesitated. By 1913 the Government's own franchise legislation had been frustrated by procedural means, and it was not clear what, if anything, they would do. Moreover, the complications of the Labour–NUWSS pact were infinitely less serious for Conservatives than for Liberals; indeed, in so far as this produced more three-cornered contests and embarrassed women Liberals it would be to his own party's immediate advantage. He stuck to his basic strategy of uniting his party around the Irish question in the hope of an early general election; meanwhile, women's suffrage remained in the wings as a counterweight to the abolition of plural voting, as the compromise worked out in 1916–17 was to show.[75]

In the long run the Primrose League surely assisted rather than retarded the cause of women's enfranchisement, in spite of not being a suffragist organization, indeed perhaps because of it; for the league steadily undermined assumptions about the political inertia and ignorance of women without driving men as a whole into opposition. Against this it may be argued that in so far as the league absorbed the political energies of women during the 1880s and 1890s it blunted their sense of alienation from the political system; some feminists will therefore be tempted to regard it as having delayed emancipation. Yet this would be to make the improbable assumption that, in the absence of outlets of this kind, the women would have advanced more rapidly into the suffrage movement or adopted a more radical or militant approach. On the contrary, an apprenticeship in organizations like the league was for many British women a precondition for their subsequent suffragism. During the 1880s and 1890s a generation of women − and men − learnt to accept a visible role for women in parliamentary elections and local government. Their enfranchisement was held up both by Liberal apprehension about further reform and by Conservative confidence in their ability to cope with the post–1885 electoral system. After 1900 the ubiquitous Dame was found to have quietly sapped the strength of anti-suffragism where it might have been strongest, and the antis found it impossible to undo twenty years of work. As in 1867 many politicians, without being outright democrats, were prepared to enfranchise a new class of people because experience had shown that it was safe to do so. What in the end was needed was the stimulus of an imminent and unavoidable measure backed by a government, which is precisely what emerged during 1916–17 and passed into law in 1918.[76] While there is plenty of evidence that the Conservatives found the new male franchise rather disturbing in 1917–18, female enfranchisement proved to be a reassuring element in the Act.[77] That Conservative MPs supported the women's vote by three to one, and went on to enact equal suffrage in 1928 was not an aberration but part of a steady evolution, which for them had begun in the 1880s.

FEMINISM AND THE PARTIES

The women of the Primrose League help the historian to perceive the history of women in Britain in a true perspective. As with the history of the labour movement it is easier to study organized minorities than masses, and women's history could easily become a history of radical women only. Yet radicalism and women clearly drifted apart in the second quarter of the nineteenth century. The 1832 reform bill formalised women's exclusion from the franchise, and even the Chartists conspicuously excluded women from their demands. By mid-century what had been an abstract matter of individual rights began to assume a disturbingly concrete form. Women were demanding education and access to professional employment; both manual workers and, by the 1880s, clerks and teachers perceived women as competitors for jobs. Despite John Stuart Mill's example, many late Victorian Liberals stopped short of fresh extensions of the electorate. Trade unionists, having won their own foothold in parliament, often regarded women as 'bourgeois women's righters', while many socialists accepted Robert Blatchford's warning that it was not yet safe to give women votes because they would use them against socialism. [78] In this somewhat hostile climate it is not surprising that women concentrated on precise objectives such as married women's property or abolishing the Contagious Diseases Acts, where some male support was forthcoming. Partly as a result the movement for women's enfranchisement remained extremely small. For example, when in 1897 the various women's suffrage groups were reorgaized to form the NUWSS they comprised barely twenty local societies. As late as 1906–7 they boasted a mere 32 and some 13,000 members; under the continued stimulus of militancy their numbers reached 54,000 by 1914. It is thus doubtful whether, even for the Edwardian period, one can reasonably speak of a mass movement for women's suffrage. Against this background the ladies of the Primrose League cannot be belittled for not asserting feminist demands in the 1880s. The point is rather that by sheer force of numbers they helped to modify the perception of women and their role in Britain.

Radicals and socialists pondered the meaning of the Primrose League and the remarkable capacity of the Conservatives to harness women to their cause. Did it mean that women were in some sense naturally Conservative? Were they basically religious and susceptible to Anglican influence, captivated by the romantic appeal of monarchy, or moved by the thrilling and awesome cause of Empire and patriotism? Or were they simply malleable in the hands of astute manipulators of deference and snobbery? One part of the explanation lies in the fact that Conservatives provided a form of politics that was readily appreciated by a group unused to formal political bodies; league activities appealed to women and often capitalized upon the skills they already possessed. This provoked a good deal of scorn from political opponents, but in the long run the criticism came to be interpreted as a tribute to the league's effectiveness. Indeed, this is corroborated by the repeated attempts on the part of Liberals to launch their own version; but the Progress League, the Red Rose League, the Lily League and the Ladies Liberal Social Council were, as the *Primrose League Gazette* gleefully observed, all more or less ephemeral and unsuccessful ventures. Of course by the 1880s the Liberals were less well endowed with wealthy, leisured ladies able to give a lead in each local community. And even though deference was by no means absent from Liberal politics, any attempt to copy the Primrose League would have been embarrassing for a party whose activists loved to excoriate the upper classes as a parasitic elite of landowners.

On the other hand the league rapidly demonstrated that women could help remedy the organizational deficiencies of the parties. No doubt Mrs Gladstone had this in mind when in 1887 she inaugurated the Women's Liberal Federation: 'There will be no Knights and no nonsense,' she announced. But there was too much friction and too few members. Inevitably a more serious-minded body than the league, the WLF was no sooner founded thanʼ it began to urge the Liberal Party to adopt a policy on women's suffrage — which was just what had deterred politicians from establishing women's sections in the first place. However, before converting the party the WLF had to settle its own view; since the organization was not committed to the suffrage for several years many women declined to join, or else devoted themselves more to the franchise issue than to the party. In 1892, when the WLF adopted a women's suffrage policy, Mrs Gladstone resigned as President and the organization was split into two hostile groups until 1919. Naturally this infighting militated against a really effective role for the WLF in Liberal electoral activities. With only 10,000 members in 1888 the women Liberals were not in any case on a level with their rivals, though the Edwardian revival lifted them to 66,000 in 1904 and a peak of 133,000 in 1912. However, it proved frustrating and demoralizing to remain loyal to a party whose leaders persistently obstructed women's enfranchisement; as a result the women often withdrew support for anti-suffragist Liberal candidates and lost members during the last two years before the war.

On the Labour and socialist side of politics there existed a variety of organizations women might join, though they seem to have faced similar difficulties to their Liberal counterparts. Much the most significant dimension was contributed by the Women's Co-operative Guild, established in 1883, which attained a membership of 30,000 in the Edwardian period under the leadership of Margaret Llewellyn Davies. Because it familiarized working women with organizational methods and encouraged them to assert their rights against their husbands, the WCG aroused a good deal of antagonism in the labour movement.[79] It enjoyed the advantage of standing on its own feet and thus freely adopted women's suffrage, but the corollary was a reluctance of men to accept the WCG as an integral part of their movement. The alternative strategy may be seen in the Women's Trade Union League, which originated in 1874 as the Women's Protective and Provident League. By 1904 it had built up a membership of 126,000, but with the exception of cotton textiles, members came from trades in which employment was almost wholly confined to low-paid women workers. To the trade union movement the WTUL was at best peripheral and at worst a threat. Leading figures like Margaret Bondfield and Mary MacArthur were tolerated at trade union conferences provided they played down the feminist cause, which meant acquiescing in adult suffrage rather than an early enfranchisement of women. They were not strong enough, numerically or financially, to exercise independent influence.

Thus the formation of the Labour Representation Committee in 1900 found women a peripheral and neglected element in a labour movement oriented around male interests. A few women were indirect members of the LRC through the Fabians and the ILP, but the neglect of a system of individual party membership hampered female recruitment. In 1906 the Labour Party recognized that its organizational weakness might be overcome by setting up a Women's Labour League. Even at this late stage the prejudice against women in local ILP branches remained remarkably strong. As one WLL organizer in 1908 reported: 'I... found some of the old trade unionists afraid we should spoil their homes by taking women out to meetings!!!'[80] Thus by 1913 the WLL's membership remained a tiny 4,000. Moreover, in view of its dependence upon the Party for annual financial assistance its leaders tended to reflect the orthodox party line on suffrage, that is, they subordinated women's enfranchisement to the adult suffrage policy which was generally acceptable to the labour movement. WLL branches often split because one faction wanted to join the WSPU rather than wait for the men to come round to their view.[81]

The experiences of women in the three political movements in this period are clearly not entirely different. All remained either segregated or outside the official party organization in some sense. All felt the same pressure to play down women's suffrage for fear of dividing the party. On the other hand the Conservative experience is distinctive in certain respects. Through the Primrose League it was vastly more successful in mobilizing women than its rivals; and it provided far more opportunity for men and women to work together throughout the country over a period of several decades. But the corollary of this co-operation was that the league's ladies would never be assertively feminist. Ladies Grand Council pointedly declined even to be represented at national and international gatherings of women on the grounds that they were not a women's organization at all.[82] In essence the league's formula worked because it allowed both sexes to retain dignity and self-respect – which historically is probably the key to the emancipation of women. Though the men perceived no threat to their status, few would have quarrelled with Lady Jersey's claim that 'no political contest can be fought thoroughly and properly without the help of ladies.' Male Conservatives rejoiced that their women had avoided the Liberal mistake of turning themselves into 'a caucus exclusively in petticoats'; they chose instead to exercise their influence in politics 'not by their talents but by their charms'.[83] Patronizing as such sentiments must seem to a later generation of women – and men – they may still be recognized as stepping stones along the path. For the conversion of British society to the full and equal participation of women in politics did not, and has not, proceeded beyond a very limited point. Evidence for a real change of attitudes has been extremely hard to find for any period before the Second World War. Such limited advances as have occurred have their origins in the Victorian period, and in the attempts of some most unlikely heroines to demolish the screen separating their sex from politics.

4

The Ideology of
Late Victorian Conservatism

It may well be an exaggeration to dignify Victorian Conservatism as an ideology. Conservatives espoused a collection of attitudes and precepts rather than a coherent or carefully devised theory: a feeling that the sphere of politics was strictly limited; a distrust of rationalism and a corresponding fondness for experience and tradition; a belief in the virtues of hierarchy as a natural and unifying element both in the family and in the nation itself; and a disposition to accept authority, both religious and political. Such general notions could, of course, be deployed so as to justify a wide variety of political ideas and policies. At certain times Conservatives appeared to lay stress on the dispersal of power in the localities, on the undesirability of central bureaucracy, and on individual self-help. Yet at others there emerged a more 'Tory' emphasis on the responsibility of the elite to the people, on the benevolent and moral aspect of the state, and on the energetic use of authority in the interests of the community.[1]

During the nineteenth century the pressures of economic and social change led Conservatives to coalesce around the notion of a 'balanced' constitution comprising the Crown, Lords, Commons and, in addition, a national Church, which, it was hoped, would help to legitimize the existing distribution of power and wealth and thereby facilitate judicious adjustments in the balance. Late Victorian Conservatives, however, were troubled by the perception that the balanced constitution, however desirable, seemed an unappetising menu for a populace now gaining the rights of citizenship. Empirically the Conservatives' eventual electoral success suggests a capacity to come to terms with this dilemma. Historians once believed that statesmen like Disraeli and Churchill somehow matched or outflanked the abrasive appeals to class interest associated with Joseph Chamberlain and the politics of the 'caucus'. However, virtually all Tories regarded a competition on Chamberlainite terms as a bleak prospect which would culminate in confiscation of wealth. Up to a point the National Union represented a Conservative equivalent of the National Liberal Federation, albeit in an emasculated form, in that it profferred to the electors the material advantages of Conservative rule, though more in terms of past achievements than of future programmes. Yet this is a false trail for those who seek to explain the Conservatives' accommodation with modern politics. The Disraelian connection with social reform has been shown to be tenuous and exaggerated;[2] the famous speeches of 1872 were not Disraeli's way of pointing to a new programmatic politics and a democratic Conservatism, but a timely reaffirmation of the centrality of Crown, Church, Lords and Empire in the party's politics.[3] Similarly, Churchill's celebrated Dartford speech of 1886, though superficially about Tory social reform, was a typical example of his favourite tactic of embarrassing the Liberals by showing up the timidity of their own ideas; in so far as Churchill held definite political convictions they were hostile to reform and essentially defensive of traditional institutions.[4]

Indeed, the real contribution of men like Disraeli and Churchill lay in the idea that those causes and institutions most dear to Conservatives, and supposedly vulnerable, might be assets rather than liabilities in electoral combat. This is the assumption which underlay the Primrose League's thinking. When a member joined the organization he put his signature to a declaration pledging himself to the maintenance of religion, the monarchy, the estates of the realm and the British Empire. Whatever lay beyond these few but fundamental principles, lay outside the league's interests; in its official conception of the world, economic man scarcely existed. Certainly the league from time to time felt obliged to notice subjects outside its sphere – 'labour questions' in 1892, tariffs after 1903 and women's suffrage intermittently – but it endeavoured to leave it to other bodies both within and outside Conservatism to expatiate upon them. For the Primrose League its official principles constituted true Conservatism, a creed which would endure well beyond the ephemeral attractions of manifestoes and legislation.

In the circumstances of the 1880s this represented a bold strategy designed to mobilize popular enthusiasm without pandering to the baser emotions that were assumed to be ultimately destructive of Conservatism. Yet it might have been considered more foolhardy than bold. Conservative experience after 1906, indeed, suggests what risks the late Victorian Conservatives took in allowing their opponents to make the running on the material aspects of politics. However, in the 1880s their approach was less anachronistic than might appear in retrospect. After all, Gladstone himself was masterminding his own version of this strategy on the Liberal side from the 1860s onwards, and not entirely without success. Equally fearful of the debilitating effect of self-interest in politics, he attempted to harness the support of the new voters through a series of moral crusades.[5] Somewhere in the combination of Monarchy, Empire and Religion might lie a Conservative version of the 'Nonconformist Conscience'; certainly the principles espoused by the League fulfilled a similar function in that they provided a coherent expression of the Conservative faith capable of attaining the same idealistic and moral tone adopted by the Radicals. Against 'Peace, Retrenchment and Reform' or 'Trust the People' would be pitted 'Fear Your God and Honour the King'. Moreover, the passage of time tended to confirm Conservatives in their dislike of the Chamberlainite approach. The Radical 'Cow' failed to materialize; and though her impresario later brought his talents to the Conservative Party, his penchant for programme politics again led to awkward and unfulfilled promises such as Old Age Pensions.

Crown; Church; Estates of the Realm; Empire. These comprised the popular Conservative tradition into which the league hoped to infuse new life. But were they popular? Were they Conservative? Were they even traditions? We have recently been reminded that what we are accustomed to regard as great British traditions are often of comparatively slight antiquity.[6] Nor were declining institutions like the Church obviously efficacious vehicles for a political campaign. In addition, the Palmerstonian hegemony, which had only begun to disintegrate in the 1860s, had left Conservatives apparently adrift from the symbols of British national sentiment. Yet to say this is only to emphasize that the idea of turning tradition to party advantage had to be worked at; it did not come ready made in 1883. Thus the role of the league lay in sedulously propagating certain traditions in a form readily comprehensible to an unsophisticated electorate, thereby extending the reach of the official party to tap the latent, unarticulated conservatism in the country. The keystone in this endeavour was to be the Crown.

THE CONSERVATIVE MONARCHY

During the twentieth century the British crown has come to be seen as above politics and to be held in equal affection by supporters of all parties.[7] Yet for most of its history the monarchy has been both powerful and partisan, and consequently its popularity has been much more limited. Throughout Queen Victoria's reign a diminution in royal government occurred, albeit gradually, but the real transition to the modern monarchy began around the 1880s. Almost in spite of herself the queen evolved into a focus of popular emotion and patriotism. Yet the novelty and the extent of this change has often been exaggerated. Even at her Jubilees in 1887 and 1897 Victoria showed herself reluctant to play her part by wearing her crown and robes of state;[8] nor had she by any means reconciled herself to the role of a strictly constitutional monarch. Edward VII was to assume the mantle of the modern monarch far more naturally. Indeed, the interest of Victoria's reign is that it lay half-way between two patterns. To concentrate on the admittedly striking manifestations of royal popularity in the late nineteenth century is to miss much of the significance of the queen's role: her known political inclinations and the political use to which they were put.

From 1837 Queen Victoria had been a much more acceptable figure than the elderly and unsavoury men whom the public had grown accustomed to see on the throne. However, she failed to exploit her early advantages, and grew into a dowdy, unregal figure, running a parsimonious and lacklustre court rather as though she were *simply* a wife and mother. She had always been subject to a certain amount of satire from the press as 'Mrs Melbourne', and later as 'Mrs Brown', but her withdrawal from public activity after Prince Albert's death in 1861 helped to stimulate an organized republican movement in the country. By the 1870s leading statesmen showed their concern at her stubborn blindness to the situation; on only six occasions between 1861 and 1886 did she consent to open parliament, for example. 'The Queen is invisible, and the Prince of Wales is not respected,' as a despairing Gladstone put it. Fortunately for her, the critics fastened upon the costs of the monarchy, especially the £385,000 Civil List and the regular requests for extra money for the queen's sons and daughters.[9] Leading parliamentary critics included Sir Charles Dilke, G. O. Trevelyan, Charles Bradlaugh, Joseph Cowen, Henry Fawcett, Sir Wilfred Lawson, Henry Labouchere, Auberon Herbert, Joseph Chamberlain and John Morley;[10] on occasion as many as sixty-four members were prepared to go into the division lobbies in opposition to royal subventions. However, this was a narrow, if tempting, line of attack which could easily be thrown back by a resumption of public activity by the queen. By concentrating on money the republicans and other critics missed the real target – the queen's political and governmental role. Perhaps because she was a woman they underestimated her political influence, a point on which Gladstone might have disabused them had he not been so loyal to her. Indeed, many critics seem to have shared a comforting expectation that the monarchy would eventually become superfluous as British democracy evolved along the lines of the much-admired American system. Since Victoria's grip seemed so slight she would be that much less of an obstacle, and there seemed no urgency in terminating her reign. On her death republicans expected the prospect of the irresponsible Prince of Wales, tainted by debts and scandals, to complete their work for them.

Yet the strength of this belief lay less in the organized republican movement, which boasted only fifty clubs and perhaps 6,000 members,[11] than in the temporary paralysis of the monarchists in the 1860s and early 1870s. Her defenders largely accepted that the queen was signally failing to perform her duty, and that the wealth and privilege of the monarch could best be justified by a flamboyant display and bold involvement by the queen in the nation's life and fortunes. Indeed, upper-class society had been fully alerted to the dangers by events in France culminating in the Paris Commune.[12] Thus by the early 1870s monarchists were only too anxious to organize a counter campaign to check republicanism. As republicanism reached its modest heights in the early 1870s the reaction was already underway, assisted by the Prince of Wales' narrow escape from death by typhoid in 1871, the queen's public appearance for the thanksgiving in 1872, and the attempt on her own life in the same year. Thus fortuitously the royal family began to co-operate in its rehabilitation.

The passage of time played its part too. As Victoria attained old age she became the focus of sympathetic interest, while her son and heir was able to lose his past in middle-aged respectability. The sequence of royal withdrawal and re-emergence contributed to that mixture of mystery and visibility which is essential to a popular monarchy. By the 1890s the queen seemed capable of defying mortality. She was seen to have done her duty as wife and mother even if her period of mourning had been excessive even by Victorian standards. Organizations like the Girls Friendly Society gladly adopted her as the very model of probity and maternity for rising generations: 'she made motherhood fashionable'.[13] Press criticism of the queen gradually dried up, and eventually a new breed of popular newspapers — the *Mail*, *Express* and *Mirror* — turned to the royal family as a staple source of copy. But long before their time, cheap magazines like *Chatterbox* had begun to satisfy the public's curiosity for royal trivia. While royal portraits and jubilee and coronation mugs came to adorn many a working-class home, the families supplemented their knowledge of the queen and her life from innumerable articles in magazines: 'father and mother never tired of hearing her read out aloud stories (*Chatterbox*) contained about the Royal Family, and Mrs Winstanley knew everything there was to know about every new Royal baby.'[14] The sense of familiarity is palpable in the terms used to refer to royal personages: 'Mother has come home' for Victoria, or 'dear old Dad' for Edward VII. At the Jubilee of 1887 criticism of the monarchy was not entirely absent, but by 1897 it appeared to have died out, at least in public. Studies of local participation in the Diamond Jubilee have confirmed that while different classes in the community wanted to celebrate the occasion in different ways, there was no disagreement about the desirability of celebration.[15] To the upper classes the popular euphoria engendered by the jubilees undoubtedly proved very comforting; indeed it was seen as a bulwark against socialism. In 1902 even the Social Democratic Federation sent a loyal address to King Edward![16]

However, the greater popularity of the monarch would not have attained much political salience but for the assiduous cultivation of the link between party and crown in this period. As early as 1872 Federic Harrison accused Disraeli of a crude attempt to appropriate the Crown as a party slogan.[17] Yet the task of exploiting the opportunity presented a delicate problem; its solution became the peculiar function of the Primrose League. On her death the league delivered a characteristic eulogy on the 'innate constitutionalism of our late Queen', and claimed 'it would be difficult to imagine a stronger fidelity to the Constitution.'[18] The proof of this, so the argument ran, lay in her readiness to accept measures such as disestablishment, of which she strongly disapproved, but which had received the endorsement of the people, precisely the line of argument used by Conservatives to justify the power of the House of Lords. In reality, not only had the queen always been a strong partisan figure, but her excitable temperament had also made her careless of showing her loyalties even when this conflicted with her proper position in the constitution. During the late 1860s the queen, like many other Palmerstonian patriots, had drifted into Conservatism. Her irritation with Gladstone's institutional reforms gathered momentum under Disraeli's ministry through the Liberal attacks on the purchase of Suez Canal shares and the Royal Titles Act of 1876. Although Disraeli welcomed the opportunity to draw together the cause of empire and the cause of monarchy, it would be an exaggeration to think that he contrived the imperial title with this in mind. It was the queen's own initiative that led to her becoming Empress of India at this point; and it was only because of Gladstone's criticism that the Conservatives found themselves virtually playing the role of queen's party over the issue. [19] Thenceforth, however, it proved tempting to interpret any dissension over imperial policy as an attack upon the *Queen's* empire. Each great imperial crisis or triumph during the 1870s tended to entrench her at the centre of the nation's affairs, and the polarization of views over the 'Bulgarian Atrocities', the Congress of Berlin and the wars in South Africa and Afghanistan left the queen firmly aligned with the Conservatives. Her most public lapse into partisanship did not come until 1885, when General Gordon's death in the Sudan provoked her notorious uncoded telegram to Gladstone: 'These news from Khartoum are frightful, and to think that all this might have been prevented by earlier action is too frightful.' Gladstone felt obliged to consider whether so public a rebuke required his resignation, though in fact the royal message did not immediately become general knowledge. [20]

As a result, Queen Victoria had adopted a position of general opposition to Liberal Governments well before the Home Rule crisis of 1886. She signalled her feelings in a number of trivial but telling ways, for example, by refusing to invite the Gladstones to events such as the wedding of Princess Beatrice. While she never set foot at Hawarden, her visits to Hughenden received full publicity. In breaking with her usual practice by opening Parliament in person in 1886 she underlined her support for Salisbury in his resistance to Home Rule. Privately the queen showed scant regard for constitutional propriety. During the Home Rule crisis, for example, she allowed Salisbury to see copies of her Prime Minister's letters and even her own replies; she also sought his views as Leader of the Opposition on the desirability of granting a dissolution on the defeat of Gladstone's Bill. In 1892 she received Salisbury's resignation 'with regret', in the words of the Court Circular; and during Gladstone's last administration when the Commons threatened to challenge the peers' legislative powers, she consulted Salisbury as to whether his party was prepared to fight an election on the issue in 1893. [21]

However, there were limits to what even the queen could do to demonstrate her partisanship. For most of the time it remained for her allies to turn her sympathy to political advantage. Too flagrant a connection with Conservatism might have reduced the crown to a mere instrument of party and thereby devalued the asset it represented. Ideally she had to be seen to be above politics and yet a Conservative; she must be hostile to Liberalism and yet difficult for the Liberal Party to attack. Such a manoeuvre would have taxed the skills of the party itself; it was far better tackled by a separate body such as the Primrose League, both because its political creed remained vague and non-programmatic, and because the royal connection embodied in its name provided a plausible reason for doing so. Every April, the pilgrimages to Hughenden for the laying of primrose wreaths at Disraeli's grave, and similar ceremonies elsewhere, kept alive the memory of the royal favour that lay behind the league's title.

To a remarkable degree royalty also formed an integral part of the week-by-week routine activity of the Primrose League. Habitation functions invariably included the singing of 'God Save the Queen' or 'God Bless the Prince of Wales'. From its popular lantern shows the Queen's image beamed sternly down upon the achievements of her people. Leading leaguers, particularly peers, assumed a major role in the life of the Court as Lords-in-Waiting or Treasurer of HM Household, while the Prince of Wales was a regular visitor to their country houses. The Ladies Grand Council would not contemplate holding one of its own meetings on a day which clashed with the Queen's Drawing Room.[22] In the pages of the *Primrose League Gazette* one finds a characteristic attempt to satisfy popular curiosity by instituting a 'Dames Column' which dwelt upon the trivial daily round of the royal family. 'The Queen continues in excellent health, and spirits', began a typical report of 1890, 'in spite of the recent execrable weather...It is quite certain that Her Majesty will, as usual, spend Christmas on the Isle of Wight.' Assiduously cultivating the impression of royal immortality the column later declared: 'The Queen still luxuriates in the arctic weather...Her Majesty drives every day, braving intense cold, snow and often sleet in an open carriage, for the sake of obtaining the fresh air for which she has such affection.'[23] Naturally the affairs of the Queen's numerous progeny — their illnesses and deaths, comings-of-age, marriages, births and jubilees — provided an endless succession of events to be marked by mourning or celebration. Such occasions as the wedding of Princess Beatrice in 1885 and the illness of Prince George in 1891 were the subject of *editorial* comment in the *Primrose League Gazette*. The death of the Duke of Clarence, who was a victim of the influenza epidemic in 1892, produced a homily on the common vulnerability of the highest and the lowest in the land, and led to a week-by-week catalogue of deaths from the same cause. Any death in the royal family involved a set ritual in which Grand Council and Ladies Grand Council composed messages of condolence to the queen and the closest relatives, followed by the publication of the royal letters of thanks in reply.[24] On Queen Victoria's own death Grand Council was specially convened to organize the procedures for mourning; every habitation in the country received instructions to send its resolution of condolence to the league's headquarters and its wreath to the Master of the Household at Windsor. Similarly the jubilees of 1887 and 1897 brought forth an abundance of loyal addresses followed by the queen's fulsome expressions of gratification.

By the end of the century jubilee celebrations had come to reflect a widespread consensus in the community.[25] This, however, was less true in 1887, and Conservatives enjoyed many opportunities to demonstrate their greater enthusiasm by outbidding and embarrassing their opponents. In 1887, when municipal authorities had to decide how to celebrate and how much might be spent, those councillors who inclined to frugality and those magistrates who showed reluctance to extend licensing hours for the day found their loyalty impugned. In the face of a grudging or parsimonious attitude Conservative organizations outdid the official arrangements by distributing beer and food to the inhabitants themselves.[26] By 1897 the novelty had departed from the celebrations: much of significance of the jubilee lies in the sense of continuity with existing activities rather than in the novelty. This is apparent when the celebration is seen in a local context. For example, in the Northumbrian villages of Stannington and Cramlington Sir Matthew and Lady Ridley presided over arrangements for the jubilee, involving a lavish tea for the entire population, with sufficient food to last for two hours, brass bands, dancing and other musical entertainments.[27] Indeed, but for the distribution of 'Empire Mugs' and the fact that the purveyors of Punch and Judy saw fit to charge four guineas instead of the usual 30/–, the occasion could well have been mistaken for a garden party or fete organized under the auspices of one of the local habitations with which the Ridleys were involved. Ridley's words on the day would have come as naturally in the party political context as in a non-partisan setting:

> It is a day of national rejoicing which even the youngest child present is never likely to see even approximately repeated. It is the celebration of a reign, the longest in English History...a reign moreover...quite unapproached in regard to the prosperity and happiness which it has brought to the subjects of Her Majesty. It will not be adequately known, until the full history of the Victorian period is written, how much the marvellous growth of the liberties, power and wealth of this magnificent empire, is due to the personal influence of the most constitutional sovereign that ever occupied our throne.[28]

All this, however, reflects the gentle, celebratory side of monarchism; it had also a sharper, more overtly political aspect. The reason why an organization like the league was well placed to reap the benefit of the burgeoning popularity of the monarchy was that it had consistently played the role of queen's champion since the 1880s. 'Never sit by silent and hear our Gracious Queen disloyally spoken of,' Mrs Rose Hubbard exhorted her habitation at Buckingham in 1886. [29] Of course, by the 1880s the republican movement had shrunk to insignificance, yet the league conjured up threats to the crown by relentlessly associating its political opponents with republicanism. In this it merely repeated the scurrilous tactics of the Fourth Party, which had managed to manoeuvre Gladstone into defending Bradlaugh's right to sit in the House of Commons. Thereafter Conservatives attempted to implicate him with secularism and republicanism by focusing on Bradlaugh's association with such causes. Thus, for example, Lady Maidstone inaugurated a habitation in 1885 by pointing to their enemy, Gladstone, 'the friend of Bradlaugh the atheist.' [30] For sheer chutzpah these tactics were probably unrivalled, yet they were not easy for the Liberals to counter except by some rather involved explanations. In 1885 the league went to some trouble to rebut suggestions that the queen had invested a million pounds in City of London ground rents, producing a letter of denial from her Secretary, Sir Henry Ponsonby, and challenging Liberal Associations to withdraw allegations made by some of their members. [31] The *Primrose League Gazette* repeatedly published figures to show the size of the Civil List when offset by the revenues paid by the Crown Estates to the Exchequer; these were compared with the costs entailed in supporting heads of state abroad, particularly in republican France and the USA, in order to prove that monarchy was really a cheap system. [32] Sensitive to accusations about the royal family living useless lives at taxpayers' expense, the league joined with Conservatives generally in emphasizing the stimulating effect of royal visits on the commercial and industrial prosperity of each community. They seized opportunities to stress both the public work and training undertaken by royal children: thus, for example, at a Conservative function in Newcastle in 1884 following a visit to the city by the Prince of Wales, the audience was reminded that his sons 'were coming up not idle lads, but were going through courses of study, and the second son had earned great honours as a sailor. (Applause)'. [33]

In this context the league's efforts to exploit the common political ground between the queen and the party, in terms of attitudes and organizations, achieved considerable credibility. It relentlessly publicized the most un-ambiguous expression of royal opinion that surfaced over the Sudan question. Indeed, the fall of Khartoum was swiftly appropriated by the league as a staple item in lantern shows, *tableaux vivants* and speeches. Three years after Gordon's death new life was instilled into the subject by the publication of a volume entitled *The Letters of General Gordon to His Sister, M. A. Gordon* which incorporated the queen's letter to Miss Gordon in which she commiserated thus:

To *think* of your dear, noble, heroic Brother, who served his country and his Queen so truly, so heroically, with a self-sacrifice so edifying to the world, not having been rescued. That the promises of support were not fulfilled — which I so frequently and constantly pressed on those who asked him to go — is to me *grief inexpressible!* — indeed it has made me ill! My heart bleeds for you...Would you express to your other Sisters and your eldest Brother my true sympathy, and what I do so keenly feel — the *stain* left upon England for your dear Brother's cruel, though heroic, fate![34]

Against such emotional Victorian overstatement the Liberals had no defence except the plea that Gordon had brought about his own demise by disobeying orders. No issue exposed more sharply the harmony of views between the monarch and the Conservative Party.

However, the queen was also involved in less blatant ways in Conservative causes, sometimes under cover of charities. In 1892, for example, there appeared the Irish Distressed Ladies Fund of which the Queen was Patron, Princess Louise President, and the Duchess of Marlborough Vice-President. Its declared object was simply to appeal for contributions to assist ladies dependent upon an income from property, who 'owing to the rent difficulty and causes beyond their control have been reduced to absolute poverty'.[35] No one needed reminding whose policies had precipitated the fall in Irish land values and the system of land tribunals since 1880. Another royal charity, though less obviously political, was established in 1899 with the characteristically florid title 'The League of Mercy'; it was intended to promote research into medicine and the relief of the suffering poor. Again, the queen assumed a role as 'Sovereign', the Prince of Wales as 'Grand President', while the members strove to win the 'Order of Merit' by their voluntary efforts for the cause.[36] Heavily publicized by the *Primrose League Gazette*, the League of Mercy must have helped to blur the distinction between the Queen and the political organization in the minds of the public. This objective is also suggested by the curious language used by the Primrose League when referring to its honours and badges. 'These decorations are an outward proof and visible sign that we have done what England expects us all to do, and that is our duty.'[37] This was tantamount to saying that the purely internal awards made by the league were of a similar worth and significance to those officially bestowed through the royal Fountain of Honour. Over the years the association of the queen with the league became so much a matter of habit and instinct that the League seemed to cast itself as her agent in the estate of Great Britain. This conviction reached its apogee in 1897 when the league arrogated to itself a singular role in what was supposed to be simply a Loyal Address:

To control the great forces set free by well-calculated legislation, this League was founded for the Maintenance of Religion, the Estates of the Realm and the Ascendancy of the British Empire. In all respects we may claim to have achieved results of vast importance. We have succeeded in binding together all classes in support of our great principles, thus guiding the nation for its own benefit and that of the colonies, towards a splendid Destiny − a direct inheritance of the Victorian Era! [38]

THE ESTATES OF THE REALM

Both republicans and monarchists assumed that a society which abolished its monarchy would inevitably decide to dispense with its aristocracy too. Similarly, the queen interpreted any attack upon the peerage as tantamount to an attack upon the Crown itself. There was thus never any doubt that the two must stand together in the 1880s. In practice this meant that both must be highly visible, surrounded by flamboyance and ceremony, and conspicuously involved in the affairs of the community, local and national; those who hid themselves and their wealth away constituted a danger to the whole order. One contemporary noticed a small but telling sign of this thinking in the practice of opening to the public such places as Hyde Park and Windsor Great Park which had previously been private pleasure grounds; [39] as we have seen, the Primrose League drew extensively on the resources of its landed patrons to emulate this idea. The ideal to be aimed at was a sense of the community as a family under its benign father figure; hence the involvement of entire communities in the celebrations occasioned by marriages and comings-of-age in the families of great magnates [40] − an echo of the royal events at national level. Aristocratic behaviour approximated most closely to the royal ideal in Ireland, where Viceroys engaged in a desperate struggle to shore up the sense of community. Back in 1865 Lady Waldegrave, the wife of Lord Carlingford, had consciously tried to encourage Irish pride in their government by restoring the traditional splendour and lavish hospitality of the Viceregal Court. Conservatives developed her example. Between 1876 and 1880 the Duke and Duchess of Marlborough took pains to cultivate the friendship of Catholics and to stimulate the lace and poplin industries by making them fashionable. The arrival in 1886 of the young Marquis of Londonderry brought the most generous spender. His wife sought to please the business community by her exhaustive programme of grand social functions, while the marquis patronized Irish sports, particularly horse racing, and even reduced his tenants' rents by fifteen per cent. [41]

Yet as the Irish example suggests, political challenges could not be contained indefinitely by invoking Merrie England. However attractive in theory, the idea of a common front of monarchy and aristocracy did not stand the test of experience. For once, radical critics proved to be tactically shrewd in shifting the emphasis of their attack from the crown in the 1860s and 1870s towards the peerage in the 1880s; with its land and constitutional position in the House of Lords it presented a more vulnerable target. Against this Conservatives deployed four defensive arguments. First, the British aristocracy gave its services to the state largely as a matter of duty with no reward beyond the 'Fountain of Honour', where other countries paid lavishly for the work of mere professionals.[42] Second, the House of Lords reflected the views of the people more accurately than the elected 'despotism' based in the Commons. Third, the league characteristically reached back to the feudal origins of land ownership, arguing that it had originated as a matter of royal assignment; in return for a perpetual lease on his land the holder contributed to the external and internal defence and prosperity of the country.[43] Fourth, inequalities of wealth were both justifiable and even necessary because 'the luxuries of the rich maintained the population who supplied them'. This, of course, extended to industrial wealth too; as J. H. Pettifer put it, 'when the capitalist moved off, he took his money with him...labour without capital, as they all knew, was just about as much use as a steam engine without fire or steam.'[44] However, while the crown appeared to gain immunity to radical attacks, it proved ultimately impossible to envelop the aristocracy in the same blanket of affection. Peers, after all, could not be simply figureheads; their active political role in the Lords and through their sons in parliamentary elections inevitably detracted from their symbolic function. Conservative electoral success in the Salisbury era obscured this flaw in the strategy and perhaps lulled the landed class into a false sense of security. After 1906 the peerage fought a losing battle in defence of its position while the crown, cocooned in non-partisan, popular affection, floated clear of the controversy.

RELIGION, CATHOLICISM AND THE ESTABLISHMENT

To Victorian Conservatives, religion, the crown and property represented but different aspects of one indivisible good. As Lady Maidstone put it in 1885: 'Take away Religion and the chief cornerstone is gone...for if the Crown and the rights of property do not derive their authority from God they have no right to exist at all.'[45] However, the Religious Census of 1851 had suggested that the cornerstone was already crumbling; the Church of England had largely failed to hold urban England, while the Nonconformists had been more successful in taking up the slack among the middle-classes than amongst workingmen. Not that active atheism attracted much support; the problem lay in apathy and the apparent gulf between the people and organized religion.

Consequently the churches invested a good deal of time and money in maintaining some form of contact by means of Sunday Schools.

Religion, however, occupied a prominent position in the nation, if only because of its political salience. In the first place, religion became tangled up in the education question. The efforts of the Anglican Church to extend its role in elementary education brought it increasingly into conflict with those reformers who believed that since many children still fell outside the voluntary school system, a compulsory state scheme was necessary. In addition the Church clashed with those who, like the Nonconformists, could not compete in school-building and therefore favoured an undenominational form of state education for their children. Forster's reform of 1870, which introduced the Board School system, left both sides aggrieved.[46] Education consequently became a party political background. Anglicans and Catholics deprecated the need for Board Schools and defended voluntary schools from state competition, while nonetheless seeking subsidies from public funds; and they frequently characterized the Board system as a radical conspiracy to eliminate religion altogether from schools. Hence the triennial board elections often turned into a struggle between Liberals and Nonconformists, standing as 'Unsectarians', and a Conservative alliance of Anglicans and Catholics.

Secondly, the steady advance of Nonconformists within the Liberal Party organization from the 1860s brought Disestablishment to the centre of controversy. Though a Churchman, Gladstone forced through Irish Disestablishment in 1869, and considered Welsh Disestablishment as 'unripe' rather than wrong. In 1885, therefore, Conservatives gleefully seized upon Disestablishment as part of Chamberlain's 'Unauthorized Programme' as a means of squeezing middle-class Anglicans out of the Liberal Party.[47] As Conservatives, the Primrose League activists could not but be influenced by these controversies. Indeed, in counties such as Dorset and Hertfordshire Anglican clergymen were conspicuous as office-holders in the habitations (see chapter 5). However, while the clergy might be an asset to the Conservative cause, it did not always follow that the political connection served to strengthen the Church of England in its struggle to hold its congregations. Where the political inclinations of the clergy conflicted with their spiritual and pastoral functions they sometimes felt obliged to subordinate the former to the latter. One Gloucestershire clergyman backed away from his local habitation in some irritation: 'I think I told you a year ago that you must not expect any more from me; the less I have to do with politics the better I shall get on with my parishioners.'[48]

For this and other reasons the Primrose League tended to avoid the question of the Establishment in its handling of religion, concentrating instead on the general threat of secularism and on the particular cause of religious education. Its canvassers were, for example, deployed in the School Board elections quite freely.[49] This emphasis, incidentally, reflected the interests of the female members such as Lady Jersey and the Duchess of Marlborough, and complemented the role already enjoyed by many middle-class women and men as Sunday School instructors. Moreover, to the men religion appeared an appropriate issue for the ladies; after all, morality fell within their sphere. It might be supposed that the Conservative Party itself was best placed to handle the political dimensions of the religious question, yet this was not by any means the case. Not only was parliamentary Conservatism wedded to the Anglican Establishment, but also grassroots Conservatism often appeared to be synonymous with militant Protestantism.[50] This obviously limited the credibility of the party's claim to defend religion as such. The league, in sharp contrast, went out of its way to encompass the full range of Christian belief: 'it does not concern itself with minor divergencies of opinion or Doctrine,' as the *Gazette* rather cheerfully put it.[51] None but atheists and opponents of the British Empire were excluded from membership; Nonconformists, Catholics and Jews were all welcome. There are some grounds for thinking that by the 1880s the more prosperous Nonconformist groups such as Wesleyans were aligning themselves with the Conservatives, partly out of sheer patriotism and because they had ceased to feel disadvantaged in British society.[52] Though the league would have been a natural target for such people in transition to Conservatism, their presence does not seem to have caused comment, though this may simply be because it was taken for granted.

Catholics, on the other hand, occupied a more conspicuous position in the Primrose League. English Catholics comprised only a minority of the Catholic population by the 1880s, though they were a key element in many constituencies in the six northern counties of England. They had been outnumbered by the immigration of Irish Catholics since the 1840s, though by the early 1880s the influx had begun to peter out. By and large the Catholic community remained peripheral politically and geographically, although the conversion of a number of able men and women who were unwilling to be deflected from public careers by their religion, helped to bring Catholics back into the mainstream of British life; Lord Ripon, for example, served in several Liberal cabinets, and Henry Matthews became Home Secretary under Salisbury. Yet the community on the whole was slow and uncertain in its approach to national politics, as is scarcely surprising in view of the obloquy regularly heaped upon the Catholic Church by both Conservative and Liberal politicians. Neither party altogether wished to surrender the 'No Popery' slogan to its rival.[53] Thus when the Pope announced the restoration of the Roman Catholic hierarchy in Brtain in 1850, Lord John Russell pronounced the new bishops a threat to the queen and introduced a draconian Ecclesiastical Titles Bill replete with penalties for those appointed. Admittedly the legislation was not enforced and was indeed repealed by Gladstone in 1871, but the relations between Liberalism and Catholics grew steadily more complicated during the third quarter of the nineteenth century. Liberal support for nationalism in Italy, for example, was interpreted as an expression of anti-papal prejudice. The growing prominence of Nonconformists in the Liberal organization during the 1860s and 1870s tended to strengthen anti-Catholicism; and the shift towards domestic radicalism under Gladstone inevitably offended many of the landed Catholic magnates and squires just as it did the Anglicans. In many ways the indigenous Catholic population of England was naturally conservative, and, but for the shrill hostility of Tory backbenchers, might have drifted to the Conservative Party much earlier. In 1858–9 Disraeli had tried to harness the support of the Catholic Members sitting for Irish seats, though without notable success.[54] Though Sir James Pope-Hennessey became the first Tory Catholic MP in 1859, the party generally had no place for Catholics as yet.

However, the emergence of Home Rule forced the pace by squeezing the already precarious position of English Catholics. The election of nationalists after 1874, and then of Ulster Unionists from the mid–1880s left very little room for English Catholics in Irish constituencies. Meanwhile in England the Liberals concentrated on mobilizing the votes of *Irish* Catholics on the nationalist ticket. Since the late 1850s constituency Conservatism had begun to benefit from the anti-Irish backlash and had acquired a militantly Protestant character; by the 1880s Conservative Associations enjoyed close relations with Orange Lodges in some areas. Consequently English Catholics were both attracted and repelled by the Conservative Party. In these circumstances their latent Conservatism could best be harnessed by an alternative organization to that provided by the official party. Both Churchill and Wolff seem to have appreciated that the Primrose League might fulfill such a role. It was fortunate that its establishment coincided with a change of allegiance by the leaders of the Catholic community.

Since the 1820s the Dukes of Norfolk had gradually shaken off the stigma of being 'aristocratic outlaws'. They had regained their right to exercise their functions as Earls Marshal at the coronations of William IV and Victoria. Emancipation in 1829 enabled the 12th Duke to sit in the Lords, and the family to take up the representation of Horsham in the Commons, as Liberals. Significantly, the new Catholic hierarchy of 1851 was opposed by the Duke of Norfolk, on the grounds that the Pope ought not to interfere in the affairs of English Catholics. Yet the family remained Liberal despite the involvement of Lord Howard of Glossop and others in the cause of Catholic education. The political initiative was taken by Henry, the 15th Duke, who came of age in 1868 and felt that since the 1820s Catholics had largely failed to exploit their opportunities. Thus in 1870 an English Catholic Union was established as a means by which laymen might co-ordinate their influence and restore Catholics to the mainstream of English politics and society. During the 1870s, however, it became apparent that this objective might be better accomplished through an attachment to Conservatism in spite of its Protestant character; indeed, perhaps because of it. Disraeli's offer of the Garter to Norfolk in 1878, though refused, was a pointer in this direction. It required the radicalism of the 1880–85 administration to tip the Duke, with others of his class, into the Conservative camp; Home Rule only made the decision easier.[55]

The League provided a convenient and congenial point of entry. From 1885 Norfolk and his wife presided over habitations in Sussex and Sheffield, while he eventually became Chancellor in 1905 and 1906. Other activists included Lord Howard of Glossop, Lord Clifford, Lord North and Lord Edmund Talbot, a future Chief Whip. Among the Dames were the Countess of Shrewsbury, her daughter Theresa, Lady Portarlington, and Lady Maidstone. Several converts to Catholicism also played a major role in the League. George Lane-Fox of Bramham, North Yorkshire, whose father disinherited him, served as paid Vice-Chancellor from 1889 to 1912. In Warwickshire the Earl of Denbigh's conversion provides an interesting example of the importance of social leadership in Conservative politics. Local landed Tories felt obliged to abandon their usual 'No Popery' propaganda at elections during the 1880s in deference to Denbigh's position at the top of county society, and the danger of dividing the Conservative forces.[56]

From the party's point of view the association with Catholics through the league and its campaigns on behalf of denominational schools helped to build bridges with what, in the north, was often a pivotal section of the electorate. Norfolk's endorsement was much in demand by Conservative candidates fighting seats which were thought to turn on the Catholic vote.[57] Moreover, the prominence of loyalist Catholics on Tory platforms constituted a valuable rebuttal of the charge that the Conservatives' Irish policy was simply coercion of Catholics by a Protestant majority. They argued, on the contrary, that English Catholics had a duty to resist Home Rule because the agitation for it was tantamount to a revolutionary movement which had been regularly condemned by Rome. This is why Radicals often alleged that the Primrose League itself had been disapproved of by the Pope. Dr Bagshawe, the Roman Catholic Bishop of Nottingham, for example, tried to get it placed under a ban by the Church on the grounds that it was a secret society, many of whose leading members were freemasons. However, he did not succeed, and a number of Catholic bishops instructed their co-religionists that they might join the league without any qualms.[58]

Yet accusations about the incompatibility of the league and Catholicism could not altogether be dismissed in view of the involvement of certain of its leaders with the Orange Order in their constituencies – the Earl of Crawford's family at Wigan and Chorley for example.[59] Nonetheless it is a measure of the seriousness with which the league regarded its non-denominationalism that Grand Council withdrew warrants when it found a habitation stubbornly using Anglican prayers with which to open its meetings.[60] Naturally, political opponents taxed Catholic members with the charge that the league's much-trumpeted commitment to Religion was merely a euphemism for defence of the Establishment. Had not Lord Curzon said that 'the Church was in danger, and would want again the Primrose League to come forward and defend that great Institution to which they were all so fondly attached'? In reply the Duke of Norfolk could only protest that 'it is altogether a mistake to suppose... that the maintenance of the Establishment is one of its objects.'[61] Though embarrassed by the question of the Established Church, the more worldly Catholic leaders had long since reconciled themselves to its existence. They seem to have entertained no expectations of dislodging the Conservative Party from its traditional attitude on the subject; had this been of vital importance to them they would have stuck to the Liberal Party in the first place. For leading Catholics the real objective was the incorporation of their community in the centre of British national life after the years spent languishing on the periphery.

Indeed, the Catholic rapprochement with Conservatism is comparable, if of lesser extent, to the Nonconformists' relationship with Liberalism in the late Victorian period. The chief difference is that the alliance with the Conservatives proved more effective in delivering honours to individual Catholics than in producing tangible gains for the community as a whole. Norfolk, however, made clear his reluctance to allow his new commitment to Conservatism to override his loyalty to Catholics. Thus in 1887 he refused to be tempted by the offer of a mere undersecretaryship which would have obliged him to support the government without giving him much influence. Salisbury found it useful to employ the duke as unofficial ambassador to the Vatican, gave him the Garter, and found him cabinet rank as Postmaster General from 1895 to 1900. In his ministerial capacity Norfolk naturally attracted the attention of Catholics seeking, for example, the appointment of their co-religionists as magistrates.[62] Yet as early as 1889 he had begun to warn the Prime Minister about the 'general feeling of disappointment and annoyance with the Government' over education. In the same year he complained bitterly at the rejection by the House of Commons of a Religious Disabilities Removal Bill for the 'slur thereby cast upon the loyalty and patriotism of the Catholics of this country'.[63] On this occasion the Conservatives threw away the opportunity of consolidating their advantage with Catholics by opening up the viceroyalty of Ireland to them, a position which Norfolk himself might have filled. Instead Gladstone was allowed to seize the chance of proposing legislation in 1890–91 designed to permit Catholics to serve as Lord Chancellor and as Irish Viceroy, thereby forcing the government to take the responsibility for thwarting Catholic expectations. The impact of this was, however, mitigated by the tendency in the late nineteenth century for Liberals, notably Sir William Harcourt, to make the running on anti-ritualist legislation.[64] Yet Gladstone's initiative successfully exposed the Conservatives' dilemma in seeking to conciliate Catholics supporters without antagonising their diehard Protestant following in the constituencies. As a result, though Catholics felt that religion was 'more likely to be safeguarded by the

Conservatives', according to Norfolk, 'they say they really do not see there is much to choose between the two parties.'[65] Consequently Catholic allegiance was apt to waver according to the issues uppermost in the community's mind. The Conservative defeats of 1892 and 1906 were both preceded by a waning of Catholic loyalties. Norfolk owed his Chancellorship of the Primrose League in 1905 to the fears of Balfour about the crumbling of Conservative support among Catholics as a result of the backbenchers' efforts to pass the Church Discipline Bill in the early 1900s.

THE EMPIRE AND THE UNION WITH IRELAND

In 1900 Lord Salisbury expressed a typical late Victorian view when he claimed that the previous twenty years had witnessed a rejuvenation of popular interest in Empire, of which the Primrose League was only one of the more important manifestations.[66] Such generalizatons provide a legitimate target for scholarly criticism. Contemporary politicians are scarcely a reliable guide for those who wish to ascertain whether the 'New Imperialism' was in fact novel or really popular. Historians have long since ceased to identify a sharp turning-point around 1880 in terms of imperial *policy*, seeing the rapid territorial expansion more as a result of stiffer international competition than of a qualitative change in British thinking.[67] Similarly, one sees continuity in popular attitudes. Jingoism did not originate in the 1880s or even 1870s. Events such as the Indian Mutiny, the Opium Wars and the Crimean War all tended to show that a highly emotional patriotism lay just beneath the surface, even in the supposedly non-imperial mid-victorian era. However, this is not to exclude the idea of a change in the extent or the character of popular imperial sentiment. For example, imperial emotions were surely aroused more *frequently* than before 1880, both because of the increase in the number of imperial powers and because of the explosion of internal agencies for the propagation of imperial information and ideas. Imperialism may well have become a more *excitable* and militaristic phenomenon owing to a perceived decline in Britain's military and strategic position and her vulnerability to invasion.[68] And the Empire may simply have grown to be more interesting and *relevant* because of shrinking economic opportunities on the one hand and the relentless commercialization of empire on the other. Indeed, it is striking to consider how all-pervasive patriotic-imperial themes became during the last twenty years of the century.[69] The ordinary Victorian grew up surrounded by reminders of his daily dependence on exotic colonial produce from the advertising campaigns of suppliers of his tea, tobacco, soap and chocolate; he could not ignore the blatant patriotism of his biscuit tins and cigarette packets, and coveted the mass-produced cigarette cards and picture postcards which portrayed the imperial cause; he applauded the songs of music hall — and sang them himself; along with literally millions of others he attended the vast Imperial Exhibitions whose character became markedly imperial during the 1880s; he imbibed imperial pride through his knowledge of history and geography, and took a vicarious thrill in empire from juvenile magazines such as the *Boys' Own Paper* and its many imitators.

Despite the impressive empirical evidence, however, it has been argued that imperialism really reflected the attitudes of an upper class or the susceptibilities of a lower middle-class, and did not affect the mass of ordinary people very deeply. This is difficult to reconcile with the fact that anti-imperial organizations such as the ILP maintained a very tiny membership and tended to suffer during periods of imperial fervour, while a body like the Primrose League, whose imperialism was quite blatant, could win mass support. During the twelve months from July 1899 to June 1900, for example, some 43,209 *new* recruits joined the league − a time when no one could have been in doubt about its imperialism. Such organizations were tapping a source of support which was on an entirely different scale to that enjoyed by their opponents. In the case of the Boer War one historian has made a distinction between the jingo mobs of lower middle-class youths on the one hand, and the huge crowds of ordinary people who turned out to celebrate on Mafeking Night without violence on the other. [70] The former is taken to indicate serious political opinion and the latter merely non-political behaviour! Yet to dismiss the spontaneous and typical patriotism of the mass of the people seems a little perverse; their behaviour was surely a sign that the working-class families were well integrated into the ideas and values of British society at that time.

There is more validity in the argument that the majority of people never subscribed to a precise policy or philosophy of imperialism. [71] Ideas such as imperial federation remained the preserve of intellectuals and academics. A vast array of pressure groups of a patriotic-imperialist character sprang up − the Imperial Federation League, the Royal Colonial Society, the League of the Empire, the Imperial South Africa Association, the Victoria League, the National Service League, the British Empire Union, the Navy League, the Women's Guild of Empire − but they were mostly small organizations; [72] and those that had specific political aims largely failed. Conservative leaders, reacting like their Liberal counterparts towards 'faddism', kept them at arms length. The Primrose League represents the other side of the coin. While obviously a very large imperial organization it remained vague, amorphous and sentimental in its imperialism, hardly ever venturing an opinion on a specific colonial question. [73] Essentially educative and propagandist, the league produced maps of the north-west frontier of India and explained the whereabouts and significance of Lake Chad; but above all it dramatized the cause of empire, using it as a focus for national pride and political advantage. Indeed, imperialism, for the Primrose League represented simply one facet of a single phenomenon which embraced nationalism and monarchism, and merged imperceptibly into a range of attitudes from Christian idealism to militarism, chauvinism and racism. Naturally this fluid quality made its imperialism all the more widely acceptable.

From the outset the Union with Ireland assumed a central place in the league's imperial strategy. It shared the basic Conservative view of Ireland as an integral part of the Empire whose loss would open up a dangerous flaw in British security. Moreover, the work of the nationalist movement in teaching the Irish people to despise their social superiors, to undermine the moral authority of their priests and to attack private property, made Ireland a crucial battle-ground for the defence of *British* society and its traditions. Consequently the league saw the question both in terms of rallying English opinion and in holding the line against nationalism in Ireland itself. To this end some thirty-five habitations were established, largely in the southern and western counties (appendix IV), which complemented the work of the Irish Unionist Alliance in the north-east of the country. While the IUA set out to demonstrate to the English the existence of a second community in Ireland, the habitations were intended to shore up the remnants of unionist sentiment in the nationalist heartlands before they disappeared altogether. In order to check English apathy towards Ireland eyewitnesses were brought across to address habitation meetings, and intrepid Dames supplied intelligence on conditions in the most disturbed districts, especially on the diminution of famine and evictions under Balfour's administration. A typical report of 1890, which emanated from Lord Clanricarde's agent, claimed that 'loyal and solvent tenants' were now taking up vacant farms on his estates, that boycotting had almost ceased, and that the Plan of Campaign had collapsed: 'in short Lord Clanricarde has beaten the Land League.'[74] In fact, by 1890 settlements had been reached in sixty of the 116 estates affected by the Plan of Campaign as a result of co-ordination among the landlords; the tenants had won in twenty-four cases, given up in fifteen, and were continuing the struggle in only eighteen.[75] Up to a point, then, the optimistic claims made for the government's policy of firmness mixed with conciliation were justified. The split in the Irish Party over Parnell and the more constructive policies for land purchase and the congested districts during the 1890s compounded the Unionists' feeling that they had regained the initiative in Ireland, as well as winning the argument in England.

However, the optimism was a little contrived. In the long run the loyalists in the south came to regard a Dublin parliament as inevitable. The habitations, though evidently attractive to the professionals and shopkeepers in the towns, withered for lack of support from the landed class: 'the natural leaders of the people have not exerted themselves as they should do,' complained the *Gazette*, overlooking the fact that the 'natural leaders' had long since ceased to be leaders in Ireland.[76] As a result, although Ireland appeared quiet by the late 1890s, this was partly because the cause of Unionism had quietly folded up outside Ulster. Policies for peasant proprietorship did little to dislodge the hold of nationalist politicians; and by 1905 the Unionists held only one more Irish constituency than they had in 1886.

Much of the significance of propagandist work in Ireland lay in the context of English opinion. Home Rule continued to be an excellent recruiting sergeant for Conservatives, especially when a return of the Liberals was expected. Indeed, the appearance of the first Home Rule Bill and the Plan of Campaign played a major part in the explosion of Primrose League membership; from 200,000 in March 1886 the figure leapt to 550,000 by March 1887. Regular contact with Ireland served to prevent the issue from becoming remote and stale to the public; it generated an endless supply of atrocity stories and outrages which the league's propagandists put to good use in lantern slides and *tableaux vivants*, designed to remind the English audiences of a beleagured loyalist people whom it would be dishonourable to desert. A lantern programme of 1889 comprised the following:

1 John Bull offering his hand to downcast Erin
2 Erin looking up and taking his hand
3 John Bull and Erin at peace watched over by Britain
4 An Irish farm in prosperous times
5 The same under the Land League
6 Inside a farm house under prosperity
7 The same under the Land League
8 Moonlighting
9 The maiming of cattle
10 A meeting of loyalists in Belfast
11 Tenants paying rent
12 The Royal Standard and the same flag without a harp
13 Justice, Law and Order.
14 Lord Salisbury with Balfour on his right and Hartington on his left
15 Disraeli encircled by a huge wreath of primroses[77]

At local level habitations involved themselves in a small way in the great question by contributing to the fund for Irish Distressed Ladies; in Dorset the Wimborne Habitation sent seed potatoes 'to help Mr Balfour's noble work'; and an advertisement in the *Gazette* in 1899 offered a 'loyal Irish lady recommended for the position of companion or Lady Housekeeper.'[78]

In a way Ireland served as a model for wider imperial propaganda by the league. Each new aspect of the struggle for Empire was made tangible and vivid; the colonies were made to assume a role in the regular life of the organization. The league, for example, spawned habitations in India, Australia, Mauritius, Cyprus, Malta, Canada and British Honduras, thereby echoing the family connections with the colonies which so many of its members experienced as a result of the massive emigration of the 1880s and 1890s. At meetings members invariably joined in the singing of such songs as 'Soldiers of the Queen' or 'Tommy Atkins', and enjoyed recitations of poems such as Kipling's 'The Absent Minded Beggar'. The league's approach to imperialism involved an attempt to tap the interest of its rank and file in broadly four ways: sheer curiosity, the cult of the hero, patriotism, and militarism.

Popular curiosity about remote territories and the exotic artefacts of empire invariably guaranteed an audience for imperial propagandists. Professor Seeley's famous lectures on 'The Expansion of England' were actually read aloud to members of the Eastville (Bristol) Habitation, but a less cerebral approach was usually employed. [79] At Forest Gate in 1890 members heard a discussion on Salisbury's treaty with the Portuguese and the need for a protectorate over Swaziland, but combined it with a vote of congratulations to H. M. Stanley for his 'splendid achievements in the dark Continent' and an exhibition of his medicine case, his photograph and autograph. Three hundred members of Ribblesdale (Settle) Habitation fortified themselves with tea before settling down to a two-hour lecture on the colonies which comprised one hundred limelight views designed to portray the vastness of empire and its commercial potential. The range of lantern lectures offered by the league in 1900 shows the reliance on imperial-military themes: 'Our Glorious Empire', 'The British Empire: its Trade and Commerce', 'The Army', 'The Army and the War', 'The Transvaal War', 'The Victorian Era', 'Landmarks of English History', 'The Navy', 'The Stately Homes of England'; each contained 45 to 90 slides and lasted 45 to 90 minutes. Later generations satisfied a similar curiosity through the cinema and the newsreels in the inter-war period, but for audiences of the 1890s the lurid images thrown up by these slides provided their only window on a mysterious and exciting world in which their countrymen were playing an heroic role.

Secondly, the league shared with other imperial bodies a tendency to hero worship. General Gordon was, of course, the favourite hero. Resurrected in wax by Madame Tussaud's in 1898, he had been kept alive as a political point since 1885 by tableaux, lantern shows and charities. Not until the end of the century was it felt that he had been sufficiently avenged by the British triumphs at Fashoda and Omdurman. In addition the league enjoyed its own hero in the shape of Colonel Fred Burnaby, a political associate of Churchill who was decorated by the Khedive Ismail in 1884, came home and joined the league, and then returned with Wolseley's rescue force to the Sudan, only to lose his life at Abu Klea. [80] Already famous for his exploits, which included crossing the Channel by balloon, fighting with the Carlists in Spain, and the 'Ride to Khiva', Burnaby seemed the very model of a Primrose Knight keeping chivalry alive in the modern world.

Thirdly, the league made a practice of equating imperialism with patriotism. The familiar Irish politicians were alleged to be conspiring with Indian nationalists, their agents to have aided Arabi Pasha and the Boers, and to have contrived the deaths of Gordon and Burnaby. As the Irish were the allies of

Britain's enemies, so the Gladstonian allies of the Irish were tantamount to being traitors. In this way the league sought to annexe patriotism for the Conservative cause, a tactic relentlessly employed by the Party itself from the 1880s onwards, as a study of its propaganda shows.[81] It was a sign of the primacy given to party over principle that when Salisbury's government faced patriotic criticism from the *Morning Post* over the early disasters of the Boer War, the league abstained, despite its dissatisfaction with the state of national defence.

Finally, it is noticeable that towards the end of the century the league's imperialism assumed a more militarist tone — a characteristic reflection of British insecurity which reached a climax with the Boer War. Prominent Leaguers, including the Dukes of Norfolk, Marlborough and Roxburghe, set an example by joining the British forces in South Africa. At home the league proclaimed its tasks in terms of 'fanning the flames of patriotism', promoting war charities and urging the case for Home Defence.[82] Indeed, the latter became something of an obsession, stimulated by leading statesmen. Lord Salisbury himself delivered extraordinarily pessimistic historical sketches on the decline and fall of earlier maritime empires — Spain, Holland, Venice and Carthage — all of which had been paralysed by an attack aimed at the heart of their domains. According to Viscount Curzon, the Chancellor, the French were in a position in 1900 to land from 50,000 to 75,000 troops on the British mainland, and, he warned, 'we have very few trained soldiers left in England.'[83] Significantly, however, military conscription found little favour even in these circumstances. Instead habitations were exhorted to draw voluntarily upon their own resources, notably their land for use as rifle ranges, and their retired army officers who were to train the rank and file to be expert marksmen. Above all the League enthused over the idea of training the cycling corps members so as to produce a force of skilled riflemen capable of rapid mobilization in an emergency. Plans were hatched to mobilize a force of 50,000 such men at Aldershot in order to repel an enemy landing at Dover; alternatively, if the enemy advanced through mid-Wales(!) the army of cyclist-riflemen would concentrate at Wolverhampton, proceeding thence to Shrewsbury and Ludlow so as to be on their line of communications. With such a force 'an invasion of this country becomes an impossibility'.[84] Such naive enthusiasm reflected the characteristic militarism of the late Victorian and Edwardian period; it was a patently dilettante, British form of militarism, perceptibly distinct from the 'Prussianism' associated with European countries.[85] This approach to national defence seems to have been acceptable throughout British society regardless of party affiliation as both the Boer War and the First World War were to show.

Ultimately the political significance of the league's brand of patriotism-imperialism-monarchism lay in its sheer woolly imprecision. By avoiding well-defined political options such as imperial federation or compulsory military training it maximized the popular appeal. Opponents found it difficult to identify a target which might safely be attacked. This was simply because the sentiments to which the league gave voice met a response that extended far beyond official Conservatism, and found an echo in the conservatism which pervaded both the Liberal Party and the emerging labour movement. The advantage this situation gave to the Conservative Party should not be exaggerated. It could scarcely guarantee the votes of a majority of the people with any regularity; but it meant that when questions of national interest assumed prime significance in the public mind, Conservatives could draw deeply upon a fund of bipartisan sentiment across the lines of class and party.

5

The Geography of Popular Conservatism

'It has been the frank and universal admission of successful Conservative candidates that they have been lifted into Parliament by the Primrose League,' declared Millicent Fawcett, the women's suffrage leader, in 1887.[1] Such claims must be treated with scepticism even when made by someone not involved with the league or the Conservative Party. Superior organization is frequently a reflection of one party's natural advantages in a constituency rather than a cause of its success; it tends to deteriorate as the party grows unpopular and to flourish as expectations of victory raise morale and draw money and volunteers back into the machine. On the other hand, where one party appears to enjoy a superiority in organizational terms that is both general and qualitatively different its approach merits consideration as a causal factor. Thus in attempting to assess the significance of a body like the league it is valuable to know how it coped where conditions favoured the opponents of Conservatism. Ideally one requires a vast amount of information not only about the number and distribution of local branches, but about their live, paid membership, whether it was actively involved in meetings or merely 'on the books', whether it was representative or concentrated in certain occupations, how it varied over time, and how far it overlapped with the membership of other political and social organizations.

After many years of study we know surprisingly little in this sense about either the Liberal, Labour or Conservative forces across the country as a whole. The evidence presented here, despite its shortcomings, will take us a little way towards a comprehensive picture of organized support for Conservatism in the late nineteenth century.[2] Some 2,300 habitations have been identified and plotted for each parliamentary constituency on thirteen regional maps. This information has been drawn from the Roll of Habitations compiled from time to time by the Primrose League, from extensive reports in the *Primrose League Gazette*, from local newspapers and the papers of habitations themselves. Some habitations have no doubt escaped attention, particularly in Scotland which enjoyed a separate and less efficient organization. Obviously

Table 5   Constituency membership of habitations on a
regional basis c. 1885–1893

Region	Constituency average	County average		Constituencies[a]	
				Sample	Total
Wessex	2,604	Dorset	3,847	4	4
		Hampshire &			
		Isle of Wight	2,936	10	10
		Wiltshire	2,930	5	6
		Berkshire	1,809	5	5
		Gloucestershire	1,614	6	7
East Midlands	2,467	Derbyshire	2,803	7	8
		Leicestershire	2,599	5	5
		Lincolnshire	2,548	11	11
		Nottinghamshire	2,019	7	7
		Rutland	1,692	1	1
South East	2,368	Sussex	3,104	6	7
England		Surrey[b]	3,028	3	4
		Kent	1,876	13	15
Central England	2,167	Hertfordshire	3,738	4	4
		Buckinghamshire	3,196	3	3
		Oxfordshire	1,772	4	4
		Northamptonshire	1,361	6	6
		Bedfordshire	1,180	3	3
South West	2,012	Devon	2,590	10	11
England		Somerset	2,279	8	9
		Cornwall	1,236	6	7
		Bristol	1,194	4	4
Wales	1,771			17	33
East Anglia	1,757	Norfolk	2,141	8	8
		Huntingdon	1,882	2	2
		Essex[c]	1,799	8	8
		Suffolk	1,645	8	8
		Cambridgeshire	1,062	4	4
West Midlands	1,699	Warwickshire	2,337	6	14
		Shropshire	2,101	5	5
		Herefordshire	1,923	3	3
		Worcestershire	1,617	4	8
		Staffordshire	1,223	13	17
North West	1,666	Cheshire	2,164	10	11
England		Lancashire[d]	1,506	31	51

Table 5 continued

Region	Constituency average	County average		Constituencies[a] Sample	Total
Northern England	1,601	Westmorland	2,643	2	2
		Northumberland	2,395	5	7
		Cumberland	1,300	6	6
		Durham	1,230	7	15
		Furness	770	2	2
Yorkshire	1,395	North Riding	2,314	6	6
		East Riding	1,303	6	6
		West Riding	1,188	23	37
London	886			46	70
Scotland	826			69	69

[a] Double-member constituencies have been counted as one.
[b] Kingston, Wimbledon and Croydon have been included in London.
[c] S.W. or Walthamstow has been included in London.
[d] North Lonsdale and Barrow-in-Furness have been included in Northern England.

the habitations recorded here were not simultaneously active. The main period in which they were established was 1885–8, when there were almost 1,900 but in the early 1890s a second wave appeared in several urban areas including Tyneside and South Wales. By the second half of the decade some inertia had set in, and the pattern of relapse and revival common to all parties prevailed. In several substantial towns like Exeter and Bradford the single original habitation was subdivided on a constituency or ward basis as soon as a large membership had been obtained; while in places such as Durham and Barnsley the original Dames habitation absorbed the Knights after a few years. Thus the picture constantly changed in detail, though this scarcely detracts from the overall impression of an extraordinarily comprehensive network.

Habitation membership figures have been recorded (see appendices V–XVIII) and should be consulted in conjunction with the regional maps in this chapter. These figures have been used to estimate the average constituency membership during 1885–93 for each English region, Wales and Scotland, and county averages where appropriate (table 5). Constituencies whose membership figures are very incomplete have been omitted from the calculations. Even for constituencies included, details are not always available for every habitation and the averages must therefore be regarded as *underestimates* on the whole; to compensate for this the higher figure has been used where several are available. Thus the interest in the averages lies less in the absolute level of membership, though this gives food for thought, than in the way they highlight relative strengths and weaknesses in regional Conservatism.

It is immediately apparent that the rank order of Primrose League regions deviates somewhat from the pattern of Conservative strength in terms of constituencies held by the party; indeed, up to a point it is a reflection of Conservative weakness. For the league prided itself on its capacity to mobilize Conservatism virtually anywhere, regardless of the political and social complexion of a constituency; this is why Wales appears comparatively high up the list despite returning few MPs. The league's only real failure was in Scotland, as we shall see. Elsewhere one is frequently surprised to discover urban, industrial districts with a contemporary reputation for radicalism supporting very large Primrose League habitations. It is not the predictably high membership of Hertfordshire, Surrey or Buckinghamshire but that of Derby, Newcastle and Rochdale which underlines the Conservatives' claim to be the national party, and reveals the extent to which they had extended their range beyond the confines of the narrow local cliques typical of a less democratic era.

SOUTH WEST ENGLAND

Despite their largely rural character the three south-western counties presented Conservatives with severe difficulties arising from the strength of Nonconformity, the prevalence of scattered, pastoral farms rather than nuclear villages, and the tendency towards small farms and comparatively few big landowners. In Cornwall, where such characteristics were most marked, the league's membership lagged well behind that of Devon and Somerset; far more habitations would have been necessary to cover the scattered population. Three points of strength, however, stand out against the general weakness. The first is the Bodmin Division which owed much to the interest taken by Earl Mount Edgcumbe and the Ladies Ernestine (RC Cotehele), Albertha and Edith Edgcumbe. The second is the town of Truro with over 900 members, significantly a centre of Anglican strength after the revival of its see in 1876. The third was Falmouth, where the 1,000 members of 'Pendennis' Habitation were a dominating element in the tiny borough seat of only 2,500 electors. 'Pendennis' like eighteen of twenty-one Cornish habitations in 1887 was under a woman RC; and one may surmise that male Conservatives, regarding the county as hopelessly radical, gladly gave the ladies full scope.

Devon provides a good example of a county where, because the odds were not too heavily stacked against them, Conservatives found it worthwhile to put their efforts behind the league. Lord Poltimore of Poltimore Park outside Exeter gave the lead.[3] As landowner and huntsman, Treasurer of HM Household 1892–4, Whip in the Lords 1892–4 and Chancellor of the league 1895–6, Poltimore was an archetypal Primrose figurehead. In Exeter itself the 'Poltimore' Habitation quickly won 4,600 members, thus providing Conservatives with a huge organizational base among the working population and the key to victory from 1885 onwards, excepting only 1906. Torquay was another rather urban constituency where, because the Liberals were strong, Conservatives had to generate an effective modern organization. Miss Harriet Mallock sister of the MP, R. Mallock (1892–1900), acted as RC of the Torquay Dames. In 1892 the habitation claimed that no fewer than 1,800 of their 2,700 members were actively electioneering on Mallock's behalf.[4] Elsewhere the pattern was more traditional. In Honiton, for example, the league enjoyed the support of the major landowners, notably Sir John Kennaway, the local MP, whose wife was RC for Ottery St Mary; Viscount Sidmouth at Honiton; Mary, Viscountess Chetwynd at Lympstone, and Lady Gertrude Rolle at Budleigh Salterton. In the Barnstaple Division there was only one moving force, Lady Chichester of Arlington Court, who was RC for Ilfracombe, Barnstaple and Arlington; when she dropped out the organization promptly diminished.[5] Seats in which leading landowners inclined to Liberalism, such as Tavistock (the Duke of Bedford) and Ashburton (the Rt. Hon. C. Seal-Hayne MP), rendered the league's efforts much less effective. However, even in a very Liberal seat such as South Molton the League was capable of building up a large membership with the backing of Lord Clinton (Beaford), Sir John Shelley (Crediton), Lady Gordon-Lennox (Torrington) and Lady Poltimore

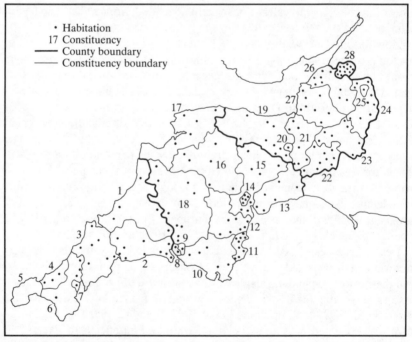

Map 1   Primrose League Habitations c. 1883–1914: South West England
Cornwall, Devon, Somerset and Bristol (see appendix V)

(South Molton) — though this was not translated into sufficient votes to win the seat. Plymouth with its dock workers and maritime traditions generated a large membership, and here the League continued to flourish as an integral part of the Conservative machine much longer than elsewhere. This was largely a result of the election of William Waldorf Astor in December 1910. His wife Nancy invigorated the habitations and kept them going in the inter-war period, when she herself was struggling to hold an essentially working-class seat.[6] The League suited Nancy Astor because it was outside the official party and could become part of her personal machine.

Somerset presented Conservatives with a similar pattern of pastoral farming, declining small-town industry and some rural Nonconformity. In the general absence of aristocratic patrons the smaller squires and their ladies took the lead and produced a dense infrastructure of habitations in every division. In the west of the county several influential landowners participated, notably E. J. Stanley, Member for Bridgwater and RC for Enmore and Spaxton, and Captain A. F. Acland-Hood, Member for Wellington and RC for Quantock Vale. The Borough of Bath, a mixture of artisans and 'villadom' was well worth working for since it returned two members; in an electorate of only 6–7,000 the habitation, with two and a half thousand members, helped to give Conservatives the edge from 1885 to 1906. The regional average is somewhat depressed by Bristol, though the city's average of 1,200 for the four divisions is impressive for a fairly radical place. Bristol held no fewer than twenty-four habitations, many clearly quite small, but covering most parts of the town. They provided opportunities for the middle-class and military residents to assume the role of Ruling Councillor or other titles. Particularly worthy of note is Bristol South, which included the business centre, some residential parts and a great deal of poor working-class territory,[7] and leant to Liberalism. The Bedminster part of the constituency, populated by miners and dockers, provides a classic example of the use of female leadership in supposedly hostile territory. Under Miss Mabel Hill the Bedminster Habitation grew to 940 in 1891 and 1,600 in 1892, almost wholly drawn from local working-class families.[8] It received the Champion Banner awarded annually to the most efficient and deserving habitation. By tackling the most intractable element in South Bristol the league tipped it into Conservative hands in 1886, 1892, 1895 and 1900.

WESSEX

With its constituency average of 2,600 Wessex plainly represented a pillar of Primrose League and Conservative strength. The elements in local society which contributed to this are quite evident: extensive aristocratic landowner-ship in each county, country seats thickly distributed, rapidly expanding residential areas especially in East Berkshire and along the south coast at Christchurch and Bournemouth. As a result servants were numerous and the labour force in general somewhat dependent on the patronage of society. Gentlemen farmers, keen on horses and hunting, found Hampshire, Gloucestershire and Berkshire attractive; nuclear villages were much more common than in the south-west, and the Established Church predominated. Finally, pride in the army and navy loomed large in the barrack towns and dockyards of the region.

In Berkshire the two best organized constituencies, Newbury and the Eastern division, were characterized by the country-house network. Newbury, dominated by big Conservative landowners like W. G. Mount, the local MP, and Lord Wantage, boasted eighteen habitations. In East Berkshire the wealthy enjoyed Thames-side establishments within ten miles of Ascot, Henley, Windsor, Eton and Sandhurst and, thanks to the branch lines of the Great Western Railway, within easy reach of London. In such country it was difficult for Conservatives to lose – and they never did. At fashionable Wargrave over 700 local gentry and their servants enlisted in a habitation led by the siter-in-law of Cecil Rhodes, while 1,400 were enrolled in the small residential town of Maidenhead by 1887. Willie Grenfell of nearby Taplow Court joined the league after quitting the Liberal Party, and became RC for Maidenhead. A famous athlete, boxer and oarsman, Lord Desborough, as he later became, was welcomed by the League and served as Chancellor in 1909–11.

The Hampshire constituencies generated one of the largest concentrations of membership in the country including 3,200 in Andover, over 4,000 in Basingstoke and 5,100 in the New Forest. One distinctive feature was the role of army and navy personnel, eighteen of whom held office in the Andover, Basingstoke, Portsmouth, Fareham and New Forest divisions. In addition, the leaders of landed society rallied strongly to the cause: in Petersfield the Earl of Northesk; in Basingstoke Lord Basing and the Hon. Diana Sclator Booth, the Duchess of Wellington and Lord Frederick Kerr; in Andover the Countess of Caernarvon and Lady Heathcote; and in the New Forest Lady Montagu of Beaulieu and Lady Hulse of Breamore. By 1890 the 'New Forest' Habitation alone boasted 2,600 members in the most radical parts of the constituency where they were regularly tended by an effective machine in the shape of the thirty-seven wardens and seventy sub-wardens.

Even Hampshire's average membership of 2,900 was comfortably exceeded by that of Dorset – at 3,800 the highest in the country. This was essentially the result of dire necessity; for Dorset, like Wiltshire and Gloucestershire, contained a good deal of rural radicalism and Nonconformity among the labourers, and the East and North divisions leant to Liberalism. The impact of the League is particularly striking when contrasted with the situation at the time of the 1880 election, when Edward Stanhope reported to Lord Salisbury that Dorset was 'without any attempt at organisation whatever';[9]

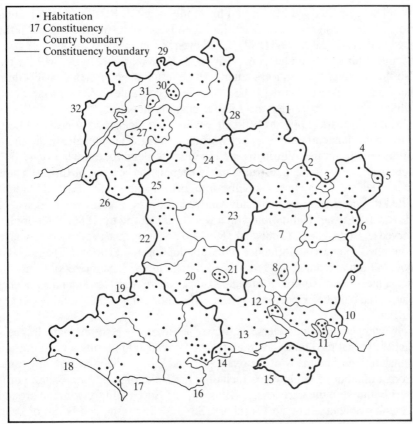

Map 2   Primrose League Habitations: c. 1883–1914: Wessex
Berkshire, Hampshire, Isle of Wight, Dorset, Wiltshire and Gloucestershire
(see appendix VI)

typically, the local Conservatives resisted pressure from the central party organization and claimed that any attempt to raise an organization locally would stimulate the Liberals and thus be counter-productive. Clearly Dorset was a county in which the league could succeed where neither the official party nor traditional methods matched the problem. Several wealthy families rallied to its attractively feudal style, encouraged perhaps by Salisbury's own example in Hertfordshire. In both North and West Dorset the Digby family of Sherborne Castle patronized several habitations. The Anglican-Nonconformist cleavage must have been conspicuous in the North, for by 1888 seven local clergymen had become RCs or secretaries in the fourteen habitations. West Dorset's huge membership (5,800) reflected the extensive habitations around Melbury led by the Earl and Countess of Ilchester, and Bridport under Sir Molyneaux and Lady Nepean. In the East, which enjoyed over 4,000 members, Lord

Wimborne of Canford Manor and his family acted as RCs in several habitations. What is significant is that the Liberals, after losing their seats in the East (1886) and the North (1892), failed even to contest the subsequent election despite their strong underlying position. J. K. Wingfield Digby, MP for the North, attributed this to sheer demoralization resulting not from national politics but from the intensive work by the Dames in the constituency between elections, which appeared to render the Liberal position hopeless. [10]

Similar remarks apply to Wiltshire, whose average stood at nearly 3,000. Two major landed families lent powerful patronage to the league in the south of the county. In the Wilton division the Earl of Pembroke, owner of 42,000 acres, and his wife were instrumental in keeping the seat out of Liberal hands from 1892 to 1906. In the small borough of Salisbury the Earl of Radnor filled the same role, he and Lady Gertrude Bouverie taking turns as RC of 'Longford Castle' Habitation which was 3,500 strong by 1886. Radnor also served as Chancellor in 1886 and 1890. No doubt these aristocrats could have continued to exercise influence without adopting the Primrose League. But both Wilton and Salisbury fell to the Liberals in 1885. Some regular institutional means was required for holding Conservatives together around a political cause; the old purely personal appeal and ad hoc campaigns would no longer suffice.

By comparison Gloucestershire showed itself largely resistant to the league's tactics, in that the county average reached only 1,600 despite a proliferation of habitations, and many of the seats remained Liberal. Support certainly came from a number of landowners including the Duke of Beaufort (Badminton), Earl Bathurst in the Cirencester Division, and Sir Gerald Codrington around Chipping Sodbury. But the Thornbury, Stroud, Cirencester and Forest of Dean divisions as well as Gloucester Borough usually returned Liberals. In some districts the Liberal inclinations of the working population were reinforced by the presence of Liberal landowners, [11] hence greater resistance to joining habitations. Sir Michael Hicks-Beach's prompt withdrawal both as candidate and as *landowner* after his defeat in 1885 may well have discouraged other landed figures from a determined counterattack. Certainly the records which survive for habitations at Chipping Sodbury, Nailsworth and Horsley and Coln Valley suggest that they were inefficiently run. Associates were charged too much, tributes invariably not collected, and men rather than women were often in charge; as a result their membership remained small and apathy soon set in. [12] The exceptions to this were Cheltenham Borough and the North or Tewkesbury Division, where the electorate included 2,000 property owners from Gloucester and Cheltenham, and 1,000 Gloucestershire outvoters for whom a separate habitation was established. Active Tory squires here became RCs for their immediate localities: the Belcher family of Swindon Hall, Lord and Lady Fitzhardinge of Berkeley Castle, G. E. Lloyd-Baker of Hardwicke Court, Mrs Dent of Sudeley Castle (Winchcombe), A. C. Dowdeswell of

Ripple Hall (Tewkesbury), Major-General Kerr of Prestbury Court, and Mrs E. Waddington of Guiting Grange. Tewkesbury and Cheltenham were regularly won by Conservatives.

SOUTH EAST ENGLAND

The whole of this region, with its attractive wooded countryside, growing seaside resorts and inland spas, drew large numbers of wealthy middle-class families in the late Victorian period; those who wished to commute to the City found northern Surrey and Kent an ideal residential area. Consequently servants bulked large in the population and Anglicanism was relatively strong.[13] Kent, though much more industrial than Surrey and Sussex, was almost as Conservative. This may well be because in such places as Dartford, Gravesend, Dover and Chatham the working population often derived its living from breweries, public houses, dockyards and port labour, which inhibited Liberalism and left them susceptible to the Conservative appeal.

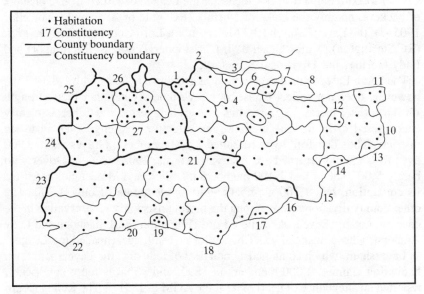

Map 3   Primrose League Habitations: c. 1883–1914: South East England Kent, Sussex and Surrey (excluding Croydon, Wimbledon and Kingston) (see appendix VII)

Each of the four Surrey seats included in this region boasted an impressive network of habitations worked by leisured middle-class ladies and often graced by aristocratic families. Clearly, though, the Conservatives stood in relatively little need of an efficient electoral machine here and the size of membership is simply a reflection of the character of local society; this is reflected in the comparatively high proportion of Knights and Dames in some of the habitations: 200 as opposed to 355 Associates at Guildford, for example, and 112 as opposed to 285 Associates at Epsom. In 1891 the Walton and Oatlands Habitation in Epsom claimed 1,861 members among a total population of 4,520; in such conditions there was little room for an effective opposition to Conservatism.

The same was true in Sussex, except where the Liberal-Nonconformist elements on the Sussex Weald impinged upon the East Grinstead and Eastbourne constituencies. On the whole little industry existed, while landed families were numerous. In Horsham Division, habitations were promoted by the Earl of Egmont of Cowdray Park and Sir Francis Montefiore of Worth Park; in East Grinstead by Lord Arthur Hill, MP; and in Rye by the Marquis of Abergavenny and Lord Richard Nevill of Eridge Castle, E. Hussey of Scotney Castle, and A. M. Brookfield, the local MP. Abergavenny was Chancellor in 1894 and a key figure in Conservative circles as patronage advisor to Lord Salisbury. In Chichester the League benefited from a phalanx of backers, notably the Duke of Norfolk (RC Vale of Arun and Chancellor 1905–7), the Earl of March (RC Molecombe), Lord Zouche of Parham Park (RC Storington), Major-General Sir Christopher Teesdale (RC Bognor) and Lady Goring, the Divisional Secretary.

The South East regional average is dragged down by Kent with 1,876. This, however, does not reflect Conservative weakness but rather their strength *vis à vis* the Liberals. For reasons already suggested the Liberals clearly encountered difficulty in generating an effective challenge even in urban districts. Thus Dartford town recruited 2,500 members; Gravesend had 900 even in 1905 and returned a Conservative in the 1906 election; Dover with barely 5,000 voters had 1,100 members by 1889; and Maidstone, noted for its corruption, had 1,700 members amid an electorate of only 4,700. The other county divisions were among the most consistently Conservative in the country, notably Sevenoaks, where Lord Hillingdon, Earl Stanhope and Lady Amherst, whose husband was Chancellor in 1889, spearheaded the League. In Faversham, which contained a good deal of industry, the Faversham town habitation claimed 2,000 members in 1890, and, what is more significant, reported an attendance of nearly 900 at the AGM in 1891.[14] The Ruling Councillor was Lord Harris of Belmont Park, another wholly typical League figure. Major Commandant of the East Kent Yeomanry, Harris captained both his county and the England team at cricket. Under-Secretary for India and for War during 1886–90, he also served as Chancellor in 1888 and 1889. In 1890 he went to Bombay as Governor, in which capacity he was thought to have done much to popularize cricket amongst Indians, returning to be Chancellor again in 1894–5.

LONDON

The average of under 900 members in the London constituencies, though low by Primrose League standards, was impressive in view of the difficult conditions prevailing in the capital; that the league existed in every constituency regardless of social character was an achievement in itself, for in London all parties struggled to establish permanent organizations and keep them alive. Considered as a purveyor of entertainment the league clearly faced rather stiffer competition here, in view of the sophisticated entertainment industry, than elsewhere in Britain, which may have detracted from its appeal. But the real difficulty lay in the mobility of population. In the poorest districts families constantly moved about in search of cheap lodgings; while in the more fashionable parts the wealthy were distracted by the demands of Society functions at home and excursions abroad. Perhaps in the expanding suburbs there was an opportunity for bodies like the league to build up a community spirit among the new residents.

As one would expect, the constituencies stretching from the City of London, the Strand and Westminster to the West End were thick with habitations flourishing among the wealthy; in Mayfair the 275 Knights and Dames in 1888 outnumbered the 137 Associates; while the 532 members of the 'Abergavenny' in the Strand Division were all Knights who also belonged to the Constitutional Club. The 3,400 members in St George's Hanover Square enlisted in the 'Belgravia' under Viscount Curzon MP, the 'Northumberland' (Mayfair) under the Duke of Abercorn, the 'Wimborne' under Lord Wimborne or the 'St George's' under Lord Algernon Percy. Only one problem troubled them – the London Season made it difficult to hold successful meetings and even hire halls; as a result some habitations felt obliged to concentrate their activities in the quieter winter months.[15] In addition, West End activists were encouraged to contribute time and money to struggling habitations in the East End. The league existed, for example, in all seven divisions of Tower Hamlets, of which Mile End, Stepney, St George's in-the-East, Limehouse and Bow and Bromley invariably elected Conservatives prior to 1906. In several cases the RC had to be brought in from outside the area: Col. W. le Poer Trench of Hyde Park Gardens for Whitechapel, Captain Spencer Beaumont of Brighton for Stepney, and W. H. Davis of Crouch End for Bow and Bromley. Moreover, the league felt it necessary to depart from its usual tactics here by embarking on a series of discussions on 'Labour' and 'Social' questions among the working-class habitations during 1892–3;[16] fortunately for the league, these seem to have petered out without raising any challenge to the rather limited political principles to which it was pledged. Lively working-class orators were produced for these occasions, capable of deflating Liberal panaceas and concentrating on more congenial topics such as patriotism, protectionism, alien immigration and the defence of public houses. In addition, it was expected that in these poverty-stricken districts candidates would continue to be generous in material matters to their constituents,[17] and habitations may well have provided a useful cover for this. Since the electorate was very small it remained susceptible to personal influence. In Mile End, for example, Spencer Charrington, whose brewery dominated the constituency, served as Ruling Councillor and MP. In the Hoxton Division of Shoreditch Claude Hay, one of the earliest members of the league, used the local habitations to dislodge the Liberal hold on the seat in 1900 and, remarkably, won it again in 1906. Hay's success in 1900 stood in marked contrast to the situation in the adjacent Shoreditch Haggerston, where the Tory Member who had been elected in 1895 decided that he could do without the Primrose League; at the election he suddenly asked for forty canvassers which the party evidently could not provide, and

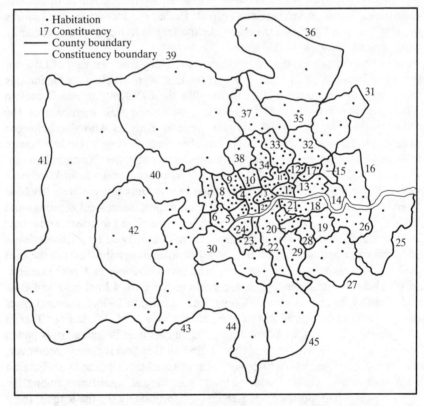

Map 4   Primrose League Habitations c. 1883–1914: London
South West or Walthamstow Division of Essex, Kingston, Wimbledon and Croydon
Divisions of Surrey, Uxbridge, Brentford, Ealing, Harrow, Hornsey, Tottenham and
Enfield Divisions of Middlesex (appendix VIII)

was defeated.[18] South of the river, Lambeth North, Southwark West, Rotherhithe and Bermondsey were also heavily working-class and frequently returned Conservatives. However, here the RCs were local men and Conservatism more firmly rooted among the watermen, lightermen, bargemen, tanners and leather workers. Moreover, for the Catholics who were numerous here the League was a congenial form of Conservatism free of protestant prejudice.

Most of the rest of London comprised a huge band of residential constituencies, both middle and working class, stretching from Wandsworth in the south-west through Clapham, Norwood, Brixton, Dulwich and Lewisham to Deptford, Greenwich and Woolwich in the south-east, and in the north from Hackney, Islington and St Pancras across to Hampstead, Hammersmith and Fulham. By and large these were areas of sharply rising population in the late nineteenth century. Affluent middle-class communities gathered in constituencies such as Wandsworth (where there were five habitations at Putney, Tooting, Balham, Wandsworth and Streatham), and Hackney North where the 'villadom' of Stoke Newington produced 955 habitation members. A number of the residential seats were characterized by clerks and other lower middle-class employees struggling to maintain respectability on low salaries. To such communities an organization like the league had much to offer, and habitations proliferated in Fulham (three), Hammersmith (five), Lewisham (six), Peckham (two), Brixton (two) and in parts of the Islington divisions. The Conservative appeal to the social pretensions of this section of the population kept these seats in their hands even in the Edwardian period except where, as in Islington, a working-class influx modified the character of the district.

Beyond these seats lay a number of peripheral suburban districts still retaining a rural ambience, which showed themselves strongly Conservative. This seems to have been true of working-class suburbs such as Walthamstow, which had five habitations and Conservative MPs from 1886–1900, as well as of the more mixed constituencies like Enfield. The emphatically middle-class Harrow, Ealing, Brentford and Uxbridge seats provided easy territory for the League and plentiful supplies of lady activists, as did the three Surrey suburban divisions Kingston, Wimbledon and Croydon. Only in the last named, where middle-class dominance was increasingly weakened by working-class penetration did Conservatives have to fight for the seat;[19] but with seven habitations and over 2,500 members Croydon remained Conservative except in 1906.

CENTRAL ENGLAND

The five counties of 'Central England' scarcely constitute a region; they comprise a band of territory between the London and Midland conurbations, largely agricultural in character but punctuated with industrial concentrations at Northampton, Bedford, Luton, Peterborough, Wolverton, Aylesbury and High Wycombe. The high membership average of 2,167 conceals two distinct political communities; on the one hand, Oxfordshire and the two weakest counties, Northampton and Bedford, all marked by patches of staunch Non-conformity, small-town skilled workers and rural radicalism; and on the other Buckinghamshire (3,196) and Hertfordshire (3,738), two of the best-organized counties in the country, both close to London, already attracting a commuter population, and studded with country seats.

For the Primrose League the *crème de la crème* was the St Albans Division of Hertfordshire with twelve habitations and up to 4,500 members.[20] The machine here was graced by the Earl of Verulam (RC St Albans) and especially by Lord Salisbury himself at Hatfield; his family seem to have participated, Lady Gwendolen Cecil on the Divisional Council, Lord Robert as RC for Hatfield and Lord Hugh as Treasurer. In the circumstances there was little scope for the official Conservative Party. Similarly in East Hertford the Marquis of Hertford provided the figurehead for the eight habitations, while in the West or Watford Division the wife of the local MP, J. F. Halsey of Great Gaddesden, organized a huge central habitation which grew from 3,600 in 1888 to 5,000 by 1900. In the North or Hitchin Division, where Lord Dimsdale was the Member, seven local clergymen acted as RC or secretary in the habitations. Buckinghamshire reveals a similar pattern especially in the South where rail communications with London made for convenient commuting and a full social life for the fashionable. The MP, Viscount Curzon (the heir to Earl Howe), was Chancellor of the League in 1900–2 and his wife RC for Iver; other leading lights included Ettie Grenfell (RC Burnham), Sir P. F. Rose (RC Tyler's Green and Penn) and the brewer T. O. Wethered (RC Marlow). In Mid-Buckinghamshire the seat was held by the Rothschilds as Liberal Unionists, and perhaps for this reason there were only six habitations. Only the North or Buckingham Division resisted the Conservatives partly because of industry in several towns and partly because of the Verney family of Claydon who were major landowners and active Liberals. In order to prise the seat out of Verney hands the Primrose League mobilized a battalion of local owners including Evelyn Hubbard (RC Buckingham) who became Lord Addington, his son Egerton (RC Wilmslow), Sir T. F. Fremantle (later Lord Cottesloe), Viscount Lewisham, (RC Olney), Sir P. D. Duncombe (RC Bletchley) and the Duchess of Buckingham (RC Wotton). They won the seat in 1886, 1895 and 1900. These Buckinghamshire families are a reminder of the institutional coherence of higher society. One finds Mrs Hubbard and Lady Fremantle assisting the local Girls Friendly Society; Hubbard, Fremantle and Wethered among the active promoters of the Volunteer Movement in their county;[21] and the same names are reported in connection with gatherings of the local freemasons.[22] The leadership of the Primrose League was evidently only one of a series of overlapping circles in local society.

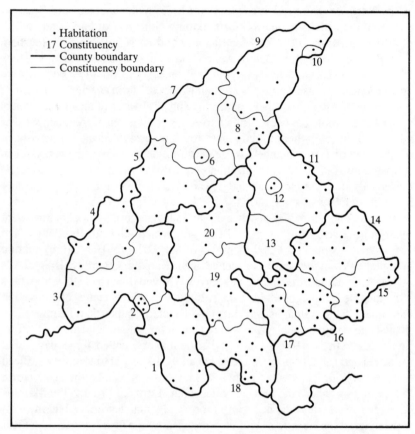

*Map 5   Primrose League Habitations c. 1883–1914: Central England
Oxfordshire, Buckinghamshire, Hertfordshire, Bedfordshire and Northamptonshire
(appendix IX)*

In Oxfordshire, the South or Henley Division strongly resembled South Buckinghamshire and East Berkshire. The expanding residential population around Henley and Caversham contributed to habitation strength under the leadership of the Earl and Countess of Macclesfield and Lady Stapleton, and enabled the Conservatives to hold off a strong challenge from Herbert Samuel in 1895 and 1900. In Mid-Oxford or Woodstock their efforts were far less effective in spite of the presence of Viscount Valentia of Bletchington Park in the Primrose League camp, the Earl and Countess of Jersey at Middleton Park, and the Duke and Duchess of Marlborough. The weakness lay in a failure to tackle the working population in places like Headington and Witney, in the slackness of the Church of England in the large rural parishes, and in the reluctance of Jersey and Valentia to accept the sitting Liberal Unionist MP. [23]

In the North or Banbury Division, Albert Brassey, brother of Lord Brassey, was both the candidate and RC for Chipping Norton; Lord and Lady North of Wroxton Abbey were RCs for Banbury and R. Nicol Byars of Rousham Park RC Steeple Ashton. But the same social characteristics as in Woodstock kept the seat in Liberal hands except in 1895 and 1900. In all three Bedfordshire constituencies Conservatives were handicapped by an extensive industrial population, the strength of Nonconformity and an absence of major landowners willing to promote the cause. In fact the county divisions were much weaker than the borough, where middle class residents provided the framework of a habitation of 1,800 members by 1891 with nine wardens and twenty-seven sub-wardens.[24] With this organization Bedford was wrested from the Liberals by Guy Pym of the Hazels, Sandy, who was also RC for Potton, but only in 1895 and 1900.

If Northamtonshire was nearly as weak in league terms it was not for want of trying. Even Northampton Borough, which elected Bradlaugh and Labouchere, contained 1,200 members of the 'Delapre' Habitation, the title being taken from the nearby residence of Sir Rainald Knightley. Knightley's own seat, South Northampton, was narrowly saved down to 1892 with wife's indefatigable campaigns on his behalf; Lady Knightley's tactics of cultivating the radical centres such as Daventry and Brackley rather than taking refuge in the Conservative countryside was typical of the league at its most effective. The East, with its radical boot- and shoe-makers, called for equally bold measures and habitations were created at all the industrial towns; they sufficed to give the Liberals a run for their money but not to take the seat. North Northampton, where the Duke of Buccleuch, Lord Lilford and the Marquis of Exeter wielded influence, was more congenial territory, but in Mid-Northampton the League's style was cramped by the loyalty of Earl Spencer of Althorp to Liberalism. No one rivalled Spencer as owner of 17,000 acres, but lesser figures, Lady Eleanor Clifton and Lady Rose Pender, steadily built up the Guilsborough Habitation to 1,500 members by 1891. Lady Rose, a noted huntswoman and RSPCA activist, sometimes addressed three or four meetings a night on behalf of her husband, Sir James, who surprised his own party by defeating Spencer's son in 1895.

EAST ANGLIA

The protracted decline of industry in East Anglia had left this, by the late nineteenth century, a markedly agricultural region. Its arable farming resulted in a large, though diminishing, labour force, and had attracted gentleman farmers. However, Conservatives lost heavily throughout the region following the county enfranchisement of 1885, and East Anglia was thus a crucial battle-ground in which Conservatives fought back by using Primrose League methods.

Though some ground was recovered the party continued to struggle, as the modest regional average membership suggests. While the large number of habitations is a sign of the effort that was made, especially in Norfolk, Suffolk and Essex, the low membership of many habitations shows the political resistance encountered. The militancy of agricultural labourers, who often joined their union here, may have been strengthened by Joseph Arch's presence as MP for North West Norfolk. Certainly Liberals in East Anglia freely derided the 'sham gentility' of the league and warned the new electors that it was a scheme hatched by the privileged to swindle them of their new power.[25] The league countered with some well-directed humour:

> Mr Barry said it was proposed to oppose the Primrose League by a counter organization to be called the Progress League...but he suggested that the Cowslip League would be a better name, the cow having given the slip to those who expected to have got her. (Laughter)[26]

In place of 'three acres' Conservatives in East Anglia talked much about allotments, and in place of a live cow the league offered dead ones: 'In the tent (at Melford Habitation's fete) were long tables on which were joints of beef, mutton, ham, pies, cake, bread and butter etc. together with tea and coffee.'[27]

Furthermore, Essex, Suffolk and Cambridgeshire were traditional Dissenting counties, while Primitive Methodism gained a hold in much of Norfolk. A combination of large parishes and a paucity of nuclear villages in the fen and heath country militated against Church influence. Nor was there a very substantial middle-class to fill the gap, except in Bury, Norwich, south Essex and some coastal resorts. The weakness of the league in rural Cambridgeshire is largely accounted for by the absence of either a middle class or a willing gentry particularly in the Wisbech and Chesterton Divisions. In addition, the tribulations of arable farmers led to some migration into the region by less affluent men from the north and Scotland, ready to take up less prestigious branches of agriculture, who tipped the balance further against the Conservatives.

At the other extreme, south Essex resembled south-east England with its large middle class, its Anglicanism, nuclear villages and country house network. Chelmsford, for example, enjoyed ten habitations, one of them led by W. J. Beadel the local MP; Epping, too, was very suburban and safely Conservative with 3,100 League members. On the other hand the Saffron Walden and Harwich Divisions shared more with the rest of East Anglia; in the absence of local landowners the habitations remained rather weak and the representation usually Liberal. Maldon, with its patches of Nonconformity and agricultural unionism, was marginal. Here the key family was the Strutts of Terling, who threw their weight behind the league. C. Hedley Strutt MP

*Map 6   Primrose League Habitations c. 1883–1914: East Anglia
Norfolk, Suffolk, Cambridgeshire, Huntingdonshire and Essex (not including the
South West or Walthamstow Division) (see appendix X)*

was RC for Maldon, Lady Evelyn Rayleigh RC for Terling and Lady Clara
Rayleigh RC for Wickham Bishops.

Throughout Suffolk the league depended heavily upon landowners' influence,
but frequently without great success. This is particularly the case in Eye, where
the major landowner, the Duke of Hamilton, remained inactive politically.[28]
The initiative rested with Lord Henniker of Thornham Hall, whose daughter
Mary grasped the opportunity to sponsor no fewer than nine habitations, all

bearing her name, within the constituency, as well as nine more elsewhere in Suffolk. Other major landed figures backed the League in the Woodbridge Division (R. H. Lloyd-Anstruther MP) and Lowestoft (the Earl of Stradbroke and Lady Hilda Rous), but they were too few in number and too frequently challenged to be a dominating force; this is underlined by the Suffolk membership figure of 1,645 per constituency. Thus in Woodbridge, Stowmarket and Ipswich victory passed from one party to another, and only Sudbury and Lowestoft went consistently against the Liberals after 1886; but in both cases the defection of the sitting Member to Liberal Unionism was probably the decisive factor.

In Norfolk, Conservatives were much provoked by the election of Joseph Arch in the North West Division in 1885, and the result of their efforts is to be seen in the average membership of 2,141. However, landlord influence in Norfolk was often absent or ineffective. In Arch's constituency, for example, major owners like the Earl of Leicester and the Prince of Wales left politics to the labourers. Though ten habitations were created, led by the local doctors and clergymen, Lord Henry Bentinck (the Conservative candidate) and the Countess of Romney, they won the seat only in 1886. The villagers at Dersingham, where the league had nearly 400 members in 1888, were stated by contemporaries to be staunchly Liberal.[29] This suggests that the labourers' families may have joined the habitation as a kind of insurance while still voting Liberal, or perhaps simply enjoyed its social activities without being seduced politically. Similarly in both East and Mid-Norfolk the presence of an active Liberal landowner, the Earl of Kimberley, helped to blunt the league's efforts politically and both seats were usually Liberal. Indeed, South West Norfolk is the only constituency in which landlord influence may have been efficacious in keeping the seat in Conservative hands through the role of Lord Walsingham (RC Wayland), Sir A. T. Bagge (RC Downham Market) and W. A. Tyssen Amherst of Didlington Hall, who sat as the local Member. On the whole the urban centres proved more favourable territory in both Norfolk and Suffolk. Large habitations catered to the workingmen in Norwich and Ipswich, both two-member seats in which the Conservatives shared the representation. King's Lynn, with under 4,000 electors, enjoyed a League membership of 2,300, and the Conservative MPs, R. Bourke and T. Gibson Bowles, worked with the League, the latter as a member of Grand Council.

THE EAST MIDLANDS

Lincolnshire, with its high average of 2,500 members, may be considered first as it strongly resembled the Norfolk pattern. In the 1880s Methodism underpinned local radicalism and arable farming was collapsing, with the result that large areas became either free from church-and-squire influence or somewhat resistant to it. The Conservatives' best chances lay in the small boroughs. Tiny Boston, for example, was dominated by 1,921 league members tended by 25 wardens. Grantham Borough, where the Countess of Brownlow was RC, claimed 3,665 (though not all in the town itself). Lincoln, a marginal seat, recruited 4,530 members, including 92 wardens, under Mrs Ellison of Boultham Hall; the scale of activities is indicated by a report that 1,100 members sat down to tea in the Corn Exchange at Lincoln in February 1890.[30] However, several of the county constituencies stubbornly returned Liberals in spite of aristocratic support for the league from the Earl of Yarborough in Brigg and Grimsby, Lady Mary Turnour in Louth, the Earl of Winchilsea in Spalding, and clergy and squires in Gainsborough. The only reliable Conservative seats — Stamford, Horncastle and Sleaford — seem to have been those dominated by landowners. In Stamford, for example, it was the Earl of Ancaster, the Earl Brownlow, and the Duke of Rutland. In Sleaford Henry Chaplin, owner of 23,000 acres, held on to the seat until 1906 with the aid of some formidable rural habitations like the 'Ellison', which covered 100 square miles south of Lincoln. It claimed that a third of the total population (7,000) were members; and at its peak ran 250 meetings a year, enrolled 467 Juveniles and had a Cycling Corps nearly 100 strong.[31]

By contrast, Derbyshire, Leicestershire and Nottinghamshire were dominated by urban and industrial districts where families relied upon mining, boot and shoe making, railway engineering, wool, silk, lace and cotton. This economy naturally generated many skilled workers, some well-supported, though moderate, trade unions, and a pattern of small-scale production, all of which contributed to the Liberal strength of the region. However, the level of Primrose League support was second only to that of Wessex, for throughout the region Conservatives not only had an incentive to organize, in view of Liberal strength, but also a means in the shape of a wealthy local aristocracy. Leicestershire, and to a lesser extent Derby and Nottingham, remained a county of pastoral farming but with nuclear villages, a sporting gentry and lordly landowners. Yet in 1885 it had not been possible to separate agricultural from industrial communities, and, as a result, the Melton Mowbray, Market Harborough, Loughborough and Bosworth Divisions were all more or less mixed in character and thus keenly fought over at elections. The Earls of Loudon, Lanesborough and de Lisle and Henry Harpur-Crewe were among the leading lights in the league, but the habitations flourished in the towns as much as in the country, including radical Leicester itself. But only Melton, graced by the Duke of Rutland, the Marquis of Granby (the MP) and Sir F. T. Fowke of Lowesby Hall, fell to the Conservatives.

In Nottinghamshire the Conservatives did better because they were more successful in mobilizing working-class support. This is noticeable in Nottingham itself where all three divisions included substantial working-class elements. Particularly interesting is the East, which was strongly working class and held a large English Catholic vote;[32] it was thus one of those seats in which the

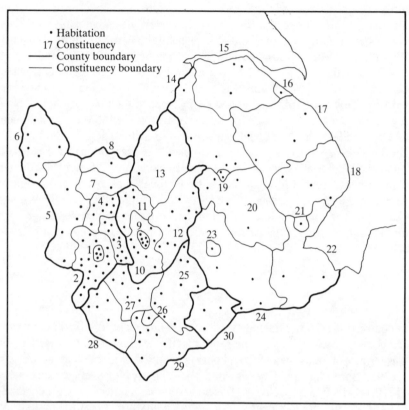

Map 7   *Primrose League Habitations c. 1883–1914: East Midlands*
Derbyshire, Nottinghamshire, Lincolnshire, Leicestershire and Rutland (appendix XI)

league could come with clean hands by contrast with the party, which was disadvantaged by its traditional militant Protestantism. The four habitations here helped Conservatives to victory in 1895, 1900 and twice in 1910. In the county Mansfield and Rushcliffe remained safely Liberal, while Newark, with 3,100 members in ten habitations, and Bassetlaw stayed Conservative. Bassetlaw seems to have been unusually well-endowed with major resident landowners: Viscount and Lady Galway of Serlby Hall, the Earl and Countess of Manvers of Thoresby Park, the Duke of Portland and Lady Bolsover at Welbeck, and the Duke of Newcastle at Clumber. The habitation for Retford and District alone had 4,500 members, and Welbeck and Clumber were the objects of summer excursions for members throughout the East Midlands Primrose League.

In Derbyshire the Chesterfield and North East Divisions were too dominated by workers in coal and iron to be winnable for Conservatism; and the Welbeck influence on the east of these seats does not seem to have been translated into habitations. The rest of the county, however, was formidably organized both as regards the number and size of habitations as the figures suggest: West (3,400), Mid (3,700), South (4,300), High Peak (3,100), Derby Borough (2,000) and Ilkeston (2,000). Two are worthy of note. In the South, where George Curzon of Kedleston was heavily defeated in 1885, the industrial workers in towns and villages around Derby made this at first a strongly Liberal seat. A systematic fight-back by the Conservatives led to the establishment of 15 habitations in the radical centres as well as the country; Sir Vauncey Harpur-Crewe of Calke Abbey patronized the habitations at Breadsall, Tickenhall and Melbourne. The seat was recovered in 1895 and 1900 though Curzon had departed long since. Derby Borough was a radical stronghold which produced but one shock Conservative victory in 1895 over Sir William Harcourt. The combination of the immediate issues of that campaign with the build-up in the six habitations in the town prior to the election helps to account for it.

THE WEST MIDLANDS

In contrast, the West Midlands were consistently Conservative in both town and country after 1886, with the result that the need for the Primrose League was far less obvious than in neighbouring counties. It is true that the western counties, Shropshire and Herefordshire, show a fairly high average membership of 2,101 and 1,923 respectively. This however, was a reflection of the character of local society: predominantly agricultural, a mixture of pastoral, arable and fruit farming in which protectionism still flourished, a numerous squierarchy and weak Nonconformity; the basis for a really effective Liberal challenge was lacking. The exception was the north-west corner of the Oswestry Division, where Welsh immigration posed a challenge which was met by the concentration of habitations there.[33]

In the more industrial counties to the east Conservatism achieved a remarkably strong hold, particularly after the Liberal split of 1886. Indeed, the Unionist alliance held all the Birmingham seats comfortably regardless of social composition. Even before 1886 the Conservatives had been obliged to seek a popular base, and the addition of the Chamberlainite following left relatively little room for the Primrose League. Although thirteen habitations have been traced in the eight Birmingham and Aston Manor seats,[34] they appear to have attracted a relatively small membership and only the 'Ladywood' under Lady Sawyer enjoyed a long existence. To some extent these remarks apply to Worcestershire as well, where the young Stanley Baldwin served an apprenticeship as Secretary to the Divisional Primrose League. Clearly some friction developed within the alliance here; in East Worcestershire for example, where there were eight habitations, the Conservatives felt reluctant to assign the seat to Austen Chamberlain in 1892.

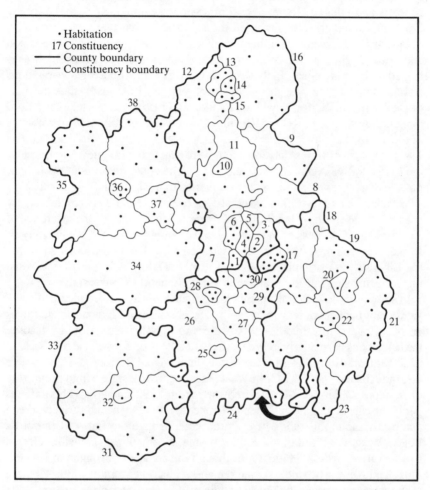

Map 8   Primrose League Habitations c. 1883–1914: West Midlands Staffordshire, Warwickshire, Worcestershire, Herefordshire and Shropshire (appendix XII)

Outside Birmingham the Chamberlainite influence steadily waned and the pattern reverts to normal. Warwickshire constituencies saw a uniformly high level of activity as the county average of 2,337 suggests. But the work was crucial in Nuneaton and Rugby because of the strength of the Liberal challenge. Since a quarter of Nuneaton's electorate were miners it is not surprising that the seat went Liberal in 1885, but it did not do so again until 1906. The nine habitations were supported by F. A. Newdegate, a major landowner and the MP from 1892 until 1906. But the seat could only be held by tapping the Conservatism of the industrial workers, and the Dames organized weekly concerts and sales of clothes at cost price in Nuneaton itself.[35] In the Rugby Division the pattern also favoured the Liberals in that there was a mixture of industry and agriculture; Liberal landlords like the Marquis of Northampton and Lord Leigh, combined with the local reputation of Joseph Arch, strengthened their rural appeal. In these circumstances Primrose League habitations were adopted as the best means of dislodging the Liberals;[36] thus the Earl of Denbigh was RC for Newnham Paddox and Prior's Hardwicke, and Lord Willoughby de Broke RC for Kineton. But it was probably the shift of votes in the towns that gave Conservatives a victory in 1895. Rugby itself gained 1,494 members of whom only forty-four were Knights and Dames. Significantly, the Conservative Agent in 1900 decided that he could do without the habitations' assistance, whereupon the seat reverted to the Liberals.[37] In South West Warwickshire or Stratford Conservative tactics were more successful largely because Conservative landlords were more dominant − the Marquis of Hertford, the Countess of Warwick, Lord Denbigh and Lord Willoughby de Broke. The reliance of their candidates on local habitations was such that the Liberals here organized a County Voters Defence Association to resist undue influence; but the seat remained consistently Conservative.

In spite of its low overall membership figure, Staffordshire included some significant pockets of league strength. The absence of titled patrons in towns encouraged wealthy middle-class owners to ape their superiors by leading the habitations particularly in Wednesbury (the 'Wilson Lloyd' and the 'Richard Mills' at Darlaston), Walsall (the 'Frank James') and Burton-on-Trent, where George Allsopp was the RC. In West Staffordshire, despite a high proportion of miners, a Unionist MP was returned from 1892 onwards. This reflects partly the capacity of the ex-Liberal Member to appeal to the industrial workers, and partly the mobilization of the rural vote through the Earl of Bradford's large 'Weston' Habitation. Similarly the North West Division elected Conservatives from 1886 to 1906, though the adjacent boroughs of Hanley, Stoke and Newcastle-under-Lyme remained Liberal except in 1900. All these seats reveal Primrose League strength in the working-class districts, the Duchess of Sutherland serving as RC for those at Hanley, Stoke and Fenton, Newcastle and Trentham. At Kidsgrove the 'Coal and Ironworkers' Habitation recruited some 700 members almost wholly drawn from the working class, 'There being scarcely any gentry or even really well educated persons belonging to it'.[38] A combination of political speeches with 'knife-and-fork' teas, ventriloquists, punch-and-judy and dances was the formula adopted here. Similarly the Audley and Alsager's Bank Habitation, some 1,270 strong, included only twelve Knights and Dames. These two were among five habitations in North West Staffordshire, led by ladies without whose work such a constituency could scarcely have remained Conservative in four successive elections.

It is not surprising to find Yorkshire, with an average constituency membership of 1,395, well down the list in terms of Primrose League strength; the social conditions that made the West Riding a consistently Liberal area are reflected in the average of only 1,188 members. The East Riding's average of 1,303 conceals a high membership in the county divisions dragged down by the three Hull seats. However, the North Riding at 2,314 is very much in line with agricultural districts further south. Clearly the Vale of York, eastern Richmond, the East Riding and Ripon and Barkston Ash in the West were all characterized by a prosperous agriculture, some big landowners, nuclear villages and a strong Anglican influence. Richmond, with 3,800 members, presented the league with a challenge in the western half, where the scattered farms and mining communities adhered to Nonconformity and Liberalism, and the advantage, in the eastern half, of an active landowning elite; the Marquis of Zetland of Aske Hall served on the Grand Council, the Hon. C. T. Dundas, Sir Henry Beresford Peirse of Bedale Hall and Sir John Lawson of Brough Hall all became Ruling Councillors. Other constituencies seem to have relied on one or two families: the Earl and Countess of Feversham in Whitby, Lady Lascelles and Lord Beaumont in Ripon, Mrs Pennyman of Ormesby Hall in Cleveland and Sir George Sitwell MP in Scarborough, where he presided over a 1,000 strong habitation in an electorate of only 5,000. In the East Riding the Earl of Londesborough, also a Grand Councillor, placed Londesborough Park at the disposal of habitations; while in Buckrose Lord Middleton and Lady Sykes gave the lead, as did two MPs, Sir Albert Rollit (Grand Councillor) and F. Grotrian in Howdenshire.

The majority of Yorkshire constituencies, however, fell within the textile, mining and steel districts or in the Pennine moorland areas where scattered farmsteads, large parishes and Primitive Methodism militated against Conservatism. In this broadly Liberal region two points should be made. First, even industrial Yorkshire included concentrations of working-class Conservatism in the habitations at Barnsley, Bradford, Doncaster, Goole, Selby, Sheffield and Huddersfield, where the workers were employed in mining or other unionized and skilled occupations. Second, although aristocratic patronage was not wholly absent, as the examples of the Earl of Wharncliffe (Hallamshire), Lord St Oswald (Pontefract) and the Duke of Norfolk (Sheffield) suggest, their role had necessarily to be filled by middle-class employers and by ladies in several constituencies: Lawrence Hardy JP in Shipley and Bradford, J. A. Brooke JP in Huddersfield, Mrs Brooke in the Colne Valley,

Miss Rawson in Sowerby, Miss Edith Milner in York and Miss Wentworth at Barnsley.

The three largest West Riding towns, Leeds, Bradford and Sheffield, illustrate the wide variation in Conservative strength. In Leeds the league was relatively weak, and none of the habitations appear to have had a large membership, which was attributed to the aloofness and even hostility of the local party.[39] Conservatives had benefited from the 1885 redistribution which gave them two seats out of five: the business constituency (Central) and the residential constituency (North). Interestingly the habitations were most numerous in Leeds West and the adjoining Pudsey division, both characterized by a substantial artisan electorate and self-help institutions.[40] Herbert Gladstone's near-defeat in the West in 1892 and 1895 suggests the Conservative potential of such communities.

In Bradford, on the other hand, the league began with a single 'Bective' Habitation which had recruited 1,800 members by 1888 and then split into

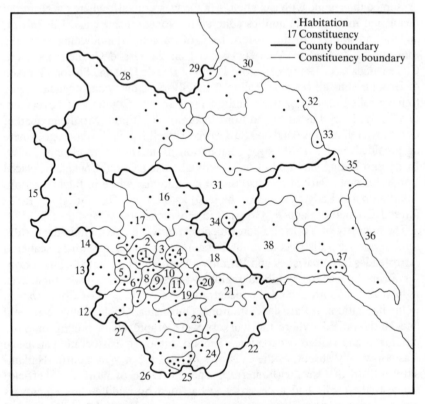

Map 9   Primrose League Habitations c. 1883–1914: Yorkshire West, North and East Ridings (appendix XIII)

three, one for each constituency; by 1893 there were 4,000 members — twice the size of the ILP in its major stronghold. [41] These habitations formed an integral part of the Conservative machine in Bradford, and attracted Sir Ernest Flower, a Grand Council member, as a candidate. The party's revival from the late 1880s reflected a bold populism which involved attacking the temperance reformers, exploiting imperialist sentiment and vigorously championing the voluntary schools' demand for additional grant aid. All three Bradford seats contained a large working-class electorate, and all three went Conservative in 1895 and 1900. Nor can this success be explained simply by the appearance of ILP candidates who split the Liberal vote, for the Conservatives won these seats in both three-cornered and straight contests. Indeed they did better in Bradford East in the absence of a Socialist, which underlines the existence of a significant body of voters willing to vote Conservative-ILP, not Liberal-ILP, at least in the pre-1900 period.

At first sight it seems remarkable that Sheffield should have returned Conservatives in three of the five constituencies throughout 1885–1914, and in four in 1900. The party clearly took advantage of certain conditions prevailing in the city. Because of the light metal trades there were large numbers of skilled workers and small workshop proprietors; from the 1880s foreign competition in cutlery and steel generally enhanced the popularity of protectionism; orders from the army and navy boosted the prosperity of Sheffield's munitions manufacturers, which given the Conservatives' patriotic and imperial stance appeared to benefit them in spite of the parsimony of Conservative Governments. [42] The potential was realized because from the early 1880s local Conservatives were keen to establish a popular organization, and large habitations sprang up in each division regardless of social composition. Relations with the party were kept close and friendly by several key figures, notably Sir Howard Vincent, the Member for Sheffield Central. As a former professional soldier, a Colonel in the Volunteers, and an indefatigable campaigner for tariffs and control of alien immigration, Vincent personified the patriotic, populist tone of Sheffield Conservatism. [43] The Duke of Norfolk, a major urban landowner here, was evidently welcome as a patron both to the Party and to the Conservative-run municipality, jealous of the pride and status of the city; but Norfolk was more than a dignified part of the machine, for he used his influence to place his nephew, J. F. Hope, in the Central Division on Vincent's death. In the salubrious residential seats on the west of the city (Hallam and Ecclesall) the large league membership is not surprising, but it was matched in Brightside and Attercliffe. Nor was the league's attraction confined to the really poor, dependent working-class, but flourished among the artisans and small entrepreneurs typical of the Central Division. Not only was this seat held in 1906 and 1910, but over the 1885–1910 period it gave the Conservtives a higher share of the poll than the two middle-class divisions.

NORTH WEST ENGLAND

In North West England one encounters a region noted for the strength of its Conservatism in both urban and rural districts, a reflection both of the immediate relevance of the Irish question socially and strategically, and of the traditional populist character of local Conservatism. Cheshire's constituency average of 2,164 reflects the residential character of those parts south of the Manchester conurbation and the role of landed families in the Primrose League including W. Bromley Davenport and the Earl of Shrewsbury (Macclesfield), Lord Egerton of Tatton (Knutsford), Sir Philip Grey Egerton (Eddisbury) and Joseph Sidebottom MP (Hyde). But Cheshire would not have been so staunchly Conservative but for its major organized support in the towns, notably Macclesfield, Congleton, Crewe, Nantwich, Stalybridge, Stockport, Northwich, Hyde and Chester.

The comparatively low average for Lancashire, which is an underestimate since we have no membership returns for many habitations in constituencies included here, conceals a number of important variations in the level and nature of support. Seats with a residential-rural mixture, such as Southport and Blackpool, were, as one might expect, well endowed with habitations. Aristocratic patronage characterized one or two industrial divisions. In particular, the Earl of Lathom became Prior of the Imperial Chapter of the league, while the Countess served on Ladies Grand Council; she and her daughter, Lady Maud Wilbraham, were responsible for most of the eight habitations in Ormskirk. The family of the Earl of Crawford and Balcarres adopted the league to perpetuate its political influence in the Wigan and Chorley constituencies. The Countess was RC for the 'Lindsay' (Wigan) which boasted 2,854 members by 1888 and won the Champion Banner in 1895. For a mining seat with an Irish Liberal vote Wigan remained remarkably consistent in its Conservatism until 1910. Lord Balcarres sat for Chorley from 1895 until his succession to the Earldom in 1913, being unopposed for much of that time.

However, this was not generally the pattern in Lancashire. For example, the Knowsley interest was not apparently behind the league until after 1903, when tariff reform drove Lord Derby to align himself with it. In Liverpool in particular and on Merseyside in general the Primrose League was never well organized;[44] for the pattern of politics there had already been set in sectarian concrete before the mid-1880s. With a popular base in the shape of Alderman Salvidge's Liverpool Workingmen's Conservative Association and a run of election victories, the party found little need for an alternative organization. Indeed, the robust Orangeism of Merseyside Toryism was antipathetic to the league, which welcomed Christians of all denominations; any attempt to recruit Catholics here would have been deeply resented by a party which needed no more than Protestant votes to win. As a result, the only large habitation was in residential Toxteth under the Baroness Henry de Worms, whose husband was the local MP; a quarter of its members were Knights or Dames, a sign of its superior social status. In addition several habitations catered for the outvoters of Bootle, who comprised a fifth of the electorate there.[45] Sir George Baden Powell, Member for Kirkdale, sat on the Grand Council but beyond that local involvement with the league was slight. The habitations in Manchester also seem to have been small, though the reason is not clear; it may reflect the separation of the middle class from the working population in the conurbation – no one was available to play the role envisaged by the League.

It is a different story in the cotton spinning towns to the north and west of Manchester: the boroughs of Oldham, Rochdale, Bury, Bolton and Ashton and the county divisions of Middleton, Heywood, Radcliffe-cum-Farnworth and Prestwich, as also in the Cheshire towns of Stockport, Stalybridge and Hyde. Here one finds no great aristocratic patrons but everywhere a large League membership rooted in the working population. Reputations are misleading here. In Middleton the supposedly 'Liberal' Todmorden and Little-borough supported habitations as strong as that in 'Conservative' Middleton. The working-class Radcliffe seat was usually won by Liberals but by small margins; Conservatives repeatedly lost with 49 per cent of the poll and in view of the 2,000-strong habitation among the Farnworth miners and the 1,600 at Radcliffe their strong performance is not surprising. Rochdale, despite its radical traditions, contained 4,000 league members led by Mrs Royds, the wife of Clement Royds, who won the seat in 1895 and 1900. Bolton, which had 1,800 members by 1888, saw a remarkable leap forward in the late 1890s when the habitation eventually topped the 6,000 mark; Conservatives took at least one and often both the seats here. Since the Irish were by no means a perennial issue in these districts historians have sometimes found the Con-servative strength in such heavily working-class constituencies puzzling.[46] It is less so if seen through the perspective of the league. Essentially the cotton spinners comprised an industrial elite whose (male) wages exceeded £2 a week by the end of the century.[47] They and their families were in a position to join organizations of all kinds for pleasure, improvement and mutual support, and their attendance at Primrose entertainments was but one expression of this. They supported Friendly Societies, Co-operatives, and trade unions, and were more likely to own their own homes than their equivalents elsewhere. It has often been forgotten how keen Conservatives were in this period to promote self-help along these lines (see chapter 6). In particular, many workers paid for the education of their children with the result that voluntary schooling became a major issue among Anglicans, Catholics and even Methodists in Lancashire. Now the defence of voluntary schools against the Board system was a chosen battleground of the league, and clearly acquired unusual salience in the north-west. In this comparatively bouyant, materialist and nationalist

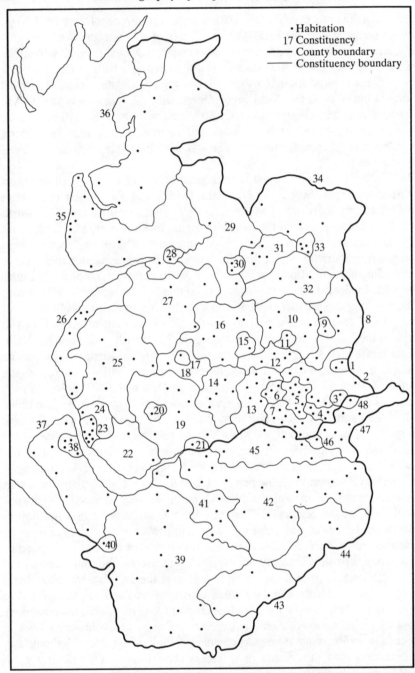

Map 10   Primrose League Habitations c. 1883–1914: North West England
Lancashire (not including North Lonsdale and Barrow-in-Furness) and Cheshire
(appendix XIV)

society Conservatism appeared to be more in tune with popular aspirations than the more dour, serious-minded Liberals — at least until the reappearance of cheap food as an issue.

To the north of the county lay another area in which weaving was a major source of employment, comprising Blackburn, Preston, Accrington, Darwen, Clitheroe, Burnley and Rossendale. Here again were pockets of great strength especially in such towns as Bacup, Darwen, Accrington and Blackburn. An additional element which goes some way to accounting for the Conservative position here is the large number of English Catholics in each constituency. In contradistinction to the situation elsewhere in the north-west the Conservative cause was better presented here under the more benign aegis of the league, so that full advantage might be taken of Catholic concern over their schools. As the Duke of Norfolk warned Salisbury, the Catholics in places like Preston could not be taken for granted by the Conservatives and would withdraw support if they thought the party's Protestant tail was wagging the dog.[48] Candidates recognised the volatility of the Catholic community not only in the seats already mentioned but in Blackpool, Southport and Chorley where they held a decisive position in the electorate.[49]

NORTHERN ENGLAND

Although the four northern counties of England were, as a whole, one of the weaker areas for the Primrose League, the high figures for Westmorland and Northumberland are reminders of two quite different sources of strength: a powerful rearguard action by several aristocratic families, and a surprising reservoir of urban support on Tyneside. In general, however, there is no doubt that it was particularly difficult to exercise landowner influence in the North by the late nineteenth century. Much of the region comprised pastoral, moorland farming; agricultural wages had risen as a result of the alternative sources of employment, and it was possible for shepherds, for example, to become tenant farmers. Though east Northumberland held some large estates the county was unfashionable and not well populated by gentlemen farmers. Not only were the old Dissenting sects strong, but Primitive Methodism flourished among many industrial workers, while Scottish immigration had brought a good deal of Presbyterianism into Northumberland. Perhaps more than anywhere else in England, rural radicalism went hand in hand with industrial. Largely as a result of the miners federations, Northumberland and Durham were the most highly unionized counties in Britain; and highly paid groups such as engineers, boilermarkers and blastfurnacemen had generated an assertive, if moderate, labour movement. Only in Westmorland did traditional influence still flourish, both in the Kendal Division where the Earl of Bective, MP, of Underley Hall (son of the Marquis of Headfort) dominated the

Conservative cause, and in the Appleby Division where the key magnate was the 'Yellow' Earl of Lonsdale, famous more for his associations with boxing, horse-racing and automobiles than with politics. In practice, his wife Lady Grace kept the Lowther interest alive through her role in the habitations at Lowther, Penrith and Whitehaven. After their old rivals the Howards split over Home Rule, there was less of a challenge to the family's position in the far north-west. However, several of the Cumberland seats leant to Liberalism and required careful handling. The Conservatives' successes may have something to do with the large Catholic population in the Egremont,

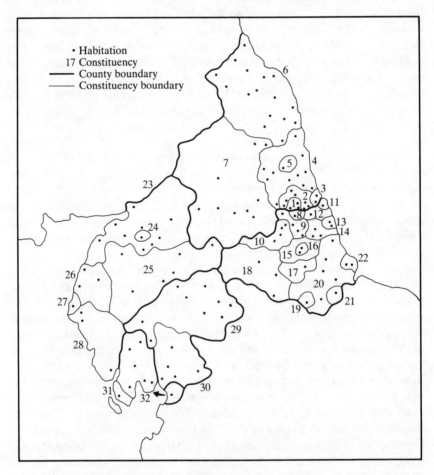

Map 11   Primrose League Habitations c. 1883–1914: Northern England Northumberland, Durham, Cumberland, Westmorland and Lancashire (North Lonsdale and Barrow-in-Furness) (appendix XV)

Cockermouth and Whitehaven constituencies. Whitehaven, for example, had a mere 2,700 electors but up to 870 Primrose League members and fell to the Conservatives in 1885, 1886, 1895 and 1900. The Egremont or West Cumberland Division held a mixture of industrial and rural interests. Lord Muncaster, the Member from 1885 to 1892, provided traditional landlord influence, but the seat would not have been won in 1885, 1886, 1895 and 1900 without the mobilization of support in the industrial districts, particularly at Cleator Moor where the habitation numbered 1,100. It seems that in both Egremont and Whitehaven the Liberals won in 1892 and 1906 only when the Irish vote came to them; otherwise much of it aligned with the Conservatives. [50]

Turning to the eastern side of the country, one finds that both the owners of wealth and their workers were inclined to Liberalism particularly south of the Tyne. In Barnard Castle, it is true, the Earl of Strathmore held extensive estates and patronised the Teesdale Habitation. But the league's effort rested largely upon a single family, that of the Marquis of Londonderry who certainly promoted large habitations at Wynyard, Seaham Harbour, Darlington, Stockton and Hartlepool. It was noted in 1890 that Londonderry's return from Ireland had stimulated a doubling in the membership at Seaham. [51] Seaham fell within the South East Durham constituency, which had been designed by the Boundary Commissioners to maximize the agricultural and minimize the mining interests which were so prevalent in the county generally; the freeholders from the neighbouring boroughs also voted in the South East. It was here if anywhere that a seat could be won for Conservatism, and the build-up of habitation strength preceded the party's victory in 1895; it was held until 1910. But Lady Londonderry refused to consider the nearby boroughs of Darlington and Stockton as irremediably Liberal. At first Darlington, a Nonconformist town dominated by the Pease family, looked unlikely. In 1885 the Ruling Councillor and candidate was W. H. Wilson Todd of Halnaby Hall, a local landowner. A split in the Pease family over Home Rule presented an opportunity, though it was not until 1895 that Darlington fell to a Unionist. Stockton, with its heavy industry and working-class electorate, seemed a formidable challenge. Thomas Wrightson a local employer and Conservative candidate led what by 1892 had become a habitation of 1,300 members organized by 150 wardens. [52] It fell to the Conservatives in 1892 and 1900. This build-up of habitation strength in the early 1890s seems to lie behind the surprising success of Conservatives in the north-east in the 1892 general election when the country returned Gladstone to office. [53] Nowhere was this more striking than in the double-member constituency of Newcastle-upon-Tyne. Of the seven habitations here five were established in or after 1890. As a result the city had 3,000 League members by 1892, when one of the seats fell to a Conservative; by 1893 some 6,000 members had been enrolled and the full mobilization of the Conservative vote eliminated the surviving Liberal Member, John

Morley.[54] The habitations appear to have covered all parts from the poverty of St Andrews to the villadom of Jesmond. Particularly interesting is the Elswick Habitation, which drew its members from the skilled engineers and mechanics of the Armstrong munitions works. Since their homes were scattered around the city they were visited regularly by one of 40 wardens who met fortnightly to co-ordinate their work.[55] The 700 members of 1891 had grown to 1,500 by 1894 and to 3,400 by 1905, a startling example of the survival of factory-based politics into the twentieth century. Lord Armstrong made his Cragside estate available to north-eastern habitations who, with Ravensworth Castle, Lumley Castle, Lambton Park and Wynyard were almost spoilt for choice. Nor was Newcastle the only part of the region to develop habitations comparatively late. In 1896 a new one appeared at Blyth in great strength which cannot have been unconnected with Thomas Burt's near-defeat at Morpeth in 1900, when his opposition to the Boer War became an issue. South Shields claimed 1,300 members in 1900; the 'Gort' at Hamsterley Colliery near Consett recruited 1,000 in 1908; and at Jarrow the 1908 by-election revived the habitation which won a surprising 1,600 members immediately.[56]

In the more extensive divisions of Northumberland — Hexham, Wansbeck and Berwick — the league looked to such magnates as Viscount Ridley and the Duke of Northumberland, though with little electoral success. In Berwick an array of squires and clergymen, spearheaded by the Percies, marshalled nearly 4,000 league members by 1888 in an effort to avenge the defeat of the Duke's son, Earl Percy, by Sir Edward Grey in 1885. However, Percy's son Lord Warkworth and F. W. Lambton consistently failed. Percy's tactics by no means reflected the true spirit the league aimed to create. He dwelt at length on his opposition to 'democracy' instead of cheerfully accepting reform and showing confidence in the people; moreover, he repeatedly defended wealth and inequality, thus drawing attention unnecessarily to his family's position.[57] In view of the fact that he was not faced with a radical expropriator on the Liberal side, this was an inappropriately negative approach. Indeed, Grey, as a gentleman of long and local standing was doubtless the ideal candidate against the Percies' somewhat feudal appeal; his success underlines the point that popular respect for birth and status could best be tapped by a light and gracious appeal.

SCOTLAND

At first sight Scotland appeared fertile territory for the Primrose League. Endowed with a romantic and sporting upper class and a stirring historical tradition still to be heard in the names of the castles and clans of the country-side, Scotland excited the imagination — from the English side of the border.[58]

The cause of the British Empire, which provided employment for many a Scot, seemed particularly popular towards the end of the century. Moreover, Scottish Conservatives, notoriously aloof from their electorate, might have been expected to appreciate the league as a builder of bridges to the people. Thus in October 1885 a separate Primrose League organization was launched in Scotland at a time when only 83 local bodies were affiliated to the NUCA for Scotland.

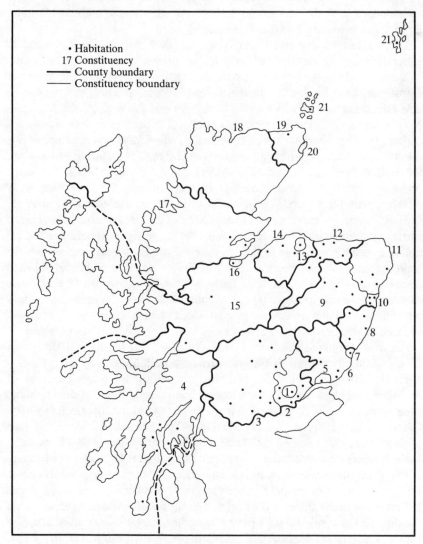

Map 12   Primrose League Habitations c. 1883–1914: Scotland (the Highlands and Islands) (appendix XVI)

The Scottish Branch had a similar structure to the parent body and ran its own finances, but was ultimately responsible to Grand Council in London. Since detailed membership returns from the Scottish habitations are very incomplete the calculation of the constituency average has been based on the total return of 56,986 members in 1891. The low average − 826 − is corroborated by the relative paucity of habitations north of the border: 158 in 1891, or a little over two per constituency, which may be compared with five per constituency in Wales, for example. In Scotland, alone in mainland Britain, large areas evidently remained untouched.

This cannot be explained simply by the fact that Scotland adhered to Liberalism for, as we have seen, the league proved quite adept at recruiting in areas hostile to the Conservatives. Unquestionably some of the pillars of Conservatism in England were absent from Scottish politics, and the league never managed to cope with the problem. [59] No real equivalent to the Anglican-Nonconformist division in politics existed north of the border. The established church, the Presbyterian Church of Scotland, was widely regarded as compatible with Liberalism. Although breakaways by the Free Church in 1843 and the United Presbyterian Church in 1847 caused division and led to some pressure on the Liberal Party to adopt disestablishment, this did not seriously interfere with the Liberals' hold on Scottish constituencies which, in 1885, favoured them by a margin of six to one. Moreover, the rather more democratic spirit prevailing within the Scottish churches was a sign that deference might not be a weapon available in the struggle for political influence. In fact the league seems to have been unsure whether to contrive a deferential or a democratic spirit. When in 1891 Lady Willoughby d'Eresby urged the use of workingmen as speakers, she was contradicted by a habitation secretary who maintained that these were English tactics which in Scotland 'never *will* succeed. There is no greater aristocrat at heart than a genuine Scotchman.' [60]

For most Primrose Leaguers it was axiomatic that the natural leaders of each community should live up to their responsibilities. Yet in Scotland it appeared that they would not or could not do so. No doubt an array of prominent families came forward to lead habitations. North of the Highland Line, for example, one finds Sir Kenneth Matheson of Lochalsh (RC Clacknacuddin, Inverness), Lady MacDonald of the Isles (RC Skye), the Earl of Strathmore (RC Glamis) and the Marchioness of Tweedale (RC Dingwall). In the Borders the Earl of Home supported habitations at Duns and Coldstream; in Dumfriess there was some Buccleuch influence, Lord James Douglas being RC for Lochar. But the only concentration of aristocratic activity occurred in Perthshire in the shape of the Earl and Countess of Ancaster of Drummond Castle, the Duke of Atholl of Blair Castle, the Earl of Kinnoull of Dupplin Castle, Lady Helen MacGregor (RC Callander), the Countess of Errol (RC Errol) and Viscount and Lady Strathallan (RC Auchterarder). However, it is significant that even here only one of the three Perthshire seats (West

Perthshire) usually elected a Conservative; and no other part of Scotland shows such intensive aristocratic involvement. Indeed the Scottish Branch constantly struggled to persuade sympathetic magnates to take an active interest; the league, it was claimed, would flourish as it did in England 'if only gentlemen of position in Scotland would lend us their influence and their houses'. [61] Thus in 1902, for example, Grand Council lamely concluded that there was no possibility of reviving Fochabers Habitation unless a member of the Duke of Gordon's family would take an interest; and in 1906 Forfarshire was felt to be hopeless so long as Lady Dalhousie remained abroad. [62] The league was in a sense a victim of the removal of the seat of government to London, which had gradually drawn the Scottish upper classes south and inevitably emasculated their involvement in Scottish affairs. Very often the best place to catch a 'Scottish' magnate was in a London drawing room, or so it seemed to the Scottish Branch. [63] For the league this was bound to be crippling, particularly in view of the fact that the middle classes were sparsely distributed in many constituencies, or were inclined to be Liberal. However, the flaw in the Scottish upper class probably went deeper than this. For Scottish landowners represented more of a liability politically than their English counterparts, and were forced onto the defensive by a strongly supported movement for land reform. Even moderate Liberals had been driven from their constituencies by Crofter candidates in 1885 and, rightly or wrongly, the radical picture of the absentee, exploitative landlord commanded more plausibility in Scotland than anywhere except Ireland. Politically, therefore, landowners seem to have cut their losses. For example, while we find the Duke of Sutherland's family actively involved in Staffordshire habitations, the Scottish estates were apparently left unworked, as were most of the Highlands.

A further complication lay in the unusual antagonism between the party and the league in Scotland. As early as 1886 the Scottish branch was urging Conservative Associations to establish habitations in each centre of population – a distinctly tentative approach by comparison with English practice; while by 1894 the Secretary was reduced to asking the party in which constituencies the league might be organized with advantage. [64] Locally one finds examples of non-cooperation such as the refusal of the Galashiels Unionist Club to allow a habitation to use its premises for functions. [65] To some extent the problem lay in the attitude of Liberal Unionists who clearly gave Conservatives the key to their gains in Scotland after 1886; the league's slightly late start meant that in 1886 it was not well entrenched and could be dismissed as irrelevant. Certainly the league itself believed that both the ex-Liberals and the Conservative Associations regarded them as competitors for membership which suggests that the female dimension was seen as less significant here. In particular, the hostility of Conservatives in the west of Scotland doubtless reflected the party's close involvement with Ulster immigrants and the Orange Order in that area. [66]

In addition there is some evidence that the character of the league differed from that south of the Border. In 1905, for example, the Council in a revealing remark urged that the tracing of removals was 'very suitable work for ladies, as they are not necessarily brought into contact with the electors at all.'[67] At habitation level things sometimes appear to have been rather dour. Deeside Habitation in Kincardineshire, which covered 16 parishes, ran strictly temperance meetings which were closed at ten o'clock 'before people get tired and politics are lost in amusements'; it reported also that 'dancing has been considered unadmissible as there is no need for it.'[68] Clearly such a straight-laced approach would not have succeeded for many English communities; but since the habitation won a thousand members perhaps it suited the local taste.

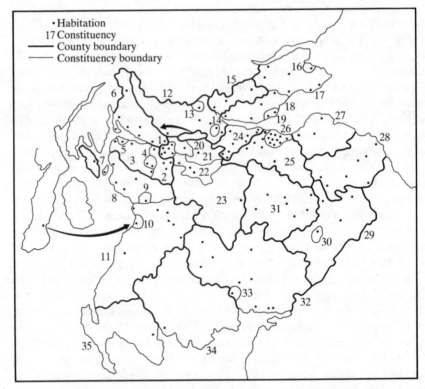

*Map 13   Primrose League Habitations c. 1883–1914: Scotland
(Central and Borders) (appendix XVII)*

The English pattern was probably better reflected in urban than in rural communities particularly in the, admittedly few, residential and suburban districts. Edinburgh, for example, was well-endowed with habitations especially in its South and West Divisions. To the north of Glasgow the residents of

Bearsden, Milngavie ('The Craigend') and Kelvinside supported habitations, as did those on the south side at Pollockshields, Thornliebank and Cathcart. In and around Glasgow the moving spirits in the League were Sir Archibald and Lady Campbell of Blythswood (MP for West Renfrew), Sir John Stirling Maxwell (MP for College) and Sir James Buchanan of Craigend Castle. [69] A significant working-class membership gathered in the habitations at Stirling, Aberdeen, Paisley and in the industrial county of Linlithgow where six habitations flourished under the patronage of the Earl of Hopetoun (Kirkliston, Bathgate and Torpichen) and Sir William and Lady Baillie of Polkemmet (Fauldhouse and Whitburn).

However, the habitations never attained the general importance for the Conservative cause which their English counterparts could claim, both because they remained comparatively sparse and because they were less well integrated into the party's electoral machinery. By the 1890s the Scottish branch seemed to be in early decline. Tributes were very slow to come in, and leading Conservative speakers proved extremely elusive. In 1897 the Duke of Buccleuch declined to serve as Grand Master; and during the Edwardian period major figures such as Ancaster and Atholl let their interest dwindle. By 1903 some eighty-five habitations existed, of which only forty were considered to be in a satisfactory condition. [71] Many of them were rapidly overtaken by tariff reform and the creation of Women's Unionist Association branches. During the war Grand Council met once or twice a year at most and not at all in 1918. Early in 1920 the Scottish branch was dissolved. [72]

WALES

In contrast to Scotland there were few areas of Wales even on the southern coalfields which escaped Primrose League activity. With its average membership of 1,771 and 166 habitations Wales is comparable with East Anglia, in that the coverage was fairly comprehensive but local membership not particularly large owing to the cultural-political antagonism towards Conservatism. Industrialized constituencies sometimes generated a high level of support. For example East Denbigh had 3,300 members by 1891, often drawn from mining villages in the classic league fashion: 'although Brymbo is described as a rough place, much good work may be done there by ladies.' [73] Similarly South Glamorgan or Gower had recruited 5,500 by 1891. Since the Liberals had polled 72 per cent of the vote in 1885 local Conservatives felt disinclined to contest Gower, but the impetus to do so came from the habitations who produced one of their RCs who held the Liberal poll to 54 per cent at a by-election in 1888. [74] With their low expectations of victory in much of Wales Conservatives were somewhat demoralised; it was thus comparatively easy for the league to fill the vacuum.

In view of the patently English and imperial character of the league one might have expected it to suffer greatly from the nationalism of late Victorian Wales. Undoubtedly habitations were alive to the difficulty, for they used literature printed in Welsh and their meetings were often conducted in both languages.[75] In counties where a high proportion of the population spoke English only — Radnor (93.6%), Pembroke (65.4%), Montgomery (52.5%), Flint (50.8%) — habitations flourished. But Cardigan, where only 6.7 per cent spoke only English, boasted nine habitations and a large membership comprising gentry, farmers and labourers.[76] In Denbighshire, where 38 per cent spoke English only, some twenty-one habitations flourished in the three constituencies. However, this apparent strength in Welsh Wales merely disguised an Anglican and Anglicized base, particularly in the small towns which historically had always been outposts of English culture and influence. This is certainly corroborated by the county of Caernarvonshire where 10.3 per cent were English-only speakers. Only one habitation existed in the South or Eifion Division, while the six in the North or Arfon Division were concentrated in the coastal resorts such as Llandudno, Colwyn and Colwyn Bay. But the Caernarvon Boroughs enjoyed a habitation in each of its six component boroughs; in particular the middle-class, Anglican Bangor, Caernarvon and Conway supported 2,200 members between them. Not surprisingly the seat was won by a Conservative in 1886 and, but for Lloyd George and the 1890 by-election, would probably have been won again.

Though Wales remained in general an economy of small, pastoral farming somewhat deficient in big landowners and gentlemen farmers, the league made good use of the limited number of sympathetic families. In the north these included the Earl of Mostyn in Flintshire and the north coast, the Earl of Powis in Montgomeryshire, the Marquis of Anglesey (RC Beaumaris), and Sir Watkin and Lady Williams Wynn in Denbighshire. In the south J. Alan Rolls, a wealthy urban landowner who was elevated to the peerage as Lord Llangattock, actively promoted habitations in Monmouthshire, as did the coal owner Lord Wimborne at Dowlais, and Lady Lewis at Aberdare and Mountain Ash in Glamorgan. Sir Charles and Lady Philipps of Picton Castle patronised the League in Pembrokeshire, as did Lord Dynevor and Viscount Emlyn in Carmarthen, the Earl and Countess of Lisburne in Cardigan and the Countess of Dunraven who was RC for Barry and Bridgend. In Cardiff Lord and Lady Windsor acted as Ruling Councillors, as did Lord Ninian Crichton-Stuart, the heir to Lord Bute, who won the seat in December 1910. However, the difficulty in south Wales, as Lord Salisbury found when trying to choose a Lord Lieutenant for Glamorgan from Lords Dunraven, Headfort, Bute, Windsor, Wimborne, Jersey, Clive and Tredegar, was to find one who was both Conservative and *resident* in the area.[77] In many cases the leadership given by these magnates to the Welsh habitations was of a purely nominal kind. Moreover, their propaganda lacked a political cutting edge; in Wales the issues

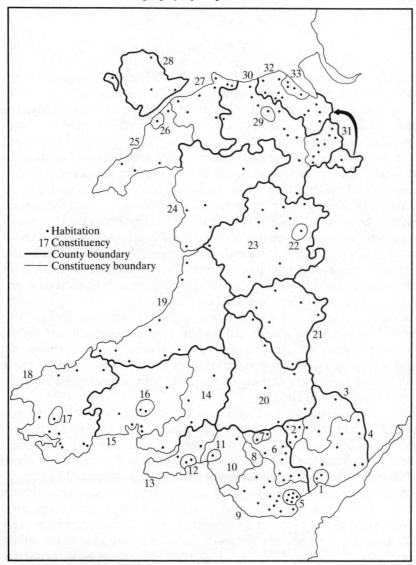

Map 14   Primrose League Habitations c. 1883–1914: Wales (appendix XVIII)

were largely Liberal ones, and the league's imported patriotic-imperialism evoked only a muted response. As a result, habitations in the Principality flourished primarily as social organizations for ladies rather than as effective electoral machines. Their main impact was in the group of small boroughs – notably Montgomery District, Denbigh District and Monmouth District – where an echo of English Conservatism gave the party a chance of victory.

CONCLUSIONS

The first general point to be made about this brief survey of England, Wales and Scotland is that it suggests vast scope for the investigation of grassroots Conservatism through the network of social leaders in each community. The prominence given here to titled leaders surely obscures the role of middle-class figures, especially after the initial novelty of the league had worn off. As to landed influence some qualification is perhaps necessary. Constituencies in which resident and politically active landowners dominated the local economy and gave a distinctly feudal quality to politics, such as the Bassetlaw Division of Nottinghamshire, were rather exceptional after 1885. In the majority of cases 'influence' fell far short of this. Aristocrats lent their names to habitations, their wives as Ruling Councillors, their houses for garden parties and their sons as candidates. But their appeal invariably consisted in something less than extensive ownership and control. They could serve as the focus for local pride and snobbery, and personify the links between Conservatism and national symbols such as Queen and Empire. By being visible they cultivated the illusion of lordly influence at a time when its reality was slipping. This helps to explain the peculiar attraction of the Primrose League for some great families; it preserved the spirit of the pre-democratic era. But it would not simply prop up a declining personal influence, as the Percies discovered in Northumberland, in the absence of a relevant political appeal and a regular organizational infrastructure.

The outstanding feature of the league in the late nineteenth century was simply its ubiquitousness. Most communities, regardless of their social character were capable of supporting a habitation. In particular, one notices the involvement of skilled workers at places such as Newcastle, Sheffield, Walthamstow and Bradford despite their traditional reputation for Gladstonianism and socialism. Only in some rural districts such as the Scottish Highlands and parts of Cornwall and Wales did the political culture prove hopelessly hostile to the league's form of Conservatism. As a result Conservatives were able to mount a comprehensive challenge to Liberalism even in the radical heartlands. As early as 1886 some leaguers began arrogating to themselves the task of pushing laggard Conservative Associations into election contests at every opportunity, regardless of the chances of victory.[78] Consequently the Conservatives came to enjoy a marked advantage in terms of unopposed returns:

	1885	1886	1892	1895	1900
Liberals unopposed	14	40	14	11	22
Conservatives unopposed	10	118	40	132	163

Finally, the nature of the league's contribution to Conservative success deserves comment. In years like 1886 it must be regarded as the beneficiary of the bandwagon set in motion by the eruption of Irish Home Rule. In 1895, despite the fulsome tributes by both Conservative and Liberal candidates to the league's effectiveness, [79] Liberal disarray rather than Conservative strength was surely decisive. Even in 1895, however, one's attention is caught by Conservative gains registered by Primrose League activists in improbable constituencies: Bedford (Guy Pym), West Bradford (Ernest Flower), Glasgow St Rollox (F. Faithfull Begg), Rochdale (Clement Royds), Mid-Northamptonshire (Sir James Pender). A much more telling case is the election of 1892, which would repay more attention from historians than it has generally received. With the tide running back in the Liberals' favour after Salisbury's long and unexciting reign, the Liberals actually emerged with only 272 MPs in England, Wales and Scotland to the Conservatives' 293; the nationalist majority in Ireland gave Gladstone his overall lead of forty. Clearly the Conservatives managed to contain the Liberal advance in spite of the fact that the political argument was not particularly helpful to them. They even gained seats which had been the subject of Primrose League effort in the immediately preceding years, notably Newcastle, Lichfield, Wolverhampton West, Dorset North, Montgomery District and Scarborough.

However, to concentrate on the league's significance in terms of the outcome of short election campaigns is probably to miss the point. Though it effectively supplemented and sometimes supplanted the party organization as an election machine, its primary contribution lay in its routine activities during the long periods in between elections when habitations could perpetrate the 'subtle work of demoralization', as the *Manchester Guardian* put it. [80] In more neutral language this meant keeping Conservatives together when the parties slackened their efforts. To be effective in this sense the habitations had to hold very regular meetings – and the successful habitations clearly met weekly. In addition they had to achieve a high level of participation and attendance – and again one can see from their reports that a 75 per cent turnout was not unusual. [81] Finally, it was essential to maintain contact through the regular visits of the wardens of the habitation to both members and, of course, electors. As we have seen, it was common for a habitation to appoint anything from twenty to a hundred or more wardens and sub-wardens to comb each group of streets or hamlet several times each year; only in this way could they hope to keep track of members who moved house or left the constituency, and capitalize upon the purely personal and family circumstances which influenced them. The effect of this work was to make popular Conservatism a social rather than a narrowly political force in Britain. This impression is corroborated by several observable facts. For example, it helps us to understand why the Primrose League should often have flourished in constituencies where the Conservatives rarely or never won elections. Further, it makes sense of a characteristic of Conservative support which was noticed by a distinguished historian of Conservatism some years ago, namely its stability.[82] The smaller the turnout at post–1885 elections, the larger the Conservative share of the poll. While Liberal support fluctuated very sharply during 1885–1910, the Conservative vote appeared relatively constant; even in 1906 their heavy defeat seemed to have owed more to a major rise in the turnout for Liberal candidates than to a transfer of votes away from Conservatives. This points to a broad distinction between the parties in the sense that the Liberals were sensitive to specific political issues, while Conservative support remained relatively immune by virtue of its grounding in the social structure. Of course the corollary was that the ideological rigidity and narrowness of the Primrose League made it an inadequate weapon in those periods in which politics were overtaken by new and controversial ideas; it could be outflanked both by its enemies and by its rivals within Conservatism.

6

Conservatism, Class and Community

Beneath the glittering surface of its social junketings the Primrose League waged a stern struggle to harness the forces of social change in British society. The confident Salisbury who played Grand Master was also the pessimistic author of 'Disintegration'. He shared with many Victorian Conservatives an acute fear that the delicate balance of the British system would be upset by the new centres of wealth and power generated by industrialization. There was always a danger that the middle classes who suffered political, religious or legal disabilities would be tempted to align themselves with the lower orders in order to capture power at the expense of the landed aristocracy. Thus the reforms of 1832 and 1846 had been necessary expedients designed to dissolve the incipient alliance of working and middle-class critics by giving the latter a foothold in the Establishment and an interest in the status quo. This strategy must be regarded as a partial success in view of the continuation of aristocratic influence on parliament and the cabinet during the mid-Victorian era.

Yet how far could the gentle process of assimilating fresh groups into the political nation safely go? In 1866 Gladstone displayed a true conservative grasp of the need to adjust the boundaries of the constitution just sufficiently to reflect social evolution; but Disraeli, with his household and lodger franchises, jumped dangerously ahead of it. The inevitable sequel was an extension of the new franchises to the counties in 1884, which delivered power into the hands of an electorate of 5.7 million men whose sheer poverty exposed them to the temptation to despoil property through the ballot box. One must remember that in the 1880s fewer than a million people paid income tax;[1] already the rights of property had been infringed by Irish land legislation; a cabinet minister had attacked those 'who toil not, neither do they spin'; and the case for taxing the 'unearned income' from land was gaining currency. No doubt the realignment of the Whigs during the 1880s represented a reassuring and logical consolidation of property under the Unionist banner, but in so far as it widened the gulf between two antagonistic nations it threatened to exacerbate rather than resolve the problem of accommodating all classes in a political system designed to maintain the status quo.

Of course nothing apocalyptic occurred. Even the Edwardian financial revolution unleashed by Asquith was intended to contain class conflict as much as to provoke it, though most Conservatives understandably failed to appreciate the point. Conservatism had in fact found its salvation in a variety of developments and expedients, some fortuitous and some contrived. As early as the 1870s the radical front had begun to break down as a result of the success of the middle classes in throwing off their disabilities; taking their places on the lower branches of the establishment they grew more aware of political assertiveness on the part of the labour movement. Consequently the rapprochement of middle and upper-class Britain required only some deliberate encouragement by the Conservative leadership. As both redistribution and suburbanization led Britain towards a class-based constituency structure, Conservatives managed simultaneously to acquire middle-class territory and to consolidate their traditional working-class strongholds.[2] This was facilitated by the Liberals' failure to exploit economic questions in place of the great moral issues in this period, a failure for which Gladstone bore much of the responsibility.

Yet things could so easily have gone wrong in the 1880s. Conservatives found class a very troublesome matter, not so much in ideological as in practical organizationl terms. Even the urban middle classes showed a propensity to rebel when inadequately rewarded for their allegiance, and for a time the National Union of Conservative Associations seemed to threaten a Conservative version of the 'caucus'.[3] Similarly the Conservative Workingmen's Clubs, which were encouraged to affiliate to the National Union, made Conservatives uneasy; if left to their own devices they could deteriorate into mere drinking clubs. but if brought into the centre of the party they might make politically embarrassing demands upon it. 'I have never been myself at all favourable to a system which would induce Conservatives who are working men to form societies confined merely to their class', said Disraeli.[4] On the whole the party failed to accommodate its working-class following within the official organization; at National Union gatherings, as one delegate put it, 'there is a great deal too much broadcloth and far too little fustian. There is not that direct representation of the workingman that there ought to be.'[5]

The Primrose League represented an attempt to come to terms with such difficulties by circumventing and obscuring the material distinctions between the wealthy, the respectable and the poor. If this seems ambitious it was not by any means a novel approach. In mid-Victorian England a variety of institutions aspired to link the classes with a view to some broad political objective. We have, for example, been reminded recently of the pervasiveness of Sunday Schools.[6] In the words of one Anglican clergyman: 'In the Sunday Schools when the children of the richer classes were young they learned to feel and sympathise with the poorer classes and in that way Sunday Schools had a great power of drawing together the sympathies of rich and poor.'[7] A generation later the activities of Primrose League habitations were said to create 'a feeling of respect and sympathy for the virtues, the struggles and the aspirations of those born to a life of toil', and to show the poor that 'people who, by accident of birth, are rich or highly-placed are not the soul-less, selfish beings depicted by the political stump-orator'.[8] This is not to assume the effectiveness of the strategy, only to underline the continuity of aim and method. Similarly, men of all social classes were attracted into the Volunteer Movement after 1859. Once the initial rush of gentlemen and middle-class volunteers had subsided the regiments came to depend heavily upon lower middle-class men and particularly on artisans, who formed the largest single element.[9] Indeed, the Volunteer Force seems to prefigure the Primrose League in several ways. Its success depended upon the support of local society leaders; it was blatantly hierarchical yet offered a ladder by which the socially ambitious might ascend a rung or two; and it underlined the contribution which patriots of each class might make to the community of which they were members. This need to find values, prejudices and loyalties capable of transcending material divisions lay at the heart of the Conservatives' popular appeal in the late Victorian period.[10] Yet it was the peculiar role of the League to try to bring the ideology and the organisation together. Class could scarcely be the natural, organic, unifying force which Conservatives traditionally claimed unless it was demonstrable in local communities rather than simply at the abstract level of the nation. The realization of this aim involved a threefold strategy. First, the league must reach deeply into each level of society for its recruits; second, it must never be found apologising about class or hierarchy, but must endeavour to cast them in a bold, appealing light; third, it must enthuse each part of the hierarchy with a sense of its value as a necessary and equal part of the political community.

Obviously some parts of this strategy were more readily attainable than others. The league held up a mirror to society in which it reflected what, in effect, were three social classes. At the base stood the mass of Associate members who paid merely a few pence and, as Grand Council put it, 'were only intended to be poor working people'.[11] Next came the Knights and Dames with their 2/6 tribute and perhaps another 3/6 for their habitation. These sums seem surprisingly low – until one remembers that they were designed to attract not real Knights but those who wished to pretend; the dignity lay just within reach for those with meagre incomes but burgeoning aspirations. Finally, those who could afford it paid a guinea to join the Ladies Grand Council or become one of the Knights Imperial.

This basic hierarchy was dramatized by the league's own 'Fountain of Honour' which spouted forth a niagara of painted enamel badges, pendants and ribbons, each of which distinguised one's class of membership, function or achievements. Any member might, on the recommendation of the habitation's council, be honoured with a Special Service Clasp awarded for work during a general election.[12] Since up to ten per cent of a habitation's members could be honoured every year the effect was akin to a regiment glorying in its battle honours. A clasp rendered the member eligible for further promotions. A Knight Harbinger of twelve months' standing might become a Knight Companion, a Dame might be made Dame Order of Merit. Even an Associate with one clasp and twelve months' membership could be a honorary Knight without paying tribute. Next came the award of the Grand Star in five grades, and, after 1887, the Grand Jubilee Star, also in five grades. George Lane-Fox observed rather smugly in 1888 that Grand Council exercised more patronage than the Lord Chancellor![13] Those who mocked the lavish distribution of baubles were told this was tantamount to deriding 'such honours as the Garter and the Victoria Cross'.[14] This effrontery on Lane-Fox's part is more explicable in the general context of late Victorian official practice which involved the creation of new honours and a return to grand ceremonials when a new Knight of the Garter was installed.[15] There is certainly evidence that the award of a Primrose League Grand Star was highly coveted even among aristocrats.[16] For the humble rank and file member the effect of the pageantry and honours system was to offer prestige and success in a local community which patently echoed the British national community.

To twentieth-century minds this emphasis on rank and distinction may sound a shade incongruous in the light of the league's claim to have 'broken down the distinction between one class and another throught the Kingdom'. 'They are all equal at the meetings,' declared one member, 'and it is one of the finest ideas of breaking down caste and levelling up ever invented by the Conservative party'.[17] Equality here took on a special and limited meaning. All were equally privileged as participants within the immediate community regardless of their status outside it. Thus all had to have equal access to the entertainments; no Knight or Dame should be allowed to buy a seat at the front while Associates were relegated to the back row. Obviously such restrictions went against the grain, so that occasionally a habitation was reprimanded for selling better seats at inflated prices. Indeed the ideal strategy meant avoiding seats in rows, which were socially divisive, and grouping them informally so as to maximize social intercourse.[18] In addition, the right of electing habitation officials and of standing for election was open to all members regardless of rank. As a result one finds habitations, such as that at Aberdeen, run by a blacksmith (as Secretary) in 1906 and an Executive Council largely comprising workingmen from the local shipyards. However, this was exceptional. The favoured role for men and women of the working class and lower middle-class was that of Warden or Sub-Warden; according to Lady Knightley, for example, sub-wardens were best chosen from those who were just a little superior in education and social status to agricultural

SOME PRIMROSE LEAGUE DECORATIONS.

Each illustration gives the actual size of the Badge represented. These Badges can only be obtained from the Head Offices of the Primrose League, 64, Victoria Street, S.W. 1.

Reversible Brooch, for Dames or Associates. 2/6

Divisional Councillor's Badge 2/-

Dame's Full Dress Badge 5/-

Knight Imperial's Badge Nickel, 10/-; Silver £1

Watch Pendant. 2/-

Ruling Councillor's or Dame President's Badge. 5/6

Knight Companion's Stud or Dame of the Order of Merit's Brooch. 2/6

Patriotic Service Badge. 1914-19. 1/-

WARDEN

Warden's Badge. 2/- Also a Sub-Warden's Badge 1/6

CHAMPION WARDEN

Champion Warden's Presentation Badge 6/6

The Grand Star 1st Grade £1

Small P.L. Cycling Corps Badge. 8d.

Majority Badge. 1/-

Deputy Ruling Councillor's Badge. 5/6

Knight Companion's or Dame of the Order of Merit's Full Dress Badge. 5/-

"Primrose League Gazette" Badge. Presented by Grand Council

Knight's or Dame's Enamel Stud or Brooch 2/6

P.L. Cycling Corps Badge 2/-

Plate 5   Primrose League decorations

labourers; they required sufficient clerical skills to enable them to maintain a membership register and record the fees paid. The duties, if socially rewarding, must have been onerous for those like the Leicester factory girl who, as a warden, made her deliveries and visits on Saturday afternoons. At Chiswick the habitation made it a practice to appoint a working man and his wife as subwardens; once they became accustomed to regular visits and collections they were promoted to Warden and took on middle-class districts as well as working-class ones, thereby helping to reduce the barriers between members. [19]

A vivid picture of the league's capacity to reach into each level of society is provided by the Cleveland habitation in north Yorkshire, where the wardens thoughtfully recorded the occupations of almost half the membership (table 5). Its social profile suggests five roughly equal sources of membership: semi-skilled manual workers, skilled manual workers, lower middle-class clerical-administrative occupations, shopkeepers, and substantial entrepreneurs and professionals. Obviously certain groups fit uneasily into any one category; many of the self-styled 'farmers' must have been small tenants nearer to shopkeepers in status and wealth; and the distinction between an artisan and a shopkeeper is blurred for men such as saddlers, who both made and sold goods on the same premises. Naturally one cannot generalize from a single surviving example. The prominence of craftsmen, farmers, shopkeepers and servants in the Cleveland membership reflects the territory of the habitation, which took in a range of agricultural villages, small towns and mining communities to the south of Middlesborough and along the North Yorkshire coast. One can only guess that farmers, for example, may have been more willing to declare an occupation than labourers. Nonetheless the *range* is impressive; it tends to corroborate the league's claims to be able to penetrate far beyond the traditional political class. Under the leadership of Mrs Mary Pennyman, wife of the landowner James S. Pennyman of Ormesby Hall, the habitation clearly mobilized a community capable of realizing the Conservative ideal of class unity.

However, critics detected some implausibility in the notion of direct social contact between the classes; the league, scoffed Herbert Gladstone, was 'only fit for duchesses and scullery maids'. Far from being embarrassed by such sallies, a Grand Councillor, Sir Kenneth Kemp, blandly riposted that Gladstone had 'let his wit run away with his brain', and claimed that any organization which 'enabled duchesses and scullery maids to meet on equal terms was of the greatest value'. [20] The idea that the high-born encountered the humble on an equal footing was of course an illusion, carefully contrived, but evidently one in which both sides gladly indulged. At a vast tea party at Seaham Hall in 1890 it was reported: 'Lord Castlereagh (heir to the Marquis of Londonderry) waited upon the guests at the tea tables (and) was the subject of gratified comment on every hand.' [21] Even a hostile observer at a huge Primrose League fete at Blenheim readily conceded the value of the occasion:

Table 6   *Cleveland Habitation: occupational analysis 1886–1888*

Category	Self-description	Male	Female	Total
Leisured	Gentleman	8		8
Higher professional	Barrister	1		
	Solicitor	4		
	Accountant	4		
	Architect	1		
	Surgeon	3		
	Vet	2		
	Officer	2		
	Clergyman	6		
	Clerk in Holy Orders	3		
	Engineer	6		
	Mining engineer	1		
	Artist	1		34
Businessmen and	Manufacturer	1		
manufacturers	Merchant	3		
	Corn merchant	1		
	Builder	5		
	Brewer	1		
	Miller	5		
	Flour dealer	1		
	Farmer	73		90
Shopkeepers	Grocer	11		
	Butcher	21		
	Draper	7		
	Milliner		3	
	Florist		1	
	Bookseller	1		
	Newsagent	2		
	Hairdresser		2	
	Ironmonger	3		
	Confectioner	3		
	Stationer	2		
	Postmaster/mistress	1	1	
	Chemist	3		
	Tallow chandler	2		
	Hotel proprietor	1		
	Innkeeper/publican	20		
	Landlady		1	

Table 6 continued

Category	Self-description	Male	Female	Total
	Shopkeeper	3		
	Milk seller	1		88
Lower professional/	Schoolmaster/mistress	13	5	
administrative	Pupil teacher	4	2	
	Music professor	2		
	Governess		1	
	Nurse		2	
	Auctioneer	2		
	Station master	1		
	Registrar of births	1		
	Gas manager	1		
	Registration agent	1		
	Policeman	3		
	Exciseman	1		
	Coast guard	2		
	Farm manager	1		
	Land agent	4		46
Clerical	Secretary	1		
	Clerk	26		
	Railway clerk	4		
	Solicitor's clerk	1		
	Cashier	1		
	Traveller	1		
	Verger	1		35
Supervisors	Foreman	2		
	Butler	4		6
Skilled manual	Engineman/driver	3		
	Carpenter/cabinet maker	2		
	Joiner	17		
	Fitter	7		
	Plumber	1		
	Plasterer	1		
	Painter	6		
	Bricklayer	3		
	Slater	1		
	Watchmaker	1		
	Tailor	11		
	Shoemaker	2		

Table 6 continued

Category	Self-description	Male	Female	Total
	Saddler	3		
	Lady's maid		2	
	Dressmaker		4	
	Blacksmith	5		
	Cartwright	2		
	Charger	1		
	Mill wright	7		
	Iron moulder	1		
	Iron presser	1		
	Stone mason	1		
	Fireman	1		
	Sexton	1		
	Apprentice	1		85
Semi-skilled manual	Miner	12		
	Quarryman	2		
	Weighman	1		
	Railway porter	3		
	Ropemaker	1		
	Hookmaker	1		
	Bill poster	1		
	Letter carrier	1		
	Shop assistant	1		
	Cab driver	1		
	Maid		10	
	Cook		2	
	Manservant	2		
	Footman	1		
	Coachman	1		
	Gamekeeper	5		
	Groom	5		
	Gardener	18		
	Laundress		1	
	Barmaid		1	
	Labourer	21		91

Total sample: 483 from a membership of 1,050
The Habitation covered Ormesby, Stokesley, Great Ayton, Normanby, Redcar, Halton, Budby, Yarm, Marton, Skelton, Eston and Stainton.
Source: Cleveland Habitation membership register 1886–88, Cleveland CRO

The strength is not always derived from a deep political conviction, but is derived partly, and sometimes wholly, from memories like those which will be handed down from today — a memory of a day spent in a stately park and a historic house, when a champagne luncheon was given to all comers (who numbered thousands) by the prodigal generosity of the Duke...when...the local merchant's wife met the squire's wife; the parish councillor's wife, whose boy is at the charity school, sat next the Member's wife, whose boy is at Eton; and the parish councillor himself met the Duke. Such social opportunities are a convenient rampart to the Conservative faith...and at the end of it all I reflected that the Liberal Party had simply nothing wherewith to match these great wells of party strength. [22]

Respect for the powerful, fascination for the lives of the high-born and wealthy, and sheer snobbery; such was the mixture of sentiments tapped by the league through its social functions. But it would be an oversimplification to characterize its appeal solely in terms of deference. No doubt it evoked a purely passive response in certain rural districts where, for example, audiences abstained even from asking questions at meetings out of respect and awe for those who addressed them. This, however, was far from being typical of the country areas in the 1880s, let alone of the towns where the rank and file could be assertive and self-confident. Working-class families might join habitations because they wanted to not simply because they were afraid not to. How, otherwise, is one to make sense of the Lancashire workers who both voted Conservative *and* participated in trade unions and strikes? Their behaviour is explicable in so far as both the union and the habitation offered members a combination of tangible advantages and an appeal to their pride and ideals.

THE ARISTOCRATIC–MIDDLE CLASS RAPPROCHEMENT

The Primrose League's strategy of class unity was most easily attainable in the relations between the middle classes and the aristocracy. Even at this level, however, collaboration required some deliberate effort, for throughout the nineteenth century middle-class men were driven into politics by their antagonism towards upper-class privilege. Although the embers of this resentment still glowed as late as 1910, however, they had diminished since the 1860s as a result of a gradual absorption of the middle classes into the social and political establishment. However, the transaction was a two-way process in which the institutional absorption of the middle class was matched by a less obvious aristocractic adoption of the values and ideals of bourgeois respectability. [23] By the 1880s several generations of males of the two classes had undergone a common educational experience in the Victorian public schools, while the females found charitable organizations an acceptable vehicle for the pursuit of common goals. As a result, the generation of aristocratic patrons who enrolled in the Primrose League in the 1880s and 1890s represented a subtle but perceptible shift away from the traditional Tory peers whose popularity reflected their association with vulgar and violent sports and pastimes, or the bucolic, unintellectual Tory squires. Archetypal Primrose leaders — men like Lord Harris, Lord Desborough, Viscount Curzon or the Earl of Crawford — leaned distinctly to respectability; manly and sporting but chivalrous types, they volunteered in peace and fought in war, rode hard, hunted well and shot expertly, but were also proficient at games such as cricket and even golf.

Increasingly, aristocrats found a ready acceptance in middle-class circles as symbols of respectability and probity. When Cecil Rhodes launched his slightly dubious British South Africa Company in 1889 he chose to dignify the board with a clutch of lordly names including the Duke of Abercorn, Albert (later Earl) Grey and the Duke of Fife.[24] More strikingly, peers began to emerge as figureheads in the municipal sphere. After 1835 the aristocratic owner of urban land and manorial rights had frequently constituted an obstacle to municipal improvers. But by the 1880s this form of conflict had diminished, for the appetite for municipal improvement had been blunted both by sheer achievement and by the pressure of rising rates. What remained was the burgeoning pride and prestige of local politicians, which might be satisfied by recourse to the trappings of municipal dignity — the royal visits, the mayoral chains, maces, aldermanic robes and coats of arms. In this context a peer was regarded as an asset, not an alien. Whereas the Sheffield press buried the 14th Duke of Norfolk with a mere six-line obituary in 1860, his successor was deemed to merit entire pages on his death in 1917.[25] By the 1890s this mood had manifested itself in a penchant for aristocratic mayors.[26] Not surprisingly, Primrose League peers relished the mayoral function, including the Duke of Norfolk (Sheffield and Arundel), the Earl of Dartmouth (West Bromwich), Lord Windsor (Cardiff), Lord Addington (Buckingham), the Earl of Dudley (Dudley), the Marquis of Londonderry (Seaham), Lord Brownlow (Grantham), the Earl of Lonsdale (Whitehaven), Lord Llangattock (Monmouth), Lord Wimborne (Poole), the Earl of Pembroke (Wilton) and the Duke of Marlborough (Woodstock). Nor was this phenomenon entirely confined to Conservatives. Peers sometimes exercised a powerful attraction upon radicals, as the Progressive majority on the London County council showed when they chose Lord Rosebery as the first chairman of the authority in 1889.[27]

However, those titled families who did not wish to be reduced merely to a dignified role in the system found it possible to maintain a foothold in politics by judicious adjustment to the new conditions of the 1880s. Many had always regarded themselves as a ruling class at local rather than national level. Hence they opted for participation in County Councils which in 1889 replaced the old pattern of government through the Quarter Sessions. Finding the county electorate and the smaller seats more congenial than parliamentary contests, many peers assumed the chairmanship of their county councils. A similar sense of continuity and tradition made the Primrose League an attractive form of political activity for such families. Indeed, of the twenty-nine peers whose gross landed income exceeded £75,000 per annum in 1883, sixteen actively supported the league at some stage.[28] For the landed gentry and sons of peers the route into the House of Commons itself became much more difficult after 1885 owing to the combination of franchise and redistribution reform. In that year the Liberals won a majority in the English county seats, while Conservatives took the lead in the English boroughs. Among the existing Tory members in 1885–6 the proportion of men from landed backgrounds as against those from industrial and professional backgrounds stood at 55 per cent and 44 per cent respectively, whereas among the newly elected members in 1885 it was 35 per cent and 61 per cent.[29] This shift in the social balance, however, did not presage a swift demise of the traditional representatives of Conservatism, for the landed element improved its share of the new members in 1886, 1892 and 1895. County gentlemen whose careers had been blighted by the new county voters in 1885 grasped a lifeline presented by the electors of the seaside resorts and suburban and commercial constituencies, which became the new heartlands of Conservatism. Thus Sir Michael Hicks Beach abandoned Gloucestershire for salubrious Bristol West; Walter Long quit Wiltshire for Liverpool and, later, the Strand; George Curzon left Derbyshire for Southport; Lord Warkworth and Sir Matthew White Ridley shifted from Northumberland to South Kensington and Blackpool respectively; and even Lord Randolph Churchill came to rest among the 'lords of suburban villas' in Paddington.

From a middle-class perspective, on the other hand, the political relationship with the upper classes had been strained up to the mid-1880s. Their shift away from Liberalism produced paltry results at first. For example, between 1868 and 1880 the Conservatives increased their poll from 37.5 per cent to 44.3 per cent in the 62 largest constituencies, but gained only two seats.[30] This exacerbated the frustration during 1880–83 among urban Tories who felt that their leaders were too absorbed by their traditional county interests to appreciate the potential support in the towns. However, they derived some satisfaction from the redistribution of constituencies in 1885, for this created many middle-class, single-member seats which, after 1886, fell easily into Conservative hands. As the party's parliamentary base grew broader the composition of the cabinet itself changed. In his short 1885 ministry Salisbury included five middle-class members out of sixteen; in 1886 five out of fifteen; and in 1895 eleven out of nineteen.[31] However, cabinet rank represented a pinnacle of success available only to a handful of men; the alternative was to appease middle-class supporters with honours. Salisbury learnt his lesson from Disraeli's mistakes by paying lip service to the pretensions of the National Union and, more importantly, by distributing knighthoods and peerages more freely. Not only did the rate of creation of peers increase during the 1880s, but the proportion of new peers drawn from the industrial and professional classes exceeded 40 per cent by the end of the century.[32] Before attaining their ennoblement middle-class families accumulated merit by sustaining their local parties, becoming candidates, making donations and subsidising party newspapers. This, of course, was only the political work of what has been called an 'urban squirearchy' of prosperous families keen to play a dignified role in their communities.[33] For the social climbers among them the habitations of the Primrose League provided a serviceable ladder. Among the more prominent examples of such men were: J. Alan Rolls, a wealthy owner of property in south London, who patronized the Monmouthshire habitations and became Baron Llangattock in 1892; Archibald Campbell, the half-millionaire Glasgow ground-rent landlord, who, with his wife, promoted the league in the west of Scotland and was raised to the Barony of Blythswood in 1892; William Armstrong, the Newcastle armaments manufacturer, who was a pillar of the league on Tyneside and received his peerage in 1887; and Ivor Guest, the South Wales ironmaster, who had already obtained a peerage in 1880 and patronized habitations in both Dorset and Wales. Perhaps the most blatant social climbers were Sir Algernon Borthwick, proprietor of the *Morning Post*, and his wife who felt insufficiently rewarded by Salisbury for their contribution to the party.[34] This is why they threw in their lot with Churchill. Lady Borthwick grasped the opportunity to ensconce herself alongside the duchesses by inaugurating the Ladies Grand Council in 1884, while her husband rose to be Chancellor of the league, and was finally ennobled as Lord Glenesk by a reluctant Salisbury in 1895. The process of absorption was underpinned by the marriage of members of each of these families, except Armstrong, into the landed aristocracy.

LOWER-MIDDLE-CLASS ASPIRATION

Of similar importance in the league's scheme of things was the lower middle class, a section of society characterized by an ambiguous and fluctuating social status. Ranging from shopkeepers to clerks, elementary school teachers and commercial travellers, they frequently came from working-class families and enjoyed an income no more and sometimes less than that of the highest paid manual workers. The nature of their work, their residence and their aspirations often cut them off from their roots, but without the resources to employ servants their families frequently maintained only the most tenuous grip on middle-class respectability. Those to whom respectability and social mobility mattered may well have seen the Primrose League as an attractive opportunity, as is suggested by the membership profile of the Cleveland Habitation, where four out of ten members fell into the lower middle class category. Clerks, for example, often aspired to the status of managers and entrepreneurs; but the days when young commercial clerks could launch out independently in, say, the tea trade had largely gone by the 1880s. Upward mobility was attainable by bank clerks but by few others. Most found themselves trapped in routine employment which drew thousands of recruits each year; by 1891 some 450,000 occupied minor commercial jobs, and by 1911 740,000. In these circumstances it was tempting to blame foreign, especially German, clerks for depressing their wages – which contributed to the strident nationalism of this section of society.[35] The majority found themselves tied to an income a little below or a little above £100 a year. For them there remained only the illusion of middle-class status, which was best attained by public association with the institutions and, thus, the values of their social superiors. Hence the prominence of lower middle-class men among the Volunteers.[36] Similarly, the titles and badges of Primrose Knighthood offered a short cut to social mobility. Even this modest expense often put a strain on precarious budgets, with the result that some who originally joined as Knights or Dames subsequently maintained their membership as Associates, thereby keeping a claim to the title without the cost. For example, in one small Gloucestershire habitation 10 Knights out of 56 affiliated as Associates in a single year. 'Villadom is not the easiest class from which to draw subscriptions,' complained the Scottish Branch Secretary.[37]

There are some grounds for seeing small shopkeepers as being in the vanguard of radicalism in the mid-Victorian era, but by the last quarter of the century they had probably ceased to be a natural liberal constituency. After 1867, of course, they lost their numerical significance among the electorate. In addition, they experienced some competition from the expanding co-operative stores and multiples; however, many flourished by catering to a specialist market, or held on to their working-class customers by offering them credit. It has also been suggested that small shopkeepers were politicized by the pressure of rising rates.[38] This could be true of small investors generally since they tended to put their money into small house properties which bore the brunt of expensive municipal improvement.[39] However, it is far from clear whether this was at the root of a drift of shopkeepers to Conservatism in the late Victorian or the Edwardian era. Ratepayers' revolts predated the revival of Conservative fortunes by many years; and their occurrence in the 1850s, for example, suggests that Liberals were just as capable as Tories of responding to the pressure at municipal level. By the 1890s councils had found ways of circumventing the complaints of small property owners.[40] However, such men may well have endorsed the national Conservative appeal in the

1880s that all owners of property, however small, had a common interest in resisting spoliation threatened by radical taxation of the land; once begun the process could be extended to 'the property of the humbler classes...the investments of the shopkeeper, the accumulated proceeds of the business of the merchants, the possessions of the small freeholders'.[41]

Among the members of the Cleveland Habitation shopkeepers were obviously very prominent, but there were few general 'shopkeepers' and food retailers, which is a warning against the assumption that there was a *general* movement to Conservatism; those at the lower end of retailing may have retained their links with the working class and with radicalism. On the other hand, butchers, long considered to be Tory because of their close connections with the farmers, loomed large in the habitation; so too did publicans, doubtless offended by the role of temperance in Liberal politics by this time. The higher-class grocers and more specialist retailers, being socially somewhat isolated from both the middle and working class, doubtless valued the opportunity for greater contact with respectable society available through the Primrose League, charities and clubs. Moreover, they were only too conscious of their dependence upon the favoured custom of well-to-do families who, by the 1880s, were likely to be Conservative; most retailers went out of their way to avoid giving the slightest offence.[42] The value placed upon patronage by the wealthy is under-lined by the experience of the Ladies Grand Gouncil of the Primrose League, which was no sooner formed than beset with requests from producers and retailers for offical recognition.[43] These were refused, but some manufacturers were engaged 'By Special Appointment' to the league, such as W. O. Lewis who produced the jewellery, and the 'Primrose League Tea Company'; in addition several companies sold 'Primrose Soap', 'Beaconsfield Skirts' and 'Beaconsfield Carriage Wraps', apparently with official approval. Even Lord Londonderry advertised 'Londonderry Primrose' Coal at 24/– a ton. Primrose Dames were frequently accused by Liberals of practising exclusive dealing. This is naturally difficult to prove, but the explanation may well lie partly in the common membership of the league and the freemasons. Where a masonic lodge included several grocers, for example, the members were sometimes required to patronize them in strict rotation to the exclusion of non-masonic grocers.[44] Thus the ladies who carried out this instruction as wives of freemasons might well have been assumed to be acting as Dames and Conservatives.

CONSERVATISM AND WORKING-CLASS RESPECTABILITY

To see working-class Conservatism simply as the creed of a 'residuum' or lumpenproletariat in British society would be to miss half of the picture. We have already noted the strength of habitations among communities of skilled and highly paid workers in various districts; for example, among the Cleveland members nearly a fifth rank as artisans. This dimension to Victorian politics has been somewhat obscured by the discussion over an 'aristocracy of labour' in the context of Liberal and Labour politics.[45] Historians who make use of this idea tend to minimize the size and the political role of labour aristocrats despite empirical findings which suggest that they were instrumental in establishing labour organizations and that they dominated ILP membership.[46] Moreover, the whole concept has begun to appear narrow and artificial. This is essentially because the 'labour aristocracy' has been seen in terms of the wage levels of male workers. Yet the position of each family in a working-class community reflected not simply the amount of income but the manner of spending it and of supplementing it, which, of course, owed more to the wife than to the male wage earner. Indeed a far more real, and hence useful, concept is that of *respectability* in the working class.[47] It involves a multitude of behavioural characteristics: the pattern of expenditure, type of shop patronized, type of housing, alcoholic consumption, indebtedness, gambling, religious involvement, membership of friendly societies and trade unions, literacy, type of schooling, electoral status, family size, attitude to pre-marital sex, violence and swearing. Not only do these traits remind us of the subtle variations of status within the working class, they also point to an infinitely larger phenomenon than an aristocracy of 10–15 per cent. By 1900, for example, some 5½ million people had become involved in friendly societies; in this form respectability was thus *typical* of the working class in Britain. Indeed, given the prevalence of respectability it would be surprising if it did not make some contribution to each political tradition. We are familiar with the self-improving Liberal and Socialist working-man, but it requires a greater effort of imagination to understand the Conservative worker as trade unionist, church-goer, co-operative society member, small-property owner and abstainer.

Its heavy reliance upon women tended to make the Primrose League a natural expression of respectability for its working-class members. Habitations drew upon their women for skills in needlework for banners and costumes, and for tableaux, as well as for decorating meeting halls and generally maintaining a decorous atmosphere. Suggestions of rowdiness were usually firmly checked. At Bermondsey the problem was tackled characteristically by the appointment of a twelve-man Primrose Guard under a Sergeant-at Arms.[48] Alcoholic drink provides a sensitive measure of the league's struggle to be respectable yet still convivial. On the one hand Grand Council reprimanded those habitations which were tempted to hold meetings in public houses. Garstang Habitation decided to refuse admission to anyone under the influence of alcohol and to eject from meetings anyone found to be using bad language. On the other hand consumption of alcohol during meetings was clearly permitted provided there was 'no suspicion of insobriety'.[49] The dilemma is well illustrated by the relationship between the Duke of Northumberland and the workingmen's club he patronized in Alnwick. In 1883 the club members voted, in the presence of Earl Percy, to add wines to the beers already available; and in 1891 they introduced 'spiritous liquor' which they justified on the grounds that the existing facilities had not been abused and that 'when a man gets a little up in life, a glass of rum or whisky will not do him the least harm'.[50] Though not enthusiastic about this, neither Percy nor the Duke felt able to use their power to refuse permission.

Up to a point the Primrose League may even be regarded as a part of the Conservative movement for temperance in which the Church of England and the lady activists played the key role. This form of temperance was distinct from that of the radical temperance reformers in two ways. First, it placed the emphasis on individual moderation and dismissed legislation or compulsion; the league's ladies mocked 'Sir Wilfred Lawson and others who think they can make people sober by Act of Parliament'.[51] Characteristically, Lady Londonderry propagated the cause of restraint both at Mothers' Meetings and through the league, arguing that women were themselves vulnerable to temptation and that they might also help to purge male society of the worst effects of drink.[52] Secondly, the league made sure it offered alternatives to alcohol; 'It is often thrown in our teeth that we are a set of tea drinkers' boasted one Dame.[53] Generous provision of solid food with tea and coffee, attractive in itself, also gave the housewives a model to emulate; for the 1880s and 1890s saw a greater variety of food, as well as lower prices, of which working-class families took full advantage.

Late Victorian Conservatives also showed themselves just as aware as Liberals of the virtues of self-help institutions. Housing was a particular favourite. One of the few specific issues raised by Conservative workingmen at National Union conferences was the proposal for state assistance for those who wished to purchase their own homes. Several backbenchers produced bills to enable workingmen to buy the freehold of their homes by means of advances from the rates.[54] However, the favoured response in the 1880s was to rely upon private initiative. In 1885 the *Primrose Record* carried advertisements for the launching of the National Conservative Industrial Dwellings Association, with one million pounds of capital, designed to finance houses which workingmen could acquire by easy payments. More typical was the emphasis on friendly societies; indeed the Primrose League took some trouble to underline how consistently Conservative governments from Pitt onwards had assisted them by legislation. Friendly Society benefits were often an expected part of membership of a trade union or a political organization, as much among Conservatives as among Liberals.[55] Nor is one justified in assuming that such benefits were enormously expensive and thus limited to an elite. For example, the Watford Conservative Workingmen's Sick and Benefit Club was open to anyone with a weekly income of 10/– in the 1880s, which scarcely suggests an exclusive membership.[56] For each 'share' (which cost 3d a week) the member gained entitlement to payments of 5/– a week for 8 weeks and 2/6 for a further 8 weeks in the year, plus £1 to his family as death benefit and a share of the remaining funds at the end of the term. Again, the importance of responsible conduct was underlined by the rule which denied benefits to men prevented from working by drunkenness. In 1886 the Primrose League followed suit with its own Benefit Society. Open to both sexes, the society linked payments to age: 1d a day for those under 30 years, 1½d for 30–39 year olds, and 2d for 40–59 year olds. [57] This scheme offered a 10/– weekly benefit for sickness and an annuity expected to be £30, but computed on the amount standing to the member's credit, when he reached the age of 65; if he died before 65 all credit would be paid to his next of kin. The point is that these practices were not novel; as one Tory delegate reminded the National Union: 'working men in the north country always wanted to see some return for their money, and would therefore more willingly join a benefit club than an association for a purely abstract object.' [58]

Historians have recently begun to place late Victorian popular Conservatism in the context of a wider evolution of working-class society by drawing attention to the decline of the traditional radical workingmen's clubs, especially in London, and the growth of a predominantly conservative culture characterized by amusement, sport and drink, though in comparatively respectable forms. [59] The popularity of music hall is taken as typical of this trend. During the 1870s music hall began to assume a more conventional, traditionalist, patriotic and imperial tone in place of the radical, anti-aristocratic bias of earlier decades. Both the proprietors and the drink trade, who influenced this shift of emphasis, reflected a strong Conservative prejudice. Obviously as a technique the music hall was highly compatible with Primrose League work, and the links are underlined by the involvement of men like Edward Terry, the comedian, who was voted onto Grand Council and became Ruling Councillor of Barnes Habition. [60]

However, others have challenged the view that the stridently imperialist, monarchist and xenophobic material of music hall entertainment was really a reflection of working-class sentiments. [61] This, of course, is to overlook the fact that people attended voluntarily and would scarcely have paid to hear songs they found offensive; while the promoters of popular entertainment may have been Tories, their prime motive was commercial, not political. Moreover, music hall represents only one aspect of the manifold interactions between the leaders of society and the mass of the population. A plethora of organizations, including Sunday schools, the volunteers and rifle clubs, mechanics institutes, music halls and the habitations of the Primrose League, all brought people of different social positions together for the purpose of influencing their behaviour. But whether they succeeded and, if so, who was influenced by whom, is not always clear.

It has rightly been argued that working-class families were not necessarily putty in the hands of their social superiors or incapable of generating their own values and habits. [62] Indeed, there are good grounds for seeing the activities of these organizations as a two-way process in which the behaviour of the higher groups underwent some judicious modification, as did that of the lower. Working-class communities, whose powers as consumers were strengthened in the late Victorian period, clearly took what they wanted from the associations they joined. Trade unions just as much as Conservative organizations were under pressure to act as friendly societies. Again, drink, though its consumption could be restricted by contriving decorous circumstances and by providing alternatives, could not be denied to a population who insisted on it, as both the league and the entertainments industry discovered. Often organizations initiated by the higher social classes tended to pass out of their hands because of their popularity with working-class people — as is suggested by the changing composition of the volunteers on the one hand and by the evolution of the game of football on the other. From 1885 onwards the Primrose League rapidly came to terms with the requirements of a popular membership, even though for some this went against the grain. This one takes to be the implication behind Lady Salisbury's response to the suggestion that the activities were a little beneath ladies and gentlemen: 'Vulgar? Of course it is vulgar, but that is why we have done so well.' [63] Nor should one forget that for those who were accustomed to political activity confined to a tight clique of friends, even a body like the league, with its internal elections and involvement of both women and workingmen in important tasks, represented a considerable compromise. Even the routine work of canvassing, which brought many middle-class Conservatives into direct contact with the problems of the poor for the first time, threatened to undermine the party's approach to social policy in the long run; as one contemporary, with understandable exaggeration, put it, their work was 'educating the Dames into Radicalism'. [64]

Up to a point all the agencies of 'social control' may be regarded as failures, and the Primrose League is no exception. While it certainly helped Conservatives to come to terms with the problem of class it is not at all clear that it led to a solution of the real dilemma. Finding the right balance between popular participation and popular deference, and the best mixture of the social and the political, proved difficult. Inevitably the formula varied from one locality to another. Even the league admitted that in some rural districts there was insufficient emphasis on participation and politics. Attendance by the squire and his lady was calculated to bring out the farmers, the servants and the labourers, but their absence meant a small audience. [65] When a family suddenly sold an estate or let their house to an outsider, or when the wife of the local member died or he retired, a habitation might collapse, deprived of its driving force. This proved a great flaw for habitations whose working-class members had not been advanced beyond sub-wardenships. For example, at Stirling the 'Rock' habitation lapsed in 1910, though it retained a large working-class following, simply because the middle-class leaders had joined a tariff reform association. [66]

Ultimately the league proved only marginally better than the Party at providing a ladder of advancement for workingmen. Its working-class orators like J. H. Pettifer, 'whose name adorns the visitors' book in many a palace and baronial hall', [67] failed to capitalize on their position in the party. As early as 1885 the Chief Whip received an offer from the London Workingmen's Association to contribute financially to the expenses of workingmen who stood as Conservative parliamentary candidates, but although both Salisbury and Northcote pronounced themselves in favour, nothing came of the initiative. [68]

In 1892 a Walthamstow bricklayer embarrassed the National Union by observing that the time had come when 'the Conservative Party should have its Burts and its Broadhursts'. [69] This was a truer remark than he probably knew. The 1890s was a critical decade for the Liberals in that they failed to overcome the reluctance of local caucuses to adopt workingmen, which might easily have deflected the path of a generation of early Labour politicians. Conservatives, meanwhile, hedged: workingmen might not command the votes of their own class let alone those of others; their election would lead inevitably to the payment of members, a reform almost calculated to corrupt; and a workingman would only be effective if he was the representative of a genuine working-class organization rather than an imposition by the party. [70] This condition, however, was not impossible to meet. James Mawdsley of the cotton spinners stood at Oldham in harness with Winston Churchill in 1899; but the experiment was not repeated and the chance to pioneer a Labour-Conservative ticket in the two-member seats slipped away. Eventually the strategy was pre-empted by the Liberal-Labour pact of 1903, and after 1906 the question of candidatures returned to trouble the party once more (see chapter 7).

Ideologically, too, Conservatives marked time, at least in the domestic sphere. To take over as champions of self-help at a time when some Liberals were losing confidence in the idea may have facilitated a broadly based Conservative aliance in the medium term. But even the league perceived that an unduly negative approach to social and economic matters was dangerous. This is why in 1892–3 it deliberately undertook a series of discussions on 'Labour and Social Questions' in working-class habitations, especially in London. [71] Issues like the Eight Hour Day and the 'Relations of Capital to Labour' were not shirked, and some plausible and lively arguments for the status quo were produced at these meetings. But they never concluded with a vote on a specific resolution, and the experiment petered out in 1893 without any conclusion. Thus the Primrose League showed little sign of wanting to lead Conservatives back to the 'Young England' tradition by adopting a reformist line on the poor law or factory legislation; if anything it reinforced their inclination towards the end of the century to retreat into the cul-de-sac of laissez-faire.

7

The Strange Death of Tory England
1901–1914

The years between the Royal Jubilee of 1897 and the early stages of the South African War marked the climax of late Victorian Conservatism; but what appeared, superficially, to be a stable national consensus based on patriotism and imperialism soon showed itself to be a brittle phenomenon. After their victory at the 'Khaki' Election of 1900 the Conservatives slithered towards the Liberal landslide of 1906 divided and demoralized; they had rallied by 1910 only to find themselves checkmated by the Liberal-Labour-Irish alliance. Thereafter the central tenets of Conservatism – the House of Lords, the Union with Ireland, the Anglican Establishment – came under effective attack at last, presenting a dilemma which drove the party into a self-defeating negativism. Finally, the combination of internal division and electoral defeat led to the removal of one leader in 1911 and very nearly a second in 1913. That Edwardian England was *primarily* a crisis for Conservatism has, however, long been obscured by the exhaustive search made by scholars for the origins of the decline of British Liberalism.

Conservative behaviour after 1900 reflected more than merely a nervous reaction to Radical revivalism and a more assertive labour movement, for its capacity to respond to the challenge was greatly complicated and inhibited by its own acute schisms. During Salisbury's reign the need to make fundamental choices in policy had been reduced by successful electoral exploitation of a traditional, defensive brand of Conservatism. But the strategy had gradually ceased to satisfy Conservative realists and intellectuals increasingly alarmed by the military, economic, demographic and educational inferiority of British society. War and failure against the Boers proved to be a catalyst for the cult of 'National Efficiency', and released a wave of frustrated nationalism into politics; as a result, by the Edwardian period Conservatism had fathered its own form of radicalism. Some scholars have characterized this as a 'new right' or a 'radical right', though it had no comprehensive contemporary label. Characteristically, however, Conservative radicals sought to modernize British government and society in various ways; and they identified the party establishment associated with Salisbury — 'Conservative mandarinism' — as an obstacle almost as serious as an effete and unpatriotic Liberalism.[1] Of course the divisions were not always clear cut. A. J. Balfour is often treated by historians as part of the traditional right, which does little justice to his intellectual response to national efficiency or to his reforming record after 1902. Walter Long's cultivated image as the feudal squire tends to obscure his consistent role as an innovator. Lord Curzon, apparently the epitomy of negative, autocratic Conservatism, showed himself, in India, to be a dedicated and ruthless modernizer. The confusion results partly from the existence of antagonism along class lines as well as intellectual. Many, though not all, of the radicals represented middle-class Conservatism and often characterized their opponents as landed-aristocratic drones — an echo of the favourite Liberal line of attack. Up to a point the modifications in the social composition of the party and the advance of the radicals went hand in hand; once the ranks of the squires had been thinned by the 1906 debacle, their places were taken by middle-class Conservatives in 1910 and 1918.[2] Simultaneously the MPs moved sharply towards protectionism and helped destroy the traditional leadership of Balfour in 1911; Bonar Law initiated a run of three bourgeois leaders which lasted until 1940.

However, it must be remembered that the British Conservative establishment never faced a challenge as extreme or as popular as that encountered in Germany at this time. Since they retained well over 40 per cent of the vote there was always a strong pressure to trim to the centre rather than lurch to the periphery. In Britain the institutional vehicles of the radical right never attained the dimensions of the million-strong Navy League in Germany, for example. In fact the British Navy League claimed a mere 15,000 members in 1900, the National Service League 35,000 in 1909, and even the Tariff Reform League, whose exact size is not known, was more intent on an internal takeover of local parties; its attempt to mobilize workers through a trade union organization, for example, produced scant response.[3]

The explanation for this lies partly in the fact that Conservatism already had its patriotic mass movement in the shape of the Primrose League. Even though in serious decline after 1900, it still drew much of popular Conservatism into its web of traditionalism and inertia, thereby sapping the momentum of the radicals. Although the Primrose League and the Tariff Reform League have been described as 'kindred organizations',[4] this is only true in that the war between them was a civil war. Both as rival institutions in the country and as upholders of rival Conservative ideologies they clashed throughout the Edwardian years, to the advantage of tariff reform, which absorbed many activists from the older body.

Thus the Conservatives' difficulties after 1900 reflected both short-term unpopularity and uncertainty about the fundamental departure from Victorian politics which British decline and the rise of Labour seemed to require. The Primrose League, anxious to revive the old formula rather than reorientate its approach to politics, found that it was by no means immune to the controversies over tariffs which deranged the party. Consequently it diminished in size, yet remained too large and valuable an asset to be written off; increasingly it became absorbed into the regular army of Conservatism.

THE CHANGING POLITICAL CLIMATE

The pre-1900 success of Conservatism had been achieved partly by default. A sense of external threat from the aggrandisement of Russia, France and Germany had engendered a closing of the ranks around the values and policies of Conservative governments. Meanwhile their Liberal opponents had been largely forced on to the defensive because they were internally divided, isolated from the national consensus, and because their constructive ideas lacked credibility after the experience of 1892–5. However, by 1900 this pattern was about to disintegrate, for the Liberals were converging on a genuine alternative in the Condition of England question, which they backed up with precise social and financial proposals and an intellectual rationale.[5] By 1900 they were able to work with the grain in addressing themselves to British social problems while the Conservatives were thrown into confusion. Thus the fillip that the Boer War gave to Conservative morale petered out rapidly in the face of intellectual criticism and popular discontent. Even the *Primrose League Gazette* admitted in 1901 that in the working-class districts 'the idea is there, that the war ought to have been over before now'.[6] As in each of Britain's twentieth-century wars, the initial patriotic mood gave way first to impatience and finally to a complete reorientation towards domestic concerns. Fears about urban deterioration were kept alive by the Report of the Committee on Physical Deterioration in 1904 and by Balfour's Unemployed Workmen's Act in 1905. In the closing stages of the war middle-class families complained of inflation and increased taxation, while the working class saw real wages slipping back after a prolonged period of improvement. Suddenly there was no mileage in imperial questions. Indeed, Liberal propagandists seized upon Sir Alfred Milner's untimely use of Chinese indentured labourers in South Africa to parade pig-tailed 'coolies' in the streets during the 1906 election, a graphic portrayal worthy of the Primrose League itself.

With the League deprived of its traditional weapon, the Liberal and Labour forces reintroduced domestic issues to the centre of the stage. However, they would not have succeeded without some co-operation from the Conservative side in the shape of Chamberlain's tariff reform crusade from 1903. The significance of this lies not simply in the obvious effects of tariffs on food prices, but in the fact that it involved Conservatives in a claim to be able to improve the material conditions of the working man both by securing his employment and by financing social reform. Thus Chamberlain's followers were challenging both the narrow free trade argument and the wider visions of the New Liberalism in social reform. It is this willingness of all the political parties to debate the social-economic question that made possible a sea-change in British politics in the early twentieth century. Yet in throwing fuel onto the fire Conservatives were contributing to conditions which they, and the Primrose League in particular, were ill-equipped to handle.

Primrose Leaguers, while not necessarily hostile to social reforms, regarded them as beyond the scope of their political creed. Thus they were even more uncomfortable than the party when faced with the problem of responding to innovations from the government in 1908. Old age pensions, as prepared by Asquith, posed the dilemma most acutely. In place of the traditional application to the Boards of Guardians many old people now became entitled to a pension collected at the post office. This cost its recipient nothing financially or in pride; no taint of pauperism or parliamentary disqualification attached to it. By thus introducing the state as a patently benevolent element into the lives of ordinary people, the pensions scheme directly challenged the Conservative belief in individual philanthropy and personal responsibility. Lady Knightley, a sympathetic if stern paternalist, soon saw the significance of this on her local workhouse visits; she still went to read to the inmates but observed how few elderly people were now present, for 'I daresay the old age pensions are beginning to tell.'[7]

Pensions immediately threw the Conservatives onto the defensive, partly through embarrassment at the unfulfilled promises made by Chamberlain in the 1890s.[8] They felt disinclined to oppose the scheme, both because of its presumed popularity and because, though costly, it appeared to have been carefully budgeted for. But when, owing to unexpectedly high applications for pensions, the cost rose well beyond what had originally been contemplated, the Opposition felt bound to be critical of the government's extravagance, if not of the principle of pensions. This led Conservatives into a somewhat negative and grudging position which lent credibility to Liberal efforts to maximize their advantage from social reform. By 1909 their claim that pensions had been introduced against Conservative wishes was being taken so seriously that one habitation at Slough began distributing leaflets outside post offices in refutation, an initiative that was soon copied by others.[9] Balfour issued a firm denial that his party would abandon pensions if returned to office. On their side some Liberal Agents had taken to issuing invitations to people over seventy to call at their offices for advice and assistance in claiming a pension, while explanatory leaflets had been printed by Liberal Publications Department.[19] While in the short term this might swing some votes, in the long run familiarity with state benefits seemed calculated to destroy the dependent status of the elderly.

Pensions also served as a reminder that domestic servants, a hitherto passive group, might be released from the fear of a penurious old age. A similar perception of the challenge to existing relationships manifested itself in the campaign to protest against the health provisions of the 1911 National Insurance Act on behalf of servants. Led by Primrose stalwarts such as the Dowager Lady Desart this phenomenon had petered out well before the scheme came into operation in July 1912. Here lay the origins of what after the First World War was known as 'the Servant Problem'; though servants continued to be plentiful they began to show less gratitude and more willingness to leave their employers.

Leading Conservatives such as Austen Chamberlain, Walter Long and F. E. Smith felt that the social reforms acquired great popularity after they had been enacted, and considered that their party would not recover the urban vote without a positive policy. However, the only definite initiative in this direction emanated from the Unionist Social Reform Committee set up under Smith in 1911. Its constructive ideas failed to tempt Bonar Law away from his belief that it would be futile to try to outflank Lloyd George on social policy.[11] Similarly the instinctive reaction of the Primrose League, even before the 1909 budget, had been to launch a purely negative anti-socialist campaign. According to the league, socialism meant state dictation in employment, the abolition of private property, state regulation of marriage and children culminating in the extinction of family life, a huge bureaucracy, and the equal treatment of good and bad citizens.[12] Whether, beyond the ranks of the party faithful, this was an effective way of attacking the modest Liberal programme seems doubtful. At most it attracted some donations and stimulated a renewed emphasis on Juvenile Branches as a means of checking the influence of the Socialist Sunday Schools.[13]

Yet the role of social reform and imperialism represented only part of the league's political dilemma, for other central causes, notably the peerage, the monarchy and the Union with Ireland, also posed problems. Laden with peers as Ruling Councillors and Grand Councillors, the league had no alternative but to defend the hereditary principle and justify the Lords' treatment of Liberal legislation.[14] Lloyd George's budget provoked the Chancellor, Lord Desborough, to warn that extra taxation would make it impossible for him to spend money on improving his estates and thus employ as many men as formerly. Though widely used by peers, this argument was a double-edged one for the league, for it suggested a rather grudging interpretation of the obligations of wealth which were central to its ideology. Their lordships' capitulation to the Parliament Bill in 1911 blew a hole in the defensive system on which the league had taken its stand since the 1880s, and left the Church and the Union suddenly vulnerable.

Among the institutional pillars of Conservatism the crown alone stood immune to attack, a symbol of authority, hierarchy and duty. Yet it no longer served the same purpose in politics as it had under Victoria. Unlike his mother, Edward VII thoroughly enjoyed the public pomp and spectacle of monarchy; and since he had not been brought up to take a close interest in policy, he assumed a more modest role in government. As a result his short reign brought the monarchy to its modern non-partisan status. Although the league issued the usual badges for Edward's coronation, neither he nor George V figured in its publications and activities as Victoria had done. Though of Conservative opinions, Edward was thought to dislike protectionism, and he enjoyed good relations with his Liberal ministers, especially Campbell-Bannermann. His view of foreign affairs and the armed forces was largely consistent with the trend of policy pursued under Sir Edward Grey and R. B. Haldane. His son, who was not known to have any political leanings, aroused considerable Conservative apprehension in 1910 for his inexperience and willingness to work with his ministers. Lloyd George had already seized the opportunity to turn the investiture of the Prince of Wales at Caernarvon Castle into a pageant, teaching him a smattering of Welsh and establishing a good rapport with the prince. [15]

However, the real test lay in the king's conduct in the House of Lords controversy. Asquith had already won an election in January 1910 over the peers' rejection of the budget, but, to the dismay of his supporters, he had obtained no undertaking from the king on the wider question of the powers of the upper house. Under pressure, George V reluctantly consented in November 1910 to ennoble sufficient Liberal peers to enact a reform of the House of Lords, but only after a second election. His refusal would have involved Asquith's resignation, Balfour's assumption of office and a general election in which the Crown would have been compromised and dragged into the party debate. However, the December election was fought without public declaration of the royal pledge to create peers, and so most Conservatives chose to believe that the Government's legislation was a bluff. Not until July 1911 were the Opposition leaders forced to accept that the king would take the advice of his ministers if the House of Lords remained obdurate. This came as a bitter blow which a number of Primrose League peers, notably Northumberland, Salisbury, Amherst, Abergavenny, Sutherland, Londesborough and Kinnoull, chose to ignore to the end. Moreover, when the Liberals proceeded to introduce an Irish Home Rule Bill in 1912, similar pressures were brought to bear. The Conservative leadership attempted to persuade the king that as the Constitution was now in suspension he was justified, as its ultimate guardian, in using his veto on the Irish legislation until popular consent had been obtained. [16] This again would have been tantamount to dismissing the prime minister and thus embroiling the Crown in controversy at a subsequent general election. Not only was the royal veto as Asquith put it 'literally as dead as Queen Anne', but so also was the special relationship between Conservatism and the monarchy. By opting to be a figurehead for his people George V had ensured the monarchy's survival in the twentieth century; but the corollary for Conservatism was the loss of another of its institutional pillars.

Ulster alone remained. In 1912 Bonar Law tied the party firmly to Sir Edward Carson in offering unlimited resistance to Home Rule, while the league grasped the opportunity to rejuvenate its strength in the country. The Londonderrys provided the hard core of the resistance to Liberal policy in Ireland. In January 1911 Lady Londonderry accepted the Presidency of the New Ulster Women's Unionist Council, which had enrolled 15,000 members by the end of 1912 drawn from every Ulster constituency.[17] 'We at this time were preparing for Civil War', Lady Castlereagh recalled later[18] – which was literally true in the case of the Primrose League. In 1913 it undertook to be responsible for refugee women and children expected to flee from Ulster in the event of hostilities. Under the auspices of the 'Help The Ulster Women' Committee the league secured promises of accommodation for 8,000 and donations of £17,000 by August 1914.[19]

However, as the ladies also recognized, the Irish were no longer arguing over Home Rule: the issue really turned upon the attitude of British electors. Thus while the Conservative leaders sought to drive the Asquith Government to yet another dissolution, the league and the Ulster Women's Unionist Council threw their efforts into the official party campaign by organizing itinerant lecturers and copious supplies of literature for the mainland. Branches adopted marginal Liberal constituencies in the hope of persuading enough voters to switch before the anticipated general election. Yet while this flurry of activity in the last ditch helped to galvanize both the party and the league in the last years of peace, there is little evidence to show that the Home Rule question was restoring the Conservative position. Indeed, after 1912, the Liberals actually began to improve their by-election performance.[20] As several historians have noticed, a number of Conservative politicians felt that they were failing to pick up support despite their campaign.[21] This is corroborated by both objective and subjective evidence from the league. For example, a mere 300 habitations signed the league's memorial to Carson in 1914 and a similar number were actively co-operating in the Ulster Women's campaign. There was 'far too much apathy in Great Britain' in the words of one activist; and even Lady Londonderry admitted that the English voters 'did not seem to mind' the approach of Home Rule.[22]

APATHY AND DECLINE

By 1911 Conservatives had adopted a mutinous mood which led to Balfour's ejection from the leadership. But a preliminary skirmish was fought over the party's organization, which was under Balfourite control and demoralized by three unsuccessful elections. The combined pressure of Curzon, Salisbury and Derby led to the appointment of the Unionist Organization Committee in February 1911 over the opposition of the Chief Whip, Sir Alexander Acland Hood. The critics mounted a powerful case to suggest how very little the Party's approach to organization had changed since 1880. [23] The Chief Whip could scarcely cope with his own office, the Central Office, the regional offices and party fund-raising. Party agents were still frequently non-professionals. Too often local work remained the responsibility of a lawyer who was the personal agent of the candidate rather than of the Association. If the candidate, whose money largely kept the Association in being, witheld funds for registration until an election was imminent, the whole constituency sank into inactivity during the long stretches between elections. Liverpool was still held up as the model organization, dependent upon a large body of paid-up members who provided a corps of volunteers at all times, but elsewhere membership of the party had little meaning. As a result the party had not responded effectively to the expansion of the electorate by one million between 1900 and 1910, nor to the new danger posed by the Labour Party, whose trade union membership threatened to deprive Conservatives of their traditional hold over a section of the working class. However, the internal controversies over the state of party organization must be taken with a pinch of salt. Conservatives would scarcely have done so well in elections since the 1880s if their attitude to organization had been quite so slack. It is always comforting to blame electoral setbacks on inadequate organization and propaganda rather than on the failures of the party in office. When morale is low and the party divided the organization is bound to look ramshackle. Thus the proposals of the Unionist Organization Committee were of limited value. The Chief Whip's functions were divided between three men including a Party Chairman and a Party Treasurer; Central Office and the National Union were merged; and there were emphatic but general strictures to local associations on the necessity for a permanent organization, regular propaganda and properly trained agents. In practice the defects of the official party organization had to a considerable extent been made good by the volunteers, the registration work and the propaganda of the Primrose League. However, the league too was in decline after 1900. Even if it could be restored, would it be a match for organized Labour? And, since the organization of the party was being rationalized, should it not be incorporated into the formal structure?

Undoubtedly the overwhelming Conservative victories of 1895 and 1900 had induced a certain complacency in Primrose League circles. Yet as a body it suffered certain inherent weaknesses. For example, the peculiar dependence of local habitations on the patronage and initiative of leading families often inhibited their political vigour; rural habitations in particular had been prone to rely upon importing outside speakers rather than raising their own orators through members' debates. [24] Some neglected their political functions in favour of an unchanging routine of social activities,[25] which left them vulnerable to a change in the political climate and to the loss of a key individual in the habitation. By 1902 the league had begun to complain of the 'Apathy of the Leisured Classes'[26] which was often the result of disillusion over a specific issue like tariff reform. In addition, by the Edwardian period many of the original officers were celebrating twenty years of activity by retiring, so that habitations frequently collapsed suddenly as a result of the withdrawal, death or departure of a key individual. By 1906 criticism was openly voiced of the 'quasi-aristocratic type (of habitation) which organizes two or three entertainments during the year, but makes no further effort to keep in touch with the working classes, of whose sentiments and wishes we are in consequence profoundly ignorant'. As a result the Edwardian elections brought a new crop of reports about league members who were thought to have voted Liberal.[27]

As early as 1895 critics at Grand Habitation business sessions had pointed out that the published membership figures tended to exaggerate the league's real strength; the 2,200 habitations in that year included 400 not listed in the current Roll.[28] Grand Council had usually protested that it would be an unduly expensive task to ascertain each year the precise condition of every habitation; however in 1901 they were sufficiently concerned to institute systematic visits by provincial agents which unearthed some depressing evidence. In Devon 11 of 42 habitations were described as 'inert', in Cornwall 7 of 26, in Somerset 13 of 35 and in Dorset 13 of 31; Lancashire habitations were ranked as: live 49, dormant 30 and dead 13.[29]

As a result of this attrition at the grass roots the league sometimes failed to provide effective assistance to the party in by-elections in the early 1900s. A notable humiliation occurred at Brighton in 1905 where the seat was defended by Gerald Loder MP, who happened to be current Chancellor of the League, on his appointment as a Junior Lord of the Treasury. The local Dames were reported to be apathetic and Loder lost the election.[30] Elsewhere, as at Barkston Ash, also in 1905, a hitherto safe seat was lost after the Conservative organization firmly declined to involve the Dames in the canvass.[31] Following the debacle at the general election in 1906 a Committee on Reoganization under the duke of Norfolk reported that as many as 115 English and Welsh constituencies had been without active habitations.[32]

Internal investigations in the Edwardian period provide, most unusually for a political organization, a picture of both its official and actual strength. For example, the official list of 2,645 habitations compares with a live total of 950 in 1914. Enrolment of members had topped two million by 1910, but Grand Council's sober estimate of current membership for 1912 showed a more modest, though still impressive, figure (see table 7).[33]

These figures are significant in that they suggest a formidable organized base for Conservatism even in a period of electoral failure and internal division. Moreover, the Conservative revival seems to have been genuine in that some

90,000 additional members were recruited in the next full year, and by the spring of 1914 a membership of 800,000 was reported to Grand Habitation. [34]

Table 7   1912 Membership figures

England and Wales habitations	495,463
Scottish habitations	22,500
Irish habitations	1,500
Juvenile branches	65,000
Estimate for habitations alive but lacking details	67,000
Total	656,269

On the other hand this revival was doubtless largely a matter of recouping lapsed members rather than winning new territory in working-class areas. 'The last election has taught us that Labour Members have come to stay,' remarked Lord Penrhyn in the aftermath of 1906. [35] Critics within the league identified a failure to involve workingmen sufficiently as the key weakness. Some suggested that more workingmen should be placed on habitation executives and represented at Grand Habitation; too often habitations were said to be in the hands of people 'whose names may be imposing in their districts, but who are not in touch with the great bulk of electors'. [36] Soon the idea of working-class Conservative candidates received an airing, as it had in the National Union a generation before. Correspondents wrote in to urge that J. H. Pettifer, the league's leading stump orator, should be adopted for Parliament. When invited to respond by the editor of the *Primrose League Gazette* Pettifer flatly rejected the notion on the grounds that the party would never run a working man for a winnable seat if he could not pay his expenses, support himself as an MP and contribute to funds: 'And I don't blame them either.' [37] Pettifer's attitude reflected traditional thinking on the subject, but the whole discussion suggested a loss of confidence in deference and class unity as the natural bedrock of conservatism on which the league's position was founded.

RIVAL VISIONS OF IMPERIALISM

While struggling with internal decay the league also suffered derangement arising out of controversies external to its organization. The growing tension over women's suffrage has already been mentioned in this connection (see chapter 3). However, tariff reform, which also ultimately involved the women, proved a far more deeply disruptive question. The origins of the movement for tariff reform lay in the deteriorating competitiveness of some sections of manufacturing industry since the early 1880s, which had rejuvenated the old agricultural protectionism, generated a new pressure group in the Fair Trade League, and attracted considerable sympathy at the annual conferences of the National Union. Colonel Howard Vincent, MP for Sheffield Central and a persistent advocate of protectionism, campaigned throughout the Conservative Party; but his attempts in the 1880s to urge Grand Council towards tariffs were firmly rebuffed. [38] Thereafter protectionism did not disturb the league's affairs until 1902, when the imposition of a 1/– duty on corn imports by the Chancellor of the Exchequer sparked off a debate on a preferential tariff for the colonies.

Initially, the league's leaders dismissed the issue as though dealing with a trivial or peripheral dispute: 'The Primrose League has nothing to do whatever with the policy of the Unionist Party. Free Trade and Protectionism are questions quite outside our province.' [39] But the issue refused to subside and after Joseph Chamberlain's dramatic resignation from office in 1903, Vincent warned Grand Council with some reason that habitations would want a definite lead; Lord Jersey persuaded them to wait for the Government to announce its policy. In a speech to the Knights Imperial Balfour promised an enquiry into fiscal matters which Grand Council gratefully grasped as a means of fending off the enquiries pouring into head office. However, while the league continued to say that it had 'no desire in any way to dictate to Habitations in the matter', it suggested that it would commit itself to the policy adopted by the Cabinet. This in itself marked an abandonment of its original position. [49]

As the split in the Conservative Party developed, some leaguers, especially the free traders, attempted to cast the league in the role of healer of the party's wounds, on the grounds that its principles were the ones on which all Conservatives could unite; the league and its causes would endure where 'other organizations working for ephemeral objects fall to pieces'. [41] This, however, was to overlook the fact that for several years nothing stirred Conservative activists so deeply as the tariff question; the Chamberlainites felt that their ideas were fundamental and wide-ranging, and provided the party with something fresh and precise in place of the 'roundabout, indefinite and ill-defined' opinions typical of the league's Conservatism. [42] Consequently even the league's official neutrality was belied by acute disagreements at the top. Apart from Vincent, Grand Council included some active tariff reformers such as Viscount Ridley (Chairman of the Tariff Reform League from 1905), Lord Ancaster, Lord Willoughby d'Eresby, the Earl of Radnor and Sir Robert Gresley; even Pettifer's speeches to habitations assumed a distinctly protectionist tone. At the local level many workers seemed to be channelling their efforts into Chamberlain's campaign. Clapham Habitation's members were reported to be angered by their Member's free trade opinions, and Peckham had to be warned against affiliating to the Tariff Reform League.[43] In Croydon, when the free trader C. T. Ritchie was pushed out of his seat, the large habitations seem to have given him no effective support against the much smaller protectionist organization.[44] In April 1908 Grand Habitation approved, with only one dissentient, a resolution endorsing the policy of retaliation laid down by Balfour at Birmingham, and in the same year Sir Robert Gresley became Chancellor of the league.[45]

In spite of this trend the league inevitably appeared something of a refuge for the free traders, who were reduced to a minority within the official party. In 1905 Lord Londonderry, a major coal owner, had blamed Chamberlain for splitting the Party in a speech which led to open hostility between Balfour and Chamberlain for the first time.[46] Londonderry and Jersey, who had long been involved with the league, were suddenly joined in 1909 by the Earl of Derby representing Lancashire and Cheshire on Grand Council. As late as 1913 a number of free trade MPs or ex-MPs retained their place on the Council, including W. F. D. Smith, Sir John Stirling Maxwell, Colonel M. F. Bowles, Gibson Bowles, Ian Malcolm, A. Rollit, G. Kemp, Hayes Fisher, W. Joynson-Hicks and Sir Edgar Vincent. On the subject of Lord Hugh Cecil, MP for Greenwich until 1906, the *Primrose League Gazette* had declared: 'For such a man to be hounded out of Parliament would be a scandal.'[47]

Thus, despite its protestations, the Primrose League enjoyed no immunity from tariff controversy. Tariff reform in fact represented a two-fold challenge to the league, partly ideological and partly organizational. Critics frequently adopted a dismissive view of protection as something which 'appeals solely to the business instincts of the nation'.[48] However, while some supporters of the tariff saw little further than a narrow protectionist argument, this did no justice to the full Chamberlainite vision, which included social reform and improvement at home and an Imperial Federation in the wider world. This latter point was grudgingly recognized by league critics who protested that they had 'the interests of the Empire at heart as he has'.[49] Essentially two different conceptions of empire had co-existed since the days of Disraeli. The league reflected the more sentimental, idealistic and intellectually passive approach. Like Disraeli, it gave little thought to what precisely the empire should become in the future; it was enough that it existed as a testing-ground for generations of English gentlemen. In the aftermath of the Boer War this seemed limp and even dangerous in view of the need for a coherent defence strategy for the empire. Many tariff reformers viewed the colonies in a hard-headed way, as a potential British Zollverein; for them, colonial preference would be a first step towards the exclusion of foreign imports, produced by cheap labour, and thus greater domestic employment. 'Why not make use of the Customs House Officials to act as your pickets against the foreign blacklegs?' as Chamberlain put it.[59] The league's staid patriotism was easily outflanked by this slightly zenophobic populism.

Yet were the protectionists not confusing means and aims? As Londonderry recognized, many of the tariff *enragés* regarded protectionism as Liberals regarded free trade, as a matter of morality rather than as a mere expedient of policy. For a true Conservative – which Chamberlain, of course, was not – tariffs, while justifiable and perhaps necessary in certain circumstances, could never attain the status of a creed or a principle. Tariffs were incidental to Conservatism, where Church and Monarchy remained fundamental.[51] After December 1910 this view did tend to reassert itself in the Party; for it now appeared that the pursuit of tariffs had led Conservatives to something much worse than three electoral failures; by throwing away the defensive weapon of the Lords' veto they had placed other institutions like the Church Establishment and Irish Union in jeopardy.[52]

Consequently the combination of traditionalism and realism proved too much for the protectionists after 1910, and the party retreated from the full Chamberlainite programme. Balfour had already given a pledge not to introduce duties on food without a referendum. His successor, Bonar Law, who was an uncomplicated protectionist, miscalculated by renouncing this pledge in 1912, only to provoke an outcry from the depleted but still lively free trade ranks. He preserved his leadership and a pretence of party unity by agreeing to surrender food duties altogether.[53] Thus in the last years before the war the primacy of the traditional Conservatism espoused by the league was reasserted. In the long run, though the party did not cease to be protectionist, the constructive imperialism associated with Chamberlain had been decisively checked, as became clear in the 1920s.

THE PARTY TAKEOVER

However, while the tariff issue was later overshadowed by Ulster, the impact of the protectionists upon the *organization* proved to be much more durable. Within eighteen months of its formation the Tariff Reform League boasted 235 branches, a figure which is not fully indicative of its strength. Its activists were capable of operating within the existing Conservative Associations and Primrose League habitations, where they drew off many of the politically motivated, leaving their rivals, already at a low ebb, seriously emasculated. With its presidential-style tours and mass rallies for Chamberlain, the TRL created a dramatic impression in the country. It echoed the pageantry and symbolism of the Primrose League while offering a hierarchy of participation including 'Vice-Presidents' at half a guinea, 'Members' at 1/– and 'Associates' at 1d.[54]

Ominously for the league, the Women's Committee turned itself into a Women's Committee of the Tariff Reform League in February 1904 and began to establish branches in the constituencies. This inaugurated a period of confusion and in-fighting within local Conservatism which lasted much longer than the debate among the parliamentarians. Inevitably the Primrose League lost ground, partly because the TRL enjoyed a more coherent and well-defined programme which appealed to the political activists, and partly because it had a more positive attitude to the party. Whereas the league valued a degree of independence, the tariff reformers consciously aimed at a takeover of the party at each level; to them the league represented the grass roots expression of the Conservative establishment which they sought to undermine at Westminster. Crucially the TRL outmanoeuvred the league through its women's organization. In 1906 its Women's Association amalgamated with the Women's Liberal Unionists to form the Women's Unionist and Tariff Reform Association under the Chairmanship of Mrs Maxse. From 1909, when the existing Women's Unionist Associations joined, the organization was known as the Women's Amalgamated Unionist and Tariff Reform Association. In 1911 representatives of both the National Union and the Liberal Unionist Council were appointed. [55] Thus although by the First World War women were still not constitutionally part of the Conservative organization, they held a recognized position in it for the first time.

All this carried dire implications for the Primrose League in that it was deprived of its functions as the women's arm of Conservatism. Those who had argued after 1900 that the league had become superfluous could now claim that the duplication of organizations was actually harmful; the league's inability to check the drift from Conservatism in 1903–6 justified merging it into the party structure. [56] For its part the league contended that habitations grew inactive 'mostly in places where the Conservative authorities are practically opposed to the PL', [57] a problem which was only exacerbated as the protectionists grew more influential. Thus a competition between the two organizations became inevitable. By 1904 a number of provincial agents confirmed that ladies calling themselves Women's Unionist Associations were drawing off their members initially in Scotland, and subsequently in Surrey, the Midlands, Lancashire and Yorkshire. [58] Grand Council clearly found it difficult to check the drift in the constituencies. Wargrave (Berkshire) Habitation disbanded in 1907 and were warned against handing over their funds to the TRL. Aberdeen remained nominally operative while its leaders worked for the WUTRA, while Dollar Habitation simply wound itself up and re-formed as a WUA. Stockport had its warrant withdrawn in 1911 for similar reasons. In addition there were cases of WUAs such as that at Coventry which turned themselves into Habitations. [59]

As early as 1901 attempts had been made, notably in the West Country, to create closer co-operation between the league and the party, though without noticeable result. Informal meetings between the league and the WUTRA in 1907 led to plans for joint canvassing, meetings and literature. In 1910 an attempt was made to delineate the territory to be covered by the rival organizations and, since this proved impossible, in 1912 it was agreed that neither would form new branches in districts where the other already existed without prior consultation.[60] However, local WUAs sometimes claimed to be ignorant of these national discussions, and the Scottish Branch of the League engaged in continuous disputes over poaching at Stirling, Dumfriess, Galashiels, Vale of Leven, East Kilpatrick, St Andrews, Lockerbie, Melrose and Dublane;[61] these, of course, were simply the cases which attracted attention. The difficultry lay in the fact that there was not much territory to which the league could not lay claim; the distinction between an inactive habitation and a wholly defunct one was not always clear, and if the warrant had not been withdrawn the league regarded a habitation as capable of revival.

Another form of duplication appeared in the 'Unionist Social Council', formed by some Chamberlainite ladies in 1910. It not only included leading Dames such as Lady Blythswood and Mrs Bischoffsheim, but also proposed to organize social gatherings, ostensibly to counter the work of the Liberal Social Council. However, this latter body was itself conceived as a way of imitating one aspect of the league's activity, and the new institution provided another harbinger of the absorption of the league into the party.[62]

However the major turning-point came with a qualitative change in the league's leadership during 1911–12. Lord Northcote, who had succeeded Desborough as Chancellor in April 1911, died in September and was replaced in November by Lord Curzon. Hitherto the league had always drawn upon second-rank figures in both Lords and Commons who, at best, held minor government office. Curzon was the first major politician, whose star was still rising, to serve in this capacity. At the same time Balfour, who had now lost three elections and failed to appease either free traders or protectionists, resigned as party leader and subsequently as Grand Master. Thus a personal struggle for the succession was imposed upon the ideological in-fighting. With the party evenly divided between Austen Chamberlain and Walter Long, Bonar Law emerged as a compromise candidate. But for the first time the party leader did not become Grand Master, the post going to Curzon. Long stepped into his place as Chancellor for two years before giving way to the Earl of Crawford, the former Chief Whip, in 1914. It may be that Law seemed too committed a tariff reformer to be generally acceptable to the league. Certainly he was ill-fitted both by status and personality for the Grand Mastership, whereas Curzon, a natural grand panjandrum, was doubtless flattered to play the part. However, the significance of the concatenation of Curzon, Long and Crawford is really their position at the centre of the Conservative Party. Long, in particular, as the figurehead of the anti-Chamberlainite wing, must have been aware of the desirability of restoring the balance in the party which had tipped so far towards the tariff reformers. The league's strength provided a potential counter-weight, but it had first to be manoeuvred into a closer relationship with the official machine.

In October 1912 the league accepted an invitation from the National Union to send five official representatives to its Annual Conference, and set up a new joint committee with the WUTRA.[63] Long, meanwhile, issued a series of memoranda calling for reform of the league. Although this led to an enlargement of Grand Council designed to give greater representation to the habitations, reform was really a euphemism for integration with the party. 'In future,' warned Long, 'the league must work in co-operation with our Unionist organizations throughout the country if it is to retain the power and influence which it held in the old days.' Grand Habitation in 1913 was invited to ratify an addition to the original declaration signed by all Primrose League members: 'and, further, in the firm belief that the Unionist Party are the defenders of these principles, I declare that I will loyally support the Unionist cause.'[64] In explanation Long offered the bland assurance that the league's principles were upheld by the Unionists alone. This had been perfectly apparent for many years, but had not been considered ground for abandoning the informal association of the league with the party in favour of a binding pledge. However, in the circumstances of 1913, when partisan emotions were reaching an unusual level owing to the Ulster crisis, the proposal passed with little public dissent. The private misgivings were vindicated a few years later when a new stage in the process of absorption was precipitated by the war.

8

The Rise of Modern Conservatism
1914–1935

However disruptive in organizational terms, the Great War rapidly proved to be spiritually reassuring for British Conservatives. To the Primrose League in particular it brought a final reassertion of the chivalric spirit so recently aroused during the South African War. As ever, the leaders led: Gerald Arbuthnot, the Vice-Chancellor, joined the Royal Naval Reserve in 1914, and Lord Crawford, the Chancellor, served in the Royal Army Medical Corps from 1915; among members of the Imperial Chapter the casualty rate stood at 36 per cent.[1] New badges were soon instituted to designate members on active service and those rendering patriotic service at home.[2] In common with many other voluntary organizations the league rapidly turned its branches over to charitable work in support of the war effort. Primroses went on sale in aid of the Red Cross, and habitations were permitted to donate up to two-thirds of their funds to war charities. At one penny each, Primrose League War Relief Stamps raised money for the Prince of Wales Fund, while a Needlework Committee was established to supply the Red Cross, the Belgian Relief Fund, Queen Mary's Needlework Guild, and the appeals by Lord Kitchener and Lady Jellicoe for warm clothing for men in the army and navy. Habitations used their expertise to arrange entertainments for the wives of the troops, and in 1915 the Juvenile Branches began to adopt British prisoners-of-war to whom they sent parcels of food and clothing.[3]

However, in spite of this flurry of patriotic activity, habitations also received strict instructions to keep their routine work going.[4] Of the 924 active habitations at the outbreak of war only 97 decided to go into abeyance, though many others undoubtedly functioned rather sporadically.[5] Despite a natural reluctance by Knights and Dames to make their usual payments, the sums collected as tribute during the war fell by only a few hundred pounds each year. Moreover, secretaries were advised to 'keep all our members together in view of the obscurity of the political outlook'.[6] This, of course, was a euphemistic way of reminding them that a general election was still expected in 1915. In fact the Conservatives, in common with their opponents, made strenuous efforts to ensure that the registration of voters was completed as usual in the closing months of 1914, and that the paid agents were retained as far as possible until the campaign had been fought. [7] Conveniently, the agents could be passed off as patriotic war-workers through their role in local recruiting activities.

Yet the Primrose League enjoyed a peculiar advantage in this respect. While party political propaganda was officially suspended in deference to the party truce, patriotic work for the war effort continued unhindered. In practice the difference between the two was difficult to discern. By November 1914 a new set of sixty lantern slides on the war had appeared, backed up by patriotic concerts and lectures on the reasons for Britain's entry into the war. During the summer of 1915 members used their skills to operate the Government's scheme for National Registration which required a door-to-door canvass; and in the autumn the Derby Scheme, designed to encourage men to attest their willingness to serve in the forces, also required house-to-house deliveries. [8] Yet when the Conservatives joined Asquith in a Coalition Government in May 1915 the league studiously ignored the fact; indeed, it would be difficult to establish, from the pages of the *Primrose League Gazette*, that a coalition existed at all. Meanwhile, Ladies Grand Council showed no compunction about holding meetings at which speakers like Arnold White delivered sustained attacks upon Liberal Ministers like Richard Haldane under the guise of a 'patriotic speech'. [9]

Up to a point the league simply benefitted from the war situation in the same way as the Conservative Party itself; untroubled by doubts about British participation in war, they could afford to be vociferously anti-German and critical of failures in the official war effort. But whereas the party was obliged to limit both its criticism and the nature of its activity during wartime, the league enjoyed virtually as wide a scope for its work as in peace – for it could plausibly claim that the kind of patriotic propaganda in which it routinely dealt was simply a part of the war effort; those who criticized it only cast doubt upon their own patriotism. In this way war had a profound effect in enabling Conservatives to keep alive their central political ideals, and indeed to restore their badly battered morale. The labour movement derived a similar advantage, though in a different way, in that it vigorously pursued its central concern – defending the conditions of the working classes – during the years when normal party political activity remained in suspension. [10] Significantly, the Liberals alone had no such outlet, morally or organizationally, during the Great War; hence the steady disintegration of their party throughout the country between 1914 and 1918.

As a result, the fresh challenge presented in 1918 by a general election fought in chaotic circumstances and with a vastly enlarged electorate, represented a far less daunting prospect for the Conservatives than for their rivals. However traumatic the experience of war had been, it left the Conservatives' sense of themselves as the national party intact. Organizationally, moreover, they had managed to preserve far more of their pre-1914 machine than the Liberals or Labour. After the 'coupon' election even Conservative candidates who admitted to having had little official organization testified to the effectiveness of Primrose League workers.[11] For the thousands of women who had served their political apprenticeship in the league the moment had now come when they could throw their full weight behind Conservatism along with no fewer than eight million others of their sex. They were to be an essential component in the new Conservatism in the inter-war period.

ORGANIZING THE NEW DEMOCRACY

Conservative participation in the wartime Coalition Governments greatly facilitated the enactment of a sweeping measure of parliamentary reform in 1918, which, had it been passed before 1914, would have been regarded as a triumph for the Liberals. The old complicated rules for the qualification and registration of voters were largely superseded by a simple residential qualification for men and a system operated by the Town Clerks and Clerks to the County Councils. The traditionally generous scope for plural voting was drastically curtailed such that each elector might use only one additional vote. Women who were themselves, or were married to, local government electors might also vote at the age of thirty. In the first new register in 1918 this produced a parliamentary electorate of over twenty-one million among whom there were only 159,000 business voters and 68,000 university voters against a pre-war plural vote of over half a million. Since the party had resisted rather similar proposals under Asquith's pre-war governments, it is not surprising that initial Conservative reactions to the proposed reforms were a mixture of apprehension and hostility; some alleged that the Liberal members of the Speaker's Conference, in which the scheme originated, had simply hoodwinked their less expert Conservative colleagues.[12] Rank and file reactions emerge from the letters sent in to the National Union by Constituency Associations, Chairmen and Agents, of which only thirty-two favoured legislation compared with 259 who opposed the idea and eighty-three who opposed it during wartime.[13] Both the current Party Chairman, Sir George Younger, and his predecessor, Sir Arthur Steel-Maitland, weighed in against a reform bill. However, the critics were checked by the insistence of a formidable group of leading Conservatives – Walter Long, Bonar Law, Austen Chamberlain and A. J. Balfour – on pushing ahead with legislation; and were mollified by a series of concessions when the bill came under detailed scrutiny in the Commons.[14]

As a result the Conservative Party faced an electorate three times as large as the pre-war one, including an influx of young voters hitherto largely excluded by the householder qualification; 40 per cent of the electors were now women; and two-thirds of the constituencies had a working-class majority of 80 per cent or more. [15] In the conditions of Edwardian politics such changes might well have been disastrous for the Conservatives. Although the Liberals were now demoralized and split, Labour contested a majority of seats from 1918 onwards and was assumed to be deriving great advantages from the doubling of trade union membership from four million in 1914 to eight million by 1920. This situation made the organization of Conservative support a priority from 1917 onwards. While it would be an exaggeration to suggest that the party turned itself into a thoroughly democratic body, it certainly moved in that direction; whole sections of the population such as women now had to be taken seriously by the official party machine. Inevitably these developments exacerbated the latent competition between the party organization and the Primrose League, the latter's decline being hastened by the assumption that it duplicated the work of the party in the inter-war years. It is important to distinguish the ideology of the league, which seemed stale by 1918, from its organizational function; as a political machine its decline was not a reflection of its obsolescence but a sign that it was now too valuable to be left outside the official party structure. In several respects, therefore, the party simply adopted the practice, as well as the personnel of the Primrose League. For example, a mass membership now seemed a necessary object if the Conservatives were to be on an equal footing with the mass battalions of the trade unions. Therefore the party tried to move towards a common, and mandatory membership fee during the 1920s. [16] A fee of 1/– was widely adopted, though some associations preferred 2/6. At least these sums were low enough to be widely acceptable to supporters of modest means, and the party began to reduce its dependence upon the subscriptions of a handful of Vice-Presidents in each constituency. Of course, large donations were still sought, but wealthy patrons could no longer expect to control constituency parties without cultivating a large body of paid members.

However, the multiplicity of Conservative organizations during the inter-war years detracted somewhat from the professional machine that emerged. As early as 1917 the National Union of Conservative Associations had begun to discuss amalgamation with the Women's Unionist and Tariff Reform Association. By April 1918 it had decided that, as a general principle, women ought to enjoy a third of the places in the party's representative bodies both at the centre and in the constituencies. At this point the WUTRA headquarters was transferred to Central Office and given three representatives on the National Union's Executive. [17] The National Union had aready set up a women's staff and begun to plan for the creation of women's branches throughout the country. Sir George Younger suggested to the Primrose League that its habitations should be represented on the local Conservative Associations and enjoy six representatives on the Council of the National Union.[18] League reactions to this were ambivalent. On the one hand a joint conference of Ladies Grand Council and the General Purposes Committee supported representation for habitations in proportion to their membership. Grand Council asked for twelve rather than six League delegates to the NU Council, in addition to three on the Executive – requests which were granted. Yet Grand Council also urged habitations to 'exercise discretion' as to whether and how to associate with local Conservative Associations, and insisted on the league maintaining its own 'identity and personality'.[19] Meanwhile, from the grass roots came the suggestion that the formal commitment to the party adopted in 1911 should be dropped so that the league might again become a 'non-party organization, pledged only to support its own principles'. Perhaps surprisingly, this idea was adopted in 1919, a decision which the National Union characterized as 'in effect a repudiation of its alliance with the Unionist Party'.[20] However, the league protested that the declaration in no way altered its attitude to the party, but allowed a 'wider scope for its educational activities'. Although the league retained representation on the National Union, attempts to re-establish habitations were generally rebuffed by the party agents thereafter.[21] Regardless of these decisions at national level, however, it is clear that by 1918 many habitations were disbanding with the intention of reforming as branches of the Women's Unionist Association; at Halifax, for example, the Ruling Councillor pointed out that as almost all the members were now women, it seemed logical to join the WUA.[22]

The only argument against this process of absorption lay in the league's claim to be able to maximize the field of recruitment so as to draw in the non-Conservatives and the non-political voters who were likely to elude the official machine. In view of the lack of comprehensive figures for party membership it is difficult to assess the validity of this claim. Examples of local party membership suggest a sharp increase to two or three thousand per constituency during the 1920s. However, this seems to have been concentrated almost wholly in middle-class areas.[23] Meanwhile, industrial and working-class seats in which the Primrose League had formerly mobilized substantial support often lost a paid Conservative membership, so that by 1930 the party had no genuinely local organization in at least a tenth of the constituencies.[24] This was tackled centrally by financing professional agents to ensure that derelict seats could at least fight elections. It does, therefore, seem unlikely that the associations picked up all the rank and file of the old habitations. This is particularly true during the 1918–22 period when disgruntlement with the Coalition made many local Conservatives unco-operative about organization; the pressure of three general elections during 1922–4 stimulated them once again. In Rutland, for example, the leaders of the habitation ceased to pay their tributes in 1919 owing to the creation of a WUA branch, thus leaving behind 3,000 rank and file leaguers as the old organization collapsed.[25] On the other hand, in Plymouth Sutton the league continued to flourish much as before under the inspiration of Lady Astor. With some 3,000 members largely drawn from the working class, the habitation helped to extend the influence of Conservatism throughout the community and thereby to hold a working-class seat.[26] Yet the example of Plymouth really underlines the cross-party appeal of Nancy Astor herself rather than that of the Primrose League. No longer a novelty, it was too widely regarded as an ultra-Tory organization for its missionary role to be plausible.

In addition there are grounds for thinking that the league had grown rather antiquated in methods and style by 1918. One habitation secretary criticized the 'disorganized charity by means of free teas, dances, parties and concerts', while another considered the badges and paraphernalia had become 'ridiculous'.[27] Such critics wanted to drop the non-political membership in order to concentrate on the politically motivated supporters. But although the league continued to lay great emphasis on such activities as dances and whist drives in the post-war period, it found itself eclipsed in the business of entertainment by commercial developments. Its tradition of lantern slides and musical entertainment had been rendered obsolete by the vast expansion of the cinema. Their first experience of the cinema had made a great impression upon British families during the Edwardian period: 'reckon us winna think o't'magic lantern after this do', was one Lancashire reaction.[28] A similar point should be made in connection with the Conservative party's own approach to propaganda after the war. It adopted the professional advertising agents, S. H. Benson, and produced its own films and mobile cinema vans. Since by 1919 the league was already spending well in excess of its income, it could not consider competing with the much better endowed party organization in such areas.

In many respects the movement of women activists was the key factor in stimulating membership, organization and financial improvement in post-war Conservatism. Yet it may be thought that the role extended to them in the party was a mere formality. At constituency level the men often found it difficult to adjust to the female presence, even though there was a separate women's organization which at first was frequently presided over by the wife of the MP or Chairman. The National Society of Conservative Agents refused to admit women members. The Junior Imperial League remained adamantly male, especially under Lord Stanley's chairmanship during the 1920s. And the direct female impact in Parliament was slight; only 1.5 per cent of Conservative candidates during 1918–31 were women, while only one woman gained election in 1922, three in 1923, 1924 and 1929, and thirteen in 1931.[29] However, this is not explicable solely in terms of the hostility of male selection committees; nor should the historian fall into the trap of denigrating the women themselves for lack of feminism. After all, we have already noted that women activists who had been Dames found the prospect of participation in the party attractive: it must have seemed a step forward to them, however modest. Those who were interested in enfranchisement and political questions were clearly tired of the Primrose League and welcomed the seriousness with which the party was prepared to treat them; by 1928 the women's department at conservative Central Office employed a staff of twenty-nine.[30] An avenue of professional advancement now opened up as some ninety-nine women organizers received training during the 1924–37 period. Miss Irene Ward, to take one example, spent four years as secretary to a WUA in Newcastle after the war, and then became parliamentary candidate for the hopeless seat of Morpeth before going on to become an MP.[31] Ironically, those who quickly became prominent as Conservative MPs, such as Lady Astor and the Duchess of Atholl, had not been suffragist campaigners before the war; they owed their advance to family position – as of course did many of their male colleagues.

Moreover, as the tide of Coalitionism ebbed, the local associations ignored their women at their peril. Though there was less need for the meticulous registration work in which the Dames had once excelled, the swollen electorate presented formidable problems; it had to be thoroughly canvassed, especially as the turnout at elections remained relatively low. As the emphasis switched from public meetings to quiet canvassing so it tended to facilitate the role of women. Women also contributed to the financial side of constituency work. The traditional reliance upon wealthy candidates to finance campaigns, registration and charities came under attack after the war, particularly from Stanley Baldwin, who argued that the practice restricted the choice of Conservative candidates to a tiny minority. Associations were therefore urged to raise their own expenses, which they did partly by collecting large numbers of small subscriptions and partly by fund-rasing events. The Dames' experience of social events, originally subsidized by the wealthy, was easily adapted to the new conditions; thus dances, bazaars, fetes and whist drives could be made to serve the dual purpose of rasing funds and maintaining contact and morale. By the 1930s between a quarter and a third of the constituencies are thought to have been entirely self-supporting.[32]

However, while fund raising for the benefit of their male colleagues, the women were also very much absorbed in building up their own organization. For example, in the twenty-eight constituencies in Devon, Cornwall, Somerset and Bristol they had recruited 76,000 members by 1927.[33] They ran their own conferences at which they debated temperance, education and questions affecting women and children generally. As a result the question of social reform began to be much more widely discussed in the Conservative Party than before the war, when it had been the preserve of arcane groups like the Unionist Social Reform Committee. For tactical reasons such subjects were presented not as feminist but as *family* matters to which male Conservatives could not easily take objection.

Plate 6 Juveniles of the Primrose League at Reeth, Swaledale, c. 1924

The post-1918 period also saw a greater interest by the Conservative party in youth, both because it had become much easier for young men and, after 1928, young women to qualify as voters, and because they were felt to be particularly susceptible to socialist propaganda. Socialist Sunday Schools had long antagonized the Primrose League, and the formation of the National Young Labour League in 1920 which, according to Lady Jersey, was going to teach 'camouflaged communism' to children, worried them even more.[34] In addition there were several offshoots of the Boy Scout movement during and after the war, led by those who wished to replace the emphasis on military activities with a romantic, pacifist, internationalist spirit; hence arose the Order of Woodcraft Chivalry (1916), the Kibbo Kift Kindred (1920) and the Woodcraft Folk (1925). All of these remained fairly small bodies and were never promoted by the labour movement;[35] yet they were taken very seriously on the right of politics.

The result was a further proliferation of organizations for youth. In so far as the party had a youth organization it dated to 1906, when the Junior Imperial and Constitutional League had been formed. By 1911 this body claimed 70,000 members in 280 branches, though it is not clear how young they were.[36] Perhaps because the JIL remained all male, a new organization was created in 1926 called the Young Britons, which by 1929 enjoyed a membership of 49,000 and 471 branches.[37] Within the Primrose League itself there had been a Juvenile Branch for under-16-year-olds since the 1890s (see chapter 2). By 1913 it had 65,000 members, and after the war the League, faced with a decline of its adult organization, seems to have laid greater emphasis on this aspect of its work. There was a Junior Imperial Chapter designed to cater for public school boys in the 16–18 age group, though this appears to have been subsumed under the Beaconsfield Branch later on.[38] In 1924 the Ladies Grand Council initiated the Young Conservative Union in order to enlist young men and women for 'social service as well as for political assistance' in the constituencies. This soon became too large for the LGC to manage and was affiliated to Conservative Central Office in 1928.[39] The activities available to the juveniles included athletics, competitions for singing, essays and public speaking, fancy dress, parties, dances, plays, patriotic songs, handicrafts and vegetable growing. 'Why is Great Britain the finest country in the world?' was the subject for the 1935 speech and essay competitions. Above all, the organizers seems to have believed in the moral and political virtues of sporting activity. As the Chancellor, W. Greaves-Lord, put it:

Both we and the Socialists realise that youth organizations cannot be successful without sport. It teaches some of the lessons of life. The most important thing in life is never to be above your job. If you take part in a cricket or football match you will not be asked which position in the field you would prefer. The thing is to do your little job well.[40]

RETREAT FROM EMPIRE

Of course, the purpose of organizational adaptation lay in winning elections; and electoral victories were supposed to ensure the survival of Conservative traditions. Yet the inter-war period found Conservative leaders engaged in a painful but relentless readjustment of their most cherished principles.

The capacity of the British for extricating themselves from empire with comparatively little trauma is a central, yet neglected, theme of modern history; it is best understood through the evolution of attitudes in that party which, up to 1900, had been most blatantly committed to the imperial cause. Conservatives retreated from empire under a barrage of protest from, among others, Primrose League supporters who, understandably, experienced the strain acutely; but while the protest bit hard in the 1920s, it had become almost a ritual by the 1930s − a sign that the transition had been accomplished without irretrievable damage to party unity.

In the aftermath of victory in 1918, when the British Empire attained its maximum territorial extent, many Conservatives understandably hoped to recreate the world as it was before armageddon. But to cling to the principles of the 1880s suggested a certain intellectual poverty. Religion had ceased to be an issue. Monarchy was scarcely in danger. Only a little mileage was to be derived from the defence of private property, appeals for volunteers during major strikes, or attacks upon Bolshevik and anarchist inspired sabotage.[41] Slipping back into the old routine the Primrose League produced a new slide lecture on 'Russia Under the Bolsheviks', and the *Gazette* ran a regular column on 'What the Reds are Doing'. In short, Bolsheviks replaced the Irish in Primrose demonology. According to the Earl of Pembroke and the Duke of Northumberland, Ireland had become a centre of conspiracies, hatched in Moscow, to initiate revolution in Britain and even murder the King. By 1924 revolutionaries had insinuated themselves into Ramsay MacDonald's cabinet, claimed the duke.[42]

Perhaps this excitable rhetoric reflected an appreciation that there were really no subversives in the Labour leadership; the real enemy lay within the Conservative citael in the shape of the unflappable Stanley Baldwin and his allies. Indeed, even before Baldwin took over the leadership, a decisive step had already been taken under the Lloyd George Coalition by the agreement of December 1921 which ushered in the Irish Free State. Since 1914 the Conservative leaders had privately accepted that the south of Ireland could no longer be denied self-government; the essential object was to save Ulster from subjection to Dublin. Beyond this it was a matter of saving face by preventing a total secession of the Irish from the Empire. The severity of British policy in Ireland during the war had obscured the wobbling at the top of the Party. After 1918 hard-liners like F. E. Smith, whose career had been grounded in the militant Orangeism of Merseyside, were prepared to make Ireland a self-governing dominion paying at least nominal allegiance to the crown.[43] As a result Lloyd George employed his Conservative colleagues to bear the brunt of Conservative resistance to his policy both in the provincial party organizations and at the crucial annual conference in November 1921, held in – of all places – Liverpool.[44] During 1921 the Primrose League received complaints and resignations over the cabinet's willingness to negotiate with Sinn Fein, and in the House of Lords prominent leaguers – the Duke of Northumberland, Lords Londonderry and Dufferin – attacked government policy. Throughout 1922 the critics condemned the failure to protect the lives of 'loyal British subjects' and charged that the Government had, 'by its dealings with rebels itself become treasonable'.[45] However, while the debate helped to weaken Conservative support for the Coalition, it exposed the difficulties of rank and file criticism in the face of a determined leadership; the dukes and marquises had become slightly peripheral to the centres of power in the Conservative party.

Defeat over Ireland was undoubtedly an emotional turning-point for Conservatives: it even meant changing their name. Significantly, the league continued to refer to the 'Unionist Party' during the 1920s, while Lady Londonderry lectured on 'The Meaning of Unionism' in spite of the fact that the original idea had 'gone beyond recall'.[46] Moreover, as the pessimists had always predicted, Ireland was not the end but the beginning of imperial disintegration. The Conservatives, observed Sir Samuel Hoare in 1930, were 'terrified of a repetition of the Irish negotiations' in the context of India.[47]

Rank and file opinion found it hard to accept their leaders' post-1918 strategy for empire. Essentially this was founded on the assumption that major party controversies over imperial questions invariably led to serious setbacks for British power. However, the labour movement had shown itself very patriotic, and in office its leaders had few ideas about empire, being chiefly absorbed by the cause of international peace. It was therefore feasible to pursue a bi-partisan approach on Empire so as to preserve continuity and moderate change.[48] However, the uncomfortable corollary of this thinking was that Conservatives must abstain from seeking electoral advantage in imperial issues as blatantly as they had done in the past. This adjustment was an essential characteristic of the Baldwin era; but it is only one aspect of the party's gradual abandonment of its role as defender of the British Empire.

Empire had always comprised three somewhat distinct elements: the white colonies, India and the less developed territories. This did not necessarily make for inconsistency of policy, but it did tend to divide and dissipate the imperial enthusiasts in Britain. During the 1920s, for example, the most constructive Conservative imperialist was L. S. Amery, whom Baldwin sent to the Colonial Office in 1924. In a way Amery's approach reflected the Imperial Federation philosophy associated with Joseph Chamberlain and

Lord Milner. In the aftermath of war it seemed to him obvious that Britain's economic survival depended upon her willingness to exploit the resources of the Empire in order to match the superior strength of the United States. Given the economic problems which plagued Britain in the inter-war period, a bold programme of colonial economic development and emigration might well have become a central part of the Conservative appeal. Yet what is striking is how little support existed for such an emphasis either in cabinet, among the Dominion governments, or even among the British public at large. Baldwin himself remained far more interested in strictly domestic affairs than in colonial or international, while many of his ministerial colleagues, notably Churchill, begrudged the financial support which an Amery strategy really required. To them his ideas seemed almost faddist; they recalled the discredited Chamberlainite obsession with tariffs before 1914 and the more recent disaster of the 1923 general election. Imperial development became so peripheral to Conservatism by the end of the decade that Sir Oswald Mosley was able to grab the idea in the early 1930s. In addition, the annexation of 'Empire Free Trade' by Beaverbrook and Rothermere in 1929 compounded the suspicion that the issue was essentially a weapon with which to belabour the party leadership.

Nor should one forget that the response from Dominion Prime Ministers continued to be as tepid in the inter-war years as it had been since the 1880s. Though willing enough to participate in Imperial Conferences in 1921, 1923 and 1926, they were chiefly concerned to establish their constitutional independence; hence their separate representation at the League of Nations, and their reluctance to be involved in the international conflicts of the British Government such as that with Turkey in 1922. In 1931 the Statue of Westminster satisfied them by giving a formal guarantee of their autonomy and equal status. They were content to remain under the British Crown and within the Empire provided that this involved no obligations for them in defence or in economic policy. None of the white dominions wished to restrict their own infant manufacturing industries in order to become a perpetual market for British exports.

It has, however, been suggested that among the British people imperial sentiment ran just as deeply after the Great War as before.[49] The agencies of imperialism – advertising, the press, schools, literature and exhibitions – flourished undiminished; and while the Edwardian generation, reared on the creed of Empire, had attained adulthood, another was growing up under similar influences. This, however, is to overlook the underlying flaws in the imperial ethos. We have already noticed the inability of popular imperialism to crystallize around precise policies for empire; and during the inter-war years the great imperial crises and triumphs which would have facilitated the mobilization of imperial sentiment failed to materialise. Even in the Edwardian period politics had already begun to re-orientate itself around questions of economic management, standards of living and social policy; no one, except discredited figures like Winston Churchill, was prepared to restore the old politics, because the rise of Labour seemed to make domestic affairs absolutely central in the party struggle. Although the protracted unemployment and economic depression between the wars might have appeared to increase not diminish the significance of Empire, in fact the economic rationale steadily faded. India, for example, had doubled her cotton textile production during the war, and against a rising tide of nationalism it seemed inconceivable that Britain should try to reverse such developments for the benefit of her own exporters. During the inter-war years India not only moved towards self-sufficiency in the capital goods industries, she also began to export more to Britain than she imported after 1931. British control over India's tariff policy and the exchange rate was surrendered. [50] In addition, the Indian Civil Service ceased to offer an attractive career after 1918. To some extent this was met by a shift of emphasis to African territories. But it is conspicuous that Amery's 1928 Empire Settlement Act largely failed to stimulate significant emigration. Indeed, though the absolute level of annual emigration – 130,000 in the 1920s – may look high, it should be compared with an average rate of 300,000 in the Edwardian period and 250,000 in the 1890s. By the 1930s emigrants were actually returning to Britain, and during the decade immigration exceeded emigration. The popular will to turn territories like Keyna or Rhodesia into major centres of British population simply did not exist. Of course, empire still aroused affection and interest; but the spirit behind it was increasingly defensive and passive.

The popular response to imperial questions must have been somewhat inhibited by the absence of a clear lead from the political parties, particularly the Conservatives, who were, in fact, bitterly divided, not simply between supporters and opponents of self-government in Asia, but between the enthusiastic imperialists themselves. 'One would have thought that if there was one cause in the world which the Conservative Party would have rushed to defend, it would be the cause of the British Empire in India,' complained Churchill in 1931. [51] Yet Churchill himself suffered a good deal of criticism over India from other keen imperialists such as Amery who dismissed him as 'fundamentally opposed to all ideas of Empire development and Empire preference . . . entirely lacking in constructive thought and imagination in the economic field'. [52] Amery, of course, felt aggrieved at Churchill's parsimony as Chancellor of the Exchequer during 1924–9, but he had a point. Churchill and his Indian supporters had nothing to contribute to the empire of Beaverbrook and Amery. To them empire was India; and India was seen in romantic, sentimental terms as a glorious field of endeavour for patriotic Englishmen; the measurable, material benefits were secondary. In so far as Churchill thought about the economics of empire he still subscribed to the traditional free trade philosophy – precisely what the constructive imperialists most deplored. In J. C. C. Davidson's words, Churchill 'believes the Tory Party is still in the 1890s where he left it'.[53]

Consequently the Conservatives were not *one* party where Empire was concerned, but three. Churchill's best supporters over India were elderly men reliving the Irish experience. To them the Montagu Declaration of 1917 and the Montagu-Chelmsford reforms represented liberal appeasement of the kind that had helped Ireland down the slippery slope. After 1924, it is true, they were reassured a little by the unsympathetic attitude adopted by Lord Birkenhead, the Secretary of State, towards Indian nationalism. But Birkenhead did nothing to undo the policy of Indian participation in government. Indeed, reform by now had a momentum of its own in that the British hoped that by judiciously expanding the Indian electorate they would expose the inability of Congress to win popular support. In addition, the Montagu-Chelmsford reforms were subject to review within ten years, a provision which Baldwin anticipated by appointing the Simon Commission in 1928. Thus the prospect of a further round of reform helped to arouse a new phase of agitation in India in 1929 as Congress under Gandhi threatened civil disobedience unless self-government were conceded within the year.

The India rebels also failed to dislodge the bi-partisan approach pursued by Baldwin and MacDonald in the 1920s and 1930s; the latter helped the Conservative leader by choosing Labour representatives of very cautious views to sit on the Simon Commission. Even when Labour regained office in 1929 the Viceroy found the new Secretary of State, Wedgwood Benn, perfectly congenial; indeed, it was Lord Irwin, who had been Baldwin's choice as Viceroy in 1926, who dictated the pace in this period. Irwin was so dismayed at the prospect of civil disobedience that he sought to regain the initiative by means of a declaration promising Dominion Status in October 1929. In order to achieve maximum effect in India this promise required all-party support in Britain. This Baldwin gave promptly and without consultation, thereby provoking a sustained revolt led by Churchill, who had left the shadow cabinet after the election of 1929 in order to be free to speak out on Indian matters. Baldwin was fortunate, however, in that MacDonald avoided exploiting his difficulties in the party, and attention was temporarily diverted by the campaign for Empire Free Trade. By the spring of 1931 Irwin recovered the initiative and brought civil disobedience to an end by means of personal negotiations and a pact with Gandhi, an action which the critics regarded as comparable with Lloyd George's dealings with the Irish in 1921.

Having survived the challenges of 1929–31 Baldwin then entered upon the calmer waters of the National Government. Although ostensibly an expedient for tackling the economic crisis, the National Government was used to further the bi-partisan line on India. The backbench opponents of official policy, such as the Indian Empire Society and the India Defence Committee, never involved more than 50 MPs, and raised, at best 80–90 votes in the division lobbies.

Amid the 554 supporters of the National Government their protests could be weathered if not ignored. Moreover, the diehards were misled for a time by the repressive tactics of the new Viceroy, Lord Willingdon, who reversed Irwin's conciliatory line quite sharply after 1932.[54] Yet in London the cabinet committee of Baldwin, MacDonald, Irwin and Sir Samuel Hoare, steadily pushed forward with their plans for further reform. Thus it was not until April 1933, when a White Paper on India was published, that the revolt surfaced again. For a time it seemed as though Churchill might successfully appeal to rank and file Conservatives over the heads of their leaders. In February 1933 the Council of the National Union upheld government policy by only 189–165, while the party conference at Bristol in 1934 did so by just 543–520. However, the party managers fought back, and secured a favourable vote of 3–1 at the National Union Council meeting in December 1934. Central Office did its best to discredit Churchill by pointing to his past record and his opportunism.[55] It was helped by the Labour by-election gains and the advance of the British Union of Fascists during 1933–4, both of which underlined the dangers of bringing down the national Government at this juncture. By bringing a general election forward to 1935 the cabinet helped to enforce a closing of the ranks upon disgruntled Conservatives, fearful of a return to Labour government.

The success of Baldwin and Hoare over the 1935 Government of India Act is explicable in the light of the behaviour of the Primrose League which, since it remained committed to the maintenance of Empire, suffered acutely during this period. Its leaders shifted uneasily between loyalty and rebellion. Despite the formal resolutions of confidence in the Grand Master − Baldwin − Grand Council left habitations free to express their views on India, at least during 1933.[56] Moreover, the Chancellorship fell into the hands of staunch opponents of Baldwin on several occasions, notably in 1928–9 (Sir Henry Page-Croft MP), and in 1931–2 (Douglas Hacking). As Member for a Lancashire constituency Hacking used his prominence in the league to attack the Indian boycott of British cotton goods.[57] However, by 1933 Grand Council was prepared to acquiesce in provincial self-government for India provided that British control was not surrendered at the centre.[58] In order to counter the criticism in the league the party managers deployed the persausive talents of R. A. Butler, then Indian Under-Secretary, and the prestige of the young Marquis of Dufferin, a former Under-Secretary for India and grandson of a Viceroy, who became Chancellor in 1933–4. The habit of loyalty helped the critics to swallow Baldwin's claim that the government was carrying out the traditional Disraelian policy towards Empire, by which was meant a closer trading relationship with the colonies. Lavish praise was heaped upon the Grand Master for his 'devotion to the cause of Empire and his determination to achieve the economic unity of Empire'.[59] Of course, the actual achievements of this policy were slight, and its Disraelian pedigree was highly dubious;

nor did it really apply to India. Yet by invoking Disraeli Baldwin managed to create some sense of continuity where little really existed. If he failed to share his party's emotional response to Ireland and India, he understood it enough to know that he had to divert its attention towards the white colonies and to the notion of a 'Commonwealth'. Thus he carefully made what he could out of patriotic sentiment by substituting his subdued but sincere celebration of England and the English for the brasher imperial rhetoric that had traditionally characterized his party.

THE DISRAELIAN LEGEND

Empire was only the most conspicuous of the pillars of Victorian Conservatism which crumbled or lost their relevance between the wars. For the House of Lords, for example, a much more muted rearguard action was fought, though with the same result. Since the 1911 Parliament Act Conservatives had professed to regard the constitutional arrangements as strictly provisional; and, in deference to the party, Bonar Law had promised that the parliamentary reform of 1918 would be followed by a measure to re-organize the upper chamber and restore its authority.[60] Deputations and committees dogged the footsteps of his successors throughout the inter-war period, but were always fobbed off with vague and unfulfilled promises.[61] Baldwin himself symbolized the fact that the Conservatives had become primarily a House of Commons party almost as much as their rivals.

Neither left nor right saw any significant political advantage to be won from the House of Lords question, and even less from the other great Conservative cause – the monarchy. In a party sense the monarchists eventually became the victims of their own success, for, as the Labour Party acquired power during the 1920s, there could be no mistaking its loyalty to the Crown as an institution and to George V in particular.[62] Like the Liberals, Labour included a few critics, but the routing of a republican resolution by 10-1 at the 1923 party conference underlines how peripheral such ideas were in the labour movement. This is attributable both to the enthusiasm of the British working class for the royal family, and to the perception of Labour's leaders that in the British system monarchy had become a useful anachronism. King George V's handling of the constitutional crisis of 1910 had reassured the left about the efficacy of parliamentary elections as the best means of changing British society; and the king's friendly relations with his Labour ministers in 1924 and 1929 reinforced this impression. By working within the system radicals could use the weight of the monarch to legitimize their own reforms in the face of Conservative resistance.

However, if the monarchy had truly become a matter of consensus in Britain, it followed that the role of its champions had also become redundant. Thus the significance of the Crown for Conservatism had undergone a change by the 1930s. As official Conservatism surrendered its bolder, brasher tone in favour of Baldwinism, so it exposed itself to rivalry from its right flank. It was plausible to suggest that the staid mandarins of the party and the Primrose League had failed to save Conservative governments from the debilitating influence of international Jewry – a favourite theme of papers like the *Morning Post* and disgruntled peers like the Duke of Northumberland. [63] Yet organizations such as the Imperial Fascist League, led by Arnold Leese from 1928 onwards, remained very small and peripheral. It was not until 1932 that the emergence of Sir Oswald Mosley's British Union of Fascists seriously threatened to outflank the older Conservative bodies. Though ostensibly confronting the left, the BUF competed with the right for support. [64] The fears, for instance, of Conservative MPs about loss of young patriots to Mosley in the early 1930s is corroborated by the urgent requests made by Primrose League habitations for guidance on the whole subject of fascism. [65] For some years local activists had been arguing that Conservatives ought to have their own 'Punching Brigade' to counter the hooliganism of socialists at elections, [66] a need which the BUF seemed more than capable of satisfying. That fascism failed to capitalize fully on its potential in Britain has partly to do with the light impact of the depression on the middle classes, the economic improvement from 1934, and its alienation from respectable Conservative opinion. But more fundamentally fascism could never exploit the longing for a great personality in Britain as it did in Europe because the void had been filled by a highly popular monarchy. By the time of George V's Silver Jubilee in 1936 the Crown had come to occupy its modern role in the system as a huge and absorbent sponge soaking up much of the popular emotion which might otherwise have found its way into partisan politics.

Any sense of loss which Conservatives might have felt during the inter-war years was mitigated both by their hold on government and by a positive shift of emphasis which led them to look inwards to the social and economic condition of Britain. In a way this represented a delayed reaction to the experience of the Edwardian period and, more immediately, to the rise of Labour; whereas before 1914 the leaders had not listened to the warnings of Conservative social reformers that the party would never recover its working-class support unless it addressed itself to the social condition of urban Britain, they now required little encouragement. The chief battleground of politics was the economy. Both the influx of women, interested in social reform, and the drastic turnover in membership of the parliamentary party at the elections of 1918 and 1931 facilitated this shift of emphasis. During the 1920s, it is true, a negative economic liberalism became prominent largely as a reaction to wartime taxation, bureaucratic controls and labour militancy. Yet even in this decade Neville Chamberlain restored the Conservatives' credentials as social reformers by his legislation at the Ministry of Health. A younger generation of MPs including Anthony Eden, Harold Macmillan, Oliver Stanley, John Loder, R. S. Hudson and Robert Boothby, many of them influenced by feelings of responsibility towards the workingmen with whom they had fought during the war, appealed to Tory tradition in a way that Chamberlain could not. For them the party was returning to the social paternalism and collectivism which Disraeli had campaigned for in his day. No doubt the Keynesian view of the economy which Macmillan espoused during the thirties would have been as alien to Disraeli as the supertax to Mr Gladstone, but the social thinking behind it could be represented as entirely consistent with his own. In his *Constructive Conservatism* (1924) Noel Skelton MP had urged his party to adjust to the new democracy by allowing the mass of the people an economic status to match their political role – a formulation not unlike that adopted by advocates of the New Liberalism a generation earlier.[67] As for the Liberals, so for the Conservatives, a sense of continuity of principle helped to mitigate a change of policy. 'A good Tory', as R. A. Butler put it, 'has never been in history afraid of the use of the state.'[68] By thus invoking Disraeli to justify domestic policies the younger Conservatives merely echoed Baldwin's own use of his name to sanction his imperial strategy. However dubious as history the tactic served to smooth the Tory transition from the heroic era of Lord Salisbury to the subdued condition in which Britain found herself after 1945.

Notes

For details of primary sources and unpublished works, see list of sources. All printed works are published in the United Kingdom unless otherwise stated.

INTRODUCTION

1 M. Duverger, *Political Parties* (1954); Sigmund Neumann, *Modern Political Parties* (1956).
2 *Primrose League Gazette*, 10/6/93, p. 5.
3 Quoted in *PLG*, 1/11/97.
4 M. Ostrogorski, *Democracy and the Organisation of Political Parties* (1902); Janet Robb, *The Primrose League 1883–1906* (New York, 1942); H. J. Hanham, *Elections and Party Management* (1959); J. P. Cornford, 'The Transformation of Conservatism in the Late Nineteenth Century', *Victorian Studies*, 7, (1963); J. A. Garrard, 'Parties, Members and Voters after 1867: a Local Study', *Historical Journal*, 20 (1977); Patrick Joyce, *Work, Society and Politics* (1980); Robert Stewart, *The Foundation of the Conservative Party 1830–67* (1978); John Ramsden, *The Age of Balfour and Baldwin 1902–40* (1978).
5 Norman Gash, 'Flower of Conservatism', *Daily Telegraph*, 26/4/83.
6 R. E. Dowse, *Left in the Centre* (1966), p. 9.
7 Brian Harrison, *Separate Spheres* (1978), p. 241.

CHAPTER 1 THE CONSERVATIVE DILEMMA

1 Lord Bath to Lord Salisbury, 5/12/85, Salisbury Papers, quoted in Spencer Hogg, 'Landed Society and the Conservative Party in the Late Nineteenth and Early Twentieth Centuries', Oxford B. Litt thesis, 1972, p. 156.
2 Lord Ronaldshay, *The Life of Lord Curzon* (1928), vol. I, p. 100.
3 Hogg, 'Landed Society', p. 158.
4 See discussion in R. E. Quinault, 'Lord Randolph Churchill and Tory Democracy 1880–85', *Historical Journal*, 22 (1979).
5 Robert Stewart, *The Foundation of the Conservative Party 1830–67* (1978), pp. 132–3. I follow Stewart for this and the following paragraph.
6 NUCCA Conference Minutes, 25/10/79.
7 Stanley Salvidge, *Salvidge of Liverpool* (1934), p. 15–16, 21–22.
8 Keighley Conservative Association Minutes, 25/4/85.

9 J. Ramsden, 'The Organization of the Conservative and Unionist Party in Britain 1910–30', Oxford D.Phil. thesis, 1974, p. 161.
10 R. T. McKenzie, *British Political Parties* (1955).
11 NUCCA Conference Minutes, 23/7/80.
12 Ibid., 13/12/92.
13 Ibid., 14/12/92; 1/10/03, 28/10/04.
14 Ibid., 26/10/86; resolutions were carried in 1887, 1889, 1891, 1894, 1907, 1908, and 1910.
15 Ibid., 26/10/86; 14/12/92.
16 R. F. Foster, *Lord Randolph Churchill* (1981), p. 75.
17 Ibid., p. 115.
18 Ibid., p. 126.
19 W. S. Churchill, *Lord Randolph Churchill* (1905), pp. 202–3.
20 J. A. Pitman, *Lord Beaconsfield K. G.: as a Writer from a Political Point of View* (1895), p. 11.
21 Ralph Nevill (ed.), *The Reminiscences of Lady Dorothy Nevill* (1906), pp. 284–7.
22 Grand Council Minutes, 15/12/83, including 'A Short History of the Formation of the Primrose League – corrected and revised by the Founders'.
23 Hon. Claude Hay, 'The First Days of the Primrose League', *Primrose League Gazette*, 24/12/87.
24 Lady Lucy Hicks-Beach, 12/9/85, correspondence of the Coln Valley Habitation (Gloucestershire CRO D1070/VIII/7).
25 Thomas Wright, *The Life of Colonel Fred Burnaby* (1908), pp. 209–11.
26 Sir Henry Drummond Wolff, *Rambling Recollections* (1908), vol. II, p. 270.
27 Wolff to Churchill, 13/1/84, Lord Randolph Churchill papers 2/255; Salisbury to Churchill, 23/12/83, Lord Randolph Churchill papers, 2/230B.
28 Salisbury to Earl Percy, (copy) 12/3/84, Lord Randolph Churchill papers, 2/315.
29 In 1884 a National Conservative League was founded, catering to workingmen, organized in lodges and using similar terminology to the Primrose League; however, it existed in only a few counties; see Janet Robb, *The Primrose League 1883–1906* (1942), pp. 147–8.
30 *PLG*, 1/5/01, p. 9.
31 M. Pinto-Duschinsky, *British Political Finance 1830–1980* (1981), p. 36.
32 *PLG*, 28/1/93, pp. 1–2.
33 Sir Alfred Slade to Churchill, 20/3/89, Lord Randolph Churchill papers, 23/3070.
34 *PLG*, 1/11/00; 1/9/08.

CHAPTER 2   THE POLITICS OF SOCIAL INTEGRATION

1 *Primrose League Gazette*, 26/11/87, quoting from the *Illustrated London News*, 19/11/87.
2 J. A. Pitman, *Lord Beaconsfield K. G.: as a writer from a political point of view* (1895), p. 11.
3 Ralph Nevill (ed.), *Life and Letters of Lady Dorothy Nevill* (n.d., New York), p. 161.
4 *PLG*, 1/2/01, p. 5.
5 Robert Blake, *Disraeli* (1966), p. 752; Pitman, Beaconsfield, p. 8.
6 *The Primrose League: its rise, progress and constitution* by one of the staff (1887), p. 2.
7 Mark Girouard, *The Return to Camelot: Chivalry and the English Gentleman* (1981).
8 Ibid., p. 103.
9 J. Riley-Smith, *The Knights of St. John In Jerusalem and Cyprus 1050–1310* (1967), pp. 230, 238–9, 245.
10 Scottish Branch Minutes, 15/10/86.
11 Helen E. Mathers, 'Sheffield Municipal Politics 1893–1926', Sheffield University Ph.D. thesis, 1980, p. 99.

12 *PLG*, 1/3/07, p. 7.
13 Grand Council Minutes, 25/4/85.
14 Scottish Branch Minutes, 16/3/86.
15 Grand Council Minutes, 15/3/84.
16 Grand Council Minutes, 22/3/84.
17 *PLG*, 24/12/87.
18 Grand Council Minutes, 25/4/85.
19 Duchess of Sutherland to Sir A. Borthwick, 4/2/84, Lord Randolph Churchill papers 2/291.
20 Salisbury to Churchill, 23/12/83, Lord Randolph Churchill papers 2/230B.
21 Sir Henry Drummond Wolff, *Rambling Recollections* (1908), vol. II, p. 270.
22 Sir Alfred Slade to the Duke of Norfolk, 17/1/87, Norfolk papers C767.
23 *PLG*, 1/5/95, pp. 6–7.
24 Whitehaven Executive Council Minutes, 8/4/92; Soweby Executive Council Minutes, 19/4/88.
25 *PLG*, 5/5/92, 1/5/95.
26 See John Garrard, 'Parties, Members and Voters After 1867', *Historical Journal*, 20 (1977); Patrick Joyce, *Work, Society and Politics* (1980) and 'The Factory Politics of Lancashire in the Later Nineteenth Century', *Historical Journal*, 18 (1975).
27 Garstang Habitation Council Minutes, 13/2/97.
28 *PLG*, 14/1/88.
29 G. Stedman Jones, *Languages of Class: studies in English Working Class History 1832–1982* (1983), pp. 205–7.
30 *PLG*, 31/5/90.
31 Ibid., 1/3/01.
32 David Rubinstein, 'Cycling in the 1890's', *Victorian Studies*, 21 (1977), p. 63.
33 *Newcastle Daily Chronicle*, 2/9/95.
34 Report from *Yorkshire Post*, 19/8/95, in Londonderry papers, 547.
35 *PLG*, 1/6/96, p. 8.
36 Primrose League Cycling Corps *Rules* (n.d.); *PLG*, 1/11/98.
37 T. H. S. Escott, *Social Transformations of the Victorian Age* (1897), pp. 69–70.
38 See the discussions in P. Bailey, *Leisure and Class in Victorian England* (1978); J. Walvin, *Leisure and Society* (1978); H. Cunningham, *Leisure in the Industrial Revolution* (1980).
39 John K. Walton, *The Blackpool Landlady* (1978), pp. 32–4.
40 *PLG*, 1/7/96.
41 Ibid., 21/7/88.
42 See correspondence for Melbury Habitation, letter book, Dorset CRO, D124, Box 343.
43 *PLG*, 17/5/90.
44 Ibid., 7/6/90; 24/5/90.
45 See, for example, Lowther Habitation correspondence, R. H. Bailey to Mrs F. Parker, 10/3/88.
46 St. Albans Divisional Council Minutes, 20/8/91, Herts CRO, D/EvZ7.
47 *PLG*, 28/1/86.
48 Ibid., 1/9/06, p. 11.
49 John Ramsden, 'The Organization of the Conservative and Unionist Party in Britain 1910–30', Oxford D.Phil. thesis, 1974, p. 350.
50 M. Pinto-Duschinsky, *British Political Finance 1830–1980* (1981), p. 26.
51 *Instructions to Habitations* (1892).
52 *PLG*, 12/12/91, pp. 8–9.
53 H. W. Wightwick and H. W. Wollaston (eds), *Parker's Election Agent and Returning Officer* (1884, 1959 edn), pp. 123, 240–1.
54 Ibid., pp. 116–17; see also the difficulty of the candidate's position in Arthur Haig to Sir John Stirling Maxwell, 26, 27/12/94, Maxwell of Pollock papers 1/6.

55 P. H. Milne to Mr Williams, 27/6/94, Melbury Habitation letter book, Dorset CRO, D124, Box 343; P. H. Milne to Mr Wells, 11/7/94; P. H. Milne to Mr Allen, 11/7/94; P. H. Milne to Mr Allen, 12/7/94.
56 P. H. Milne to Mr Williams, 14/7/94.
57 Wightwick and Wollaston, *Parker's Election Agent*, pp. 116–17.
58 R. H. Bailey to Lady Lonsdale, 15/6/97, Lowther Habitation correspondence.
59 *PLG*, 30/7/92; Whitehaven Habitation Council Minutes, 18/7/92, Cumbria RO.
60 Grand Council Minutes, 17/2/10.
61 Sowerby Habitation Council Minutes, 6/5/87; 'Primrose League Scrapbook', St. Andrews Parish Records, Northumberland CRO, EP 13/110.
62 Garstang Habitation Membership Register, Lancashire CRO, DDFZ; St. Albans Divisional Council Minutes 1890–9, Hertfordshire CRO,D/EV27.
63 *PLG*, 1/2/90; 12/11/92; 1/5/94.
64 John Springhall, *Youth, Empire and Society* (1977), p. 24.
65 *PLG*, 1/8/98; *Juvenile Branch Rules*.
66 *PLG*, 1/11/04.
67 Grand Council Minutes, 24/6/09; 8/7/09.
68 *Scouting For Boys* (1909), p. 270.
69 *PLG*, 1/8/13, Springhall, *Youth, Empire and Society*, p. 138.
70 M. Duverger, *Political Parties* (1964 edn), pp. 62–79.
71 Sigmund Neumann (ed.), *Modern Political Parties* (1967), p. 405.

CHAPTER 3   WOMEN AND CONSERVATIVE POLITICS

1 Constance, Lady Battersea, *Reminiscences* (1922), p. 181.
2 Mrs George Cornwallis West, *The Reminiscences of Lady Randolph Churchill* (1908; 1973 edn), p. 61.
3 Robert Blake, *The Unknown Prime Minister* (1955), p. 88; Frances, Countess of Warwick, *Afterthoughts* (1931), p. 45.
4 See press cuttings in Londonderry papers, D/Lo/F/543.
5 L. Davidoff, *The Best Circles* (1973), p. 61.
6 Ralph Nevill (ed.), *Life and Letters of Lady Dorothy Nevill* (n.d., New York), pp. 116–17; Frances, Countess of Warwick, *Life's Ebb and Flow* (1929), p. 143.
7 Warwick, *Life's Ebb and Flow*, pp. 189–91; Lady St. Helier, *Memories of Fifty Years* (1909), pp. 181, 189; Marchioness of Londonderry, *Retrospect* (1938), p. 23.
8 N. Ellenberger, 'The Souls and London Society at the End of the Nineteenth Century', *Victorian Studies*, 25, 2 (1982), p. 151.
9 Brian Harrison, 'For Church, Queen and Family: the Girls Friendly Society 1874–1920', *Past and Present*, 61 (1973).
10 Lady Knightley's Diary, 16/7/84.
11 Sir Edward Cook, *Florence Nightingale* (1913), vol. II, p. 97.
12 Countess of Jersey, *Fifty-One Years of Victorian Life* (1922); Voilet Powell, *Margaret, Countess of Jersey* (1978).
13 R. F. Foster, *Lord Randolph Churchill* (1981), pp. 39–40.
14 Brian Masters, *The Great Hostesses* (1982), p. 45.
15 Jersey, *Fifty-One Years*, p. 54.
16 Julia Cartwright (ed.), *The Journals of Lady Knightley of Fawsley* (1915), p. xiii.
17 Grand Council Minutes, 22/12/83; Reginald Lucas, *Lord Glenesk and the Morning Post* (1910), pp. 222–4, 229; *PLG*, 1/7/96; Cornwallis West, *Reminiscences*, p. 98–9.
18 Lady Knightly's Diary, 12/5/85.

19 See David Howell, *British Workers and the Independent Labour Party 1883–1906* (1983); Women's Labour League correspondence, 1/93, 1/46.
20 Meresia Nevill in the *Bury and Norwich Post*, 20/4/86.
21 *PLG*, 1/10/96, p. 15.
22 Lady Lucy Hicks-Beach, letter of 12/9/85, papers of the Coln Valley Habitation, Gloucestershire CRO, D/1070/VIII/7.
23 *Primrose Record*, 18/6/85; Lucas, *Lord Glenesk*, p. 299.
24 Grand Council Minutes, 5/5/87; Ladies Grand Council Minutes, 12/11/86.
25 Ladies Grand Council Minutes, 29/10/86; 10/12/86.
26 Lord Harris to Churchill, 29/10/86, Lord Randolph Churchill papers 16/1939.
27 Lady Knightley's Diary, May–November 1885.
28 Grand Council Minutes, 25/6/86.
29 *PLG*, 1/10/98; also 9/1/92.
30 Ibid., 10/6/93, p. 5; 19/11/87.
31 Ibid., 14/7/88.
32 Ibid., 1/12/93, p. 5; 1/12/96, p. 5.
33 *PLG*, 29/10/87; *Primrose Record* 22/10/85.
34 Lady Knightley's Diary, 1/9/85; see also Londonderry papers F/580, 'Electioneering 1911 and 1912 Maidstone'.
35 *PLG*, 19/11/87.
36 Ibid., 1/10/98.
37 Ladies Grand Council Minutes, 2/11/90; Grand Council Minutes, 6/1/10.
38 Duncan Tanner, 'The Parliamentary Electoral System, the "Fourth" Reform Act and the Rise of Labour in England and Wales', *BIHR*, 56, 134 (1983).
39 *PLG*, 2/12/95, p. 9.
40 See news cuttings, 20/4/89, Strutt papers, Essex CRO, D/DRa F88; also the pamphlets of the Conservative and Unionist Women's Franchise Association in the Catherine Marshall papers 8/14 (see list of Sources).
41 *PLG*, 24/1/91.
42 Lady Knightley's Diary, 2/4/80; 27/11/85; 28/11/85; Cartwright, *Journals of Lady Knightley*, p. xiii.
43 *PLG*, 8/12/88; 8/4/93; Scottish Grand Council Minutes, 3/7/90; 2/8/92; 11/7/01; Ladies Grand Council Minutes, 27/4/88. It is erroneously stated in C. Rover, *Women's Suffrage and Party Politics in Britain 1886–1914* (1967), p. 56, that the Conservative and Unionist Women's Franchise Association was within the League.
44 Ladies Grand Council Minutes, 27/4/88; *PLG*, 21/2/91; 8/12/88.
45 *Women's Suffrage Journal*, 2/9/89.
46 *Primrose Record*, 26/11/85.
47 *PLG*, 9/4/92; 19/11/87.
48 Report in the *North Star*, 4/11/95, Londonderry papers 548.
49 Ladies Grand Council Minutes, 28/11/88; *PLG*, 18/8/88; 15/11/88.
50 *PLG*, 24/5/90.
51 Brian Harrison, *Separate Spheres: The Opposition to Women's Suffrage in Britain* (1978), pp. 83, 118–19.
52 Cromer to Curzon, 18/7/10, Curzon papers D/1/6.
53 Harrison, *Separate Spheres*, pp. 119–23.
54 Lady Jersey to Curzon, 21/9/10; Cromer to Curzon, 28/9/10; 13/10/10, Curzon papers D/1/6.
55 *PLG*, 10/12/87; see also Earl Percy recanting, 15/10/92, Northumberland Household Press Cuttings, vol. III.
56 Editorial in the *Bury Post and Suffolk Standard*, 7/6/87.

57 Cromer to Curzon, 5/2/12, Curzon papers D/1/7; see also Catherine Marshall papers 3/24,33.
58 *PLG*, 20/2/92.
59 C. Rover, *Women's Suffrage and Party Politics in Britain 1866–1914* (1967).
60 *PLG*, 15/12/88.
61 Quoted in Sandra Holton, 'Feminism and Democracy: the Women's Suffrage Movement in Britain with particular reference to the NUWSS 1897–1918', Ph.D. thesis, Stirling University, 1980, p. 25.
62 Lady Salisbury to Frances Balfour, 11/2/97, Lady Frances Balfour, *Ne Obliviscaris: Dinna Forget* (1930), vol. II, p. 48.
63 Lady Knightley's Diary, 31/5/12.
64 Grand Council Minutes, 7/11/07, 4/3/09; Grand Council Minutes (General Purposes Committee), 6/10/10, 22/12/10.
65 *PLG*, 1/9/10, p. 12.
66 Grand Council Minutes (Agency Committee), 15/11/06.
67 *PLG*, 1/11/11.
68 Ibid., 1/12/07, p. 10.
69 A. J. Balfour to Christabel Pankhurst (copy), 23/10/07, Balfour papers 49793.
70 M. D. Pugh, *Electoral Reform in War and Peace 1906–18* (1978), pp. 149–53.
71 'Absolutely confidential' memorandum on talks with Lytton and Cecil, undated, Catherine Marshall papers.
72 Christabel Pankhurst to A. J. Balfour, 6/10/07, Balfour papers 49793.
73 Arnold Ward to Curzon, 5/2/13, Curzon papers D/1/8.
74 Marshall to Steel Maitland, 11/7/14, Steel Maitland papers GD/193/163/3.
75 'Notes on the Report of the Speaker's Committee', 3/2/17, Steel Maitland papers vol. 202; *Conservative Agents' Journal* no. 40, April 1916.
76 Pugh, *Electoral Reform*, 56–69, 79–85.
77 'Notes on the Report of the Speaker's Committee', 3/2/17, Steel Maitland papers vol. 202.
78 R. Blatchford, *Some Words to Socialist Women* (SDF Women's Committee, n.d.), p.3.
79 Margaret Llewelyn Davies, *Life as We Have Known It: by Co-operative* Working Women (1931, repr. 1977), p. 48.
80 Women's Labour League papers 1/93; see also WLL 1/46.
81 Betty Ralphs to Mrs Middleton, 29/9/07, WLL 1/39.
82 Ladies Grand Council Minutes, 3/6/92.
83 *PLG*, 1/8/95; 1/4/96, p. 6; 2/7/94, p. 5.

CHAPTER 4   THE IDEOLOGY OF LATE VICTORIAN CONSERVATISM

1 W. H. Greenleaf, *The British Political Tradition* vol. II (1983), pp. 189–93; N. O'Sullivan, *Conservatism* (1976), pp. 102–18; F. J. C. Hearnshaw, *Conservatism in England* (1933), pp. 19–33; R. Barker, *Political Ideas in Modern Britain* (1978), pp. 7–71.
2 See Paul Smith, *Disraelian Conservatism and Social Reform* (1967).
3 R. Blake, *Disraeli* (1966), pp. 522–4.
4 R. F. Foster, *Lord Randolph Churchill* (1981), pp. 26, 115.
5 See D. A. Hamer, *Liberal Politics in the Age of Gladstone and Rosebery* (1972).
6 E. J. Hobsbawm and T. Ranger (eds), *The Invention of Tradition* (1983).
7 R. Rose and D. Cavanagh, 'The Monarchy in Contemporary Political Culture', *Comparative Politics*, 8. (1976), pp. 554–5; see also E. Shils and M. Young, 'The Meaning of the Coronation', *Sociological Review*,' 1, 2 (1953); and J. G. Blumler et al., 'Attitudes to the Monarchy: their structure and development during a ceremonial occasion', *Political Studies*, 19 (1971).

8 D. Cannadine, 'The Context, Performance and Meaning of Ritual: the British Monarchy and the "Invention of Tradition" *c.* 1820–1977', in Hobsbawm and Ranger, *The Invention of Tradition*, pp. 133–4.

9 G. O. Trevelyan, *What Does She Do With It?* (1871); Charles Bradlaugh, *The Impeachment of the House of Brunswick* (1875); Frank Hardie, *The Political Influence of Queen Victoria 1861–1901* (1935).

10 E. Royle, *Radicals, Secularists and Republicans: Popular Free Thought in Britain 1866–1915* (1980), pp. 192–205; Fergus A. D'Arcy, 'Charles Bradlaugh and the English Republican Movement 1868–78', *Historical Journal*, 25,2 (1982).

11 N. J. Gossman, 'Republicanism in Nineteenth-Century England', *International Review of Social History*, 7 (1962), pp. 58–9.

12 The Countess of Jersey, *Fifty-One Years of Victorian Life* (1922), p. 52.

13 Brian Harrison, 'For Church, Queen and Family: the Girls 'Friendly Society 1874–1920', *Past and Present*, 61 (1973), p. 128.

14 Margaret Penn, *Manchester Fourteen Miles* (1947), pp. 145, 149, 189.

15 E. Hammerton and D. Cannadine, 'Conflict and Consensus on a Ceremonial Occasion: the Diamond Jubilee in Cambridge', *Historical Journal*, 24,1 (1981), pp. 134, 143.

16 W. Kendall, *The Revolutionary Movement in Britain 1900–21* (1969), p. 19.

17 Kingsley Martin, *The Crown and the Establishment* (1965), p. 46.

18 *Primrose League Gazette*, 1/5/01, p. 10.

19 L. A. Knight, 'The Royal Titles Act and India', *Historical Journal*, 11, 3 (1968).

20 Frank Hardie, *The Political Influence of the British Monarchy 1868–1952* (1970), p. 47.

21 Ibid., pp. 18, 43.

22 *PLG*, 7/3/91.

23 *PLG*, 13/12/90, p. 4; 3/1/90.

24 Ibid., 21/12/91; 16/1/92; 30/1/92; 20/2/92.

25 Hammerton and Cannadine, 'Conflict and Consensus'.

26 Patrick Joyce, 'Popular Toryism in Lancashire 1860–1890', Oxford D.Phil. thesis, 1975, p. 384.

27 See correspondence relating to Diamond Jubilee Celebration, Ridley papers, Northumberland RO, ZR1 56/2.

28 Ridley to F. J. Snowball, 20/6/97, Ridley papers 56/2.

29 *Buckingham Herald* 27/2/86, Addington (Additional) papers vol. 5.

30 *Primrose Record*, 15/10/85.

31 Ibid., 8/10/85.

32 *PLG*, 14/6/90.

33 *Newcastle Daily Journal* 6/9/84, Northumberland Household Press Cuttings vol. 2.

34 *PLG*, 17/3/88.

35 Ibid., 20/2/92; 3/12/92.

36 Ibid., 1/4/99.

37 Ibid., 1/10/00.

38 Ibid., 2/8/97, p. 1.

39 T. H. S. Escott, *Social Transformations of the Victorian Age* (1897), pp. 69–70.

40 See for example reports in the Strutt papers (*Essex County Chronicle* 4/9/96), Essex RC, Ra/F85; Northumberland papers (*Alnwick Mercury* 5/5/83), Northumberland Household Press Cuttings vol. 2.

41 Osbert Wyndham Hewett, *Strawberry Fair: a Biography of Frances, Countess of Waldegrave* (1956), pp. 189–90; R. F. Foster, *Lord Randolph Churchill* (1981), pp. 39–40; Londonderry papers (*Lady's Pictorial* 21/8/86), Durham RC vol. 543.

42 *PLG*, 14/6/90.

43 Ibid., 22/8/91, pp. 5–6.

44 Earl Percy, 31/1/90, Northumberland Household Press Cuttings vol. 3; *PLG*, 8/3/90.
45 *Primrose Record*, 15/10/85.
46 James Murphy, *The Education Act 1870* (1972), pp. 54–63; D. W. Bebbington, *The Non-conformist Conscience* (1982), pp. 127–30.
47 A. Simon, 'Church Disestablishment as a Factor in the 1885 General Election', *Historical Journal*, 18 (1975).
48 F. G. Hobbs to Mr Iles, 9/1/90, Coln Valley Habitation correspondence, Dorset RC D1070/VIII/7.
49 Sowerby Habitation Minutes, 9/12/97.
50 Patrick Joyce, *Work, Society and Politics* (1980), pp. 252, 256, 258.
51 *PLG*, 22/10/87.
52 S. E. Koss, 'Wesleyanism and Empire', *Historical Journal*, 18 (1975).
53 Joseph Altholz, 'The Political Behaviour of the English Catholics 1850–67', *Journal of British Studies*, 4, 1 (1964); G. A. Beck, 'The English Catholics in 1850', in Beck (ed.), *The English Catholics 1850–1950* (1950).
54 K. T. Hoppen, 'Tories, Catholics and the General Election of 1859', *Historical Journal*, 13 (1970), p. 48.
55 J. M. Robertson, *The Dukes of Norfolk* (1982), pp. 191; 228.
56 R. Quinault, 'Warwickshire Landowners and Parliamentary Politics 1841–1923', Oxford D.Phil. thesis, 1975, pp. 342–3.
57 Mr Jenningham to Norfolk, 17/9/85, Norfolk papers C765.
58 *Primrose Record* 17/4/86; *PLG*, 3/6/93, p. 6; Ibid., 22/10/85; 1/4/95; *Morning Post*, 29/3/86.
59 Joyce, 'Popular Toryism', p. 218.
60 Grand Council Minutes, 14/4/87.
61 D. Lysaght to Duke of Norfolk, 7/2/98, Norfolk papers C769; Norfolk to D. Lysaght (copy), 8/2/98, Norfolk papers C769.
62 See Norfolk papers C770.
63 Norfolk to Salisbury, 2/6/89, Salisbury papers, Norfolk–Salisbury correspondence 1879–1902, fol. 77; Norfolk to Salisbury 25/6/89, ibid., fol. 108.
64 H. C. Deb., 26/11/90, c. 101; 4/2/91, c. 1733. G. I. T. Machin, 'The Last Victorian Anti-Ritualist Campaign 1895–1906', *Victorian Studies*, 25, 3 (1982), pp. 290–3.
65 Norfolk to Salisbury, 8/10/93, Salisbury papers, Norfolk–Salisbury correspondence 1879–1902, fol. 149.
66 *PLG*, 1/6/00, p. 12.
67 See C. C. Eldridge, *England's Mission* (1973); D. K. Fieldhouse, *Economics and Empire 1830–1914* (1973); R. E. Robinson and J. A. Gallagher, *Africa and the Victorians* (1961).
68 I. F. Clarke, 'The Battle of Dorking 1871–1914', *Victorian Studies*, 8 (1965); P. A. Duane, 'Boys' Literature and the Idea of Empire 1870–1914', *Victorian Studies*, 14 (1980).
69 See John M. MacKenzie, *Propaganda and Empire* (1984).
70 R. Price, *An Imperial War and the British Working Class* (1972), pp. 132–77.
71 See Henry Pelling, 'British Labour and British Imperialism', in *Popular Politics and Society in Late Victorian Britain* (1968).
72 MacKenzie, *Propaganda*, pp. 148–71.
73 See for example *PLG*, 21/6/90, on Salisbury's failure to acquire territory south-west of Lake Victoria which would have linked British East Africa with Nyasaland.
74 Ibid., 6/9/90; 13/9/90.
75 Joseph Lee, *The Modernisation of Irish Society 1848–1918* (1973), p. 114.
76 *PLG*, 13/6/91, p. 9. On support in Tralee, see *PLG*, 15/12/88; 5/4/90.
77 Janet Robb, *The Primrose League 1883–1906* (1942), pp. 190–1.
78 *PLG*, 23/12/90; 1/3/99.

79 Ibid., 6/9/90; 22/2/90; 26/4/90.
80 Thomas Wright, *The Life of Colonel Fred Burnaby* (1908).
81 See R. T. MacKenzie and A. Silver, *Angels in Marble* (1968).
82 *PLG*, 1/2/00.
83 Ibid., 1/6/00, p. 13; p. 10.
84 Ibid., 2/4/00, esp. pp. 10–11.
85 See A. Summers, 'Militarism in Britain Before the Great War', *History Workshop*, 2 (1976).

CHAPTER 5   THE GEOGRAPHY OF POPULAR CONSERVATISM

1 *PLG*, 15/10/87.
2 Two published works are absolutely invaluable in this connection: Henry Pelling's *Social Geography of British Elections 1885–1910* (1967) and H. J. Hanham's *Elections and Party Management* (1959).
3 *PLG*, 1/1/96.
4 Ibid., 10/7/92.
5 Grand Council Minutes, 13/12/00.
6 Viscountess Astor papers 1416/1/1/1734–5.
7 Pelling, *Social Geography*, p. 146.
8 *PLG*, 16/5/91.
9 Quoted in J. P. Cornford, 'The Transformation of Conservatism in the late Nineteenth Century', *Victorian Studies*, 7 (1963), p. 47.
10 *PLG*, 1/8/95, p. 12.
11 Pelling, *Social Geography*, p. 155.
12 See Gloucestershire CRO 1070/VIII/4–10; 2219/6/8; 1610/X31.
13 Pelling, *Social Geography*, pp. 60–62.
14 *PLG*, 30/5/91.
15 Ibid., 6/7/91.
16 See ibid., 3/12/92; 10/12/92; 28/1/93; 4/3/93.
17 Pelling, *Social Geography*, p. 44.
18 Grand Council Minutes, 18/10/00.
19 Pelling, *Social Geography*, pp. 64–5.
20 See membership details in Minutes of the St. Albans Divisional Council 1890–99, Hertfordshire CRO D/EVZ7.
21 Ian F. W. Beckett *Riflemen Form: a study of the Rifle Volunteer Movement 1859–1908* (1982), pp. 78, 79, 108, 114.
22 Addington papers, Buckinghamshire CRO, AR 109/83.
23 Jersey to Lord Salisbury, 20/6/86 (Villiers correspondence 1882–1900/2), Salisbury papers.
24 *PLG*, 2/5/91.
25 *Bury and Norwich Post and Suffolk Herald*, 13/10/85, p. 7; 14/12/86, p. 6.
26 Ibid., 26/1/86.
27 Ibid., 27/7/86, p. 7.
28 Pelling, *Social Geography*, p. 101.
29 Ibid., p. 97.
30 *PLG*, 1/3/90.
31 Ibid., 1/5/01, p. 5.
32 Pelling, *Social Geography*, p. 209.
33 Ibid., p. 199–200.
34 *Ladywood Primrose Magazine*, March 1887.
35 *PLG*, 10/3/88.

36 Roland Quinault, 'Warwickshire Landowners and Parliamentary Politics 1841–1923', Oxford University D.Phil. thesis, 1975, pp. 220–35.
37 Grand Council Minutes, 25/7/01.
38 *PLG*, 21/7/88.
39 Ibid., 1/8/95.
40 Pelling, *Social Geography*, p. 292.
41 W. D. Ross, 'Bradford Politics 1880–1906', University of Bradford Ph.D. thesis, 1977, p. 225.
42 For an excellent analysis of Sheffield politics see Helen E. Mathers, 'Sheffield Municipal Politics 1893–1926', Sheffield University Ph.D. thesis, 1980, pp. 40, 51, 78, 85, 98, 101.
43 S. H. Jeyes and F. D. How, *The Life of Sir Howard Vincent* (1912).
44 Grand Council (General Purposes Committee) Minutes, 19/2/02.
45 Pelling, *Social Geography*, p. 251.
46 Ibid., p. 259.
47 David Howell, *British Workers and the Independent Labour Party 1883–1906* (1983), p. 54.
48 Norfolk to Lord Salisbury, 8/10/93 (Norfolk–Salisbury correspondence 1879–1902/149, Salisbury papers).
49 Salisbury to Norfolk, 7/6/85; H. Jenningham to Norfolk, 15/9/85, 17/9/85, Norfolk papers C765.
50 Pelling, *Social Geography*, p. 340.
51 *North Star* 17/9/90, Londonderry papers Lo/F/545.
52 Ibid., 16/9/92.
53 Leon Kitchen, 'The 1892 Election in the Tyneside Area' Newcastle University M.Litt thesis, 1979.
54 *PLG*, 2/4/94.
55 Ibid., 2/4/94; 1/6/96.
56 *Jarrow Guardian*, 30/7/09.
57 Speeches 9/9/89, 31/1/90, Northumberland Household Press Cuttings vol. III, 1888–93.
58 See H. Trevor Roper, 'The Highland Tradition of Scotland' in E. Hobsbawm and T. Ranger (eds), *The Invention of Tradition* (1983).
59 For the background of Scottish politics see J. G. Kellas, 'The Liberal Party in Scotland 1876–95', *Scottish Historical Review*, 44 (1965); D. C. Savage, 'Scottish Politics 1885–86', *Scottish Historical Review*, 40 (1961); D. W. Urwin, 'The Development of the Conservative Party Organisation in Scotland until 1912', *Scottish Historical Review*, 44 (1965).
60 *PLG*, 14/11/91, p. 5.
61 Ibid., 1/6/98.
62 Scottish Branch Grand Council Minutes, 28/3/02; 12/3/06.
63 Ibid., 10/5/00.
64 Ibid., 22/6/88; 20/7/94.
65 Ibid., 7/2/95.
66 *PLG*, 3/9/92; Scottish Branch Grand Council Minutes, 10/5/00; Ladies Grand Council Minutes, 28/4/93.
67 Scottish Branch Grand Council Minutes, 16/12/85.
68 *PLG*, 19/11/92, p. 4.
69 Ibid., 1/10/01.
70 Scottish Branch Grand Council Minutes, 13/1/97.
71 Ibid., 10/2/03.
72 Ibid., 25/2/19; 3/2/20.
73 *PLG*, 1/10/87.
74 Ibid., 31/3/88.
75 *Cardigan and Tivyside Advertiser* 4/4/90; 11/7/90.

76 Ibid., 4/5/88; 29/6/88; 6/6/90.
77 Marquis of Abergavenny to Salisbury 21/1/90 (Nevill correspondence 1866–1901/82, 86, Salisbury papers).
78 *Primrose Record* 11/3/86; *PLG*, 31/3/88.
79 For example see *PLG*, 1/8/95.
80 Ibid., 1/11/97.
81 Ibid., 1/5/89 on Whitehaven.
82 J. P. Cornford, 'The Transformation of Conservatism in the Late Nineteenth Century', *Victorian Studies*, 7 (1963), pp. 54–6.

CHAPTER 6   CONSERVATISM, CLASS AND COMMUNITY

1 Bruce K. Murray, *The People's Budget 1909–10* (1980), p. 37.
2 J. P. Cornford, 'The Transformation of Conservatism in the late Nineteenth Century', *Victorian Studies*, 7 (1963).
3 H. J. Hanham, *Elections and Party Management* (1959), pp. 365–8.
4 Speech at Glasgow, 22/11/73, quoted in M. Ostrogorski, *Democracy and the Organisation of Political Parties*, 1 (1902), p. 256.
5 NUCCA Conference Minutes, 26/10/86.
6 Patrick Joyce, *Work, Society and Politics* (1980), pp. 246–8.
7 Quoted in David G. Smith, 'The Social and Political Significance of the Church of England in Mid-Nineteenth Century Textile Lancashire with Particular Reference to Preston 1851–70', Lancaster University MA thesis 1984, p. 37.
8 *PLG*, 10/6/93, p. 5.
9 Ian F. Beckett, *Riflemen Form* (1982), pp. 81–3; 44–8; 78.
10 See Alan J. Lee, 'Conservatism, Traditionalism and the British Working Class, 1880–1918', D. E. Martin and D. Rubinstein (eds), *Ideology and the Labour Movement* (1979); F. Parkin, 'Working-class Conservatism: a Theory of Political Deviance', *British Journal of Sociology*, 18 (1967).
11 Grand Council Minutes, 25/7/01.
12 *PLG*, 31/3/88.
13 Ibid.
14 Ibid., 24/12/92.
15 David Cannadine, 'The Context, Performance and Meaning of Ritual', in E. Hobsbawm and T. Ranger (eds), *The Invention of Tradition* (1983).
16 Ladies Grand Council Minutes, 28/1/87.
17 *PLG*, editorial, 4/1/90; E. Donkin, *PLG*, 1/9/98.
18 Ibid., 28/2/91, p. 3; 15/5/86.
19 Ibid., 1/8/06, p. 13; 16/3/89; 1/7/06; 1/8/10, p. 10.
20 *Bury and Norwich Post* 8/3/87.
21 *North Star*, 17/9/90, Londonderry press cuttings F/545.
22 *PLG*, 2/9/01, p. 7.
23 See Harold Perkin, *The Origins of Modern English Society* (1969), pp. 271–308.
24 J. Marlow, *Cecil Rhodes* (1972), p. 122.
25 J. M. Robertson, *The Dukes of Norfolk* (1982), p. 231.
26 David Cannadine, *Lords and Landlords: the Aristocracy and the Towns 1774–1967* (1980), p. 33.
27 Robert Rhodes James, *Rosebery* (1963), pp. 197–8.
28 W. D. Rubinstein, *Men of Property* (1981), p. 194; Duke of Buccleuch, Duke of Northumberland, Earl of Derby, Duke of Sutherland, Earl of Dudley, Earl of Ancaster,

Marquis of Anglesey, Marquis of Londonderry, Duke of Portland, Marquis of Hertford, Duke of Rutland, Marquis of Downshire, Earl Brownlow, Earl of Yarborough, Earl of Pembroke, Duke of Norfolk.

29 J. P. Cornford, 'Parliamentary Origins of the Hotel Cecil', in R. Robson (ed.), *Ideas and Institutions of Victorian Britain* (1967), p. 310.
30 Cornford, 'Transformation of Conservatism, p. 58.
31 W. L. Guttsman, *The British Political Elite* (1965), p. 78.
32 R. Pumphrey, 'The Introduction of Industrialists into the British Peerage', *American Historical Review*, 65 (1959–60), p. 7.
33 John Garrard, *Leadership and Power in Victorian Industrial Towns 1830–80* (1983), pp. 28–35.
34 Reginald Lucas, *Lord Glenesk and the Morning Post* (1910), pp. 222–4.
35 Gregory Anderson, *Victorian Clerks* (1976), pp. 22–5, 60–2.
36 Beckett, *Riflemen Form*, pp. 83–4.
37 Scottish Branch Minutes, 12/2/90; *What Is Done With Our Money?* (PL pamphlet no. 291); Chipping Sodbury membership list, Codrington papers D 1610/X31; Scottish Branch Minutes, 8/3/04.
38 Michael Winstanley, *The Shopkeeper's World 1830–1914* (1983), pp. 46–7.
39 E. P. Hennock, 'Finance and Politics In Urban Local Government in England 1835–1900', *Historical Journal*, 6, 2 (1963), p. 216.
40 Ibid., pp. 220, 224–5.
41 Lord Cranbrook, 3/10/83, Northumberland Press Cuttings vol. 2, 1881–5.
42 Winstanley, *Shopkeepers' World*, pp. 54, 140.
43 Ladies Grand Council Minutes, 29/10/86; *Primrose Record* 15/5/86.
44 Winstanley, *Shopkeepers' World*, p. 192.
45 See R. Q. Gray, *The Aristocracy of Labour in Nineteenth Century Britain 1850–1914* (1981).
46 D. Hopkin, 'The Membership of the Independent Labour Party 1904–10: a Spatial and Occupational Analysis', *IRSH*, 20 (1975).
47 Brian Harrison, 'Traditions of Respectability in British Labour History', in *Peaceable Kingdom* (1982).
48 *PLG*, 14/1/88.
49 *PLG*, 21/3/91; Garstang Council Minutes, 1/2/02; *PLG*, 26/11/87.
50 30/1/83, report in Northumberland Press Cuttings, vol. 2, 1881–5; 31/1/91, report in Northumberland Press Cuttings, vol. 3, 1888–93.
51 *PLG*, 16/5/91.
52 Lady Londonderry, speech, 30/10/11, Londonderry papers F/580.
53 *PLG*, 16/5/91.
54 NUCCA Conference Minutes, 13/12/92; *PLG*, 1/4/96.
55 *Primrose Record* 8/10/85; *PLG*, 31/10/91, pp. 7–8; NUCCA Conference Minutes, 25/10/79.
56 *Rules*, Hertfordshire CRO, D/ESa 186.
57 Special Committees Minutes, 12/8/86.
58 NUCCA Conference Minutes, 25/10/79.
59 G. Stedman Jones, 'Working-class culture and working-class politics in London, 1870–1900: notes on the remaking of a working class', in *Languages of Class* (1983).
60 *PLG*, 1/7/01.
61 L. Senelick, 'Politics as Entertainment: Victorian Music Hall Songs', *Victorian Studies*, 19 (1975).
62 F. M. L. Thompson, 'Social Control in Victorian Britain', *Economic History Review*, 34 (1981).
63 Janet Robb, *The Primrose League 1883–1906* (1942), p. 87.
64 *PLG*, 20/4/89.

65 Ibid., 1/11/95.
66 Scottish Branch Minutes, 21/6/10.
67 *PLG*, 1/2/03, p. 11.
68 Viscount Chilston, *Chief Whip: the political life and times of Aretas Akers-Douglas* (1961), pp. 174–8.
69 NUCCA Conference Minutes, 13/12/92.
70 Chilston, *Chief Whip*, p. 177.
71 *PLG*, 29/9/92; 5/11/92; 12/11/92; 26/11/92.

CHAPTER 7   THE STRANGE DEATH OF TORY ENGLAND 1901–1914

1 See G. R. Searle, *The Quest for National Efficiency* (1971); P. Kennedy and A. Nicholls (eds), *Nationalist and Racialist Movements in Britain and Germany Before 1914* (1981).
2 J. M. McEwen, 'The Coupon Election of 1918 and the Unionist Members of Parliament', *Journal of Modern History*, 34 (1962), pp. 298–302.
3 Anne Summers, 'The Character of Edwardian Nationalism: Three Popular Leagues', in Kennedy and Nicholls, *Nationalist and Racialist Movements*.
4 Ibid., p. 72.
5 See H. V. Emy, *Liberals, Radicals and Social Politics 1892–1914* (1973).
6 *PLG*, 1/10/01.
7 Lady Knightley's Diary, 5/8/11.
8 *PLG*, 30/1/92.
9 Grand Council Minutes, 9/12/09; 7/10/09, 9/12/09; *PLG*, 1/11/09, p. 7.
10 *PLG*, 1/10/08, p. 1; 1/11/08, p. 8.
11 D. J. Dutton, 'The Unionist Party and Social Policy 1906–14', *Historical Journal*, 24, 4 (1981); J. Campbell, *F. E. Smith* (1983), pp. 354–7.
12 Grand Council Minutes, 3/10/07; *PLG*, 1/11/06, 'The Warden's Handy Sheet Supplement'.
13 *PLG*, 1/7/07.
14 Ibid., 1/2/06, 1/1/07; 1/7/09.
15 Harold Nicolson, *King George V* (1952), p. 148.
16 Robert Blake, *The Unknown Prime Minister* (1955), pp. 133–4, 150–3.
17 Speech at Antrim 20/9/11, Londonderry papers F/580.
18 Speech 15/11/26, Londonderry papers F/615.
19 Grand Council Minutes, 6/11/13; *PLG*, 1/12/13.
20 P. F. Clarke, 'The Electoral Position of the Liberal and Labour Parties 1910–14', *English Historical Review*, 90 (1975), pp. 829–35.
21 Dutton, 'The Unionist Party and Social Policy', p. 879; P. F. Clarke, *Lancashire and the New Liberalism* (1971), p. 387.
22 *PLG*, 1/1/14 and 1/3/14; E. Sinclair to Lady Londonderry, 11/3/11, Londonderry papers, C686; 'Electioneering in 1911 and 1912 in Maidstone', Londonderry papers F/580.
23 J. Ramsden, *The Age of Balfour and Baldwin 1902–40* (1978), pp. 45–56.
24 R. S. Woof to Lady Lonsdale 20/12/94, 1/3/06; R. H. Bailey to Lady Lonsdale, 19/4/97, Lowther Habitation correspondence.
25 Grand Council Minutes, 15/2/06; see for example, Garstang Habitation Minute Books 1894–1911.
26 *PLG*, 1/4/02, p. 8.
27 Ibid., 1/5/06, p. 13; Grand Council Minutes, 1/3/06; 17/12/10.
28 *PLG*, 1/5/95, pp. 6–7.
29 Grand Council Minutes, 25/7/01; 19/12/01.
30 *PLG*, 1/5/05.

31 Ibid., 1/11/05, p. 6.
32 Grand Council Minutes, 12/7/06.
33 *PLG*, 1/5/14; Grand Council Minutes, 31/10/12.
34 *PLG*, 1/5/14.
35 Ibid., 1/4/06, p. 6.
36 Grand Council Minutes, 15/2/06; *PLG*, 1/2/06, p. 10.
37 *PLG*, 1/3/06, p. 5; 1/4/06, p. 11.
38 Grand Council Minutes, 3/6/87.
39 *PLG*, 1/7/02, p. 5.
40 Grand Council Minutes, 25/6/03; 16/7/03; 5/11/03; 7/6/07.
41 Lord Londonderry, speeches 29/8/04, Londonderry papers F/554; 11/9/05, ibid., F/557; Lady Ancaster, *PLG*, 1/12/07, p. 10.
42 General Purposes Committee Minutes, 15/2/12.
43 Agency Committee Report, 17/12/03; General Purposes Report, 16/6/04.
44 D. Porter, 'The Unionist Tariff Reformers 1903–12', Manchester Ph.D. thesis 1976, p. 355.
45 *PLG*, 1/5/08, p. 7.
46 Richard Rempel, *Unionists Divided* (1972), pp. 132–3.
47 *PLG*, 1/3/05, p. 9.
48 Ibid., 1/11/03, p. 10.
49 Ibid.
50 Quoted in Porter, 'Unionist Tariff Reformers', p. 291.
51 Londonderry, speech 14/9/03, Londonderry papers F/552.
52 Alan Sykes, *Tariff Reform in British Politics 1903–13* (1979), pp. 105–6.
53 Ibid., p. 264–70.
54 Porter, 'Unionist Tariff Reformers', p. 256.
55 See *WUO Report and Programme* (1927).
56 *PLG*, 1/5/01, p. 9; 2/12/01, p. 9; 1/3/06, p. 19.
57 Agency Committee Report, 19/12/01.
58 Scottish Branch Minutes, 12/1/04, 8/3/04, 12/7/04, 10/3/08, 14/4/08; General Purposes Committee Report, 13/12/06; Agency Committee Report, 4/6/07. General Purposes Committee Report, 3/11/10, 1/6/11, 15/2/12.
59 General Purposes Committee Report, 6/6/07; Scottish Branch Minutes, 17/1/10, 25/5/09; General Purposes Committee Report, 1/6/11; Agency Committee Report, 20/10/10.
60 *PLG*, 1/5/01, p. 6; General Purposes Committee Report, 22/10/07; Grand Council Minutes, 21/7/10; General Purposes Committee Report, 31/10/12.
61 Scottish Branch Minutes, 9/6/08; 7/7/08; 13/10/08; 20/11/08; 25/5/09; 5/10/09; 18/3/10; 19/4/10; 20/2/12; 19/3/12.
62 General Purposes Committee Report, 7/7/10.
63 Ibid., 17/10/12; 31/10/12.
64 Grand Council Minutes, 21/11/12, 13/3/13; *PLG*, 1/12/12, 1/5/13.

CHAPTER 8　THE RISE OF MODERN CONSERVATISM 1914–1935

1 Grand Council Minutes, 5/2/20.
2 General Purpose Committee Minutes, 14/1/15.
3 *Primrose League Gazette*, 1/10/14; General Purposes Committee Minutes, 8/10/14; *PLG*, 1/2/15; 1/11/15.
4 General Purposes Committee Minutes, 14/1/15.
5 Finance Committee Minutes, 3/4/19.
6 *PLG*, 1/10/14, p. 5.

7 Martin Pugh, *Electoral Reform in War and Peace 1906–18* (1978), pp. 48–51.
8 *PLG*, 1/8/15; 1/11/15.
9 Ibid., 1/7/15, p. 5.
10 Martin Pugh, *The Making of Modern British Politics 1867–1939* (1982), pp. 177–9.
11 *PLG*, 1/2/19.
12 Pugh, *Electoral Reform*, p. 88.
13 National Union Executive Minutes, 8/5/17.
14 Pugh, *Electoral Reform*, pp. 92–4, 105–18.
15 D. Tanner, 'The Parliamentary Electoral System, the "Fourth" Reform Act and the Rise of Labour in England and Wales', *BIHR*, 56, 134 (1983); M. Kinnear, *The British Voter: an Atlas and Survey 1885–1964* (1969), pp. 122–4.
16 J. Ramsden, 'The Organisation of the Conservative and Unionist Party in Britain 1910–30', Oxford University D.Phil. 1974, pp. 169–70.
17 Minutes National Union Executive, 9/4/18; W.U.O. Annual Report, 1927, Astor papers 1416/1/816.
18 Sir George Younger to Lord Crawford, 6/3/18, Grand Council Minutes, 13/3/18.
19 Grand Council Minutes, 13/3/18.
20 Ibid., 11/4/18; Thomas Cox to Reginald Bennett, 16/7/19, Grand Council Minutes, 24/7/19.
21 Grand Council Minutes, 13/12/23.
22 General Purposes Committee Minutes, 5/6/18; Grand Council Minutes, 4/7/18; Finance Committee Minutes, 3/10/18; 6/2/19; Grand Council Minutes, 4/7/18.
23 Ramsden, 'Organization of the Conservative and Unionist Party', pp. 191–2.
24 John Ramsden, *The Age of Balfour and Baldwin 1902–40* (1978), p. 255.
25 General Purposes Committee Minutes, 6/2/19.
26 *PLG*, 1/3/27, p. 9; C. G. Briggs to Miss Jenkins 26/9/22, Astor papers 1416/1/1735.
27 *PLG*, 1/11/17, p. 9; Halifax Report, 19/6/18, Grand Council Minutes, 4/7/18.
28 Margaret Penn, *Manchester Fourteen Miles* (1947), p. 152.
29 Brian Harrison, *Separate Spheres* (1978), p. 234.
30 Ramsden, *Age of Balfour*, p. 229.
31 *PLG*, 1/2/25, p. 9.
32 Ramsden, *Age of Balfour*, pp. 245–6, 248.
33 Private and Confidential Report, 1927–8, Astor papers 1416/1/816.
34 Grand Council Minutes, 7/10/20.
35 J. Springhall, *Youth, Empire and Society* (1977), pp. 110–18.
36 JIL Annual Reports, Minute Book, 1906–22.
37 NUCUA Report, 1929.
38 *PLG*, 1/2/20, p. 3; Grand Council Minutes, 5/2/31, 5/3/31.
39 Lady Jersey, circular letter, April 1924, Astor papers 1416/3/820; LGC Annual Report, 1928, Astor papers 1416/1/820.
40 *PLG*, 1/1/27, p. 8.
41 Ibid., 1/10/19; 1/11/19.
42 Ibid., 1/1/22, p. 7; 1/4/23, p. 8; 1/1/24, p. 8.
43 John Campbell, *F. E. Smith* (1983), pp. 557–8.
44 Sir Robert Sanders' Diary, 1/11/21.
45 Grand Council Minutes, 20/10/21; 27/7/22.
46 Speech, n.d. Londonderry papers F/615.
47 Martin Gilbert, *Winston S. Churchill*, vol. V (1976), p. 367.
48 This argument is well articulated in Dennis Dean, 'The Contrasting Attitudes of the Conservative and Labour Parties to Problems of Empire 1922–36', London Ph.D. thesis, 1974, pp. 7–8.
49 John M. MacKenzie, *Propaganda and Empire* (1984), pp. 217–18, 256.

50 B. R. Tomlinson, *The Political Economy of the Raj: The Economics of Decolonisation 1914–47* (1979).
51 Quoted in Dean, 'Contrasting Attitudes', p. 421.
52 Gilbert, *Churchill*, vol. V, pp. 1, 444.
53 quoted in Dean, 'Contrasting Attitudes', p. 242.
54 Gilbert, *Churchill*, vol. V, p. 432.
55 Ibid., p. 387.
56 Grand Council Minutes, 2/3/33.
57 *PLG*, 30/3/31, p. 14.
58 Grand Council Minutes, 2/3/33.
59 Lord Strathcona, *PLG*, 1/2/30; *PLG*, 1/5/30.
60 Pugh, *Electoral Reform*, p. 157.
61 Sir Robert Sanders' Diary, 14/7/26; 2/7/27; 12/5/32; 3/6/34.
62 J. A. Thompson, 'Labour and the Modern British Monarchy', *South Atlantic Quarterly*, 70 (1971).
63 G. C. Lebzelter, *Political Anti-Semetism in England 1918–39* (1978), pp. 18, 67, 69.
64 Robert Skidelsky, *Oswald Mosley* (1975), pp. 409–10.
65 Grand Council Minutes, 7/6/34.
66 *PLG*, 1/1/27, p. 5.
67 W. H. Greenleaf, *The British Political Tradition*, vol. II (1983), pp. 247–8.
68 Quoted in H. Glickman, 'The Toryness of English Conservatism', *Journal of British Studies*, 1 (1961–2), p. 134.

Sources

PRIVATE PAPERS

Addington — Egerton Hubbard, 1st Baron Addington
Astor — Nancy, Viscountess Astor
Bayford — Sir Robert Sanders, Lord Bayford
Baldwin — Stanley, Earl Baldwin of Bewdley
Balfour — Arthur James, Earl of Balfour
Churchill — Lord Randolph Churchill
Galway — George Edmund Milnes Monckton, 7th Viscount Galway
Halsey — Sir Thomas Frederick Halsey, Bt.
Henniker — Arthur Henry Henniker, 6th Baron Henniker
Knightley — Lady Louisa Knightley
Londonderry — Theresa, Marchioness of Londonderry; Charles Vane-Tempest-Stewart, 6th Marquis of Londonderry; Edith, Marchioness of Londonderry.
Marlborough — Frances, Duchess of Marlborough and John, 7th Duke of Marlborough
Marshall — Catherine Marshall
Maxwell — Sir John Stirling Maxwell of Pollock
Norfolk — Henry Fitzalan-Howard, 15th Duke of Norfolk
Northumberland — Algernon George Percy, 6th Duke of Northumberland; Henry George Percy, 7th Duke of Northumberland
Ridley — Sir Matthew White Ridley, 1st Viscount Ridley
Salisbury — Robert Gascoyne-Cecil, 3rd Marquis of Salisbury
Selborne — Maud, Countess of Selborne
Stradbroke — George Edward Rous, 3rd Earl of Stradbroke
Strutt — Charles Hedley Strutt and Clara, Lady Rayleigh
Walsingham — Thomas de Grey, 6th Lord Walsingham

PRIMROSE LEAGUE — CENTRAL RECORDS

Minutes of the Grand Council 1883–87; 1900–1935 (including reports of the Committees on Finance, General Purposes, Agency, Literature, Juvenile Branch and Sports)
Minutes of the Ladies Grand Council 1886–1901

Special Committees Minute Book 1886–1900
The Roll of Habitations 1886, 1890, 1897, 1899, 1904, 1912
Primrose League Manuals 1897, 1898, 1899
Juvenile Branch Rules (n.d.)
Cycling Corps Rules (n.d.)
Primrose League Pamphlets
The Primrose April–May, 1884
The Primrose Record June 1885–January 1887
The Primrose League Gazette October 1887–December 1935
'A Short History of the Formation of the Primrose League', corrected and revised by the founders, 1883, Grand Council Minutes
The Primrose League: its Rise, Progress and Constitution (1887), by one of the staff
G. A. Arbuthnot (ed.), *The Primrose League Election Guide* (1914).

PRIMROSE LEAGUE – LOCAL RECORDS

Alnwick – 'Percy' Habitation. Duke of Northumberland Household Press Cuttings
Badminton – 'Beaufort' Habitation. Cash Book 1886–7
Birmingham – 'Ladywood' Habitation. *The Ladywood Primrose Magazine* 1887
Bishops's Castle Habitation – Warden's Book 1893–8
Bournemouth Habitations – *The Primrose* 1887
Buckingham Habitation – Addington Press Cuttings
Cardiganshire Habitations – *The Cardigan and Tivyside Advertiser*
Chipping Sodbury 'Codrington' Habitation. Correspondence of Sir Gerald Codrington 1886–1914
Cleveland – 'Pennyman' Habitation. Membership Register 1886–8
Coln Valley Habitation (Gloucestershire) – Minute Book 1885; Membership Register 1886–7; Correspondence 1885–6; Receipts; Accounts Book 1886–90; Ephemera
Edinburgh – 'Scott' Habitation. Minute Book 1897–1909
Garstang Habitation (Lancashire) – Minute Books 1894–1911; Membership Register 1894–1909
Lowther Habitation (Cumbria) – Letter Book 1886–97; Minute Book 1886–94; Wardens Books 1887–9; Accounts Book 1886–92; Receipts; Ephemera
Melbury Habitation (Dorset) – Letter Book 1894–1913; Membership Registers 1886, 1894–1901; Accounts Book 1884–90
Nailsworth and Horsley Habitation (Gloucestershire) – Minute Book 1887–99
Newcastle-upon-Tyne – 'St Andrew's' Habitation. Press Cuttings and Ephemera 1905–9
St Albans Habitations – Divisional Council Minute Book 1890–99
Scottish Branch – Grand Council Minute Books 1885–1920
Seaham Harbour – 'Londonderry' Habitation. Londonderry Press Cuttings
Sowerby – 'Rawson' Habitation. Minute Books 1887–1900, 1912–13
Suffolk Habitations – *Bury and Norwich Post and Suffolk Herald*
Whitehaven Habitation – Minute Book 1888–1902; Membership Registers 1889–97; Receipts; Ephemera
Wynyard – 'Londonderry' Habitation. Londonderry Press Cuttings

CONSERVATIVE PARTY RECORDS

NUCCA Council Minutes
NUCCA Executive Minutes
NUCCA Conference Reports
NUCCA Pamphlets
Campaign Notes 1885–1914
Conservative and Unionist Women's Franchise Association Pamphlets
Junior Imperial and Constitutional League Minute Books 1906–22
The Tory 1892–97
Conservative Agents Journal 1898–1917

THESES

Dean, Dennis William 'The Contrasting Attitudes of the Conservative and Labour Parties to Problems of Empire 1922–36, 'London Ph.D. thesis, 1974.

Hogg, S. A., 'Landed Society and the Conservative Party in the late Nineteenth and Early Twentieth Centuries', Oxford B.Litt thesis, 1974.

Joyce, Patrick, 'Popular Toryism in Lancashire 1860–90', Oxford D.Phil. thesis, 1975.

Kitchen, Leon, 'The 1892 Election in the Tyneside Area', Newcastle M.Litt. thesis, 1979.

Mathers, Helen E., 'Sheffield Municipal Politics 1893–1926: parties, personalities and the rise of Labour', Sheffield Ph.D. thesis, 1980.

Porter, Dilwyn, 'The Unionist Tariff Reformers 1903–14', Manchester Ph.D. thesis, 1976.

Quinault, Roland, 'Warwickshire Landowners and Parliamentary Politics 1841–1923', Oxford D.Phil. thesis, 1975.

Ramsden, John, 'The Organisation of the Conservative and Unionist Party in Britain 1910–30', Oxford D.Phil. thesis, 1974.

Ross, Duncan, 'Bradford Politics 1880–1906', Bradford Ph.D. thesis, 1977.

Appendices

APPENDIX I   LEADING OFFICE HOLDERS OF THE PRIMROSE LEAGUE

Chancellor

1883 Lord Randolph Churchill MP
1884 Earl of Abergavenny
1885 Sir William Hardman
1886 Viscount Folkestone
1887 Lord Harris
1888 Lord Harris
1889 Earl of Amherst
1900 Earl of Radnor
1891 Lord Borthwick
1892 Sir William Marriott
1893 Duke of Abercorn
1894 Lord Borthwick
1895 Lord Poltimore
1896 Lord Harris
1897 Lord Glenesk
1898 Duke of Marlborough
1899 Duke of Marlborough
1900 Viscount Curzon MP[a]
1901 Viscount Curzon MP
1902 Earl of Powis
1903 Lord Willoughby de Eresby
1904 Gerald Loder MP
1905 Duke of Norfolk
1906 Duke of Norfolk
1907 Lord Llangattock
1908 Sir Robert Gresley
1909 Lord Desborough
1910 Lord Desborough
1911 Lord Northcote/Lord Curzon
1912 Walter Long MP
1913 Walter Long MP
1914 Earl of Crawford and Balcarres
1915 Walter Long (acting)[b]

1916 Walter Long (acting)
1917 Walter Long (acting)
1918 Earl of Crawford and Balcarres
1919 Earl of Clarendon
1920 Earl of Clarendon
1921 Earl of Pembroke
1922 Earl of Pembroke
1923 Earl of Pembroke
1924 Sir W. Joynson-Hicks MP
1925 Duke of Sutherland
1926 W. Greaves-Lord MP
1927 W. Greaves-Lord MP
1928 Sir Henry Page-Croft MP
1929 Lord Ebbisham
1930 Lord Strathcona and Mount Royal
1931 Douglas Hacking MP
1932 Lord Greenwood
1933 Marquis of Dufferin and Ava
1934 Lord Ebbisham
1935 Lord Ebbisham

Grand Master

1885 Marquis of Salisbury and
     Earl of Iddesleigh
1887 Marquis of Salisbury
1903 A. J. Balfour MP
1912 Lord Curzon
1925 Stanley Baldwin MP

Vice-Chancellor

1883 T. B. Cusack-Smith
1889 George Lane-Fox
1912 Gerald Arbuthnot[c]

[a] The son of Earl Howe.
[b] While Crawford was serving with the Royal Army Medical Corps.
[c] He was killed in action in 1916 and the post left vacant.
The Vice-Chancellor's post was a salaried one; the holder was in charge of the administration of PL headquarters. Chancellor and Grand Master were honorary positions. The Chancellor was effectively the League's leading public voice; he presided at most functions and travelled around the country to address habitations; official Precepts appeared in his name. The Grand Master simply addressed Grand Habitation once a year in April.

APPENDIX II   SOME LEADING FIGURES COMMON TO THE LEAGUE
AND THE CONSERVATIVE PARTY ORGANIZATIONS 1883–1895

In the Primrose League		*In the National Union/ Parliamentary Party*
Chancellor	Duke of Abercorn	President
Chancellor	Earl of Abergavenny	President
Grand Councillor	Sir T. J. Agg-Gardner MP	Council
Ruling Councillor; Chancellor	Earl of Amherst	Chairman
Grand Councillor	Sir Ashmead Bartlett MP	Council
Chancellor; Ruling Councillor	Earl of Crawford	Chief Whip
Ruling Councillor	Duke of Beaufort	President
Chancellor; Trustee	Lord Randolph Churchill	Chairman
Ruling Councillor	Earl of Dartmouth	President
Grand Councillor	A. Akers-Douglas	Chief Whip
Ruling Councillor; Grand Councillor	Earl of Feversham	President
Ruling Councillor	Marquis of Hertford	President
Grand Councillor	Sir F. Dixon Hartland MP	Chairman
Ruling Councillor; Grand Councillor	Sir M. Hicks-Beach MP	Chairman
Grand Councillor	Earl of Jersey	President
Prior; Ruling Councillor	Earl of Lathom	President
Ruling Councillor	Marquis of Londonderry	President
Ruling Councillor	Earl of Londesborough	Chairman
Chancellor; Ruling Councillor	Duke of Norfolk	President
Ruling Councillor	Earl Percy	Chairman
Knight	Duke of Portland	President
Grand Councillor	H. C. Raikes MP	Chairman
Ruling Councillor	James Rankin MP	Chairman
Prior; Ruling Councillor	Sir M. W. Ridley	President Northern Federation
Grand Councillor	Sir A. Rollit MP	Chairman
Ruling Councillor	Viscount Valentia MP	Whip
Grand Councillor	Col. H. Vincent MP	Council
Ruling Councillor	Earl of Wharncliffe	President
Ruling Councillor; Grand Councillor	Lord Windsor	President

APPENDIX III   PRIMROSE LEAGUE JUVENILE BRANCH

Examination questions set for members of the Juvenile Branch of the Grantham Dames (Croydon)
Habitation 1898 (*Primrose League Gazette*, 1/11/98, p. 12)

Q.   Compare and contrast the reigns of Queen Victoria and Queen Elizabeth.
A.   There were no baths fitted in houses in Queen Elizabeth's time, but there were in Victoria's
reign. We have gas, trams, omnibuses and trains but they had not. (8-year old)
A.   Elizabeth chopped off Mary's head. Victoria did not chop off anybody's head. In
Elizabeth's reign they had very few sweets. Now they have lots of them. (10-year old)

A. Queen Elizabeth ate with her fingers. We have knives, forks and spoons. In Elizabeth's reign everybody had to go to church on Sunday. Nobody need go to church on Sunday now. (10-year-old)

Q. What are your reasons for wishing to join the Primrose League?

A. So that I may grow up a Conservative. (9-year-old)

A. My father and mother are both members, and I go with them to the meetings, which are very nice, and I like the entertainments; when I grow old enough I shall join the League because I want to learn about the Queen, and the things they talk about at the meetings. (8-year old)

Examination questions set for members of the Juvenile Branch of the Hastings and St Leonards Habitation 1901 (*Primrose League Gazette*, 2/9/01, p. 11)

Q. Why should we honour King Edward VII?

A. We must be loyal to King Edward VII because our late beloved Queen Victoria was his mother and he was her eldest son, so he is ruler over the British Isles and many other places over the sea. He is a good, kind gentleman, and we must love and honour him. He has many names – Sovereign, Monarch and sometimes spoken of as His Highness. (George Arthur Denton, 7-year-old)

Q. How do you propose individually to help on the cause of Religion and Conservatism by being a member of the Primrose League?

A. By joining the Primrose League I hope I may be able to induce my companions to be members, and they in turn may influence their brothers and parents, and so strengthen the cause of Conservatism, which, really, all true English people who love their king and country should belong to. I attend Church and Sunday School, and, by trying my hardest to be a good girl, I hope to show that a member of the Primrose League may set a good example to others. (Evelyn Glenister, 12-year-old)

Complete question paper set for Juveniles of the Grantham Dames (Croydon) Habitation in 1900 (*Primrose League Gazette*, 1/12/00, pp. 18–19)

1   What was the origin of the Primrose League? Give three good reasons for belonging to it.
2   To what fundamental principle is every Primrose Leaguer pledged with regard to all educational questions? Instance results of the rejection of this principle.
3   Name a few important events that occurred during Earl Beaconsfield's life, and give a short descriptive history of the Berlin Treaty.
4   What reasons can you adduce for your adherence to the monarchical system? Contrast it by example with the republican form of Government.
5   What is meant by the phrase 'Britannia rule the waves'? Give a small sketch of our naval flag.
6   Give a brief account of the great naval battle of Trafalgar, and the death of Lord Nelson.
7   Give the names of six English statesmen who have influenced history, with a short sketch of the life and work of your favourite one.
8   Write a short history of Lord Clive
9   In what year was the last Irish Parliament held? Why was it dissolved, and who was the Prime Minister?
10 What circumstances led to the union of the Crowns of England and Scotland?
11 Explain in simple language the word Federation as regards our colonies.
12 What Bill has been recently passed by the English Parliament that has great importance for some of our colonies? Who has been appointed Governor-General under it?
13 When was Australia discovered and by whom?
14 What is a treaty port? Give the names and some account of those in China.
15 What is a Chinese Boxer, and how did the recent troubles in China originate?
16 What would be the advantages of European supremacy in China?
17 Give a short sketch of the war in South Africa, its cause and progress. What good is expected to result from it?
18 Give an account of the founding of the First English colony in North America.

19   'Worse evil can fall on a nation than war.' Comment on this.
20   Show that we have an individual liberty beyond that enjoyed in any other European
      country.

'Hymn of the Primrose Buds'
(*Primrose League Gazette*, 1/3/09, p. 9)

Children of the Empire,
Primrose Buds are we,
Marching, ever marching,
On to victory,
Wearing still the emblem,
Just a tiny flower
From our native woodland,
Every joyful hour.

We a pledge have taken
Ever to be true
To our King and Country,
And the Empire too −
True to our religion,
Ever serving Him
Who is loved by angels
And the Seraphim.

APPENDIX IV   IRISH HABITATIONS
(with membership figures where available)

Belfast	'Premier' (1890) − 965 (1893); RC Lord Londonderry 'Balfour' (1892) Larne (1894)
Cavan	Redhills (1886)
Carlow	'Carlow Royal' (1885)
Cork	Blackwater Vale (Youghal) (1886); RC Earl of Mount Cashell 'St Patrick's' (1886) − 3,500(1888); RC Countess of Bandon Bandon and West Cork (1891) Castle Townshend (1886) − 1,841(1890) Mallow and N.E. Cork (1891); RC The Lady Mary Aldworth Kinsale (1892) Mitchelstown (1892) Dunmanway (1892)
Down	'The County Down' (1885) Kilkeel (1886) Holywood and Bangor (1894)
Dublin North	'Londonderry' (1890)
Dublin South	'Victoria' (Kingstown) (1887) − 603(1890) Killiney (1887) Rathmines (1887) Blackrock (1889) − 2,207(1890)
Dublin St Stephens	'Beaconsfield' (1885) − 850(1885); 865(1889); 1,200(1890); RC Lord Ardilaun 'Londonderry' (Rotunda Ward) (1889) − 2,250(1890)
Fermanagh	'Castle Archdale' (Irvinestown) (1886)
Galway	Athenry (1886)
Galway Borough	Galway (1886)

Kerry West	'St Brendan's' (Tralee) — 700(1888); 1,137 (1890); RC Lord Ventry
Limerick	Garryowsen (1890)
Meath	'Headfort' (1885); RC Marquis of Headfort
Tipperary Mid	Killahara (1886)
Tipperary South	'Rock of Cashel' (Cashel (1892); RC Lady Clementina Maude Nenagh (Kilroy) (1895)
Tyrone South	'Union' (Ballygawley) (1885)
Waterford Lismore	Upper Blackwater Vale (1886)
Westmeath North	'Shamrock' (Killucan) (1885)
Wexford	Ardcandrisk (1886) — 500(1888)

APPENDICES V–XVIII   TABLES OF HABITATIONS

The constituency numbers correspond to the numbers used in the regional maps in chapter 5.

The bulk of the habitations were first established during 1884–89, and for them no date has been entered in the tables. For those founded from 1890 onwards the date has been entered in brackets immediately after the name of the habitation.

The figures show membership during the year given in brackets; they are derived from the surviving Rolls of Habitations, the *Primrose League Gazette*, habitation records and local newspaper reports.

APPENDIX V   SOUTH WEST ENGLAND

1 Cornwall North East or Launceston

Launceston — 250(1887)
Cotehele (Callington, Gunnislake, Calstock) — 620(1887)
'Bevil Granville' (Stratton) — 380(1887)
'King Arthur's Round Table' (Camelford and Port Isaac) — 250(1887)
St Kew (Lanarth) (1894)

2 Cornwall South East or Bodmin

Lostwithiel — 181(1887); 346(1891)
Mount Edgcumbe — 403(1887)
Antony — 228(1887)
Bodmin — 132(1887)
'Tre, Pol and Pen' (Sheviok) — 130(1887)
'Liskerret' (Liskeard) — 252(1887)
Fowey — 652(1887)
Essa (Saltash) — 201(1887)
Looe and Sandplace
Tywardreath (1892)

3 Cornwall Mid or St. Austell

St Austell — 544(1887)
St Wenn and Trewollack — 73(1887)
Padstow — 137(1887)
St Columb — 85(1887)
'Pencalenick' (Grampound Road and Probus)
Newquay
Par (1890)

4 Cornwall North West or Camborne

'Carn Brea' (Camborne) — 166(1887)
'Carnmarth' (Redruth) — 116(1887)
Hayle (1901)

5 Cornwall West or St. Ives

6 Truro

Truro — 362(1887); 912(1891)
'The Godolphin' (Helston) — 195(1887)

'Carclew' (Mylor and Perranarworthel) −
  230(1890); 384(1901)
Treslissick

7 Penryn and Falmouth

'Pendennis' (Falmouth) − 198(1887);
  962(1980); 765(1891)

8 Devonport

Stoke Damerell − 255(1887). 600(1891)
'Victoria Regina' (East Stonehouse) −
  240(1887)

9 Plymouth

'The Beaconsfield' − 965(1886);
  1,463(1887); 1,984(1890); 1,166(1901)

10 Devon South or Totnes

'The Iddesleigh' (Kingsbridge) − 1,295(1887)
Ivybridge − 86(1887)
'Lopes' (South Brent) − 88(1887)
'Start Bay' (Dittisham) − 228(1887)
Plympton − 110(1887)

11 Torquay

'Torbay' (Brixham) − 60(1887)
'The Torquay Dames' − 1,239(1887);
  2,700(1892)
Mount Braddon (Torquay) − 334(1887)
'St Mary Church' (Babbacombe) −
  259(1887); 443(1891)
'The Dart' (Dartmouth) − 179(1887)
Paignton − 223(1887); 326(1906)
Cockington
Kingswear
'Teign' (Shaldon)

12 Devon Mid or Ashburton

'The Clinton' (Ashburton)
Bovey Tracey − 135(1886); 257(1890);
  400(1891)
Newton Abbot ('Teign Bridge') − 87(1886)
Dawlish and Luscombe − 264(1886)
Chudleigh
Teignmouth − 460(1888); 875(1889)
Bishop's Teignton

13 Honiton

Honiton − 699(1887)
'The Chetwynd' (Lympstone and Exmouth) −
  510(1887)
Axminster − 613(1887); 942(1890);
  1,043(1891)

'The Sid Vale' (Sidmouth) − 465(1887);
  600(1890)
'The Kennaway' (Ottery St Mary) −
  178(1887)
Budleigh Salterton ('Bicton') − 303(1891)

14 Exeter

'Poltimore' − 4671(1887) − subdivided into:
St David's and St Sidwell's − 813(1891)
Rougemont − 450(1891); 632(1901)
'Florence' (Heavitree) − 229(1901)
'Beaufort' (St. Thomas) − 380(1901)

15 Tiverton

Tiverton − 78(1886)
'Exe Vale' (Brampton) − 364(1887)
Topsham
Starcross
Culm (1891)
Cullompton (1892)
Haldon (1906)

16 South Molton

'The Bampfylde' (South Molton) −
  1,056(1886); 989(1887)
'The Northcote' (Crediton) − 46(1887)
'Trefusis' (Beaford) − 421(1887)
Chumleigh − 190(1887)
North Tawton and District (1908)
Torrington and District − 970(1909)

17 Devon North or Barnstaple

'The Iddesleigh' (Bideford) − 629(1886);
  859(1891); 1,000+(1906)
'The Chichester' (Ilfracombe) − 826(1886);
  589(1891)
Barnstaple − 700(1886); 548(1891);
  1,000+(1906)
'The Northcote' (Lynton, Lymouth and
  District) − 113(1886)
Arlington − 355(1891)

18 Devon West or Tavistock

Tavistock − 72(1887)
Tavistock (Dames) − 264(1887)
Hatherleigh − 70(1887); 90(1900)
Maristow − 490(1891)
'The Stanhope' (Holsworthy) − 493(1889);
  522(1891)
'The Valletort' (Bere Ferris)
Whitleigh
Bradworthy (1890) − 82(1890)
Okehampton (1895)

19 Somerset Western or Wellington

Poundisford — 304(1888)
Crowcombe — 68(1888)
Wiveliscombe — 431(1888)
'The Bisset' (Minehead) — 148(1888);
   380(1901)
Quantock Vale — 343(1888)
Wellington
Dulverton
Milverton

20 Taunton

Tone Valley (1893) — 530(1900)

21 Bridgwater

Crickleaze — 823(1888)
'Quantock' (Bridgwater) — 227(1888)
North Curry — 231(1888)
Cannington — 437(1888)
Enmore and Spaxton — 421(1888)
Combe Beacon (1893)
Ilminster

22 Somerset Southern

Crewekerne — 421(1888); 300(1891)
South Somerset Dames (Merriott, N. Perrott)
   — 751(1888); 701(1891)
'The Digby' (Yeovil) — 1,129(1888);
   1,019(1891)
Martock — 944(1888); 1,385(1890);
   2,050(1891)
Chard — 1,192(1888); 1,089(1890)
Ilchester (1892)
Curry Rivel (1892)
Coker (1892)
West Chinnock

23 Somerset Eastern

Somerton — 217(1888)
'Blackmoor Vale' (Wincanton) — 1,125(1888)
Milborne Port — 221(1888)
Evercreech – 252(1888)
The Butleigh
Stratton-on-the-Fosse (1890)
Shepton Mallet — 114(1890); 226(1891)

24 Frome

'The Wickham' (Frome) — 627(1888)
Road
'Vale of Avon' (Batheaston) — 500(1888);
   604(1891)
Newton St Loe — 208(1888)
Weston — 100(1888)
Norton St Philip

'The Theobald' (Nunney)
Freshford and Limpley Stoke
'The Paget' (Cranmore) — 500 + (1886)

25 Bath

Bath — 2,440(1888)

26 Somerset Northern

Harptree — 561(1888)
Farrington Gourney — 124(1888)
Nailsea
'The Llewellyn' (Yatton)
Vale of Chew
Clevedon
Portishead
'St George' (Easton-in-Gordano)
Backwell (1892)

27 Wells

Mendip — 1,247(1888)
Wells — 650(1888); 563(1890)
Glastonbury — 500(1891)
Weston-Super-Mare; 351(1891)
'The Loyal' (Burnham-on-Sea)
Lympsham
Isle of Wedmore (1906)
Brent Knolls (1906)

28 Bristol West

'The Colston' — 730(1886); 1,092(1888)
Hotwells — 41(1888)
Clifton — 421(1911)
Westbury — 58(1888)
Salisbury Club
St Michael's Ward — 125(1886)
St Augustine's 78(1886)
Horfield and Bishopston — 90(1886)
Redland

Bristol North

Fishponds — 140(1886); 186(1888)
St Paul's — 39 (1888)
'The Eastville' (Stapleton) — 191(1886)
The District Ward — 90(1886)

Bristol East

Bissell — 75(1888)
'Travers F. Fox' (Easton) — 52(1888)
'Forest of Fillwood'
'The Salisbury' (Russeltown) — 44(1886)
St George's

Bristol South

Knowle and Totterdown — 207(1890)

Bristol City — 332(1886)
Bedminster — 940(1891); 1,600(1892)
Bristol Ward — 58(1888)

St Philips Conservative Club
Redcliffe

APPENDIX VI WESSEX

1 Berkshire North or Abingdon

'The Abbey' (Abingdon) — 90(1887)
'St Helen Dames' (Abington) — 170(1887)
'St Stephens's' (Wallingford) — 138(1890)
Wantage
Faringdon — 115(1886)

2 Berkshire South or Newbury

Newbury — 177(1887)
Greenham — 160(1887)
Aldermarston — 386(1887)
Shaw-cum-Donnington — 326(1887)
Falkland — 214(1887)
'Crookham House' (Thatcham) — 351(1887)
Arlington — 117(1887)
Winchcombe — 127(1887)
Hungerford — 152(1887)
Purley, Tylehurst and Sulham — 450(1887);
    718(1890); 792(1891)
Kintbury — 177(1887)
Basildon — 15(1887)
Burghfield and Sulhamstead — 194(1887)
Mortimer — 315(1886)
Englefield — 490(1891)
Bradfield (1891)
Streatley (1892)
Compton (1895) — 200(1897); 305(1900)

3 Reading

Reading Borough — 246(1886)

4 Berkshire East or Wokingham

Wargrave — 733(1887)
'Desborough' (Maidenhead) — 1,371(1887);
    600(1912)
Wokingham — 377(1887)
Sunninghill and Ascot — 105(1886)
Easthamptstead — 861(1886); 536(1888)
'Queen's Arbour' (Waltham St Lawrence)
    (1890)
Binfield (1893)
Crowthorne (1898)

5 Windsor

'The Royal Windsor' — 187(1886);
    230(1890); 850(1891)

6 Hampshire Northern or Basingstoke

Winchfield — 968(1888)
Basingstoke — 584(1888)
Farnborough — 209(1888)
Oakley — 159(1888)
Aldershot — 253(1886); 409(1888)
Candover — 202(1888)
Blackwater — 452(1886); 505(1888)
'The Victoria' (Ewshott) - 222(1886);
    473(1888)
Hartley Witney — 386(1888)
Strathfieldsaye — 185(1888)
Sherborne St John (1892)

7 Hampshire Western or Andover

Hursley — 403(1886); 509(1888)
Burghclere — 410(1888); 440(1890)
Andover — 391(1886); 691(1888)
Anna Valley (Abbott's Ann/Amport Firs) —
    364(1886); 486(1888)
Kingsclere — 332(1886); 543(1888)
Twyford — 63(1888)
Stockbridge and District — 66(1888)
Itchen Valley — 117(1888)
Highclere — 281(1886); 340(1905)
Broughton
Longparish

8 Winchester

'The Caer Gwent' — 385(1886); 647(1888)
Winchester — 235(1886)

9 Hampshire Eastern or Petersfield

'The Palace' (Bishop's Waltham) —
    438(1886); 741(1888); 1,250(1891)
Longwood — 118(1888)
Bentworth and Shalden — 212(1888)
Alton — 105(1886); 492(1888)
Bramshott — 340(1888)
Hinton Daubnay — 142(1888)
Farringdon and District — 427(1888)
Hambledon — 104(1888)
'The Gilbert White' (Selborne)
Petersfield
Alresford — 78(1888)

10 Hampshire Southern or Fareham

Gosport – 316(1886); 550(1888); 224(1891)
Eastleigh – 332(1888)
Fareham – 86(1886); 169(1888)
Wickham – 147(1888)
Netley – 321(1888)
'Place House' (Titchfield) – 296(1888)
'West End' (Southampton) (1890) –
    92(1891)
Havant and Hayling (1891)
'Leigh' (Emsworth) (1891)

11 Portsmouth

'The Bruce' (Southsea) – 865(1886);
    2,424(1888); 2,164(1891)
The Portsea – 35(1888)
'The Naval and Military' (Southsea)
'The Fitz-Wygram' (Southsea)
'The Palmerston'
'Elphinstone' – 288(1888)
'St Alphege' – 46(1888)
'St Luke's and St Bartholomew's Wards
    (1895)

12 Southampton

Southampton – 500(1886); 778(1888)
Millbrook – 401(1891)
Bitterne – 44(1886)

13 The New Forest

'New Forest' – 2470(1888); 2,658(1890);
    subdivided into:
    Beaulieu
    Totton
    North Eling
    Lyndhurst
    Bramshaw
    Ringwood
'Palmerston' (Romsey)
Minstead (1896)
Copythorne and Netley (1896)
Lymington – 1,030(1886); 1,395(1888)
Breamore – 979(1886); 1,009(1888)
'St Boniface' (Nursling) – 115(1888)

14 Christchurch

Bournemouth – 183(1888)
'Drummond Wolff' (Bournemouth) –
    800(1885); 1,752(1888); 3,961(1900)
'The Malmesbury' (Christchurch) –
    1,700(1886)
Boscombe and Pokesdown (1895)

15 The Isle of Wight

'Medina' (East Cowes) – 263(1888);
    304(1890)
'Stanhope' (West Cowes) – 1,002(1888)
Ryde – 153(1888)
Ryde Dames – 162(1886); 456(1888)
Undercliffe – 72(1888)
'The Central' (Newport) – 305(1886);
    681(1888); 765(1890); 460(1905)
Shanklin – 141(1888)
Sandown – 105(1888)
Freshwater and Yarmouth – 221(1888)
Wootton Bridge
The Ward

16 Dorset East

'Cornelia' (Poole) – 450(1888)
Wimborne Minster – 379(1888); 654(1906)
'The Guest' (Wimborne) – 331(1888)
'The Churchill' (Hampreston) – 387(1888)
Cranborne – 396(1888)
Corfe Mullen – 136(1888)
'The Frances' (Kinson) – 140(1888);
    255(1906)
'The Corisande' (Heatherlands) – 299(1888)
Parkstone
Branksome
'The Peverill' (Swanage)
'The Lytchet' (Lytchet Matravers) –
    152(1886)
'Sandford' (Wareham) – 464(1888)
'Mansel' (Corfe Castle) – 436(1888)
'Henbury' (Sturminster Marshall) –
    165(1888)
'The Radclyffe' (Bere Regis) – 294(1888)
'The Handley' (Sixpenny Handley)
Witchampton

17 Dorset South

Weymouth – 1,960(1888)
Melcombe Regis (1893)
'Floyer' (Dorchester)
'Brymer' (Puddletown) – 404(1888)
'Fyler' (Wool) – 580(1888)
'Wyke' (Wyke Regis) (1893)

18 Dorset West

Lyme Regis – 149(1888)
Broadwindsor – 82(1888)
Beaminster – 1,049(1888)
'Nepean' (Bridport) – 1,552(1886);
    1,943(1888)
'Ilchester' (Bridehead) – 605(1888)
Chalmington – 452(1888)

'Melbury' (Melbury, Evershot & District); −
  1,045(1886); 790(1888); 666(1894);
  653(1900)
Hawkchurch − 47(1888)
'The Digby' (Cerne Abbas) − 136(1886)
Abbotsbury − 293(1886)

19 Dorset North

Blandford − 247(1888)
Childe Okeford − 156(1888)
Sherborne − 295(1888)
'The Rock' (Shaftesbury) − 110(1888)
Motcombe − 102(1888)
'Stour Vale' (Marnhull) − 327(1888)
'The Hambro' (Milton Abbey) − 197(1888)
Holwell − 257(1888)
Bourton − 77(1888)
Thornhill (Stallbridge) − 151(1888)
Haselbury Bryan − 233(1888)
Gillingham − 306(1888)
Tarrant Valley − 157(1888)
'Jubilee' (Thornford) (1897)

20 Wiltshire South or Wilton

'Wilton House' (Wilton) − 3,114(1889)
'Chafyn Grove' (E. and W. Knoyle) −
  290(1891) (later 'Knoyle Vale')
'Wardour' (Donhead/Ludwell) − 320(1889)
Nadder Vale − 471(1889); 554(1890)
Broad Chalke − 615(1889)
Shrewton
Hindon (1890)
Wyle Vale (1890)
Norrington (1890)
Downton (1890)
Durnford (1890)

21 Salisbury

'The Longford Castle' − 3,481(1886);
  2,326(1889); subdivided in 1890:
  St Martin's Ward
  St Thomas's Ward
  St Edmund's Ward
  Milford and Wyndham Park
  Fisherton

22 Wiltshire West or Westbury

Melksham − 197(1889)
Freshford − 54(1889)
Bradford-on-Avon − 290(1889)
Trowbridge
'Beaconsfield' (Trowbridge Dames) −
  315(1889)
Warminster − 588(1889)
Westbury − 513(1889)

Longleat − 547(1889)
'Thynne' (Melksham Dames) − 167(1889)
'The Long' (Keevil and Steeple Aston) −
  141(1889)
Holt − 107(1889)
Seend (1896)

23 Wiltshire East or Devizes

Marlborough
'The Dorothy' (Marlborough)
East and West Lavington − 172(1889)
Devizes
'Avon Valley' (Amesbury)
Pewsey District (1902)

24 Wiltshire North or Cricklade

Swindon − 307(1889)
Lyneham − 173(1889)
Cricklade − 192(1889)
Highworth
'The Lady Somerset' (Broad Town) −
  52(1889)

25 Wiltshire North West or Chippenham

Calne − 375(1889)
Colerne − 215(1889)
Chippenham − 1,296(1889)
Kington St Michael − 91(1889)
'King Athelstan' (Malmesbury)
'The Bruce' (Somerford, Dauntsey and
  Brinkworth)
Corsham − 270(1889); 600+(1903)
'The Beaufort' (Sherston) − 97(1889)
Crudwell − 210(1889); 290(1891)

26 Gloucestershire South or Thornbury

'Kingsweston' (Henbury and Avonmouth) −
  318(1888); 291(1891)
Thornbury − 333(1888)
'Blathwayt' (Dyrham Park) − 70(1888)
Coalpit Heath and Frampton − 47(1888)
Hambrook District − 213(1888)
Bitton − 184(1886); 89(1888)
Mangotsfield
'Codrington' (Chipping Sodbury) −
  130(1886)
Wick − 151(1886)
'The Beaufort' (Badminton)
Stoke Bishop
Hanham (1890)
Westbury-upon-Trym (1893)

27 Gloucestershire Mid or Stroud

'The Hicks-Beach' (Dursley) − 130(1888)
Bisley − 216(1888)

Woodchester — 177(1888)
Nailsworth and Horsley — 159)1887);
   185(1888); 300+(1891)
'Lypiatt' (Chalford) — 94(1888)
Frocester — 71(1888)
Painswick
'Beaufort' (Wotton-under-Edge) — 90(1886)
Stroud — 400(1886)
Minchinhampton

22 Gloucestershire East or Cirencester

'Cotteswold' (Cirencester) — 488(1888);
   990(1906)
Stow-on-the-Wold — 756(1888)
Campden — 890(1886); 1,087(1888)
Coln Valley — 182(1886)
Northleach — 350(1886)
Barrington Park
Ampney Crucis
Shipton Moyne (Tetbury) (1892)
Mickleton (1892)
Redesdale (Morton-in-Marsh) (1895)

29 Gloucestershire North or Tewskesbury

Tewkesbury — 220(1888)

Swindon Hall — 139(1888)
Guiting Grange — 125(1888)
'The Helen' (Fretherne) — 313(1891)
Prestbury — 76(1888)
Hardwicke — 303(1888)
Winchcombe — 279(1888)
'The Puckrup' (Twyning)
'Salisbury' (Berkeley)

30 Cheltenham

Cheltenham — 447(1886); 519(1888);
   1,985(1901); 3,016(1902)
Salterley — 114(1888)
Leckhampton Ward — 96(1886)
Charlton Kings

31 Gloucester

The Gloucestershire Outvoters — 28(1886)
Gloucester — 15(1886); 1,107(1906)

32 The Forest of Dean

Lydney — 985(1888)
Dymock — 213(1888)
'St Michael's' (Newent)
'Forest Acorn' (Newnham-on-Severn)

APPENDIX VII   SOUTH EAST ENGLAND

1 Kent Western or Sevenoaks

'Louisa' (Seal) — 383(1888)
Chislehurst — 280(1888)
Sevenoaks — 528(1888); 694(1891)
Chevening — 1693(1888)
Farnborough — 408(1888)
Bromley — 252(1888)
Beckenham — 329(1888)

2 Kent North Western or Dartford

'Oakfield' (Dartford) — 1780(1888);
   2,425(1891)
'The Frognal' (Sidcup)
Orpington and Cray Valley

3 Gravesend

Borough of Gravesend — 160(1886);
   240(1888); 900+(1905)
Northfleet and Perry Street (1898)

4 Kent Mid or Medway

Wierton — 184(1888)
Wrotham — 314(1888)
'The Nevill' (West Malling — 1685(1888)

'The Chilston' (Harrietsham) — 130(1888)
'Medway' (Wateringbury) (1891)

5 Maidstone

'Howard de Walden' (Dames) — 461(1886);
   752(1888); 980(1890)
'Ross' — 600(1886); 733(1888)

6 Rochester

'The Cecil' (Rochester) — 130(1888);
   500+(1891)

7 Chatham

'The Gorst' (New Brompton and Gillingham)
   — 59(1888)
Borough of Chatham
'The Gordon' (Chatham) (1894)

8 Kent North East or Faversham

Faversham — 1695(1888); 2,000+(1890);
   393(1906); 1,779(1909)
Isle of Sheppey — 296(1888)
Queensborough (1892)

9 Kent South West or Tonbridge

'The Nevill' (Tonbridge Wells) − 944(1888)
Tonbridge
'The Torrington' (Mereworth) − 593(1888);
701(1891)
'The Bayham' (Lamberhurst) − 1,249(1888);
475(1891)
'The Sidney' (Penshurst)

10 Kent East or St Augustine's

Herne Bay
Chartham and Mystole − 201(1888)
'Akers-Douglas' (Deal and Walmer) −
398(1888); 471(1904)
Kingsdown − 1,838(1888)
St Margaret's-at-Cliffe
Evington − 265(1888)
Wingham − 300(1888)
The Eastry
Lydden-Ewell and Rivers('Dour Valley' 1890)
'Bifrons' (Bourne Park, Patrixbourne)
Sibertswold and Waldershare (1894)

11 Isle of Thanet

Thanet (Margate) − 167(1888)
'The King-Harman' (Ramsgate)
Westgate-on-Sea
Birchington

12 Canterbury

Canterbury − 150(1886); 436(1888)
St Augustine's

13 Dover

'Premier in Kent' − 455(1888); 1,100(1889);
2,000(1900)

14 Hythe

Folkestone
'Saltwood' (Hythe) − 700(1886); 203(1888)
Cheriton, Newton and Sandgate − 229(1886)

15 Kent Southern or Ashford

Cranbrook − 887(1888)
Ashford − 915(1888); 1,212(1906)
'The Hope' (Goudhurst) − 210(1888)
Staplehurst − 502(1888)
'The Maytham' (Rolvenden)

16 Sussex Eastern or Rye

'Waterloo' (Bexhill) − 252(1888)
'The Bayham' (Lamberhurst) − 950(1888)
Rye − 649(1888)

Battle − 2140(1888)
Eridge − 800+(1890)
Ticehurst(1890)
Mayfield(1903)

17 Hastings and St Leonards

'South Saxon' (Hastings and St Leonards) −
250(1886); 147(1888)
Hastings and St Leonards Dames −
720(1886); 947(1888); 1,130(1890)
'The Premier Cinque Port' − 148

18 Eastbourne

Hailsham − 800+(1907)
Eastbourne
'Davies Gilbert' (Eastbourne)
Newhaven (1890)
Ringmer and Laughton ('Royal Delves')
(1901)

19 Brighton

Brighton Dames − 50(1884); 372(1886)
540(1888) 1,200(1891)
'The Beaconsfield' (Brighton) − 301(1886);
178(1888)
'The Coningsby' (Brighton) − 222(1888);
347(1891)
'The Constitutional' (Hove) − 138(1888)
Preston − 401(1886); 561(1888)
'The Royal York' (1893)

20 Sussex Mid or Lewes

Henfield − 153(1888)
'The Weald of Sussex (Barcombe) −
509(1888); 553(1890)
'The Gundrada' (Lewes) − 463(1888)
Wolstonbury − 310(1888)
Ditchling − 75(1888)
'The Hughenden (Worthing) − 86(1888)
Kingston-by-Sea − 149(1888)
'Southdown Dames' (Kingston) − 142(1888)
'Braose' (Bamber and Beeding) − 126(1888)
Harold or Brookside − 192(1890)

21 Sussex Northern or East Grinstead

Lindfield
Worth
Burgess Hill − 103(1888)
Wakehurst
East Grinstead − 223(1888)
Uckfield − 410(1888)
Framfield − 56(1888)
Warninglid − 117(1888)
Warninglid Dames − 90(1888)
Hurstpierpoint − 181(1888)

Hayward's Heath
Cuckfield
Ardingley (1895)

22 *Sussex South Western or Chichester*

Bognor
'Molecombe' (Chichester) – 1,788(1888)
Storrington
Westbourne – 765(1888)
'The Slindon' (Walberton) – 128(1888)
'Vale of Arun' (Arundel and Littlehampton)
   – 112(1888)
Angermering – 43(1888)
Stanstead

23 *Sussex North Western or Horsham*

'The Cowdray' (Midhurst) – 712(1888);
   787(1890)
Horsham – 1,367(1888); 1,432(1890)
Milland
Crawley
Petworth – 895 (1888)
Kirdford and Wisborough – 334(1888);
   381(1890)
Pulborough

24 *Surrey – Guildford*

Guildford – 555(1888); 576(1890)
Peper Harrow – 978(1888)
Godalming – 218(1888); 396(1891)
Haslemere – 185(1890)
'Cranleigh' (Ewhurst) (1893)
Tillingbourne Valley (1896)
Farnham (1896)
'The Victorian Era' (Bramley, Shalford and
   Wonersh) (1897)

25 *Surrey – Chertsey*

Weybridge
Egham – 1,030(1888)

Chertsey
Woking
Addlestone – 234(1888); 222(1890)
Horsley
'The Pine Wood' (Frimley)
Byfleet
Bagshot (1893) – 401(1893)
Windlesham and Chobham (1897)

26 *Surrey – Epsom*

Walton-on-Thames and Oatlands –
   330(1884); 717(1885); 1,084(1887);
   1,861(1890)
Esher – 233(1888)
Hersham
Epsom – 397(1888)
Molesey
Ashtead – 193(1888)
Banstead – 609(1888)
Cobham – 576(1888)
'The Nonsuch' (Worcester Park) –
   219(1888); 160(1891)
Sutton – 567(1888)
Mickleham – 270(1888)
Leatherhead
Bookham – 329(1888)
Claygate – 30(1888)
Ewell(1890)
'The Dittons' (Thames Ditton) (1891)

27 *Surrey – Reigate*

Redhill – 440(1888)
Dorking
Ford
Reigate
Ockley – 301(1888)
Charlwood
Tilberstow (Godstone)
Chipstead – 165(1888)
Horley
Vale of Holmesdale

APPENDIX VIII   LONDON

1 City of London

City of London – 157(1886); 1,500(1912)
The Corn Exchange – 13(1886)
City Carlton Club
'Marquis of Salisbury' – 61(1888)
Tower – 49(1886)
'Lloyd's Patriotic'

2 Westminster

The Westminster – 500(1886); 1,144(1888)

3 The Strand

'The Premier' – 14(the original founding
   members, November 1883)
'Abergavenny' (Constitutional Club) –
   532(1888)
The Conservative Club – 114(1888)
The Tavistock
The Primrose Club

4 St George's Hanover Square

St George's – 422(1888); 1,120(1890);

1,051(1901); 1,344(1905)
'The Wimborne' − 404(1888)
Belgravia − 1,103(1888); 1,088(1890)
'The Northumberland' (Mayfair) −
412(1888); 500(1890)
The Grosvenor − 350(1886)
'The Limerick' − 199(1886)

5 Chelsea

Cheyne − 337(1888); 226(1898)
Cadogan − 268(1888)
'Stanley' − 361(1886); 758(1888)
Knightsbridge and Upper Chelsea −
511(1886); 467(1888)
'St Mary's' (Queen's Park)

6 Fulham

Fulham Conservative Club − 201(1888)
Fulham Dames − 144(1886)
'The Empire' (West Kensington) − 31(1886)

7 Hammersmith

'Albert' − 274(1888)
'The Churchill' (Shepherd's Bush) −
118(1888)
'Victoria Dames' − 320(1886); 176(1890)
Hammersmith − 212(1888)
'The Goldsworthy'

8 Kensington North

'Hamilton' − 346(1888)
'Coronation' (1902)

Kensington South

'The Borthwick' − 241(1888)
'The Bective' − 90(1888)
'Jubilee' − 235(1888)
Old Court Suburb − 400(1900)
Earl's Court − 57(1886)
'The Wynstay' (Queen's Gate)

9 Paddington North

'The Lionel Cohen' − 400(1886); 529(1888)
Paddington (No. 1 Ward) − 279(12888)

Paddington South

'St Stephens' − 77(1886)
Bayswater(1890) − 60(1890); 660(1894);
1,400(1900)
'The Randolph Churchill' − 430(1886)
'Minchin' (Westbourne Park) − 215(1890)

10 St Marylebone East

'Beresford' − 860(1886)

St Marylebone West

West Marylebone and Montagu − 38(1886)
Marylebone − 490(1886)

11 Finsbury − Holborn

'The Doughty' − 71(1888)
'The Cecilia' (Bloomsbury) − 243(1888)
Inns of Court (1890)
Holborn (1892)
St Andrews

Finsbury Central

Clerkenwell − 122(1886); 140(1888)

Finsbury East

Bigwood
East Finsbury (1891)

12 Shoreditch − Hoxton

Caxton − 115(1888)
Montagu (1892)

Shoreditch − Haggerston

Haggerston and Dalston − 300(1886);
220(1889)

13 Tower Hamlets − Whitechapel

'Trench' − 529(1888)

Tower Hamlets − St George's in the East

Riverside (1893)

Tower Hamlets − Stepney

'Beaumont' − 114(1888)
'Isaacson'

Tower Hamlets − Limehouse

Limehouse and Shadwell (1891)

Tower Hamlets − Mile End

'Spencer Charrington' − 164(1886);
148(1890); 202(1891)

14 Poplar

'The Welby' − 2,320(1888)

15 Bow and Bromley

'The Beaconsfield' − 259(1888)

16 West Ham South

'The Henniker'
Silvertown and Cannington — 51(1886)
'The Churchill' — 331(1886)

West Ham North

'The David Howard' (1891)
'The Forrest Fulton' (Upton Park) —
68(1888)

17 Bethnal Green North East

'Sir Michael Hicks-Beach' — 121(1888);
200(1890)

Bethnal Green South West

'The Montefiore'

18 Southwark West

'The Christchurch'
Blackfriars

Southwark — Bermondsey

St Mary's — 192(1886)
'The Grange' — 157(1888)
'The Lafone' — 93(1886)
St George's — 56(1886)

Southwark — Rotherhithe

'The Hamilton' — 329(1886); 501(1888)
Rotherhithe — 220(1886); 721(1888)

19 Deptford

'The Chichester' (Deptford)

20 Camberwell North

North Camberwell
'The Brunswick' (1895)
Camberwell — 177(1886)

21 Newington West

West Newington (1892)
'The Burnaby'

Newington — Walworth

Walworth

22 Lambeth North

'The Knightley' (Tulse Hill)
'The Craufurd Fraser'

Lambeth — Kennington

'The Churchill' — 200(1886); 412(1888)
'Princes' (1891)

Lambeth — Brixton

Brixton — 59(1886)
The Norwood Dames — 80(1888)

Lambeth — Norwood

'The Crystal Palace' — 52(1886)
'The Bristowe' — 340(1886)
'The Knightley'

23 Clapham

Lavender Hill — 130(1888)
'The Iddlesleigh' — 276(1888)
'The Bolingbroke' — 51(1886)
'The Bourke' — 75(1886)

24 Battersea

'Meresia' — 330(1888)
Old Battersea — 72(1886)
'The Beaconsfield' — 20(1886)
'The Bolingbroke' (Clapham Jnction) —
13(1888); 170(1890)

25 Woolwich

Woolwich — 162(1886)

26 Greenwich

'Charlton' — 238(1886); 364(1888)
'Spencer' (Greenwich) — 57(1886)
Blackheath
Kidbroke and Coombe
'Vansittart' (West Greenwich) (1890);
152(1891)

27 Lewisham

The Borough of Lewisham
Forest Hill
Lee Green — 110(1886)
Lower Sydenham and Perry Hill — 52(1888)
South Lee — 98(1886)

28 Peckham

Peckham — 457(1886); 115(1888)
'The Baumann'

29 Dulwich

Anerley — 30(1886)
Hamlet of Dulwich — 66(1888)

Dulwich and East Dulwich — 121(1886);
400+(1891)
Alleyn (1893) — 340(1900)

30 Wandsworth

'St Leonard's' (Streatham) — 312(1888)
Wandsworth — 444(1888)
Tooting — 18(1888)
Putney — 101(1886); 249(1891)
Balham and Upper Tooting — 140(1886)

31 Essex South West or Walthamstow

Walthamstow — 108(1886)
Woodford — 254(1888)
'Beaconsfield' (Leyton)
Grange Park
Leytonstone

32 Hackney North

Stoke Newington — 411(1886); 952(1888)
Upper Clapton

Hackney Central

'The Cranborne' — 160(1886); 358(1888)
'Sir Guyer Hunter' — 159(1886); 210(1888)

Hackney South

'The Tyssen Amherst' — 1,216(1886);
1,125(1888); 1,993(1891)

33 Islington East

Highbury Vale — 72(1888)
Highbury — 201(1888)
Highbury Dames — 190(1886); 295(1888)
Canonbury — 36(1886)

Islington South

St Mary — 150(1888)
Barnsbury — 248(1888); 341(1890)
St Peter's — 88(1886)

Islington West

Holloway
St George — 180(1888)

Islington North

'The Duncan'
Islington — 40(1886)

34 St Pancras East

'The Churchill'
'The Salisbury' (1897)

St Pancras South

South St Pancras — 95(1886)

St Pancras West

'The Rutland' — 1,400(1886); 1,374(1888)

St Pancras North

North St Pancras — 107(1886)
Parliament Hill — 268(1886)

35 Tottenham

'The Howard' (Tottenham) — 331(1888)
Wood Green — 269(1888)

36 Enfield

Enfield — 972(1888); 1,100(1900)
Myddleton — 1,034(1900); 3,000+(1911)
Potter's Bar
Edmonton
Southgate

37 Hornsey

Hornsey — 205(1888)
Finchley — 642(1888)
Crouch End — 85(1888)
Stroud Green
Brownswood (Finsbury Park)

38 Hampstead

'The Pitt' — 535(1886)

39 Harrow

Stanmore — 305(1888)
Harrow and Sudbury — 302(1888)
Hendon — 314(1888)
Pinner — 192(1888)
Mill Hill
'The Hamilton' (Willesden)

40 Ealing

Chiswick — 269(1888)
Ealing
Acton

41 Uxbridge

Uxbridge — 225(1888)
Ruislip — 162(1888)
'The Dixon-Hartland' (Yiewsley and West
Drayton) — 207(1888)
Teddington and Hampton Wick
Sunbury and Shepperton — 760(1888)
Hampton Hill
Staines

42 Brentford

'Osterley' (Hounslow) − 217(1888)
'The Brent' (Hanwell) − 195(1888)
Brentford − 130(1888)
Twickenham − 234(1888); 247(1892);
   666(1900); 711(1904); 658(1905)

43 Kingston-on-Thames

Mortlake − 222(1888)
Surbiton − 329(1888)
Kingston-on-Thames − 268(1888); 802(1891)
Richmond
Richmond Dames − 400(1888); joint
   membership with Richmond 1,100(1890)
Barnes
Coombe and Maldon − 30(1888)
Kew
'The Beresford' (Sheen) − 420(1890)

44 Wimbledon,

Wimbledon − 632(1906)
Wandle (Carshalton)
Kenley

45 Croydon

Croydon − 112(1888)
'The Grantham' (Croydon Dames) −
   310(1886); 486(1888); 910(1891);
   1,660(1909)
South Norwood − 28(1886)
'The Herbert' − 182(1888)
'The Edridge' (Thornton Heath) −
   1,300(1909)
'The Beaconsfield' (Addiscombe)
'The Beatrix' (South Ward, Croydon) −
   98(1888)

APPENDIX IX   CENTRAL ENGLAND

1 Oxfordshire South or Henley

Henley-on-Thames − 506(1888); 504(1890);
   526(1891)
Thame − 512(1888)
Watlington and Tetsworth − 684(1888)
Wheatley − 197(1888); 209(1891)
Milton − 130(1888)
Whitchurch − 333(1888)
Caversham
Stokenchurch
Dorchester − 438(1890)
Chinnor Polling District
Nettlebed(1892)

2 Oxford Borough

'Gordon' − 246(1886); 475(1888) (Divided
   into the Summertown and Chesney 1893)
'A. W. Hall' − 297(1888)
'Randolph Churchill' − 64(1888)
Oxford University − 156(1886)

3 Oxfordshire Mid or Woodstock

'Golden Fleece' (Witney) − 75(1888);
   211(1890)
Burford − 291(1888)
'Valentia' (Bletchington) − 273(1888)
Shelswell − 396(1888)
Bicester
Woodstock
Bampton
Stanton St John

'St Stephens' (Clanfield)
'St Denys' (Eynsham) (1890)

4 Oxfordshire North or Banbury

Banbury − 687(1888)
Chipping Norton − 874(1888)
Steeple Ashton − 425(1888)
Shipton-under-Wychwood − 130(1888)
'King's Oak' (Chastleton)
Charlbury
Deddington
Hook Norton
Wardington (1893)
'The Three C's'

5 Northamptonshire South

'Knightley' (Daventry) − 858(1888)
Brackley − 912(1888)
'Beatrice' (Byfield) − 366(1888)
'Hesketh' (Towcester)
Canon's Ashby
Deanshanger

6 Northampton Borough

'Delapre' (Northampton) − 707(1888);
   1,200(1891)

7 Northamptonshire Mid

Guilsborough − 1007(1888); 1,548(1891);
   600(1912)
Rothwell − 91(1888)

8 *Northamptonshire East*

Hamfordsho − 421(1888)
'Hatton' (Wellingborough) − 1,037(1890);
  400+(1903); 700(1904)
Kettering
Irthlingborough
'Chichele' (Higham Ferrers) − 221(1891)
Little Addington (1890)
Wollaston (1891)
Rushden (1893)
Earl's Barton − 260(1904)

9 *Northamptonshire North*

'Rockingham Forest' (Thrapston) −
  745(1888)
Latimer − 200(1888)
Castor and Wansford − 150(1888)
'Rockingham Castle' (Corby area)
Oundle − 380 (1890)
'St Matthews' (Eye)

10 *Peterborough*

Peterborough − 38(1886)

11 *Bedfordshire North or Biggleswade*

Harrold − 122(1887)
'Salisbury' (Langford) − 113(1887)
'Crown' (Northill) − 86(1887)
'Stuart' (Tempsford) − 231(1887)
Ampthill − 205(1887)
Potton
'Union Jack' (Eaton Socon) (1894)
Blunham (1895)

12 *Bedford*

Bedford Borough − 1,790(1891); 1,696(1900)
Sir John Burgoyne − 120(1888)

13 *Bedfordshire South or Luton*

Shillington − 108(1888)
Woburn − 189(1888)
Dunstable and Haughton Regis − 225(1887)
Luton − 351(1886)

14 *Hertfordshire North or Hitchin*

Hitchin − 646(1886); 757(1888)
Stevenage − 591(1888)
Welwyn − 226(1886); 277(1888)
Offley − 306(1886); 290(1888)
Baldock − 411(1886); 445(1888); 448(1890)
Watton − 102(1887)
Bennington − 243(1887); 393(1890)
'Dimsdale' (Walkern) − 236(188)
Lilley − 120(188)

Buntingford − 293 (1888)
Benstead − 193(1886)
'Julians' (Rushden) − 171(1888)
Whitwell − 236(1888)
Mundens
Kimpton

15 *Hertfordshire East or Hertford*

Bishop's Stortford − 140(1888)
Hertford − 1,192(1888); 1,591(1890);
  1,750(1891)
Ware − 350(1886); 527(1888)
Sayesbury − 495(1888)
Stanstead Abbotts − 123(1888)
Broxbornebury − 169(1888)
Cheshunt
Hoddesdon − 200(1886)
'Myddleton' (Waltham Cross)

16 *Hertfordshire Mid or St Albans*

'Salisbury' (Hatfield) − 1,846(1888);
  1,094(1891); 623(1894); 800(1899)
'Verulam' (St Albans) − 400(1888);
  564(1891); 633(1895); 549(1899)
Barnet − 89(1888); 250(1890); 284(1895)
Essendon − 132(1888); 130(1891);
  124(1895); 84(1899)
Great Gaddesden − 155(1888); 162(1891);
  150(1893); 119(1895)
Ridge and London Colney − 287(1888);
  258(1890); 302(1894)
'Lamer' (Wheathampstead) − 173(1888);
  330(1891); 360(1895)
Aldenham and Elstree − 40(1891);
  315(1893); 500(1894); 152(1898)
Shenley and Radlett (1891) − 87(1891);
  227(1894); 207(1895)
Little Gaddesden (1891) − 24(1891);
  24(1894)
Markyate St (1893) − 132(1894); 255(1895)
North Mymms (1896) − 230(1898);
  301(1899)
Hamstead − 51(1891); 63(1895)

17 *Hertfordshire West or Watford*

'West Herts' (Hemel Hempstead Dames) −
  3,641(1888); 5,000+(1900)
Watford (1899)
Bushey (1903)
Abbotts Langley (1904)
Boxmoor

18 *Buckinghamshire South*

Slough − 317(1887)
Taplow − 144(1887)

Burnham — 319(1886); 344(1891)
Marlow — 370(1887)
High Wycombe — 205(1886)
Beaconsfield — 189(1887)
Amersham — 481(1886)
'Curzon' (Iver) — 115(1887)
Tyler's Green and Penn — 261(1887)
Chalfont St Peter — 104(1887)
Chalfont St Giles — 105(1887)
Fulmer — 430(1887)
Denham — 165(1887)
Bourne End (1902)

19 Buckinghamshire Mid

Aylesbury — 583(1887)
'Velvet Lawn' (Wendover) — 720(1887)

Dinton — 211(1886)
Chesham
Bradenham (1890)
Lacey Green (1891)

20 Buckinghamshire North or Buckingham

'Addington' (Winslow) — 1181(1887)
Buckingham — 1935(1887)
Newport Pagnell — 364(1887)
'The Dartmouth' (Olney) — 102(1887)
'Duncombe' (Bletchley and Fenny Stratford)
 — 402(1887)
'Radcliffe' (Wolverton) — 488(1887)
Wotton — 373(1886)
Nash

APPENDIX X   EAST ANGLIA

1 King's Lynn

'The Bentinck' — 775(1888)
Bourke — 1,366(1886); 1,562(1888)

2 Norfolk North West

'Salisbury' (Lynn and Castle Rising) —
 1370(1888)
'Loyalty' (Hunstanton) — 187(1888);
 225(1903)
'Bentinck' (Terrington) — 221(1888)
Central Marshland — 515(1888)
Dersingham — 392(1888)
'Bellamy' (Walsoken) — 116(1888)
Fakenham — 617(1888)
'Rolfe' (Sedgeford and Heacham) —
 291(1888)
Inglethorpe
'Romney' (Grimston and East Walton) (1890)

3 Norfolk North

Holt — 623(1888)
Cromer — 98(1888)
Foulsham — 441(1888)
Aylsham — 400(1888); 660(1902)
North Greenhoe — 203(1888)

4 Norfolk East

Coltishall — 392(1888)
'Nelson' (North Walsham) — 431(1888)
'The Flegg' (Ormesby) — 76(1886)
Taverham — 509(1888)
Catton and Sprowston — 330(1888);
 474(1890)
Scottow

Hickling — 178(1888)
Beeston — 342(1888)
Woodbastwick

5 Norwich

'The Alexandra' (Dames) — 1,070(1890);
 1,554(1891)
Norwich Borough No. 320
Norwich Borough No. 721

6 Norfolk South

'The Mary' (Diss and district) — 441(1888)
Hethersett — 300(1888)
Dunston — 504(1888)
Harleston — 283(1888)
'Depwade' (Morningthorpe) — 178(1888)
Ditchingham
Brooke

7 Norfolk Mid

Launditch and Dereham — 600(1886);
 1,031(1888)
Shadwell — 209(1888)
Wymondham and Hingham — 57(1888)
East Dereham — 503(1888)
Honingham
'Quidenham' (Guilt Cross Union)

8 Norfolk South West

Downham Market — 621(1888)
Wayland — 946(1888)
'The Buckworth' (Swaffham)
'The Nelson' (East and West Bradenham)

Didlington (1891)
Feltwell and Methwold (1893)

9 Great Yarmouth

Great Yarmouth − 1,015(1886); 1,556(1888)
'The Nelson' (Dames)
Gorleston

10 Lowestoft

'The Rous' (Wangford) − 816(1888)
Lowestoft − 898(1886); 1,058(1888)
Beccles (1893)

11 Suffolk East or Eye

'The Mary in Suffolk' (Eye) − 829(1886)
'The Mary' (Stradbroke) − 173(1886)
'The Mary' (Saxmundham) − 685(1886);
    1,033(1888)
'The Mary' (Bottesdale) − 265(1886);
    442(1888)
'The Mary' (Framlingham) − 309(1886);
    78(1888)
'The Mary' (Bacton) − 152(1888)
'The Mary' (Weybread) − 332(1888)
'The Mary' (Debenham) − 134(1886)
'The Mary' (Thorington and Yoxford) −
    200(1886)
Leiston (1893)

12 Stowmarket

Pakenham, Ixworth and Woolpit −
    314(1887); 400(1888)
'The Elizabeth' (Mildenhall) − 218(1886);
    436(1887); 750(1888)
Brandon − 16(1886)
'The Seven Hills' (Ingham) − 157(1888)
'The Hepworth' (Barningham) − 296(1887);
    520(1888)
'The Mary' (Stowmarket) − 93(1887)
'The Mary' (Thedwastre) − 63(1886)

13 Bury St Edmunds

Bury St Edmunds − 148(1887); 7 6(1888)

14 Suffolk South or Sudbury

'The Mary' (Hadleigh) − 193(1888)
'The Mary' (Melford) − 257(1886);
    348(1887); 374(1888)
'The Trundley' (Great Thurlow)
'The Clarence' (Clare) − 26(1888);
    202(1890)

15 Ipswich

'The Mary' (Dames) − 1,246(1886);
    1,680(1890)

16 Suffolk South East or Woodbridge

Campsea Ashe − 333(1888)
Woodbridge − 174(1886)
'The Mary' (Holbrook) − 198(1886)
'The Mary' (Felixstowe) − 293(1888)
'The Mary' (Claydon) − 299(1888)
Grundisburgh − 65(1886); 127(1888)
'The Mary' (East Burgholt) − 329(1888)
Aldeburgh (1893)

17 Cambridgeshire North or Wisbech

'The Selwyn' (Wisbech) − 1090(1887);
    1,100(1891)
March − 369(1887)
'The Salisbury' (Leverington) − 202(1887)
'Yorke and Manners' (Elm) − 160(1887)
'The Churchill' (Chatteris) − 510(1886)
'The Hereward' (Littleport)
'The Cranborne' (Wisbech St. Mary) −
    13(1886)

18 Cambridgeshire East or Newmarket

Bottisham − 291(1887)
Ely − 71(1887)
Newmarket − 453(1886)
'The Etheldreda' (Soham) − 120(1886)

13 Cambridge

'The Fitzgerald' − 207(1886); 404(1887);
    573(1905); 1,300(1906)
Cambridge − 74(1886)
Cambridge University − 51(1887)

20 Cambridgeshire West or Chesterton

'Thornhill' (Swavesey) − 76(1887)
'St Michael's' (Willingham) − 76(1887)
'The Northcote' (Shelford) − 59(1887)
Cottenham − 92(1887)
Histon − 116(1887)
'The Victoria' (Wilburton)
Meldreth − 13(1886)

21 Huntingdonshire South or Huntingdon

'The Montagu' (Huntingdon) − 1506(1888)
'The Sandwich' (St Neots) − 586(1886);
    683(1888)
Kimbolton

22 Huntingdonshire North or Ramsey

'The Rosamond' (St Ives) − 362(1886);
    272(1888)
Elton − 62(1888)
'The Belnheim' (Somersham) − 126(1888)
'The Fellowes' (Earith) − 81(1888)

'The Ailwyn' (Warboys) — 150(1888)
Ramsey Abbey — 795(1888)

23 Saffron Walden

Saffron Walden — 361(1886); 865(1888);
1,050(1891)
'The Quendon' (Newport) — 1020(1886);
1180(1888)
Finchingfield
Manuden (1901)
Hedingham

24 Epping

'The Premier of Essex' (Loughton) —
364(1888)
Epping — 15(1888)
Chigwell — 124(1888)
Buckhurst Hill — 180(1888)
Nazing and Waltham Abbey — 384(1886)
'The Eden' (Matching) — 241(1888)
Dunmow — 325(1886); 540(1888)
'The Budworth' (Little Laver) — 700(1886);
819(1888)
Sheering — 25(1886)
Chipping Ongar

25 Essex South or Romford

Romford — 102(1888)
'The Cranborne' (Ilford) — 379(1888)
Wanstead (1892) — 2,432(1900); 1,393(1906)
Broadway Polling District (1891)
Cann Hall and Wanstead Slip (1898)
East Ham (1899)
Stratford

26 Essex Mid or Chelmsford

Chelmsford — 926(1886); 481(1888)
Upminster — 236(1888)

Great Waltham — 400(1886); 361(1888)
Springfield — 227(1886); 336(1888)
Stock — 73(1888)
Broomfields — 160(1888)
Brentwood
Danbury
Runwell
Great Baddow — 100(1886); 229(1888)

27 Essex South East

Southend-on-Sea — 152(1886)
Dengie Hundred No 1 — 495(1886);
508(1888)
Southminster (Dengie Hundred No 2)
Orsett — 143(1888)
'Rochford' — 80(1888)
'The Unionist' (Shoeburyness)
Rainham
Grays — 227(1888)

28 Maldon

Witham — 171(1886); 157(1888)
Terling and Fairsted — 180(1886); 162(1888)
Halstead — 477(1886); 642(1888); 370(1891)
Maldon — 273(1888)
Kelvedon — 250(1886); 261(1888)
Wickham Bishops — 171(1888)
Braintree and Bocking — 1,045(1886)

29 Colchester

Colchester — 287(1886)

30 Harwich

Harwich — 251(1886); 328(1888)
Thorpe-le-Soken — 593(1886); 820(1888)
Boxted, Horkesley and Wormingford —
345(1888)
Manningtree — 313(1886)
Ardleigh — 113(1886)

APPENDIX XI   EAST MIDLANDS

1 Derby

'The Jervis' — 716(1890)
'The Balfour' — 500+(1890)
'The Wilmot' — 330(1886); 1,920(1887)
Friargate
Babington and Becket Wards
'The Salisbury' (Arboretum and Litchurch)

2 Derbyshire South

Melbourne — 371(1887)
Kedleston — 235(1886); 680(1887);
456(1905)

'The Harpur Crewe' (Tickenhall) —
239(1887)
'The Derwent' (Spondon) — 339(1887)
Littleover — 133(1887)
Barrow-on-Trent — 227(1887)
Catton and Walton — 976(1887)
Etwall — 175(1887); 340(1890)
'The Harpur Crewe' (Breadsall) — 163(1887)
Repton and District — 95(1887)
Chaddesden Hall — 267(1887)
Little Eaton — 211(1887)
The Mickleover
Winshill — 260(1890)

Stapenhill (1892)
Alvaston, Osmaston and Elvaston (1904)

3 Ilkeston

'The Alexandra' (Ilkeston) — 464(1888)
Stainsby — 438(1888)
'The Victoria' (Ripley) — 406(1888)
Sandiacre District — 338(1888)
Mundy — 283(1888)
Long Eaton
'The Balfour' (Sawley)
Ockbrook and Borrowash
Heanor and Shipley

4 Derbyshire Mid

Longwood — 71(1887)
Duffield — 589(1886); 623(1887)
Alfreton — 719(1887)
Belper — 784(1887) 1,200(1890)
Alderwasley — 432(1887)
Swanwick — 159(1887)
Carnfield — 181(1887)
Riddings and Somercotes — 159(1886);
  270(1890); 324(1891)

5 Derbyshire West

Ashbourne — 428(1887); 360(1891)
Wirksworth — 473(1886); 618(1887)
'The Rutland' (Bakewell) — 251(1886);
  466(1887); 620(1890); 733(1891)
Foston — 278(1887)
Willersley — 804(1886); 1,096(1887);
  1,070(1890)

6 Derbyshire High Peak

Buxton — 479(1886); 580(1887)
Fernilee (Whaley Bridge) — 252(1887)
Hope Valley — 322(1886); 365(1887)
'The Peveril' (Chapel-en-le-Frith) —
  119(1887)
'Bowden Middle-Call' (New Mills District) —
  72(1887)
Glossop and Hayfield — 700(1886);
  1,505(1887)

7 Chesterfield

'The Salisbury' (Chesterfield)

8 Derbyshire North East

Norton — 265 (1887)

9 Nottingham West

Bulwell — 234(1888)
'The Byron' — 244(1886)

Nottingham East

Manvers — 223(1888)
'The Robin Hood' — 350(1888)
Mapperley Ward
'The Duchess of Portland'

Nottingham South

Trent — 171(1888)
Meadows Ward — 104(1888)
Castle Ward — 506(1886)
St Mary's Ward — 60(1886)
Bridge Ward (1892)
Market Ward (1892)
'The Forest' — 105(1886); 313(1888)

10 Nottinghamshire Rushcliffe

Ruddington — 212(1888)
'The Victoria' (Colwick) — 260(1888)
Clifton — 647(1888)
'The Rushcliffe' (Widmerpool and Bunny
  Park) — 1,043(1891)
Cossall
Arnold (1890)
Beeston (1892)

11 Mansfield

Mansfield — 552(1888)
Mansfield Woodhouse
'Robin Hood' (Eastwood)
Annesley — 512(1888)
Skegby and Teversall (1892)

12 Newark

Wiverton — 402(1888)
Southwell — 849(1888)
Collingham and District — 609(1888)
'The Cranmer' (Whatton) — 405(1888)
'The Staunton' (Farndon) — 405(1888)
Thorney Wood Chase (Bulcote) — 513(1888);
  601(1890)
Pierrepoint
Newark
Caunton
Coddington (1890)

13 Bassetlaw

Worksop — 935(1888)
'The Galway' (Retford) — 4512(1888);
  3,146(1907); 5,500(1909)
Welbeck

14 Gainsborough

Gainsborough — 2897(1888); 622(1902);
  2,395(1907)

Isle of Axholme − 332(1888)
Scothorne − 137(1888)
Nettleham and District − 187(1888)
Brattleby (1890)

15 Brigg

North Lindsey (Brigg/Ulceby) − 2427(1888)
Barton-upon-Humber (1890)
New Holland and Barrow

16 Grimsby

'Yarborough' − 204(1886); 650(1888)

17 East Lindsey or Louth

Wragby − 638(1888)
Louth and District − 647(1888)
Marsh − 505(1888)
Market Rasen − 564(1888)

18 Horncastle

'The Stanhope' (Horncastle) − 377(1888);
740(1890); 930(1891)
'The Eresby' (Spilsby) − 678(1888)
Wainfleet (1891)

19 Lincoln

City of Lincoln − 2,300(1886); 4,530(1888)
(divided into Central and Lindum)
Bracebridge (1897)

20 Sleaford

Sleaford − 1831(1888)
Harmston, Navenby and Caythorpe (1896)
Branston, Heighington and Washingboro
(1896)
Boultham and Hartsholme (1896)
'The Ellison' − 2,300(1901)

Boston

'Hughenden' (Boston) − 1,150(1886);
1,921(1888)

22 Holland or Spalding

Spalding − 1361(1888)
Long Sutton − 200(1888)

23 Grantham

'The Brownlow' (Grantham and District) −
2,325(1886); 3,665(1888)

24 Stamford

Bourne − 2084(1888); 1,834(1890);
2,040(1891)

'The Burghley' (Stamford) − 1385(1888)
Market Deeping − 222(1888)
Colsterworth − 245(1888)

25 Leicestershire East or Melton Mowbray

Melton Mowbray − 296(1888)
Ilston − 406(1888)
Syston − 237(1888)
Belgrave − 191(1888)
Knipton and District − 371(1888)
Bottesford and District − 155(1888)
Wymondham (1890) − 270(1890)
Vale of Belvoir (1890)
'The John o'Gaunt' (Thurnby) (1891)

26 Leicester

Leicester Borough − 140(1886); 1,639(1888);
1,220(1890)

27 Leicestershire Mid or Loughborough

Loughborough and District − 849(1888);
603(1891)
Charnwood Forest − 816(1888); 856(1890)
'The Grace Dieu' (Whitwick) − 439(1888);
398(1891)
Wolfdale − 188(1888); 211(1891)
'West Goscote' (Lockington) − 122(1888);
324(1890); 395(1891)
'Ferrers' (Breedon and Staunton) (1890) −
384(1890); 355(1891)

28 Leicestershire West or Bosworth

Ashby-de-la-Zouche − 453(1888)
Bosworth − 541(1888)
'The John o'Gaunt' (Hinckley) − 428(1888)
'The Beaconsfield' (Coalville) − 36(1888)
'The Seale' (Netherseale) − 616(1888)
Measham (1904)

29 Market Harborough

Wistow − 819(1888)
'The Charles Brook' (Enderby) − 670(1888)
Bitteswell − 1743(1888)
'The Everard' (Narborough) − 49(1888)
'The Border Forest' (Glenfield/Leicester
Frith) − 298(1888)
Market Harborough − 646(1888)
Wigston Magna and S. Wigston (1891)
Aylestone (1892)

30 Rutland

Empingham − 734(1888)
Oakham − 415(1888)
Uppingham − 543(1888)

APPENDIX XII   WEST MIDLANDS

1 Dudley

'The Beauchamp' (Dudley Dames) −
140(1886); 190(1889)
'The Walker' (Netherton)

2 West Bromwich

'The Dartmouth' (West Bromwich) −
209(1888)

3 Handsworth

'The Jubilee' (Great Barr) − 97(1888)
'The Calthorpe' (Birchfield and Perry Bar) −
309(1890)

4 Wednesbury

'The Wilson Lloyd' (Darlaston) − 215(1886)
'The Richard Mills' (Darlaston) − 267(1888);
830(1910)
Tipton − 670(1910)

5 Walsall

'The Frank James' (Walsall) − 360(1888)

6 Wolverhampton West

Graisley and Merridale Wards (1898)
'The Churchill' − 470(1886); 1,038(1888);
790(1891)

Wolverhampton South

'The Beacon' (Sedgley)
'Hickman' (Whitmore Reans) (1890) −
125(1891)

Wolverhampton East

'The Dartmouth' (Bilston) − 234(1888)

7 Kingswinford

Seisdon − 118(1888)
Brierley Hill − 75(1888)
Tettenhall − 246(1888)
Bushbury (1891)

8 Lichfield

Lichfield − 184(1886); 731(1888)
Rugeley − 458(1888); 632(1891)
'The Lane' (Alrewas)
Burntwood

9 Burton-on-Trent

Burton-on-Trent − 532(1888)
Barton-under-Needwood − 334(1888)

10 Stafford

'Harrowby' − 1,100(1886)

11 Staffordshire West

Weston − 981(1886); 1,428(1888);
1,520(1890)
'The North Chase' (Colwick) − 259(1886)
'The Churchill' (Hednesford) − 61(1888)
Newnham (1898)
Gnossall
Penkridge

12 Staffordshire North West

Trentham − 958(1886); 563(1888)
Eccleshall − 416(1888)
Chebsey
'The Coal and Ironworkers' (Kidsgrove) −
704(1888)
'Apedale' (Audley and Alsager's Bank) −
1,270(1888); 1,587(1890)
Keele
Betley and Madeley − 365(1888)
Blore Heath − 184(1888)

13 Newcastle-under-Lyme

Newcastle-under-Lyme − 558(1888)
Norton-in-the-Moors
Tunstall and Wolstanton − 420(1888)

14 Hanley

Hanley and Shelton
Burslem
Bucknall − 85(1888)

15 Stoke-on-Trent

Stoke and Fenton − 847(1888)
Longton

16 Leek

'The Beresford' (Sheen)
'The Cruso' (Leek) − 1,001(1888);
1,200(1890)
Farley − 775(1888)
'The Dove Valley' (Rocester)
Cheadle (1891)

17 Birmingham Edgbaston

'The Hatfield' − 121(1888)
The Birmingham Dames
'The Victoria' (Rotton Park) − 37(1888)

Birmingham Central

Central Birmingham − 77(1888); 80(1890)
Ladywood − 240(1888)
'The Dartmouth' (St Thomas' Ward)
'The Birmingham' (Market Hall Ward)

Birmingham South

'The Matthews' (Duddeston and Nechells
    Wards) − 94(1888)
'The Jubilee' (Deritend) − 25(1888)
'The Gooch'

Birmingham Bordesley

'The Burns' (Bordesley) (1891)

Birmingham East

'The Princess' − 203(1888)

Birmingham North

'The Burnaby' − 130(1888)

Birmingham West

Aston Manor

18 Warwickshire North or Tamworth

'The Ferrers' (Knowle) − 648(1888)
Lozells − 363(1888)
Solihull − 191(1888)
Tamworth (1890) − 600+(1890)

19 Warwickshire North East or Nuneaton

Brandon and Wolston
Nuneaton − 819(1888)
Foleshill − 230(1888)
Hartshill − 213(1888)
'The Newdegate' (Bedworth) − 100(1888);
    360(1890); 486(1891)
Stockingford − 142(1888)
'The Arbury' (Chilvers Coton)
Atherstone (1890)
'The Bagot' (Bulkington) (1893)

20 Coventry

City of Coventry

21 Warwickshire South East or Rugby

Dunsmore − 1,434(1888)
'The Venetia' (Kenilworth) − 432(1888)
Rugby − 989(1886); 1,494(1888)
Southam − 379(1888)
Kineton
Bourton − 322(1888)

Newnham Paddox (Monk's Kirby)
'The Fielding' (Priors Hadwick) (1890)

22 Warwick and Leamington

Leamington − 133(1886); 295(1888)
Warwick − 354(1886); 647(1888)
'The Aylesford' − 348(1886); 645(1888)

*23 Warwickshire South West or
    Stratford-on-Avon*

'The Shakespeare' (Stratford) − 630(1888)
'The Hertford' (Alcester) − 1,544(1888)
Ettington − 406(1888); 349(1890)
Hockley Heath − 74(1888)
Henley-in-Arden − 111(1888)
Feldon − 289(1888)
Charlecote − 705(1891)
Wolford − 192(1888)
Temple Grafton − 91(1888); 122(1891)
Barford − 292(1891)

24 Worcestershire South or Evesham

Evesham − 425(1889)
Upton-on-Severn − 270(1889)
Broadway − 460(1889); 484(1890)
'Dovedale' (Blockley) − 628(1889)
Shipston-on-Stour
Inkberrow and Feckenham − 252(1889)

25 Worcester

Worcester Dames

26 Worcestershire West or Bewdley

'Lord Randolph Churchill' (Bewdley)
Malvern − 1,278(1889)
Teme Valley − 203(1889)
Ombersley − 384(1889)
'The Kyre' (Tenbury)

27 Worcestershire Mid or Droitwich

'The Beaconsfield' (Stourport) − 148(1889)
'The Packington' (Droitwich) − 280(1889)
Stourbridge − 131(1889)
Chaddesley Corbett
Clent − 96(1889)
Wolverley (1900)

28 Kidderminster

Kidderminster
'The Northcote'
'The Victoria' (Kidderminster Dames) −
    650(1891)

29 Worcestershire East

'The Clive' (Bromsgrove) – 176(1889)
Hewell – 333(1889)
Yardley – 705(1889)
'The Windsor' (Redditch) – 628(1889)
Moseley and King's Heath
Wythal – 301(1889)
King's Norton (1899)
Catshill

30 Worcestershire North

Weoley (1898)
Halesowen

31 Herefordshire South or Ross

Ledbury – 645(1886); 1,021(1888)
'The John Kyrle' (Ross) – 532(1888)
Harewood – 290(1888)
The Kerne – 224(1886); 380(1888)
St Michael's – 31(1888)
Stoke Edith – 210(1888)
'Doward' (Whitchurch) – 103(1888)
Vennwood – 313(1888)
Sugwas – 124(1888)
Fownhope
Muchmarcle
Pontrilas (1894)

32 Hereford

'Wyeside' – 198(1886); 451(1888);
    481(1890)

33 Herefordshire North or Leominster

Shobdon – 236(1888)
Buckland – 420(1886); 730(1888)
'North Central' (Leominster) – 476(1888)
Cradley Dames – 158(1888)
Kington – 256(1886); 422(1888)
Bromyard
Eardisley
'Bright' (Colwall) – 263(1890)

34 Shropshire South or Ludlow

Wistantow – 622(1888)
Worfield – 329(1888)
Bishop's Castle – 534(1888)
Bridgnorth
Ludlow – 1,424(1889); 1,555(1890)
Cleobury Mortimer

35 Shropshire West or Oswestry

Ellesmere – 212(1888)
'St Oswald's' (Oswestry)
Condover – 717(1886); 1,038(1888) (includes
    Shrewsbury)
Knockin – 229(1888)
Wallop – 785(1888)
Sweeney and Trefonen – 402(1888)
Brogyntyn – 130(1888)
Halston and Whittington – 252(1888)
Park Hall – 236(1888)
'The Lodge' (Weston Lodge) – 108(1888)

36 Shrewsbury

Condover – 717(1886); 1,038(1888)
    (includes Shrewsbury and rural parishes)
'The Disraeli' – 240(1886)

37 Shropshire Mid or Wellington

Wellington No. 1 (Dames) – 450(1888)
Wellington No. 2
Broseley – 47(1888)
'The Victoria' (Leighton) – 329(1888)

38 Shropshire North or Newport

'The Clive' (Market Drayton) – 486(1888);
    600+(1891)
Leaton Knolls – 1,000(1888)
Whitchurch – 701(1888)
'William Pitt' (Child's Ercal)
'The Salisbury' (Adderley) – 271(1888)
'The Dartmouth' (Albrighton) – 435(1888)
Wem – 90(1888); 351(1905); 578(1906)
Shifnal
Shawbury (1891)
Tern Vale

APPENDIX XIII   YORKSHIRE

1 Bradford West (The 1893 total for the
    three Bradford seats was 4,000)
'The Bective' – 997(1886); 1,805(1888)

Bradford Central

'The Disraeli' – 220(1890)

Bradford East

East Bradford

2 Shipley

'The Hardy' (Shipley) – 540(1891)

North Bierley and Clayton
'The Hardy' (Low Moor and Wibsey) –
    546(1890)

3 Pudsey

'The Salisbury' (Pudsey) (1898)
'The Victoria' (Bramley) – 202(1891)
'The Pickwick' – 15(1886)

4 Leeds West

'The Victoria' (Armley) – 220(1886);
    164(1891)
Holbeck (1898)
'The Albion' (New Wortley) – 190(1888)

Leeds Central

Leeds Central – 249(1888)
Walker

Leeds North

North Leeds – 495(1890)

Leeds South

West Hunslet (1898)

Leeds East

5 Halifax

Halifax Borough – 685(1888); 1,375(1904)

6 Elland

Greetland – 15(1886)
Rastrick – 122(1888)
Queensbury (1902)
Hipperholme and Lightcliffe (1902)
Illingworth (1903)

7 Huddersfield

Huddersfield Borough – 750(1886)

8 Spen Valley

'The Shirley' (Birstall) – 586(1888)
Woodlands(1901)

9 Dewsbury

Dewsbury Borough

10 Morley

'St Oswald' (Ossett) – 84(1886)

11 Wakefield

'The Dr Primrose' (Dames) – 653(1888)

12 Colne Valley

'The Brook' (Meltham) – 357(1888)
'Drummond Wolff' (Linthwaite)
Saddleworth (1890) – 400(1901)

13 Sowerby

'The Rawson' (Sowerby) – 578(1888);
    654(1890); 500(1900)
Luddenden (1895)
'Hinchcliffe' (Hebden Bridge) (1905)
Todmorden Valley – 1,153(1888);
    1,450(1901) (partly in Middleton,
    Lancashire)

14 Keighley

Keighley – 198(1886); 250(1891)

15 Skipton

'The Roundell' (Skipton) – 85(1886);
    512(1890)
'North Ribblesdale' (Settle) – 333(1888);
    468(1890); 406(1891)
'Vale of Wenning' (Bentham) – 157(1888)
Hellifield and Long Preston (1894)

16 Ripon

Harrogate – 142(1886)
'St Wilfred's' (Ripon) – 1,508(1886);
    554(1888)
Kirk Hammerton – 300(1886)
'Slingsby' (Knaresborough) – 841(1890);
    1,020(1891)
Pannal
'St Robert's' (Boroughbridge) (1892)
Pateley Bridge (1892)

17 Otley

Ilkley – 491(1888)
'Wharfedale' (Otley)
Cullingworth
Burley-in-Wharfedale (1895)
Bingley (1901)

18 Barkston Ash

Selby – 1,240(1886); 1,297(1888)
'Gunter' (Wetherby) – 280(1886); 790(1888)
'The Calcaria' (Tadcaster) – 173(1886);
    158(1888)
'The Aberfordia' (Aberford) – 257(1886)
Collingham – 530(1886)

19 Normanton

Oulton – 36(1886)

Sandal Magna
Woodlands (1901)

20 Pontefract

'The St Oswald' − 25(1886)

21 Osgoldcross

Goole − 620(1900)
'St Cuthbert' (Ackworth) − 440(1888)
Snaith − 210(1888)
'The Roland Winn' (Knottingley) −
    201(1888)
'Legiolium' (Castleford)
'St Helen's' (Skellow)

22 Doncaster

Doncaster − 1,808(1886); 1,892(1890)
Hatfield Chase − 107(1886); 45(1888)
'The Scarborough' (Tickhill) − 280(1886);
    579(1888)
Mexboro' (1890)
Thorne and District (1891)
Hooton Pagnell (1893)

23 Barnsley

'The Wentworth' (Barnsley) − 200(1886);
    552(1888)
'The Canning' (Barnsley Dames) −
    1,078(1888); amalgamated with
    'Wentworth' − combined membership
    2,138(1890)

24 Rotherham

Rotherham − 246(1886); 458(1888)
Rawmarsh − 292(1888)

25 Sheffield Central

The Central − 850(1886); 1,267(1888)

Sheffield Brightside

Brightside − 863(1886); 1,250(1888)

Sheffield Attercliffe

Attercliffe (No.1138) − 418(1886)
Attercliffe (No. 1468) − 43(1886)
Handsworth − 175(1886)

Sheffield Hallam

Hallam − 773(1886); 1,694(1888);
    1,478(1890); 210(1905); 780(1907)

Sheffield Eccleshall

Ecclesall − 3,500(1909)

26 Hallamshire

Hillsborough − 164(1888)
Wath-upon-Dearne − 228(1888)
'Sheffield County' (Norton)
Wortley − 226(1888); 246(1890)
Wincobank − 50(1886)
Bradfield and Stannington − 175(1888)
Oughtybridge
Bolsterstone − 180(1888); 197(1890)
Chapeltown (1890)

27 Holmfirth

'The Stanhope' (Penistone) − 100(1886);
    454(1888)
Kirkheaton and Lepton

28 Richmond

Richmond − 320(1886); 1,130(1888)
Northallerton − 330(1886); 941(1888)
Leyburn − 391(1888); 690(1907)
Middleham
Swaledale − 78(1888)
Bedale − 100(1886); 539(1888)
Catterick − 156(1888)
Barton − 64(1888)
Middleton Tyas
Teesdale − 980(1888), partly in Durham
    (Barnard Castle)
Kirkby Fleetham

29 Middlesborough

'Erimus' (Middlesborough) − 361(1886)

30 Cleveland

'The Pennyman' (Cleveland) − 1,378(1888)
Saltburn-by-Sea (1892)
Skelton (1893)
Yarm-on-Tees (1893)
Great Ayton (1893)
Stainton-in-Cleveland (1894)

31 Thirsk and Malton

'Vale of Mowbray' (Thirsk) − 500(1888)
Hovingham − 204(1888)
'Flaxton' (Sand Hutton)
Forest of Galtres − 213(1888)

32 Whitby

'St Hilda' (Whitby) − 286(1886);
    1,552(1888)
Pickering − 210(1886); 656(1888)
Grosmont − 322(1888)
Helmsley − 280(1888)
'Vale of Mowbray' (Gilling) − 68 (1888)

33 Scarborough

Scarborough Borough − 1,000(1886)

34 York

'The Milner' (City of York) − 1,370(1886);
  1,168(1888); 700(1891)
'The Ebor' (1891)

35 Buckrose

'Buckrose' (Norton); 291(1886); 256(1888)
'St George's' (Beeford)
Bridlington − 402(1886)
'The Sykes' (Driffield) − 378(1888)
'The Darley' (Filey) − 173(1888)
Sledmere

36 Holderness

Hornsea − 379(1888)
Beverley − 200(1886); 1,290(1888)
'Holderness' (Patrington/Withernsea) −
  169(1886); 486(1888); 559(1890)

37 Kingston upon Hull West

'De La Pole' − 410(1888)

Kingston upon Hull Central

Hull − 120(1886)

Kingston upon Hull East

East Hull − 400(1890); 450(1891)
Hull Dames − 79(1886)

38 Howdenshire

Wilton Beacon (Picklington/Wilberfoss) −
  1,405(1886); 1,594(1888)
Weighton (Market Weighton) − 184(1886)
Hunsley Beacon (Cottingham) − 466(1886);
  641(1889); 870(1890)
Hessle − 134(1886)
Howden − 111(1886)
West Hunsley − 292(1888); 370(1891)
'Ouse' (Heslington) − 26(1886)

APPENDIX XIV   NORTH WEST ENGLAND

1 Oldham

The Oldham − 1,255(1888)
Heyside

2 Prestwich

Droylsden and Fairfield − 85(1888)
'Wilton' (Prestwich) − 420(1886); 620(1888);
  560(1891)
'Clayton' − 171(1888); 235(1890)
Mossley
Heaton Moor
Audenshaw (1894)
Blackley and Moston (1896)

3 Ashton-under-Lyne

Ashton-under-Lyne − 1,663(1888)

4 Gorton

Gorton − 108(1888)
Denton and Haughton
Haughton Green
Openshaw and Fairfield

5 Manchester South

Moss Side

Manchester South West

'Hamilton' (Hulme) − 237(1888)

Manchester North West

Manchester Conservative Club − 37(1888)

Manchester North

North Manchester − 238(1888)

Manchester North East

Ancoats − 153(1888)
Newton Heath

Manchester East

'Fergusson' − 126(1888)

6 Salford North

Carlton

Salford West

Pendleton
Seedley and Weaste (1897)

Salford South

7 Stretford

Old Trafford − 133(1888)
Stretford − 195(1888)
Chorlton-cum-Hardy − 128(1886)
Withington − 76(1886)

Didsbury(1892)
Whalley Range (1890)
Albert Park (1893)

8 Middleton

'Valley' (Todmorden) − 1,153(1888);
  1,450(1901) (partly in Sowerby, Yorkshire)
'Assheton' (Middleton) − 425(1886);
  474(1888)
Whitworth Vale − 657(1888)
Littleborough − 483(1890); 619(1891)
Milnrow (1900)

9 Rochdale

Rochdale − 3,979(1888); 1,913(1897);
  3,946(1898)

10 Heywood

'The Balfour' (Ramsbottom) − 513(1888);
  699(1889); 738(1891); 1,300(1902)
Norden (1890)
Heywood (1894)
'Kemp' (Tottington) (1901)

11 Bury

'The Grant Lawson' (Bury) − 1,920(1888)

12 Radcliffe-cum-Farnworth

Farnworth − 2,020(1888)
Radcliffe − 1,587(1886)
Whitefield (1891)
'Pilkington' (Unsworth) (1891)

13 Eccles

Pendlebury
Eccles − 235(1886); 162(1888)
Worsley − 453(1886); 603(1888)
Swinton − 360(1888)
Ringley and Kersley (1891)
Patricroft (1893)

14 Leigh

'Wetherall' (Astley) − 286(1888)
'Lilford' (Leigh) − 1,335(1888)
Atherton − 760(1888)
'Withington' (Culcheth) − 181(1888)
Ramsden

15 Bolton

Bolton − 1,826(1888); 837(1895);
  1,062(1896); 2,616(1897); 5,057(1898);
  6,227(1899)

16 Westhoughton

Westhoughton
Blackrod
Egerton − 61(1886)
'Stanley' (Horwich) (1891)
'Lees Knowles' (Turton) (1904)

17 Wigan

'Lindsay' (Wigan) − 2,854(1888)

18 Ince

Ince, Pemberton and Orrell (1896)

19 Newton

Newton-le-Willows and District −
  1,036(1888)
'The Legh' (Rainhill) − 73(1888)
Billinge and Winstanley
Padgate and Orford
Golborne
Garswood − 22(1886)

20 St Helens

'Gerard' (St Helens)

21 Warrington

Warrington − 102(1886)

22 Widnes

Huyton − 257(1888); 636(1890)
Widnes (1892)

23 Liverpool Walton

'Gordon' − 263(1888)
Wavertree − 112(1888) (includes Bootle
  outvoters)
Walton-on-the-Hill − 23(1886)

Liverpool Everton

Everton − 123(1886); 30(1888)

Liverpool Kirkdale

Liverpool Scotland

Liverpool Abercromby

Liverpool − 228(1886)
Central
Rodney − 106(1888)

Liverpool West Toxteth

Toxteth − 300(1886); 671(1888); 1,020(1891)
  (includes Bootle outvoters)

Liverpool East Toxteth

Toxteth (see Liverpool West Toxteth)

Liverpool Exchange

Exchange
'The Forward'

Liverpool West Derby

24 *Bootle*

Sandys − 206(1886); 304(1888)

25 *Ormskirk*

Ormskirk
Halsall (1891)
Lathom and Burscough (1891)
Skelmersdale and Bickerstaff (1891)
Kirby and Melling (1893)
Maghull (1893)
Aughton (1894)
Upper Holland (1895)

26 *Southport*

Southport − 670(1886); 1,589(1888)
Birkdale − 354(1888)
Scarisbrick − 432(1888)
'Curzon' (Ainsdale) − 162(1888)
'Dale' (Blowick) − 117(1888)
Formby − 405(1888)
'Beaconsfield' (Waterloo) − 162(1888);
    440(1900); 987(1901); 1,320(1902);
    1,078(1903)
Blundell − 167(1888)
Great Crosby

27 *Chorley*

Chorley − 1,644(1886); 2,252(1888)
Adlington − 402(1888)
Leyland − 50(1886)
'Yarrow' (Charnock Richard, Coppull and
    Euxton) (1892)
Withnell and Hoghton (1893)

28 *Preston*

'Beaconsfield' (Preston)

29 *Darwen*

'Graham' (Darwen) − 1,436(1886);
    1,592(1888)
'Salisbury' (Great Harwood) − 304(1888)
Longridge

30 *Blackburn*

'Cranborne' (Wilton)
'Cranborne' (Hitton and District) −
    2,456(1888)

31 *Accrington*

Church − 329(1888)
'Benjamin Hargreaves' (Accrington) −
    830(1886); 607(1888)
Oswaldtwistle
'Beaconsfield' (Rishton)
Clayton-le-Moors (1891)

32 *Rossendale*

'Beaconsfield' (Bacup) − 700(1890);
    1,026(1891)
Haslingden − 57(1886)
'Victoria' (Newchurch)
Lumb

33 *Burnley*

'Thursby' − 374(1888)
'St Andrews' − 329(1888)
'General Scarlett' (Gannow Ward) −
    156(1888)
Kirkham

34 *Clitheroe*

Pendle − 127(1888)
Padiham(1901)
Nelson
Pendle Forest (1894)

35 *Blackpool*

'Beaconsfield' (Blackpool No. 2)
Blackpool Brunswickers − 176(1886)
'Stanley' (Blackpool Dames)
'Gibson' (Blackpool) − 88(1888)
South Shore (Blackpool) − 60(1888)
Poulton-le-Fylde − 236(1888)
Freckleton − 78(1888)
Fleetwood − 171(1888)
Penwortham − 1,111(1886)
'White Ridley' (Thornton) (1898)
Kirkham − 217(1888)
'Clifton' (Lytham) − 223(1889); 344(1890);
    726(1891)

36 *Lancaster*

'Duke of Lancaster' (Lancaster) − 410(1888)
'Salisbury' (Morecambe) − 281(1888)
Hornby
'Wyre' (Great Eccleston)
Caton and Halton (1890)

Cockerham (1892)
Garstang (1894) – 427(1901); 312(1906);
 279(1909)
Preesall and District (1897)
Vale of Wenning

37 Wirral

West Kirby – 109(1887)
Shotwick – 336(1887)
'Arrowe' (Upton-in-Wirral) – 103(1886)
Whitby and Ellesmere Port
Neston
Heswall – 135(1891)
Wallasey (1901)

38 Birkenhead

Wirral
Oxton
'John Laird' (1900)
Rock Ferry – 63(1886)

39 Eddisbury

Eddisbury – 718(1886); 1,966(1887)
Delamere Forest – 690(1887); 461(1900)
Morland – 357(1887)
Broxton – 373(1887)
'Watling Street' (Kelsall and Tarvin) –
 171(1887)
Frodsham District – 254(1887)
Bunbury
Tarporley
Malpas
Wrenbury
Cholmondeley
Acton (Worleston)
Bridgemere and Dodington
Farndon (1890)

40 Chester

Chester – 1,820(1886)

41 Northwich

'Vale Royal' (Northwich) – 1,277(1886);
 1,604(1887)
Runcorn – 402(1887)
Halton – 121(1887)
Great Budworth
Winsford and Over – 807(1890)
Davenham (1892)

42 Knutsford

Knutsford – 785(1886); 267(1887);
 410(1891)

Disley – 147(1887)
Bollington – 785(1887)
Adlington – 42(1886)
Lyme
Grappenhall
Daresbury
Siddington (Lower Withington) – 309(1889);
 911(1890); 1,000(1891)
'Beaconsfield' (Alderley Edge) – 96(1887)
Wilmslow – 51(1887)
Appleton
Arley (1892)
Whitley (1892)
Prestbury (1893)
Lostock Graham (1894)
Over Peover (1893)

43 Crewe

Nantwich – 643(1887)
'Brookside' (Sandbach) – 770(1886);
 1,017(1887); 1,300(1891)
'The Grey Egerton' (Crewe) – 514(1887)
'Rode Hall' (Alsager and Lawton) –
 193(1887)

44 Macclesfield

Congleton – 1,404(1887); 1,497(1890)
Macclesfield – 1,442(1887); 1,558(1890)
Higher Sutton (1900)

45 Altrincham

Lymm – 759(1887)
Bramhall – 50(1887)
'The Tatton' (Altrincham) – 714(1887)
'The Egerton' (Timperley and Bagaley)
Cheadle and Gatley (1895)
Ashton-on-Mersey – 360(1886)

46 Stockport

'Beaconsfield' (Stockport) – 654(1887);
 752(1889)

47 Hyde

Romiley – 140(1887)
'Clarendon' (Hyde) – 661(1887)
Bredbury – 149(1887)
Marple
'Longdendale Valley' (Mottram, Broadbottom
 and Hollingworth) (1896)
Compstall

48 Stalybridge

Stalybridge – 969(1887)

APPENDIX XV   NORTHERN ENGLAND

1 Newcastle upon Tyne

'Eldon' − 107(1888)
Newcastle-upon-Tyne Dames − 53(1886)
All Saints North Ward (Shieldfield) (1891) − 212(1891); 678(1893)
St Andrews (1891) − 777(1891)
Jesmond (1891) − 600(1891)
Elswick (1891) − 702(1891); 1,568(1894); 3,453(1905)
Byker and Heaton (1895)
'Tyne' (1890)

2 Tyneside

Wallsend (1891)
Gosforth − 68(1886)
St Michael's (West Denton) − 143(1888)
Weetslade (N. Gosforth) − 75(1888)
Willington Quay (1894)
Walker-on-Tyne (1895)
Newburn (1895)

3 Tynemouth

'St George's' (Tynemouth) − 81(1886); 184(1891)
North Shields (1893)

4 Northumberland − Wansbeck

'The Ridley' (Stannington) − 492(1886); 485(1888)
Mitford − 200(1888); 275(1890)
Wylam − 49(1888)
Hartburn − 281(1888)
Warkworth − 470(1888); 415(1892)
Cresswell (1890)
Whalton
Delaval (Seaton Delaval) (1901)
Bedlington (1904)
Whitley Bay (1904)

5 Morpeth

Morpeth (1892)
Blyth (1896) − 377(1896); 519(1897); 786(1898); 1,100(1903)

6 Berwick on Tweed

'Percy' (Alnwick) − 1,505(1887); 1,855(1888); 1,790(1892); 1,714(1893); 1,561(1895)
Norham-on-Tweed − 243(1888)
'Hotspur' (Lesbury) − 394(1888)
'Tankerville' (Chatton) − 122(1888)
Bamburghshire (N. Sunderland) − 209(1888)

Pallinsburn and Cornhill-on-Tweed − 379(1888)
'Lindisfarne' (Eglingham) − 105(1888)
Kirk Newton − 133(1888)
'Glendale' (Wooler) − 119(1888)
Whittingham − 231 (1888)
Felton − 107(1888)
Berwick-on-Tweed
Ellingham
Belford
Dunstanboro'
Lowick and Ancroft (1891)

7 Hexham

Hexham and North Tyne − 300(1886); 1,316(1891)
Haltwhistle − 177(1886); 435(1888); 531(1891)
Rothbury − 196(1888); 200(1889)
Broomhaugh and Riding Mill − 200(1888)
Haydon Bridge (1891) − 300(1891)
Framlington (1892)
Corbridge (1896)
Pont Valley (1897)
Bellingham − 666(1909)

8 Gateshead

'Ravensworth' (Gateshead) − 242(1886)

9 Chester-le-Street

Chester-le-Street
'Glamis' (Whickham) − 176(1888)
Lumley
Beamish (1906) − 400(1906)

10 Durham North West

Consett − 157(1886)
Ebchester and Medomsley − 40(1888)
Derwent Valley (Shotley Bridge) (1891) − 300(1891)
'Gort' (Hamsterley Colliery) (1908) − 1,000+(1908)

11 South Shields

'Salisbury' (South Shields) − 1,300(1900)

12 Jarrow

'St Bede's' − 150(1888); 1,680(1908); 2,000(1909)

13 Sunderland

'James Hartley' − 60(1886)
Monkwearmouth

14 Houghton-le-Spring

'Bernard Gilpin' (Houghton) − 321(1888);
609(1890)
'St Cuthbert' (West Rainton) − 337(1888)
'Lindsay Wood' (Hetton-le-Hole) −
103(1888)

15 Durham Mid

16 Durham

'Dunelm' (Durham) − 86(1888)
'The Queen Philippa' (Durham Dames) −
167(1888); joint membership with 'Dunelm'
from 1890: 427(1894); 686(1900);
705(1901)

17 Bishop Auckland

Tudhoe and Ferryhill − 60(1888)

18 Barnard Castle

'Teesdale (Barnard Castle) − 980(1888);
partly in Richmond, Yorkshire
'Weardale' (Stanhope)
'Wear Valley' (Witton Tower)

19 Darlington

Darlington − 662(1888); 530(1903)

20 Durham South East

'Londonderry' (Seaham Harbour) −
145(1888); 1,142(1890)
'Londonderry' (Wynyard) − 2,830(1891);
1,105(1906)
Sedgefield − 131(1888)
Haughton-le-Skerne − 110(1888)
'Garden of Eden' (Castle Eden) − 301(1888)

21 Stockton on Tees

'Tees' (Stockton) − 501(1886); 808(1888);
1,300(1890); 1,366(1892)

22 Hartlepool

'St Hilda' (1895) − 768(1898); 800(1910)
West Hartlepool

23 Cumberland North or Eskdale

Aikton − 187(1891)
'Vale of Eden' (Wetherall and district) −
350(1891)
'Eden' (Stanwix and district) − 300+(1891)
Longtown (1901)

Brampton and District (1902)
'Vale of Petterill' (Wreay and district) (1906)
Bowness-On-Solway (1910)
Dalston and Cummersdale (1910)
Silloth and District (1910)

24 Carlisle

Carlisle − 461(1887); 124(1890); 480(1891);
1,300(1901)

25 Cumberland Mid or Penrith

Penrith − 675(1887);
Ullswater − 639(1887); 689(1890)
'Forest of Inglewood' (Lazonby/Salkeld) −
537(1887); 874(1890); 737(1891)
The Mid-Cumberland
'Skiddaw and Derwentwater' (Keswick) −
246(1890)
'The Mountain' (Alston)

26 Cockermouth

'The Mayo' (Cockermouth) − 51(1887)
'The Valentine' (Workington) − 308(1887)
'Senhouse' (Maryport) − 84(1886)

27 Whitehaven

Whitehaven − 396(1889); 514(1890);
870(1892); 484(1899)

28 Cumberland Western or Egremont

'Lindow' (Cleator Moor) − 1,100(1887)
'Millom Castle' (Millom) − 1,140(1887)
'Lady Muncaster' (Egremont) − 446(1887)

29 Westmoreland North or Appleby

Ambleside
Windermere − 370(1888)
'Lowther' (Clifton, Lowther, Askham,
Helton, Melkinthorpe) − 294(1887);
336(1888); 387(1891); 352(1894)
Morland and Shap − 355(1888)
Brough and Helbeck − 140)1888)
Appleby − 573(1886); 809(1888)
Warcop − 141(1888)
Orton − 415(1888)
Kirby Stephen − 474(1888)

30 Westmoreland South or Kendal

Underley (Kirkby Lonsdale)
Kendal − 1,850(1891)
'Dallam Tower' (Milnthorpe)
Dalton, Burton and Holme − 200+(1891)
'Oakfield' (Arnside) − 146(1888)

31 Barrow-in-Furness

'The Queen's Own (Barrow) − 62(1888)

32 North Lonsdale

'Stanley' (Carnforth) − 225(1886); 391(1888)

Hawkshead − 482(1888)
'Old Man' (Coniston) − 227(1888); 170(1890)
'Eagle' (Grange-over-Sands) − 159(1888)
Ulverston − 200(1886)
Crake Valley − 20(1886)
Cartmel and Grange (1892)

APPENDIX XVI   SCOTLAND: THE HIGHLANDS AND ISLANDS

1 Perth

'Fair City' (Perth)

2 Perthshire East

'Carse of Gowrie' (Errol) − 1,000(1890); 534(1893)
Bridge of Earn
'Balgawan' (Methven) − 871(1890); 908 (1891)
St Madoes
Middle Strathearn

3 Perthshire West

Auchterarder − 400(1890)
Dunblane
Muthill (1896)
Comrie and Lawers − 316(1892)
Crieff
Dunkeld
'Ben Ledi' (Callander)
Pitlochry
Blair Atholl
'Weem District' (Aberfeldy)

4 Argyll

'Loch Fyne' (Tarbert)
'Loch Ridden' (Cowal and District)
Lochgilphead
Ardrishaig
'Kyles of Bute' (Tighnabuaich)
Dunoon (1890)

5 Dundee

'Victoria' (Dundee) − 1,178(1890)

6 Forfarshire

'The Strathmore' (Glamis)
Monifieth and District (1903)
Monikie
'The Lindertis' (Kirriemuir)

7 Montrose Burghs

Montrose

8 Kincardineshire

Howe of the Mearns (Laurencekirk and District)
Stonehaven
'Deeside' (Banchory)

9 Aberdeenshire West

Dunecht
Kildrummy
'Central Aberdeenshire' (Alford) (1896) − 1,047(1896); 1,300(1900)

10 Aberdeen North

North Aberdeen
'St Machair' (Old Aberdeen)

Aberdeen South

'St Nicholas' (South Aberdeen) − 594(1890)

11 Aberdeenshire East

Ellon
Newborough
'The Errol' (Cruden)
'The Udny' (Fortmartine)

12 Banffshire

'The Carnousie' (Aberchirder)
'The Strathisla' (Keith)
'The Glenfiddich' (Dufftown)
'West Banff' (Buckie and Port Gordon)

13 Elgin Burghs

Elgin
'The Seafield' (Cullen and Portsoy)

14 Elgin and Nairn

Fochabers
Mayne

15 Inverness

'Valley of the Ness' − 160(1887); 236(1892); 380(1897); 490(1899); 530(1900)

Lochaber
'Clacknacuddin' (Inverness)
Isle of Skye (1894)

16 Inverness Burghs

'Clacknacuddin' (Inverness)
Forres
Nairn

17 Ross and Cromarty

'Easter Ross and Black Isle' (Cromarty)
'Mary Jane Matheson' (Stornoway)

18 Sutherland

19 Caithness

'The John o'Groat's' (Thurso)

20 Wick Burghs

'Wyviss' (Dingwall)
'Easter Ross and Black Isle' (Cromarty)

21 Orkney and Shetland

'North Isles' (Orkney)
'The Dundas' (Lerwick)

APPENDIX XVII   SCOTLAND: CENTRAL AND BORDERS

1 Glasgow – Blackfriars and Hutchestown

'Lady Campbell of Blythswood'

Bridgeton

'Salisbury' (also covers *Camlachie*)

Camlachie

'Salisbury' (also covers *Bridgeton*)

Glasgow Central

'Iddesleigh'
'The Blythswood'

College

'The Montrose'

St Rollox

Dennistown

Tradestown

Govan (Lanarkshire)

'Britannia' (Govan)

Partick (Lanarkshire)

'Arthur Balfour' (Kelvinside) − 1,880(1899);
   1,835(1900)

2 Renfrewshire East

'Stirling Maxwell' (Pollockshields)
'Lady Isabella Gordon' (Cathcart)
'Lady Alice' (Thornliebank)

3 Renfrewshire West

'West Renfrew' (Gourock)
Barrhead

4 Paisley

'Abercorn' (Paisley)
'The Number One'

5 Greenock

'The John Scott'

6 Dumbartonshire

East Kilpatrick (Bearsden)
Old Kilpatrick
'The Lennox' (Vale of Leven) − 1,500(1893)
Helensburgh (combined with Gareloch Head
   in 1886)
'The Colquhoun' (Gareloch Head)
Balloch
Roseneath − 184(1890); 200+(1900)
Arrochar − 158(1900)

7 Bute

Rothesay
'Earl of Glasgow' (Isle of Cumbrae)

8 Ayrshire North

West Kilbride
'St Columba' (Largs) − 273(1891)
'St Wining' (Kilwinning) − 1,030(1890);
   1,095(1891)
'The Aiket' (Dunlop)

9 Kilmarnock Burghs

Kilmarnock
'Augusta' (Renfrew)
'Newark' (Port Glasgow)

10 Ayr Burghs

Ayr and Newton
Campbelltown

11 Ayrshire South

'Vale of Lugar' (Auchinleck and Cumnock)
Old Cumnock
'Ballochmyle' (Mauchline)
'Ballochmyle' (Catrine)
'Afton' (New Cumnock)
Wallacetown (1893)
Troon

12 Stirlingshire

'The Craigend' (Milngavie) − 657(1891)
Polmont
'Sir William Wallace' (Larbert) − 217(1890);
  231(1891)
'Larbertshire' (Denny)

13 Stirling Burghs

'The Rock' (Stirling) − 950(1890);
  1,017(1901)
Dunfermline
South Queensferry

14 Falkirk Burghs

Falkirk
Linlithgow
Airdrie
'The Cadzow' (Hamilton)

15 Clackmannan and Kinross

Kinross
'The Mar' (Alloa)
Dollar

16 St Andrews Burghs

St Andrews − 1,000+(1888)
Coupar
'East Neuk of Fife' (Anstruther)

17 Fife East

'North of Fife' (Newburgh)
Colinsburgh and Elie
Leven
'Stratheden' (Auchtermuchty, Falkland and
  Strathmiglo)

18 Fife West

Lochgelly
'The Tulliallan' (Kincardine-on-Forth)
'The Balbirnie' (Markinch)

19 Kirkcaldy Burghs

'The Dunnikier' (Kirkcaldy)
Burntisland

10 Lanarkshire North West

Glenboig

21 Lanarkshire North East

22 Lanarkshire Mid

Cambuslang
Bothwell

24 Linlithgowshire

'Hopetoun' (Kirkliston) − 313(1890)
'Hopetoun' (Bathgate and Torpichen) −
  1,050(1890)
'Baillie' (Fauldhouse) − 644(1887
'Baillie' (Whitburn)
'Strathbrock' (Uphall and Broxburn)
'Union' (Livingstone and West Calder)

25 Midlothian

'The Glencorse' (Penicuik)
Mid Calder
Gogar and Ratho
Corstophine
'Riccarton' (Currie)
Cramond
The Conservative Club

26 Edinburgh Central

'The Iddesleigh' (Edinburgh University)

Edinburgh West

'The Scott' − 388(1912)
'St Bernard's' − 281(1890); 319(1891)
'St Stephen's' − 200+(1900)
'Marquis of Salisbury'

Edinburgh South

Craigmillar − 220(1890); 250(1891)
'The Wauchope'
'The Warrender'

Edinburgh East

(Worked by 'The Scott')

Leith Burghs

'The Hamilton' (Portobello)
'Honest Town' (Musselborough)

27 Haddingtonshire

Prestonpans
'Tantallon Castle' (North Berwick)
'The Abbey' (Haddington)

28 Berwickshire

Duns
Chirnside
'Scottish Border' (Coldstream)
Earlston
'Priory' (Coldingham)
Lauderdale
Greenlaw

29 Roxburghshire

'St Mary's' (Melrose)
Kelso
'Jedforest' (Jedburgh)
'Upper Teviotdale' (Hawick)

30 Hawick Burghs

'Upper Teviotdale' (Hawick)
'Gala Water' (Galashiels)
Selkirk

31 Peebles and Selkirkshire

Innerleithen
Stobo
'Haystoun' (Peebles)

Ettrick
Traquair

32 Dumfriesshire

'Upper Annandale' (Moffat)
'The Solway' − 656(1890)
'The Nithsdale' (Thornhill)
'Upper Nithsdale' (Sanquhar)
Ruthwell (1890)
Moniavie
Lochar

33 Dumfries Burghs

'The Buccleuch' (Dumfries)
Annan − 137(1891)
'Robert the Bruce' (Lochmaben) −
 1,000(1908)

34 Kirkcudbright

'Ellangowan' (Creetown)

35 Wigtownshire

Wigtown

APPENDIX XVIII   WALES

1 Monmouth District

'The Rolls' (Monmouth) − 176(1888)
'Tredegar' (Newport) − 390(1888);
 1,000(1890 including Newport Dames)
'Talbot' (Newport Dames) − 198(1886);
 327(1888)
Usk (1890)

2 Monmouthshire West

Tredegar (1896)
Blaina and Nantyglo (1897)
Abertillery and Cwmtillery (1897)
Blackwood (1900)

3 Monmouthshire North

'Hendre' (Abergavenny) − 481(1888)
Grosmont and Skenfrith − 400(1890)
'Cranborne' (Blaenavon) − 250(1891)
Goytre
Panteg (1890)

4 Monmouthshire South

Llanfrechfa − 220(1888)
'Beaconsfield' (Risca) − 229(1888)

Wyve Valley and Trelleck − 59(1888)
Raglan
Chepstow
'The Caradoc' (Shirenewton)

5 Cardiff District

Grangetown
Cardiff
Canton − 103(1886)
Cardiff Docks
Cathays
'Clive' (Cardiff Dames) 1890
Roath − 169(1886)
Newtown
'Vale of Glamorgan' (Cowbridge)
'The Tyn-y-Cymmer' (Llantrisant) −
 232(1891)

6 Glamorgan East

'Senghenydd' (Caerphilly) − 118(1891)
Pontypridd − 416(1891)
'Lady Lewis' (Mountain Ash) − 226(1890);
 243(1891)
Ystrad Mynach, Nelson and Gellygaer −
 594(1891)

Taff's Well (1890) − 100(1891)
Penlottyn and Deri (1890)
Rudry and Macken (1894)
Maesruddud − 302(1891)

7 Merthyr Tydfil

'The Guest' (Dowlais) − 317(1891)
'Lady Lewis' (Aberdare)

8 Rhondda

*9 Glamorgan South (Total membership
1890 − 5,019; 1891 − 5,459)*

'The Ogmore' (Bridgend) − 400(1886)
Ely
'Upper Ely' (Peterston)
Llandyfodwg
Llandaff
'The Windsor' (Barry) − 46(1886)
Penarth
'The Fonmon' (Llancarfan)
Talygarn − 45(1886)
'Caerau' (Wyndham) − 600(1886)

10 Glamorgan Mid

Glyn Neath

11 Swansea District

'The Gwyn' (Neath) − 575(1886)
'The Gower' (Swansea) (also Swansea Town)
'The Beaconsfield' (Swansea) (also Swansea
  Town)

12 Swansea Town

'The Gower' (Swansea) − 945(1890);
  1,012(1891)
'The Beaconsfield' (Swansea)

13 Glamorgan West or Gower

Swansea Valley
Gowerton (1893)

14 Carmarthenshire East

Llandilo − 1,048(1901)
'The Vicar Pritchard' (Llandovery)
Ammanford

15 Carmarthenshire West

St Clears − 490(1890); 525(1891)
Llanstephan
'The Cothi' (Brechfa)
'The Picton' (Ferryside) − 85(1890)
Kidwelley

16 Carmarthen District

Carmarthen District − 90(1886)
'The Emlyn' (Carmarthen)
'The Iddesleigh' (Llanelly)

17 Pembroke and Haverfordwest District

Haverfordwest − 322(1886)
Pembroke and Castle Martin
'The Premier in Wales' (Tenby) −
  500+(1890)
'The Lord Nelson' (Milford Haven) −
  81(1886)
Fishguard
Pembroke Dock

18 Pembrokeshire

Newport − 134(1886); 300(1901)
Boncath − 500+(1888); 690(1891);
  500+(1893)
'The Haven' (Neyland)
Pembrokeshire Dames − 390(1886)
'Roose' (Haroldstone West)

19 Cardigan

Aberystwyth
Llanarth
Cardigan − 2,600(1886)
Lampeter
Aberayron
Newcastle Emlyn − 400(1888)
Llanbyther − 500(1888)
Blaenporth
Borth (1893)

20 Brecknockshire

'The Brecknock' (Brecon) − 600(1891)
'The Salisbury' (Builth)
Crickhowell − 205(1886); 457(1891);
  533(1901)
Llanwrthwl
Gwernyfed
'North' (Vaynor)

21 Radnorshire

'The Ithon' (Llandrindod) − 90(1886)
Presteign − 57(1886)
'The Tene Valley' (Knighton) − 117(1886)
Rhayader − 133(1886)
Llanbadarnfynydd − 21(1886); 100(1891)
'The Lower Elvel' (Glasbury)
Llangunllo (1892)

22 Montgomery District

'The Powis' (Welshpool)

'The Gordon (Llanidloes) — 147(1886)
'The Hafren' (Newtown) — 332(1886)
Llanfyllin

23 Montgomeryshire

'The Meifod' (North Montgomeryshire) —
  300(1886)
Mid Montgomery (Llanfair)
Machynlleth
Llanwyddyn and Llanfihangel
Sant Ffraid
Cann Office (Llangadfan)

24 Merionethshire

'The Idris' (Dolgelly) — 160(1891)
'The Penllyn' (Bala) — 438(1891)
'The Merioneth-Londonderry' (Corris)
'The Marlboro' (Aberdovey)
'Mawddach' (Barmouth) — 38(1886);
  49(1891)

25 Caernarvonshire South or Eifion

Port Dinorwic

26 Caernarvon District

'The Gloddaeth' (Conway) — 288(1886);
  600+(1891)
'The Menai' (Bangor) — 1,041(1886)
Caernarvon — 602(1890)
Nevin
Pwllheli
Criccieth and District

27 Caernarvonshire North or Arfon

'The Mostyn' (Llandudno) — 176(1888)
'The Penryhn' (Bethesda)
'The Gwydyr' (Trefriw) — 143(1891)
'Eryri' (Llanfairfechan) (1891) — 125(1891)
Colwyn (1895)
Colwyn Bay (1895) — 193(1897)

28 Anglesey

Beaumaris — 584(1886)
Amlwch
'The St Cybi' (Holyhead)
Llangefni

29 Denbigh District

Wrexham — 246(1886)
Holt and Marchwiel
Ruthin — 586(1886)
Denbigh — 816(1886)

30 Denbighshire West

Llangollen — 76(1886)
'The Vale of Clwyd' (Henllan) — 553(1886)
Elwy — 113(1886); 196(1891)
Abergele
'The Vale of Conway' (Llanrwst) —
  119(1886)
Llandyrnog — 70(1886)
Llangedwyn — 300(1891)
'The Yale' (Llandegla)
'The Eyarth' (Llanfair)

31 Denbighshire East (Total membership 1891 — 3,349)

Ruabon — 571(1886)
Brynhinalt (Chirk) — 43(1886)
Rosset — 208(1886)
Gresford — 150(1886)
'The Plas Power' (Bersham)
Cefn and Rhosymedre
'Sir Watkin' (Brymbo)

32 Flintshire

Rhyl
The Hundred of Maelor — 336(1886)
Chwilr, Bodfari and Caerwys — 167(1886)
'The Mostyn' (Whitford)
'The Plas Teg Hope' (Hope)
'The Mostyn' (Hawarden)
'Llewelyn' (Skeifog)
Llwynegrin
Connah's Quay (1896)

33 Flint District

'The Mostyn' (Mold) — 525(1886)
St Asaph
'The Mostyn' (Holywell) — 50(1886)
'The Mostyn' (Flint)
'The Mostyn' (Greenfield)
Bagillt
Caerwys (1894)

Index